ANTHROPOLOGICAL PAPERS

MUSEUM OF ANTHROPOLOGY, UNIVERSITY OF MICHIGAN
NO. 30

THE JUNTUNEN SITE AND THE LATE WOODLAND PREHISTORY OF THE UPPER GREAT LAKES AREA

BY
ALAN McPHERRON

ANN ARBOR
THE UNIVERSITY OF MICHIGAN, 1967

ISBN (print): 978-0-915703-68-5
ISBN (ebook): 978-1-951519-38-4

Browse all of our books at sites.lsa.umich.edu/archaeology-books.

Order our books from the University of Michigan Press at www.press.umich.edu.

For permissions, questions, or manuscript queries, contact Museum publications by email at umma-pubs@umich.edu or visit the Museum website at lsa.umich.edu/ummaa.

PREFACE

The present report is a slightly revised version of my doctoral dissertation, submitted to the University of Michigan, and based on field work performed in the summers of 1960 and 1961. Excavations were made possible by grants from the National Science Foundation[1] and by funds from the Horace H. Rackham School of Graduate Studies[2] and the Museum of Anthropology, both at the University of Michigan.

Publication of this report was made possible through the generosity of a summer resident of the island and frequent visitor to the site, Mr. H. Earl Hoover. A. T. Steegman was field assistant the first summer, and G. R. Peske the second. Their contributions were of very great value. The crews, mostly students, were as follows. The first summer: Christy Cogan, John Dowling, Stase McPherron, Sudha Saksena (née Srikrishen), and Louis Wojnaroski. The second summer: Robert Bettarel, Christy Cogan, John Fritz, Stase McPherron, Thomas Nemec, Sally Peske, Raymond Silverstein, A. T. Steegman, Fred Wilding-White, Henry T. Wright, Louis Wojnaroski, and Gerald Zahler. Their various insights and suggestions also contributed greatly to any successes of the operation.

Particular gratitude is due to Mr. and Mrs. Charles Juntunen for permission to excavate on their property. Help was given us by many residents of Bois Blanc Island, in particular Mrs. John Bible, Mrs. Ina Juntunen, and Ray Plaunt.

During the analysis of data, a grant from the Rackham School of Graduate Studies enabled me to visit museums and archaeologists in the Upper Great Lakes. I benefited much from their experience. Discussions with Lewis R. Binford were of importance in guiding my thinking and influencing the methods used to analyze the data. I am grateful to James C. Lingoes for help in undertaking the work done on computers. Access to the facilities of the University of Michigan Computing Center and the University of Pittsburgh Data and Computation Center enabled me to do the machine processing. Throughout all phases of the work, Dr. James B. Griffin encouraged and helped me, particularly with respect to the use of novel methods of analysis.

[1]Number 12969, 19469, G-11901, G-15719.

[2]Rackham Research Project No. 518; Michigan Alumni Fund—Faculty Research Equipment Project No. 44.

The work is dedicated to the memory of Christy Cogan, a member of the field party both summers and an assistant in analyzing the materials from the site in the Museum, who died in a vehicle accident while returning from the field the second summer, August 1961.

TABLE OF CONTENTS

Part I. Introduction. 1

1. Brief Orientation 1
2. Geography and Geology 5
3. Excavations at the Juntunen Site 22
4. Geomorphological and Depositional History 29

Part II. Description and Analysis of Archaeological Material 43

5. Pottery 45
6. Stone Industry 124
7. Copper 164
8. Worked Bone 176
9. Aboriginal Pottery Pipes 180
10. Postcontact Artifacts 183
11. Plant and Animal Remains 185
12. Burials 201
13. Habitation Features 233

Part III. Interpretations and Conclusions 251

14. Distributional and Functional Analysis 251
15. External Relationships and Dating 269
16. Anthropology and Cultural Ecology of the Juntunen Site 281
17. Summary and Conclusions 296

Appendix Attribute List for Juntunen Pottery with Descriptive Statistics on Attribute Frequencies 303

Literature Cited 307

TABLES

1. Frequencies of artifacts, by phase 28
2. Rock-stratigraphic units, occupations, and cultural phases 33
3. Stepwise regression analysis of pottery attributes 68
4. Deviation of pottery types from actual results of regression formula, based on GUTREG 70
5. Variables ranked according to association with all other variables 75
6. Juntunen pottery typology 79
7. Tests of significance for differences among some Juntunen pottery types 85
8. Summarized data on pottery attribute frequencies 87
9. Chi Square tests for independence of pottery type frequencies, through time 98
10. Frequencies of chert types in occupation phases 126
11. Chi Square test of independence of chert type on phase . 128
12. Chert debitage category frequencies and percentages . . . 130
13. Test of significance for difference in size of bipolar cores between Juntunen and other sites 134
14. Analysis of variance in length between two types of bipolar cores 139
15. Frequency distribution of projectile points and bifaces . . 145
16. Attribute list for projectile points 146
17. Summary statistics on projectile points and bifaces 151
18. Attributes in which Juntunen Triangular and Juntunen Notched points differ 152
19. Copper artifact categories and frequencies 170
20. Distribution of copper-bearing provenience units 172
21. Distribution of copper pieces 172
22. Relation between frequency of copper and frequency of copper-bearing units 173
23. Plant remains identified by Yarnell 188
24. Relative frequency of identified animal species 191
25. Molluscs of the Juntunen site 197
26. Feature 10: personal kit inventory 209
27. Small pits 246
28. Distribution of provenience units by sherd frequencies and weights 255
29. Distribution of sherd frequencies and weights in log transformation 255
30. Links through matching sherds 260

FIGURES

1. Cross section of island at area of Juntunen site 7
2. The Straits of Mackinac and surrounding areas 9
3. Aerial photograph of the west end of Bois Blanc Island and adjacent tip of Round Island, showing water depths in feet 11
4. Map of the Juntunen site 19
5. Map of central area of site showing grid system and features 23
6. Generalized composite cross section of the Juntunen site in a plane approximately normal to the shoreline . . 31
7. Cross section of central area of Juntunen site 35
8. Cross section of Southwest Area 36
9. Typical rim profiles 57
10. Sherd profile tracer 57
11. Dominant decorative motifs 62
12. Interassociations of pottery attributes, based on TOP. . . 74
13. Plotting of intermediate types with type numbers as grouping variable 77
14. Plotting of computer-generated types, "Decorative Motif" as grouping variable 78
15. Relationships among the final pottery types. 80
16. Cumulative percentages of pottery wares through time . . 99
17. Density of chert types and flaking techniques, by occupation. 127
18. Two basic bipolar core types 136
19. Split bipolar core 136
20. Bipolar core with cortex on back 139
21. "Gouged-end" artifact 141
22. Varieties of flaking done on Juntunen points 150
23. Weight distribution and summary statistics for scrapers. 157
24. Horizontal artifact distributions 174
25. Percentage of animal species in the three cultural phases 200
26. Topography of mound area 202
27. Features in mound area 202
28. Section of mound and Feature 11 204
29. Plan of bottom section of Feature 11. 204
30. Plan of upper level of burials in Feature 11. 207
31. Feature 10, personal kit. 208
32. Some bone artifacts from Feature 10. 208
33. Profile of Feature 21. 223
34. Profile of Feature 43. 224
35. Feature 43 227
36. "Longhouse" and other features. 234

37. Disturbances in square 710-180 237
38. Trench X-X' across Feature 22 238
39. Feature 4, pit 243
40. Relative frequencies of some artifact classes, by occupation 252
41. Relative frequencies of some artifact classes, by phase . 253
42. Units linked through matching sherds, distribution of Mackinac-ware vessels, and distribution of Juntunen-ware vessels 261
43. Comparative chronology of some upper Great Lakes manifestations 270

PLATES

I. Views of the Juntunen site 317
II. Lakeward-dipping lenses of sand and gravels and burned root pattern of a tree in Layer $IIIA_2$ 318
III. Profile from +875-100 to +875-090, and detail of black laminae 319
IV. Profile from 700-110 to 700-140 320
V. Profile from 720-180 to 720-170, and profile from 890-125 to 880-125 321
VI. Sherd casts showing cord-loop impressing. 322
VII. Sherd casts showing "cord-wrapped cord" impressions 323
VIII. "Cord-wrapped-object" impressions on sherds 324
IX. Some examples of relatively elaborate decoration. . 325
X. Rare vessel rim treatments 326
XI. Sherds of Mackinac Undecorated and Mackinac Punctate 327
XII. Mackinac Punctate vessels and sherds. 328
XIII. Mackinac ware 329
XIV. Partly restored Mackinac Banded vessels 330
XV. Mackinac Banded decorative styles 331
XVI. Mackinac Banded exteriors and interiors, showing the variability in interior decoration 332
XVII. Sherds of Blackduck Banded and Bois Blanc Braced Rim 333
XVIII. Bois Blanc Braced Rim 334
XIX. Rim fragments of Bois Blanc Braced Rim and an aberrant vessel 335
XX. Fragments of Bois Blanc Beaded, Bois Blanc Castellated Corded and Juntunen Linear Punctate vessels 336
XXI. Juntunen Drag-and-Jab 337

XXII. Juntunen Drag-and-Jab 338
XXIII. Mississippian tradition pottery 339
XXIV. Miniature and children's vessels 340
XXV. Rare and unique sherds 341
XXVI. Pottery pipe fragments. 342
XXVII. Polyhedral bipolar cores 343
XXVIII. "Gouged-end artifacts". 344
XXIX. Representative bladelets produced by the bipolar technique 345
XXX. Largest bladelets from the site produced by the bipolar technique 346
XXXI. Unique artifact of Eastport chert and bladelets produced by the bipolar technique 347
XXXII. Small projectile points 348
XXXIII. Medium sized and large notched and stemmed points . 349
XXXIV. Bifacial ovates and "cache points" 350
XXXV. Five gravers 351
XXXVI. Scrapers and ground-stone objects 352
XXXVII. Palette or whetstone from personal kit, adze, and bipointed pecked objects of unknown function 353
XXXVIII. Juntunen copper artifacts 354
XXXIX. Juntunen copper artifacts 355
XL. Bone awls 356
XLI. Harpoon heads and fragments, and a broken pointed bone object 357
XLII. Heaped gravels in mound area, and loose human bone near surface above Feature 11 358
XLIII. Feature 11 359
XLIV. Personal kit found at pelvic region of Burial 3, Feature 11 360
XLV. Burial 3 after removal of personal kit, and Burial 2 361
XLVI. Items from "personal kit" 362
XLVII. Feature 11 363
XLVIII. Feature 11 364
XLIX. Feature 11 365
L. Feature 11 366
LI. The best-preserved Juntunen crania 367
LII. Features 34 and 21 368
LIII. Four stages in the excavation of Feature 18 369
LIV. Features 43 and 45 370
LV. Postmolds of part of longhouse, view of site during excavations in August, 1961, postmold with decayed part of original post preserved at edges, and part of profile cut across longhouse 371
LVI. Feature 5 and Feature 28 372
LVII. Feature 23 and Feature 20 373

PART I

INTRODUCTION

I
BRIEF ORIENTATION

1.1 NATURE OF THE JUNTUNEN SITE

The Late Woodland Juntunen site consists of stratified deposits of habitation debris about 200 by 400 feet in extent on a sandy ridge some 600 feet from the shore of Lake Huron, on the west end of Bois Blanc Island in the Straits of Mackinac. The reason for its existence seems to have been the abundance of fish occurring seasonally in protected sandy-bottom shallows offshore. The main portion of the site was occupied at intervals between about A.D. 800 and A.D. 1400, spanning much of the Late Woodland period; a partially overlapping but mostly areally separate Middle Woodland site (Arrowhead Drive) was also located; it was occupied from at least A.D. 60.

Throughout its aboriginal history, the Juntunen site represented primarily a lakeside fishing village where large fish — predominantly sturgeon and whitefish — were taken in great numbers during their spawning seasons, probably with the use of nets, certainly by spearing. Some corn was eaten, though whether it was grown locally or obtained through exchange is unclear; various wild plants and animals were also utilized.

The evidence suggests that the site was occupied for most of the year except during the dead of winter, by 20-50 people, which is in accord with ethnographic accounts for the area. House types for most periods of occupation were not ascertained, but during at least one of the later occupations a longhouse was constructed.

Activities other than for subsistence include the making of pottery whose styles reflect shifting relationships with contemporary groups in surrounding areas, a flint industry with a "bipolar" component adapted to the utilization of small pebbles, and — in the latest phase — a copper industry with artifacts of very small size. Many of these activities reflect changes through time in the intensity of interaction with different surrounding groups, but the adaptation itself – primarily to the exploitation of large fish that come into shallow waters at certain times of the year – was highly stable over the 600-odd years the site was occupied.

1.2 HISTORY OF INVESTIGATIONS

In the summer of 1932, Robert Braidwood, then an undergraduate at the University of Michigan, discovered what is now named the Juntunen site and prepared a brief report, on file since then in the University of Michigan Museum of Anthropology. In August of 1959 the present owner of the property, Mr. Charles Juntunen, reported to the Museum of Anthropology, through a friend, the uncovering of burials during bulldozing. The site was immediately visited by Dr. James B. Griffin, director of the Museum of Anthropology, who directed excavation of an ossuary uncovered by Mr. Juntunen. Pottery fragments scattered about the area indicated the presence of an extensive Late Woodland village, and reports of local pothunting operations suggested the existence of a number of other ossuaries. The site was seen to be favorably located for correlation with former lake beaches.

At that time, the Museum was commencing a program entitled "A Correlation of Prehistoric Cultural Complexes and Post-Pleistocene Ecologies in the Upper Great Lakes," with grants from the National Science Foundation. This project involved studies of associations of archaeological materials with geologic formations, the investigation of paleoecologic interrelations between biota and prehistoric cultures, and investigations of problems relating to the human populations of the Great Lakes area. A number of promising archaeological sites were selected for investigation, and the Juntunen site was chosen to fill in the late end of the prehistoric sequence and to provide samples of a skeletal population that could be compared with other samples from Woodland sites in Michigan.

Formal excavations were begun in 1960, when a crew of six, under my field direction, surveyed and tested the vertical and horizontal extent of the site, removed a second and much larger ossuary burial, and examined the island for indications of other sites.

The 1961 field season had the following objectives: (1) study of the highly complex stratification of the Late Woodland site (wherein occupation layers often occurred as thin lenses, making horizontal correlations exceedingly difficult) so as to clarify the sequence of occupations; (2) collection of larger samples of vegetal and faunal remains associated with undisturbed deposits for study of the ecology; (3) investigation of settlement patterns and possible changes in them over time; (4) recovery of a more adequate sample of features, such as hearths, pits, houses, and ossuaries; (5) further study of the Middle Woodland site (Arrowhead Drive).

A few weeks of excavation in the summer of 1963 under the field direction of Charles Eyman were devoted to the recovery of additional skeletal material.

1.3 PROBLEMS OF ANALYSIS

The general problem in analyzing materials recovered may be defined as the evaluation of similarities and differences among provenience units in terms of their form and contents, with a "provenience unit" being defined as any unit of earth excavated, sifted and bagged separately, and, it was hoped, representing a unit deposited as such.

The general problem is approached through a series of subproblems: temporal ordering, possible effects of functional differences from one unit to another, effects of subsequent disturbance. Theoretically, differences among provenience units may represent:

(1) Effects of statistical sampling error
(2) Time (where the occurrence of change over time is assumed)
(3) Different function of two contemporary units
(4) Later disturbance
(5) Combinations of 2, 3, and 4.

How are these factors to be isolated, and how can it be shown that they account for the observed variation?

The large sample sizes suggested that automated techniques would be desirable in order to facilitate treatment of the samples by statistical methods. Considerable time was spent planning the analysis of materials, and both traditional techniques and new methods developed during the process of study were employed. Data were ultimately encoded and placed on punched cards, and computers were utilized in efforts to validate traditional sorting techniques, to obtain more objective classifications, and to analyze the "behavior" of one artifact class with respect to others.

Concurrently with this line of approach, other students in the Museum of Anthropology were working with certain artifact classes and non-artifactual remains from the site. These individuals and their projects are as follows:

Charles Cleland . . . . animal bone
Charles Eyman and Robert Bettarel . . human skeletal remains
(Miss) Sidney Harrison . . . . chert varieties
Barry Kent and Ronald Vanderwal . . copper-working industry
David Taggart . . . . points and scrapers
Henry Wright . . . . geology and geomorphology
Richard Yarnell . . . . botanical remains
Gerald Zahler . . . . postmolds

Yarnell's work on the Juntunen plant materials forms part of his doctoral dissertation (1964) as does bone analysis of Cleland (1966); completed reports submitted by Eyman (1964), Eyman and Bettarel (1965), Kent and Vanderwal (1962), and H. Wright (1962, 1964) are on file in the Museum of Anthropology, University of Michigan.

As a result of the geological and artifactual analysis, a series of six periods of occupation was postulated by H. Wright and assigned letters A through F (earliest to latest in the Late Woodland sequence at the site). This series was later transformed into three cultural phases, whose names and approximate time spans are indicated in the accompanying table.

Occupation	Cultural Phase	Approximate Time Span (A.D.)
F, E	Juntunen	1200-1400
D	Bois Blanc	1000-1200
C, B, A	Mackinac	800-1000

1.4 TEMPORAL SEQUENCE

Throughout the entire Late Woodland sequence, no significant change could be observed in the adaptive pattern: fishing remained the primary subsistence activity at all times. The later periods of occupation saw the growth of a copper-working industry, and there were minor changes in technology, but most temporal change was stylistic, evidently related to shifts in cultural contacts; such shifts are understandable in the light of the geographic position of the site—on major routes both east-west and north-south.

Temporal continuity from Middle Woodland into Late Woodland is not observable. There seems also to have been a gap in occupation for a hundred years or so just prior to European contact, and no early historic period occupation was located.

II
GEOGRAPHY AND GEOLOGY

2.1 THE UPPER GREAT LAKES

2.1.1 PHYSICAL CHARACTER AND POSTGLACIAL HISTORY

The drainage basin of Lakes Superior, Michigan, and Huron, with land of the adjoining states and provinces, forms a natural region characterized by a predominance of water features, with many rivers and inland lakes, and by a topography lacking natural barriers — all these largely attributable to glacial action.

Ground deposits are mostly unaltered glacial till and lake deposits, with the result that soils are generally thin and well drained. Many glacially produced lakes are now in stages of desiccation; most non-tillic soils are found in swamps, marshes, and bogs.

Glaciers had melted from most of the region by about 9000 B.C., after which time the large periglacial lakes underwent a series of changes in level — with such extreme ranges as from 620 to 230 feet above sea level — events controlled by the opening and closing of water outlets with retreat of glaciers and the rising of the land as a result of removal of the weight of the glacial ice.

Men seem to have advanced into the area close upon the retreating glacial front, the first occupations in the previously glaciated zone being represented by rather sporadic occurrences of projectile points and other stone tools, many in forms similar to those made in adjacent regions, where they are known under such names as Plano, Quad, and Suwanee. Most of these materials apparently represent big-game hunting adaptations; we may infer that relatively little exploitation of the presumably already abundant aquatic resources of the Great Lakes was being done. The stage of the Great Lakes at that time is called Lake Algonquin, 806 feet above sea level at the Straits. Wave-cut cliffs and fossil beaches of the stage, now elevated far above the present water level because of land uplift and water subsidence, are to be seen on Mackinac Island in the Straits of Mackinac, but the other two channel islands, Round Island and Bois Blanc Island, were at that time under water.

Evidence of cultural occupation for the period approximately 6000-3000 B.C. is exiguous, possibly because that was the time of the low-water stage of the Great Lakes, and many sites of that period are now under water. During that phase, Lake Michigan consisted of two much smaller lakes connected by a channel, and the Straits of Mackinac was reduced to a river.

When the lake levels rose again to the Nipissing stage about 2200 B.C., levels higher than those at the present time were once more reached (635 feet above mean sea level at the Straits). Owing to the constant rise of land, however, Bois Blance Island seems not to have been totally inundated at this time, a portion of the western end remaining above water. The period from 3000 to 1000 B.C. is the time of the Late Archaic archaeological phase, when the types of cultural adaptation that continued in many places to the historic period were in the process of forming. These adaptations may be termed the "inland waters hunting-fishing complex"; they extend over most of the Upper Great Lakes area, with widespread interaction among local groups evidenced by similarities over considerable areas in functional traits, artifact styles, and burial practices.

The last suggested major "lakes stage" before stabilization at the present levels is called Algoma. The "Algoma level" of 610 feet indicated for the Straits probably represents an unexceeded maximum rise in a series of rises and drops culminating in the present lake level of 580 feet at the Straits. On Bois Blanc Island there is a fairly even series of undulations representing fossil beaches both above and below the Algoma beach elevation. They begin at an altitude of about 598 feet and continue upward and inland for several hundred yards or more. The vertical section of the island shown in Figure 1 illustrates the undulatory nature of these crests and swales; the crest at about 612 feet is regarded as "the" Algoma beach, although it is clearly only the most pronounced of a series. It is suggested that the west end of Bois Blanc Island would be a suitable place to study lake-level phenomena between the Nipissing stage and some time after the Algoma stage (when conditions of deposition changed) because of the well-preserved series of elevations.

2.1.2 PLANT AND ANIMAL LIFE

The Upper Great Lakes area is described by Dice (1943) as an ecotone or zone of biotic transition between a truly northern biome — the "Hudsonian Biotic Province" — and a southern biome — the "Carolinian Biotic Province." Assigning to it the name "Canadian Biotic Province," Dice describes it as being characterized by forest types that differ from the montonously uniform conifer forest to the north and the species-rich deciduous forest

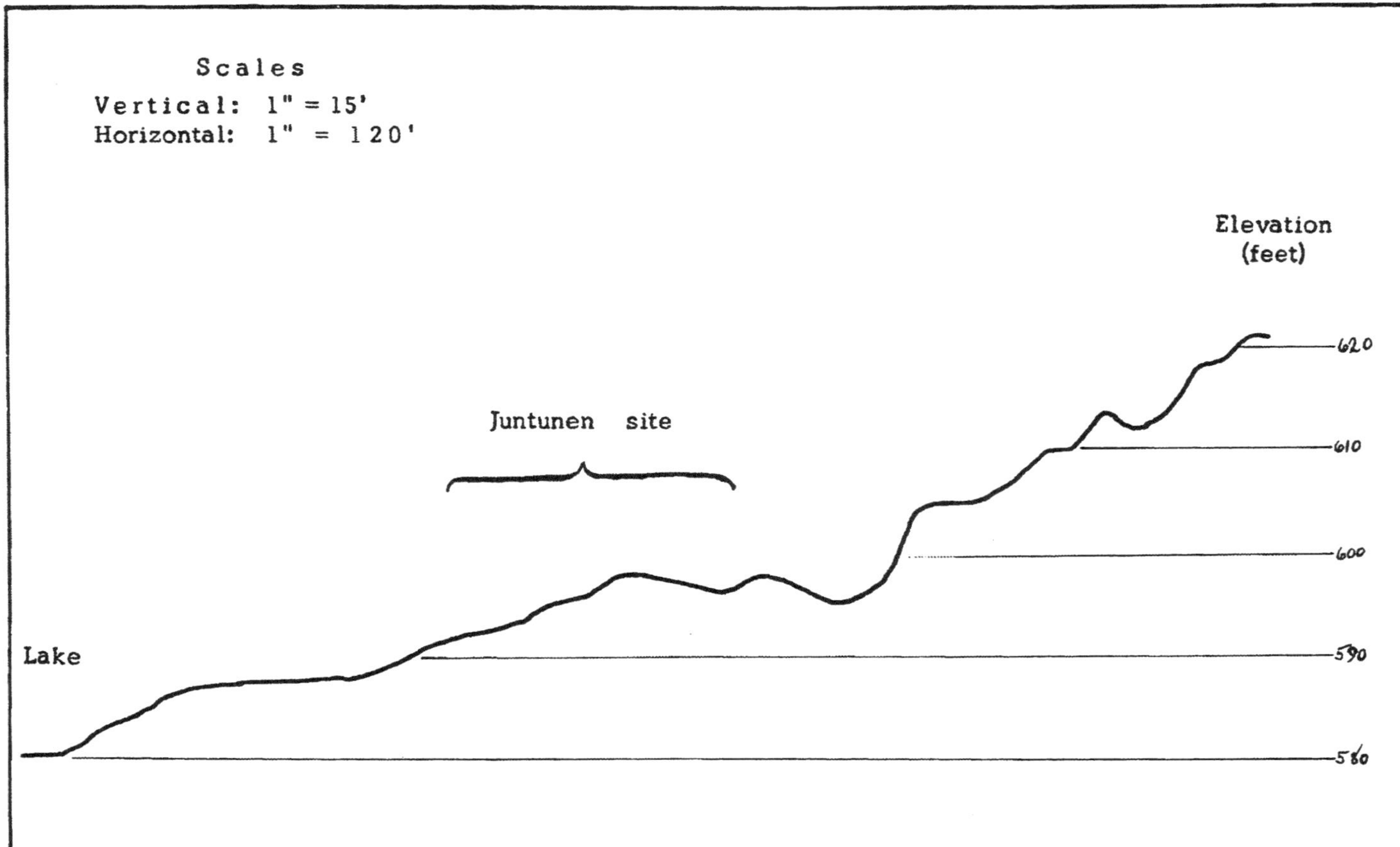

Fig. 1—Cross section of island at area of Juntunen site (compressed in horizontal dimension)

climax to the south; it is predominantly birch, beech, maple, and hemlock, with pines often forming a significant element. The north-south gradients in species predominance emphasize the transitional nature of the zone.

The northern part of the Upper Great Lakes area is described by Potzger (1946) as the "Lake Forest Formation," thus joining the factor of the many lakes and other waterways to the biotic characterization of the zone, a conjunction of some significance from the point of view of cultural ecology. Cultures exhibited considerable homogeneity over a long period of time in the Lake Forest or Canadian zone, and there is a notable sparsity of sites in areas covered by coniferous forest, which can be explained by the relative availability of wild products in deciduous compared to coniferous forests. The former yield acorns, nuts, and other products, as well as support a much larger mammalian fauna, whereas few important food sources are obtainable in the coniferous forests themselves. The importance of lakes and rivers as sources of animal food that can be gathered in quantity at certain places in various seasons of the year gives the area much of its significance in terms of cultural adaptation. (For a treatment of various aspects of the relationships between cultures and natural resources, with special reference to plant life, the monograph by Yarnell [1964] is suggested; for animal life see Cleland [1966]).

2.2 THE STRAITS OF MACKINAC

Located in the geographic center of the Canadian province and almost precisely in the geographic center of the Upper Great Lakes drainage basin (Pincus 1962, map in endpapers), the Straits of Mackinac also forms a natural crossroads for movement of people or goods north-south and east-west. The large inland lakes in the northern part of the lower peninsula of Michigan are accessible, via the Cheboygan River, to the Straits. The Straits also lies along the route of water transport between Lakes Huron and Michigan, as well as between Lakes Superior and Michigan.

2.2.1 LANDFORMS

By reference to Figure 2, the Straits may be seen to consist of the approximately 3.75-mile-wide passage between the tips of Michigan's upper and lower peninsulas. Water flowing from Lake Michigan here takes several routes. The South Channel, fairly shallow, with depths seldom greater than 80 feet, separates Bois Blanc Island from the lower peninsula mainland. The Straits proper, however, continues as the passage between Mackinac

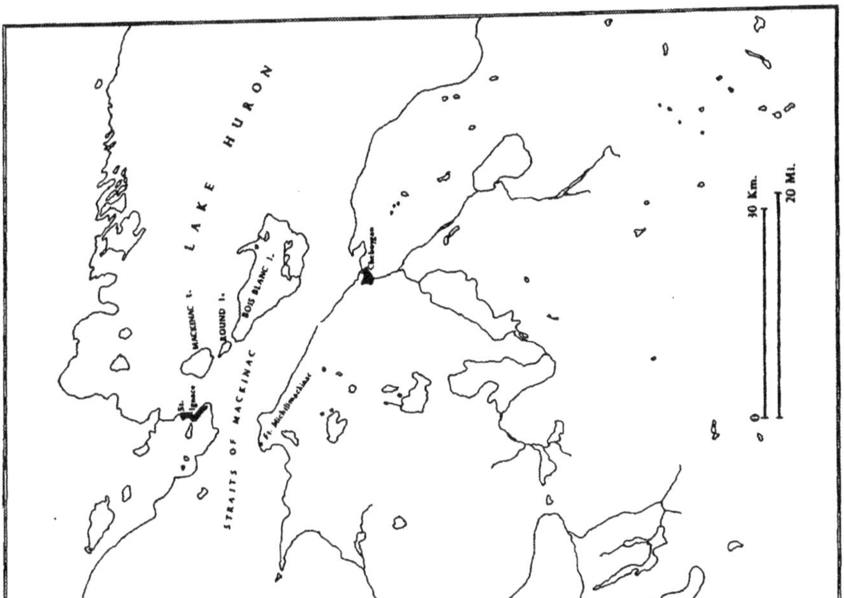

Fig. 2.—The Straits of Mackinac and surrounding areas

and Round Islands. The drowned Mackinac River, which connected what are now Lakes Michigan and Huron during the Chippewa-Stanley low-water stage, passes between Mackinac Island and the mainland at St. Ignace. The route between Mackinac and Round Island is the route used at present by all freight vessels plying between Lakes Michigan and Superior. The shallow passage between Round and Bois Blanc Islands (depths are shown in Fig. 3), only 0.64 miles wide, has a fair current flowing through it and was occasionally used by sailing vessels in the days when races were run through the Straits. It required an experienced pilot.

The tips of both upper and lower peninsulas are especially rich, even for this area, in lakes and rivers. The large inland lakes (see Fig. 2) of the top of the lower peninsula, particularly, with their various navigable rivers, should have been of importance to aboriginal populations because they provided both routes of transportation and habitation sites rich in natural resources. Mullett and Burt Lakes offer direct canoe connections via the Cheboygan River with the Straits (at Cheboygan) and fairly easy connections with Little Traverse Bay. Black Lake is connected with the Cheboygan River via the Black River. Thus, sizable portions of the upper end of the lower peninsula of Michigan have easy access to the Straits region.

The three islands in the Straits — Mackinac, Round, and Bois Blanc — differ considerably in a number of respects. Mackinac is a rather high island, with heights up to 750 feet and elevated Algonquin beaches. Its occupational history since the late seventeenth century is known: the island was long occupied by Chippewas, the Hurons had a village for a short time after their expulsion from the east by the Iroquois, and subsequently there was an Ottawa village. A fort was built by the British in 1781 and surrendered to the Americans in 1796. At present, the island is a major summer-resort center.

Round Island — the Marquette National Forest — has no human inhabitants at all and is densely covered by forest, with berry thickets in the many swampy places. Its name derives not from its outline on a map — which is anything but round — but from its appearance as one sails past it, when it appears as a great dome rising out of the water. One site was located in a clearing on the south shore near the passage separating it from Bois Blanc Island; it is marked with a hemispherical white line in Figure 3. It may be one of the two sites listed for Round Island on Map 20 of Hinsdale's (1931) atlas. The corresponding clearing at about the same place on the north shore, visible in Figure 3, seems not to have been occupied. It was the area where the

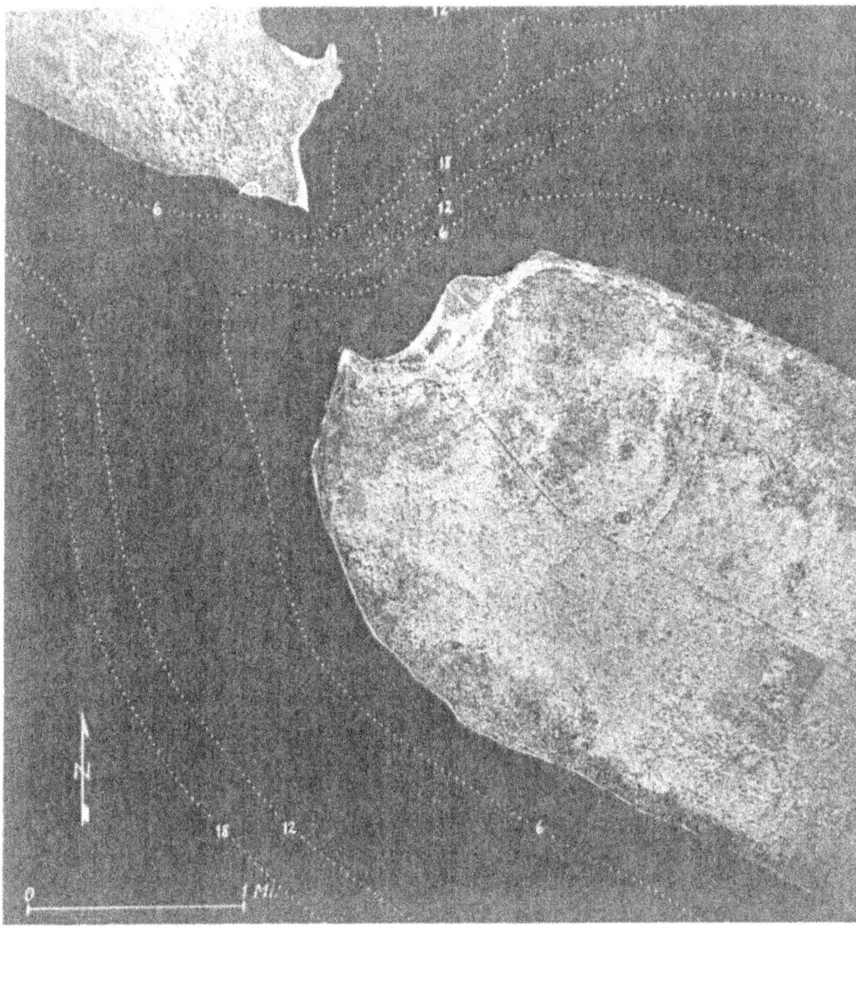

Fig. 3.—Aerial photograph of the west end of Bois Blanc Island and adjacent tip of Round Island, showing water depths in feet.

formation of a modern beach was studied by H. Wright.

Bois Blanc Island will be described in section 2.3.

2.2.2 WATERS

The waters of the Straits can be characterized as being cold and extremely clear. The July surface temperature of approximately 18°C. is about the coldest surface reading in the Lake Huron basin; the water transparency is 15 meters. On calm days one could study the bottom around Bois Blanc Island from a boat. The bottom consisted of deposits of reddish clay (thus either deposited Valders till or the parent material thereof) and varying proportions of boulders, bedrock, and sand. There was certainly no apparent muck or silt. Water plants were observed occasionally, mostly in the calmer shallows.

There are considerable seasonal variations in the amount and type of flow and in lake levels. Since lake deposits intrude upon cultural deposits at the Juntunen site, the contemporary lake-level changes, divisible into variations in the annual cycle and long-term changes, are of some interest. The annual range in variation in the Straits is about one foot (Ayers 1962:80) while a maximum range of 6.3 feet was noted between 1886 and 1926 (Laidly 1962:99). Short-period fluctuations caused by winds, pronounced changes in barometric pressure, and seiches, produce maxima that might well confuse the study of former long-term lake levels, in the absence of an ability to distinguish between high water storm beaches and beaches fossilized by land uplift. The profound change in beach profile caused by a single violent storm is illustrated by Thompson (1937). Laidly cites Lake Erie as an extreme example of short-term level fluctuations: "Simultaneous level recordings at the ends of this lake during a storm have varied by more than 13 feet" (1962:99). One wishes that studies had been made of beach cross sections before and after such events.

Icing conditions in winter can alter beach profiles and in general have a bearing on the problem of people and animals at the Straits. While the Great Lakes do not freeze over, ice builds out from shore, causing from 60 to 90 per cent of the water surface to be ice covered (Powers 1962:37).

The Straits does freeze over; freezing may be a smooth process, in which case iceboats appear in the South Channel area, or it may be a result of the piling-up of ice in ridges and windrows that may rise from 10 to 20 feet above water level, making any transit hazardous. Lake shipping is usually suspended by the first of December and opens again between the middle of March (in the south) and early April or even early May (in Lake Superior). In suitable years, then, people and animals could have walked to and from points in the Straits normally separated by water.

2.2.3 CLIMATE

While the waters of the Straits are cold the year round, there are considerable variations in air temperature. At Sault Ste Marie, the mean annual temperature is 39.4°F., the January average 13.7°F., the July average 63.4° F. (Yarnell 1964:133).

For maize horticulture, length of growing season is of critical importance. The strategic location of the Juntunen site in this respect was noted by Yarnell:

> A strip of territory with frost-free season above 140 days runs northward along the western side of Lower Michigan terminating in the area around the Straits of Mackinac. It includes the western half of Bois Blanc Island where the Juntunen site is located [Yarnell 1964:133].

A growing season of 140 or more frost-free days is suggested by Yarnell as essential for effective maize horticulture.

2.3 BOIS BLANC ISLAND

2.3.1 GEOGRAPHY

Bois Blanc Island is from 3 to 4 miles in breadth and 10 to 12 miles in length. It is thus by far the largest island in the entire Straits region. The maximum height of the island is 680 feet, but considerable portions of it are lowlands, with many bogs and swamps. There are a number of inland lakes; in Figure 2 (p. 9) the three largest of these lakes in the southern part stand at 615 feet.

There are very few places along the shore where access by canoe would have been really difficult. Much of the shore consists of smooth exposures of bedrock, generally dolomite with much splitting at joints. This bedrock is often partly covered by sand. There are sandy beaches — considered by some the *sine qua non* for a lacustrine aboriginal settlement — at several locations. The heaviest deposit — the deepest dune formation noted on the island — occurs at Sand Bay along the south shore. Examination of a 9-foot vertical face in an excavation for a septic tank indicated that the deposit was homogeneous for the entire depth; there was no sign of different types of sand, occupation debris, herb stabilization, or soil formation.

Few streams drain the interior; much drainage evidently occurs underground, and only very meager streams drain the inland lakes.

Bois Blanc Island is at present politically attached to Mackinac County, and considerable portions of it are part of the Black Lake State Forest. Only six families are permanent residents of the island; of these, all but one live in the major settlement on the south shore, Point aux Pins. At the height of the summer season the human population is swelled by hundreds of vacationers, many of whom own summer houses along the shore. These people are attracted by the wildness and great natural beauty of the island rather than by the amenities of a civilized resort. There was no electricity on the island at the time excavations were conducted, and until recently there were only one small hotel and a very small store. Most goods are brought in via a ferry which plies between Cheboygan and Point aux Pins. During the deer-hunting season, the island is again invaded by mainlanders, whose demographic and sociological structure and habits differ somewhat from those of the summer vacationers. The deer retreat into the swamps.

There is one dirt road that goes along the shore for about half the island, starting at Point aux Pins. In the opposite direction, the road leads inland. Its last few miles to the west end can be seen in the aerial photograph, Figure 3. Here the road is straight; however, for most of its length it winds between swamps and around natural obstacles, having been laid out, it is said, partly with an eye to timber rights. Its length from Point aux Pins to the west end is about nine and one-half miles, a good half-hour's drive.

Figure 3 (p. 11) reveals other features. The vegetational pattern varies, partly in response to elevation. The rather sharp line in color change from light to dark along the south shore marks fairly sharp cliffs, along the tops of which remnants of Nipissing beaches (whose elevations were not surveyed) may be found. In the lower right portion, an abandoned farm can be seen. Parts of it are long overgrown and retimbered; the smaller portion, still a clearing, was an orchard in the 1920's. There is no farming at all on the island at present, and it was never very successful.

The white-lined rectangle at the west end roughly represents the portion mapped as Figure 4 (p. 20) and includes all the Juntunen site. It may be seen that the site lies in a clearing that parallels the shore for nearly a mile, becoming only fifty yards or so wide at some points. This long clearing, roughly the same in elevation throughout, will be discussed further in section 2.4.1.

2.3.2 GEOLOGY

Reports on aspects of the geology of Bois Blanc Island were prepared by H. Wright (1962, 1964) and S. Harrison (1963); this section is heavily based on those studies.

Bois Blanc Island forms almost the mid-point in a broad arc of silurian rocks that border Lake Michigan on the west and form the Door Peninsula in Wisconsin, continue through the Straits region, run the length of Manitoulin Island, form the Saugeen Peninsula, and extend into New York State (see Hough 1958:14). These rocks, mostly dolomite, are further subdivided on Bois Blanc Island into dolomites of the Bois Blanc and of the St. Ignace formations. According to Landes and Ehlers (1945), the west end of the island should be St. Ignace dolomite. Examination of outcroppings near the Juntunen site, however, indicated that cherts and dolomites of the Bois Blanc series also outcrop at the west end. Glacial deposits blanket bedrock on the island to varying depths and are capped in places by formation of dunes, beaches, and bogs.

As mentioned earlier (sec. 2.1.1), the island was partly above water during the Nipissing stage. Material referable to that stage was found in an area approximately two-thirds of a mile south of the site; following Figure 3, (p. 11) one goes half a mile on the road starting at the beach, then turns right for half a mile. Beach deposits were found on the inland side of the ridge encountered here, suggesting that only a relatively small proportion of the west end was not awash during that stage, because only a few hundred yards to the southwest a precipitous dropoff in elevation is encountered. It is in this beach area that Bois Blanc cherts, dolomites, and "cherty dolomites" outcrop. These particular sources of chert are not likely to have been the ones utilized by aboriginal inhabitants, however, because they are of exceptionally poor quality, besides being heavily frost-fractured. No other beaches of probable Nipissing age were examined on the island. The lack of a topographic survey for the island and the dense vegetation make the search for post-glacial geologic and archaeological features exceedingly difficult.

Following removal of glacial ice, uplift of land began to take place and is still going on at present, though at a greatly reduced rate — about 20 centimeters or 8 inches of rise per century at the Straits (Powers 1962:37). This phenomenon together with the former higher lake levels combined to produce the elevated fossil beaches in the Upper Great Lakes area and to alter land outlines, the type of material and its topography at shores, and water depths. Thus (referring to Fig. 1, p. 7) on Bois Blanc Island the beach west of the Juntunen site is at present formed of gravels and pebbles, with little sandy matrix, and if one were looking for sites and expected to find them only at sandy beaches, the Juntunen site would very likely be overlooked. At the time of occupation, however, the site — now some 17 feet above lake level and several hundred feet away from the shore — was on a sand-ridge coast very close to the water, with extensive sand deposits offshore, at times apparently including bars, which if above water level would have partly enclosed a lagoon.

2.3.3 PLANT AND ANIMAL LIFE

The flora of Bois Blanc Island was studied by Yarnell (1964). The following account of the contemporary situation is abstracted from his monograph.

> Unfortunately there is no published report of the flora of Bois Blanc Island, and as a result it is poorly known. . . .The vegtation of Bois Blanc is varied and includes both coniferous and hardwood forests. A generalized forest cover map, made up in 1945. . .shows four types of vegetation. Each of three forest types is well distributed throughout the island. They are "spruce—balsam—cedar," "poplar—spruce—balsam—cedar," and "hardwood—second growth." The fourth vegetation type, "open—farm—grass," consists of seven relatively small areas that are rather widely scattered. I observed, however, a number of grassy openings which were not indicated on the map.
>
> There is one area on the island that is said to be in virgin forest. This is on and around a large point that projects into Lake Huron from the northeastern side of Bois Blanc. Here I found very few food plants. Only the western part of this forest was examined and it was found to be made up mostly of white and red pine, white cedar, yellow birch, and hard maple.
>
> The largest area of hardwood forest is to be found inland at the west end of the island. My observation is that this forest is almost pure beech-maple with very few economic food plants other than beech and maple except around clearings and bogs. The surrounding coastal area here is spruce—balsam—cedar. It is in this latter type of forest that the Juntunen site is situated. . . .
>
> At the edge of the clearing (in which the site is located) there are a number of plants which produce berries in the summer. They include bearberry, Juneberry, fire cherry, bunchberry, elderberry, and partridge berry; and the common milkweed grows abundantly within the clearing. Some other economic plants which grow upon the island more or less abundantly include paper birch, white cedar, sugar maple, beech, oak, viburnum, sumac, and sand cherry, gooseberry, blackberry, chokecherry, two-leaved Solomon's seal, beach pea, strawberry, marsh marigold, and blueberry. Of course basswood, called bois blanc by the French, also grows on the island [Yarnell 1964:30-31].

Strickland, describing the island in 1860, stated that "the larger portion of it is covered with a. . . forest of elm, maple, oak, ash, white-wood and beech" (1860:131). If his list does in fact reflect the predominant tree species at that time, then the forest composition has changed considerably in the past hundred years because of commercial exploitation of the timber on much of the island: elm and ash are not reported at all by Yarnell, and basswood ("white-wood" = *bois blanc*) is of minor importance.

At present, the fauna of the island is marked by an apparently overwhelming preponderance of two animal species: deer and mosquitoes. The deer population is one of the most concentrated in the United States. Deer were regularly encountered on the site when we arrived in the morning, and it was rare not to see at least a few when driving from Point aux Pins to the west end. That this plenitude is a departure from the aboriginal situation, however, is suggested by the fact that a total of only four deer bones were recovered from the excavations at the Juntunen site. The great change in deer frequency no doubt reflects the changed ecological situation resulting from the lumbering industry. Aside from deer, most other contemporary plant and animal species on the island also occur archaeologically.

2.4 THE JUNTUNEN SITE: SETTING

The Juntunen site (20 Mk 1; Fig. 4) is located in Section 14, T39NR2W, Mackinac County, Michigan. Coordinates are 45° 49' N. lat., 84° 35' W. long. The site's dimensions are approximately 200 x 400 feet, with the long axis paralleling the shore. The clearing in which the site is located is shown together with contours and the location of excavation units in Figure 4. The area of this site map is indicated in white on Figure 3 (p. 11). From the latter figure it may be seen that the northwestern tip of Bois Blanc Island contains a series of parallel elevated beach ridges that can be traced inland as far as a half-mile in some places. The general impression given to anyone walking inland from the shore is of an even series of gentle waves extending nearly a half mile, with no one ridge or trough being uniformly more prominent than the others, although one can be identified as the Algoma beach. The soil is nearly everywhere an unaltered sand.

Following one of the beach ridge contours for nearly a mile is a clearing, easily seen on the aerial photograph (Fig. 3 p. 11), that widens to a meadow at the area of the site, inclosing a small copse of trees. (Note that Arrowhead Drive, bulldozed by

KEY TO EXCAVATION UNIT NUMBERS OF FIGURE 4

Number on Fig. 4	Designations of Included Units
JUNTUNEN SITE	
1	490-10
2	530-100 535-97 535-100
3	600-130 605-130
4	600-200
5	600-70
6	670-245 675-255 680-240 680-245 680-255
7	F-45
8	700-120 700-130 700-140 710-140
9	700-160
10	780-180 700-190 700-200 700-210
11	695-265 700-250 700-265
12	705-405
13	730-190
14	735-230 740-230
15	740-250 740-260
16	740-305
17	F-22
18	750-230
19	780-204
20	780-300
21	790-135
22	790-220 800-210
23	810-225 815-210 820-225 825-210 835-210
24	840-260
25	870-100
26	870-120
27	870-140
28	870-160
29	880-130 890-125
30	890-190 890-200
31	890-285
32	970-185 970-190 970-195
33	1100-95 1100-100
34	1090-150
ARROWHEAD DRIVE SITE	
35	Test Unit 1
36	" " 2
37	" " 3
38	" " 6
39	" " 7

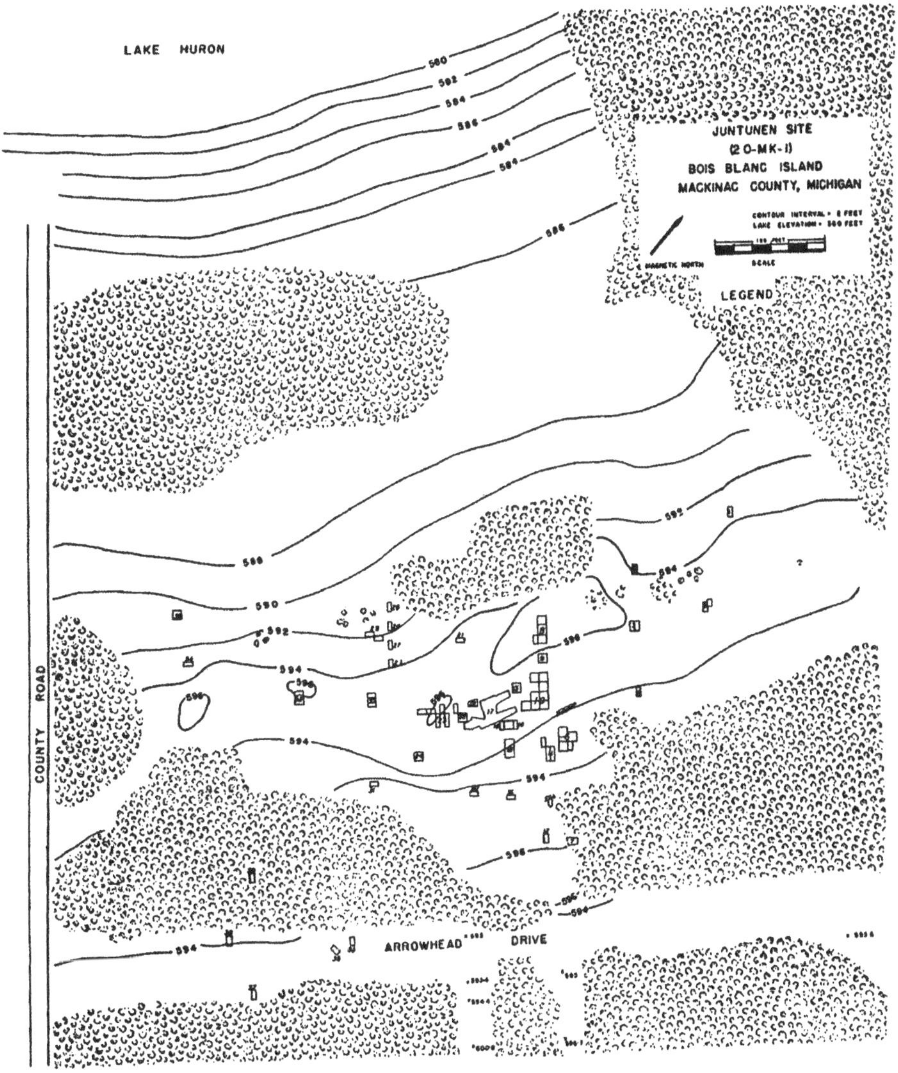

Fig. 4.—Map of the Juntunen site

Mr. Juntunen, and a few other features of the site map do not appear in the 1953 aerial photograph.) Plate I, taken after backfilling at the end of the first field season, shows two views of the meadow: *a* was taken from a position facing a few degrees east of north, and a gentle slope left toward the lake can be observed. Plate I, *b*, was taken with the photographer facing a few degrees north of west, standing where one can view the meadow open down to the lake.

The history of this clearing on an otherwise predominantly forested island is of some interest, and several pertinent facts may be mentioned. First, it will be shown in the next section that at least part of the clearing was once forested heavily enough to allow formation of a distinct soil profile of the podzol type; this soil formation seems to have preceded the Late Woodland occupation. If reforestation occurred after this, it was not sufficient to create podzolization, even though up to 300 years may have intervened between the last prehistoric and the earliest historic occupation.

It is worth noting that the area of clearing is roughly coterminous with the area of extensive aeolian sand deposition at the west end of the island, stabilized through formation of a meadow (with typical meadow-soil profile) only after the last prehistoric occupation. It has probably been the logging and farming operations since the late nineteenth century that have prevented encroachment by the surrounding forest.

Determining the horizontal extent of the site was not easy, since there were virtually no surface materials except in places where "blowouts" occurred as the result of breakdown of vegetation cover. From the excavations, however, it could be seen that the concentration of artifacts thinned out along an axis paralleling the present shore but ended sharply along a contour line of about 591 feet altitude above sea level, some 600 feet back from the water and 11 feet above it. The absence of aboriginal artifacts below 591 feet suggests that, in much of the period during which the site was occupied, the water lay close to the site. If this was the case, then reasoning from the present topography indicates that the water may have been no more than five feet deep as far as 200 feet from the shore at that time and would have had a sandy bottom forming an ideal fish spawning ground and a good place to beach canoes.

On an 1839 map of the island, a "U.S. House" — presumably a customs house — is indicated for the west end, but its exact location could not be determined from the map. Historic-period materials found at the southwestern part of the site date to this period, but no intensive search for this historic structure was made.

Traces of old cabins and other structures, some of which may date to the days of the logging camp on the site, were found in various places. Old residents of the island recall that there were cabins occupied by Indians in the first quarter of this century, who are said to have logged, farmed, and fished there until they were forced to move through the machinations of the owner, a Mr. Todd, who is reported to have been murdered and burned in his house by a servant. His barn was still stand- in 1932 when Robert Braidwood discovered the site.

III
EXCAVATIONS AT THE JUNTUNEN SITE

3.1 METHODS EMPLOYED

The field methods employed were based to a large extent on a mimeographed field manual that was prepared in order to standardize techniques for the field crews of the Museum of Anthropology at the University of Michigan and that is now in print (Papworth and Binford 1962).

3.1.1 SURVEY

The site and areas around it were surveyed topographically with plane table. Higher beaches were mapped by following trails and roads that led up into the woods.

With a transit and steel tape, a center axis and grid system were laid out and numbered in such a way that the origin of the resulting Cartesian system would be offshore, and all the site would lie within the upper left quadrant. Thus the coordinates for any point on the site would be of the form "+00-00," the object being to avoid the confusion of "left—right" or "negative-positive" that sometimes occurs. The polar orientation of the axis that roughly paralleled the shore (the "center" or "+" axis) was decided upon without reference to compass positions; an attempt was made, for ease in surveying, to have the center axis follow the most unobstructed path through the middle of the meadow.

Surveyor's stakes were placed along the center axis every 100 feet, and individual excavation units were laid out from them as required, using transit and tape. The convention for identifying excavation units was to call them by the coordinates of the east corner of the unit — the "designator corner" — citing first the position on the central axis, then the position on the axis perpendicular to it. In Figure 5, the axis parallel to the central axis that passes through most of the site is shown by the line of dots and dashes, and hundred-foot squares are indicated by dotted lines. Thus the designation of the square including Feature 18 is +710-210.[1]

1 In this map and all subsequent discussion, 1,000 feet has been subtracted from every horizontal measurement to simplify the system. In the field, the square just cited was designated "1710-1210." The "+" preceding the designations may be omitted without causing confusion.

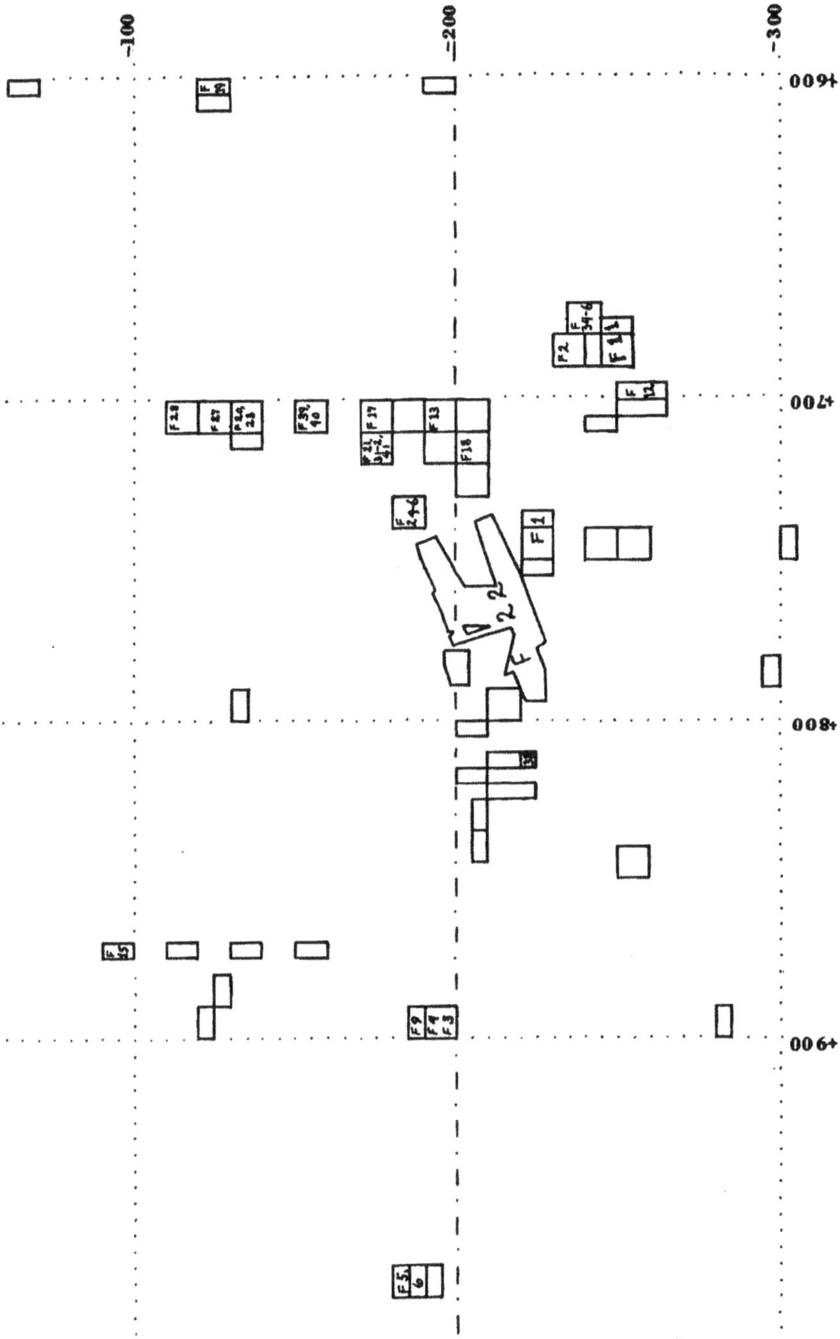

Fig. 5.—Map of central area of site showing grid system and features

Vertical controls were established, in the absence of a bench mark or any permanent marker, with reference to a flat stump, whose elevation was arbitrarily called "100 feet" for purpose of field measurement. Its true elevation was shot in from the lake level on two exceptionally calm days. The water table of the Straits for those days and hours was later obtained from the Water Level Section; U.S. Lake Survey, Detroit.

3.1.2 THE STRATEGY AND TACTICS OF EXCAVATION

Since almost no materials appeared on the surface to be collected, excavation during the first summer was directed to a number of exploratory problems.

1. Was the area of occupation continuous or discontinuous – that is, did horizontal gaps occur in clustering of artifacts? If the latter were the case, was there one site or two?
2. What were the limits of the area of occupation?
3. Did vertical spatial gaps occur in occupation? If so, do they indicate temporal gap in occuaption only or the existence of several components?
4. If multicomponent, what were the areas of overlapping and non-overlapping components?
5. What is the cultural nature of the occupation(s) – that is, temporary camp, fortified village?

In general, the strategy of excavation may be viewed as including two phases. First, efforts were made to sample the entire area of occupation and test in areas beyond the limits of the site, in order to determine the horizontal distribution of occupation and the nature of stratification, and to locate areas of particularly intense occupation (it being assumed that the latter would be the best places to dig). Second, large areas were uncovered in places where the testing suggested that a fair sample of such constructional features as house remains, pits, hearths, and burials would be encountered.

For uniformity in sampling, most digging consisted of 5 x 10- or 10 x 10-foot excavation units with vertical sides, dug in such a manner as to attempt to isolate and remove layers of soil in the reverse order of that in which they were originally deposited. Success was dependent upon the skill of the particular excavator, especially since ancient ground surfaces usually did not run parallel to later ones; it was also dependent on such factors as erosion and subsequent disturbance by man and animals.

Most excavated units are shown on Figure 4, while Figure 5 shows the units in the central area of the site within the framework of the grid system and with features indicated. In addition to those shown, a number of small "potholes" were dug in other areas of the site, and exploratory units were dug at wider intervals in most directions around the site, off the area of the map.

A major concern in excavating was the attempt to remove as units entities that had been deposited as units. Digging by arbitrary levels was done only where no way of visibly separating units was possible yet where it was desired to maintain some separation between what was above and what was below. In soft sands inhabited by people who built no enduring structures, changes in soil texture are slight and much practice is required to tell when one is encountering a transition from a loose to a compacted zone, for example, especially when little difference in color can be perceived. Color difference, of course, was the most common way of determining when the limits of a unit of deposition had been reached.

All excavated material — except when particular caution was indicated — was sifted through quarter-inch screens. This was done even for immense amounts of what appeared to be sterile sand, so that a statement "no contained artifacts" can be said to have been demonstrated. All artifactual material that could be recognized was collected, including flint chippage and sherds down to crumb size; all faunal and vegetal matter was likewise collected. Postcontact material was saved — even window glass, nails, and bottle caps — for the light it might throw on both modern occupations and the extent of disturbance. Samples of soil were preserved unsifted when a different color or texture was encountered.

When the limits of a color or texture zone or lens — however slight — was reached in digging or, in the absence of any such change, when a maximum of 0.5 feet had been removed, bags were closed, the elevations of the four corners measured, and a plan drawing of the clean-troweled floor was drawn to scale on specially prepared forms called "square sheets." A "provenience unit" is defined as any parcel of soil and its contents handled as a unit. A provenience unit thus might consist of one artifact, the total artifact content of a refuse pit, or the artifacts recovered between the drawing of two square sheets — at most a 0.5-foot layer — in a 10 x 10 foot square. An attempt was made in drawing to include as much detail as could be observed. Colors and textures were noted, and in addition to measuring and recording the elevations of the four corners, the elevations of other points would also be recorded if higher or lower than the level as a whole. In summary, reasons to stop digging and start drawing a square sheet (an example of a square sheet is included in Papworth and Binford 1962) included: 0.5 feet removed without change; color or texture change; observed change in artifacts; occurrence of new elements, such as concentrations of sherds, bone, charcoal, etc.

Square sheets were numbered consecutively for each square, so artifacts recovered up to the time of drawing the first square sheet in a given square would be labeled "Surface to Square Sheet 1." This system for identifying artifacts from units of soil horizontally and vertically will be used in this report. Thus 790-120 (2-3) refers to artifacts recovered in square 790-120 between the levels at which square sheets 2 and 3, whose elevations are indicated on the sheets, were drawn.

Considerable difficulty was experienced in obtaining uniformity in description of colors. One man's "yellowish tan" was the other man's "tannish gray," and neither conveys much to someone who has not seen the original. I attempted to achieve uniformity by collecting ten or so of the common soil types and gluing them like sandpaper to board do not look alike, and the experiment was considered a failure. Munsell color charts might well be the answer, although even here the problem of transfer from one texture to another is still unsolved.

Photographs were taken of levels cleaned for drawing square sheets when it seemed appropriate. Digging preceeded until unmistakably sterile gravels were reached, and in places even these were dug into for positive assurance and so that profiles of the bedding might be made. After completeion of a square — or ideally while the digging proceeded — profile drawings and photographs of at least two of the walls were made.

3.2 DATA RECOVERED

During the first (1960) field season of ten weeks, a crew of seven excavated 2,380 square feet of the site in 2,540 man-hours of actual digging, meaning that slightly more than one hour was required in the field to remove a square foot. Over the two field seasons combined, a total of 4,750 square feet were opened in sixty-nine 5 x 10- or 10 x 10-foot units, with 5,860 cubic feet of material being excavated, which indicates that slightly more than one cubic foot was excavated per man per hour in the field. One may wonder where the time went. The answer lies mostly in the recording; more time was spent writing, measuring, drawing, photographing, and pondering how to proceed than was actually spent with shovel and trowel. A total of 523 provenience units were bagged and recorded in the 1960 and 1961 seasons.

If the site may be assumed to measure 80,000 square feet (200 x 400 feet), then the square footage excavated represents a 6 per cent sample of the site — rather small, as samples go, to represent a universe in the statistical sense and drawn in a non-random fashion.

The figures given above represent only work done on the Juntunen site proper. In answer to problem 1 of section 3.1.2, two sites could be recognized, with a high degree of horizontal separation and artifact difference. The Late Woodland site occupies the area of the meadow (Fig. 4 p. 20). The Middle Woodland site, called Arrowhead Drive, occurs as a thin scattering of artifacts for nearly a mile on a ridge whose surface is in most places not significantly higher than the Juntunen site but is somewhat more inland.

The data recovered can be divided, first, into artifactual and non-artifactual material. An artifact is here defined formally as anything whose form or presence is the result of human activity. Artifacts can further be divided into recoverable items, such as arrowheads and potsherds, and "features"—such artifacts as hearths, pits, and traces of decayed posts, which are inherently non-recoverable, which are destroyed in excavation, and whose only form of preservation is in the records kept by the archaeologist.

The major classes of recoverable artifacts from the Juntunen site are presented in Table 1 by frequency and level. It will suffice at this point to refer to the totals, where we see that potsherds constitute by far the major kind of artifact, although the actual number of vessels inferred to be represented is not unduly large. On the average, 17 sherds were recovered per cubic foot of earth shifted. The total of over 100,000 sherds weighed 276.4 kilograms or 608 pounds. Chert artifacts were second in frequency for tools, followed by copper artifacts.

In sum, the data included (1) artifacts, animal bones, and plant remains collected with quarter-inch screen; (2) profiles and floor plans of each provenience unit in every excavation unit; (3) notes on strata and features; (4) black-and-white and color photographs; (5) pollen samples and bags of soil whose proveniences were noted on profile drawings and square sheets.

TABLE 1

FREQUENCIES OF ARTIFACTS, BY PHASES

Occupation	Cultural Phase	Provenience Units	Cubic Feet	Pottery: Vessels	Pottery: No. of Sherds	Pottery: Sherd Wt. (Grams)	Chipped Flint: Number	Chipped Flint: Weight	Chipped Flint: Bois Blanc Chert	Chipped Flint: Non-Bois-Blanc	Bipolar: Cores	Bipolar: Flakes	Non-Bipolar: Cores	Non-Bipolar: Flakes	Scrapers	Projectile Points Bifaces	Decortication Flakes	Shatter	Utilized Flakes	Others	Unclassified	Copper: Finished	Copper: Unfinished	Bone Tools: Awls	Bone Tools: Harpoons	Bone Tools: Others	Animal Bone	Maize Kernels
E-F	JUNTUNEN	98	1043	269	14333	42395	4103	8046	433	3177	142	583	65	1070	51	19	290	274	56	45	1113	34	217	18	3	12	7104	11
D to E-F	Intermediate II	64	706	410	22270	58052	1123	8970	506	3149	186	864	49	1232	96	36	299	210	50	21	871	24	241	8	--	2	3219	1
D	BOIS BLANC	53	594	142	15043	47141	2057	3776	471	1586	119	332	76	1032	17	12	121	772	31	8	598	12	75	5	--	6	6509	1
A-C to D	Intermediate I	29	277	174	15246	30578	3655	2126	206	917	77	219	10	378	22	12	100	68	10	--	427	4	44	5	--	3	14535	--
A-C	MACKINAC	194	1662	438	21023	72357	3610	7875	1777	2326	94	449	70	1944	25	39	225	287	40	50	1042	5	16	20	2	10	14102	2
Unassigned		85	1579	183	13533	25905	2713	7614	941	1772	126	438	69	796	34	80	209	246	30	32	831	11	35	13	4	9	2494	4
		523	5861	1616	101447	276428	17261	38407	4334	12927	744	2885	339	6452	245	198	1244	1157	217	156	4882	92	628	69	9	42	47963	19

IV

GEOMORPHOLOGY AND DEPOSITIONAL HISTORY

4.1 METHODS OF ANALYSIS OF THE GEOLOGICAL DATA

The deposition of cultural remains on the site occurred in the context of several geological conditions, principally dune formation, which caused the stratification to be exceedingly complex. The task of ordering and interpreting the deposits utilizing mainly data of geologic significance was undertaken by Henry Wright, whose preliminary paper (1962) is largely summarized here.

His task was not an easy one. Excavation was conducted primarily for archaeological objectives, with roughly equidimensional and generally discrete excavation units. Geologic data, however, are best obtained from long continuous profiles, minimizing the problems of correlating isolated exposures. Whereas efforts were made to "trench the site — the series of units perpendicular to the major or "y" axis seen in Figure 5 (p. 24) were laid out for this purpose — that fact that the trenches were not continuous resulted in problems of geological analysis. They were, in fact, laid out for economy so as to skip every other ten feet, and archaeological data were simultaneously being collected and recorded with as much care as in any other part of the site. It would have been greatly preferable to employ power equipment and run a long narrow trench from which a profile could be obtained, sacrificing a small amount of cultural data. Techniques for recovery of non-artifactual data were imperfect. Wright suggests that two, rather than one, types of soil samples should have been collected:

> first, the usual sack of soil for sieve analysis of grain size and chemical studies; second, a microsample (perhaps five 1 cc samples from five randomly selected points on a ten foot exposure) for grain shape or wear counts, or a water-settling analysis of grain size. All of these soil samples should be measured into the profile drawings. A standardized Munsell color rating of each stratum should be made in the field before the colors fade [1964:2].

The analysis of the geological data commenced with study of the stratigraphy. Based on profile drawings and photographs, two full-color cross sections of the site ridge — one at +700 and the other at +870 on the center axis — were prepared. The locations of soil samples and the altitudes of the square sheets were noted wherever possible. These cross sections of the site roughly perpendicular to the beach ridges were then subdivided by Wright into morphologically defined zones. As shown in the composite generalized cross section, Figure 6, these zones were, in order, as follows. The "beach zone" was an area showing evidence of direct wave action during the earlier part of aboriginal occupation by gravel layers, black laminae, and waterworn artifacts. The "foreslope zone" was defined as the area that showed evidence of considerable aeolian deposition by crossbedded dunes and thick sand layers but that showed no evidence of wave action during or after aboriginal occupation had commenced. The "topslope zone" was defined as the area composed primarily of flat-lying soil formations with relatively little evidence of wind deposition. The logical complement of these three zones, the "backslope zone," showed no evidence of accumulation of deposits during the period of aboriginal occupation and was therefore not studied geologically.

Along the major axis, the site was further subdivided into three areas: a "northeastern area" along the line perpendicular to the center axis at +600 feet on that axis, a "central area" (+700 to +800 on the center axis), and a "southwestern area" along the line of 5 x 10-foot units at +870 on the center axis.

The soil samples were first studied for grain-size differences; sieve analysis failed to show significant differences among samples. Microscopic examination likewise failed to show significant differences in proportion of quartz to non-quartz mineral grains but did reveal marked differences in the degree and type of grain wear among samples. Grains varied from round to angular and had fractured, pitted, frosted, or polished surfaces. Subjective judgments of the proportions of these attributes were made by Wright for each sample.

Wright made three assumptions in order to infer a general sequence of stratigraphic layers from the local sequence in each subarea. These assumptions were that (1) the developed podzolic soil (A in Fig. 6), the lowest soil horizon on the site and containing the earliest cultural remains, was of essentially the same age wherever it occurred; (2) the marked angular unconformity appearing in three subareas (between D-E and F in Fig. 6) was of essentially the same age wherever it occured; (3) similar sequences of lithologically similar strata occuring between these two features could be correlated.

The analysis next involved comparing the gross morphology, types of grain shape, and types of grain wear within each unit, between units, and with control samples from a live beach on

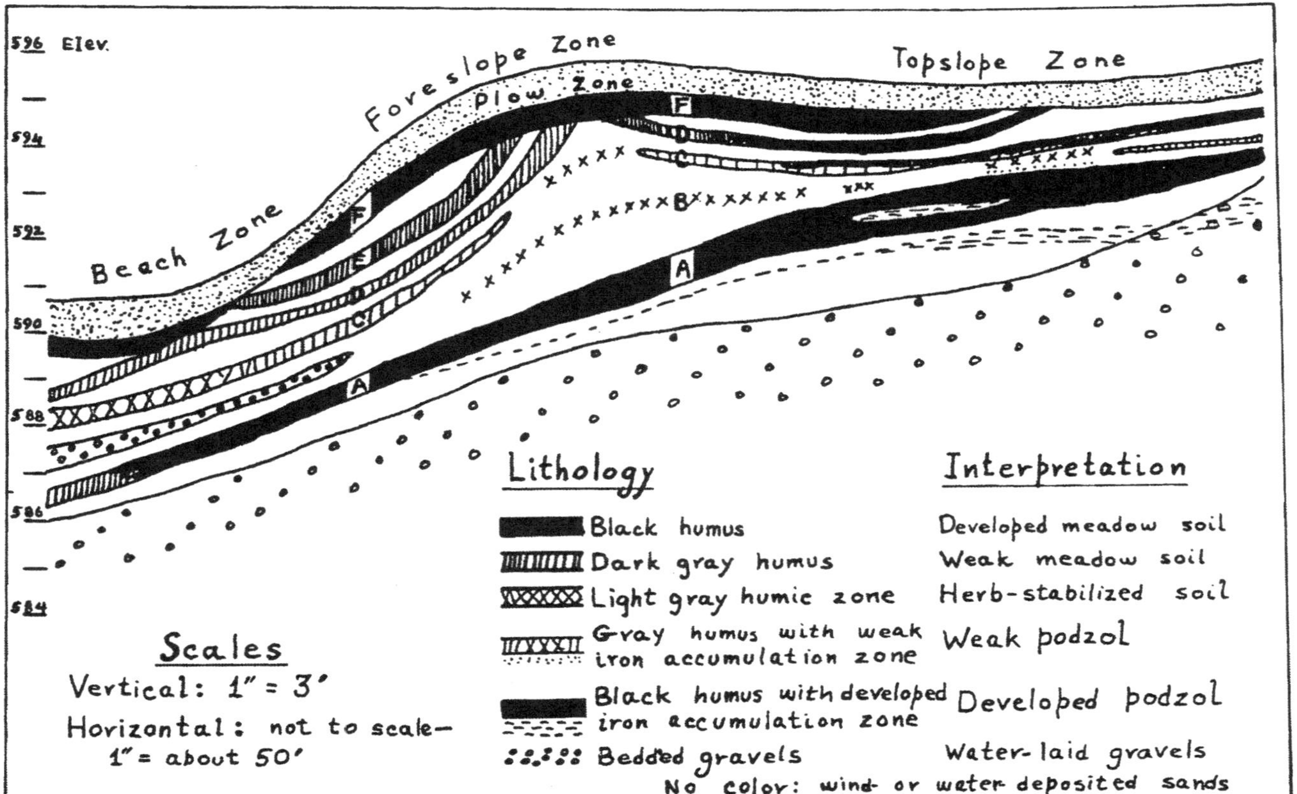

Fig. 6.—Generalized composite cross section of the Juntunen site in a plane approximately normal to the shoreline.

Round Island forming under what are believed to be the same conditions as operated to produce the Juntunen site ridge. This Round Island beach is on the opposite side of the island from the site marked with a white ellipse; it can be seen in Figure 3 (p. 11) to be protected by cuspate headlands in much the same fashion as the west end of Bois Blanc Island. The geologic processes at work on the various areas of the Juntunen ridge at different times were then inferred, and these inferences were integrated by Wright into a general history of the geomorphological changes of the Juntunen site.

The series of stratigraphic layers developed by Wright are listed in the second column of Table 2 while the third column shows the frequency of culture-bearing provenience units that could be assigned to these layers. A brief description (based mostly on Wright, 1962) of the layers follows. It may be noted that the word "layer" is used here as a purely conventional term to avoid the confusion that results from overuse of the word "unit"; it is not intended to describe or specify morphology.

4.2 SEQUENCE OF DEPOSITIONAL UNITS

Layer I. — (see Plate II, *a*.) Basal unit consisting of overlapping lenses of coarse and fine gravel slanting toward the lake. Wright infers that the gravel core of the ridge upon which the site is located was first formed as an offshore bar when the water stood higher than a plane now at an altitude of 596 feet above mean sea level and that the lenses were deposited on the lakeside flanks of this core as the lake level decreased and land rose.

Layer II. — Veneering the gravel ridge in most places is tannish-white sand, of variable thickness, deposited mostly by wind action, but with black laminae in some places nearest the beach, suggesting that deposition occurred very near the waterline.

Layer III. — A podzol soil horizon formed in places on the site on top of Layer II, stabilizing the sand deposits. It is most strongly developed in the central portion of the site (note the A1, A2, and B horizons in Pl. II, *a*), suggesting a long-standing forest cover, but is weak or lacking in southern portions, suggesting a non-tree cover. The concentrations of charcoal in the A1 zone of this layer and the burned-root pattern of a tree in the central foreslope zone (see Pl. II, *b*) suggest that the tree cover was burned off, quite possibly by some early occupants.

Layer IV. — Variable in thickness, color, and morphology, this layer of sand appears to have been derived partly from beach sand and partly from Layer III_{A1}.

TABLE 2

ROCK-STRATIGRAPHIC UNITS, OCCUPATIONS, AND CULTURAL PHASES

Absolute Dates	Stratigraphic Layers	Number of Culture-bearing Provenience Units Assignable	Occupation	Cultural Phase	Number of Provenience Units Assignable to Phase
A.D.					
	XXV$_1$	2			
	XXV$_2$	6	F		
1330 ± 100	XXV$_3$	17		Juntunen	98
	XXIV	5			
	XXIII	2			
	XXII	3	E		
	XXI	--			
	XX	2		Intermediate II	64
	XIX	--			
	XVIII	4	D		
1070 ± 75	XVII	21		Bois Blanc	53
	XVI	10			
910 ± 75	XV	11		Intermediate I	29
	XIV	1	C		
	XIII	8			
	XII$_1$	5			
	XII$_2$	1			
	XI	8			
	X	--	B		
	IX	1			
	VIII	--		Mackinac	194
	VII	--			
	VI	1			
835 ± 75	V	22			
	IV	8			
	III$_{A1}$	10	A		
	III$_{A2}$	--			
	III$_B$	1			
	II	3			
	I	--			
Unassigned Provenience Units		371			85
Total Prov. Units		523			523

Layer V. — Only in places separable from Layer III_{A1}, this layer is a gray-black sand, representing the deposit of Layer IV subsequently stained by heavy occupation and humus formation. Calcareous clayey sand lenses indicate intensive occupation in the northeast and central areas of the site. Leaching of portions of Layer IV directly below this layer suggests reforestation and resumption of podzolization. Layer V is the upper part of zone A of figure 6 (p. 32) and is seen above III in Figure 7 between +700-110 and +700-130. A carbon date of A.D. 835 ± 75 on charcoal was obtained (M-1142, Crane and Griffin 1961).

Layers VI through X. — These depositional units represent a series of processes known to have directly affected only the southwestern beach zone. As seen in Plate III, Figure 6 (p. 32), and Figure 8, they cut into and overlap earlier depositional units. Layer VI is a tan-white sand with thin black laminae, clearly seen in Plate III, *b;* VII is a lens of gravel offlapping VI; VIII is very similar to VI, while IX, seen in Plate III *a*, is a fairly thick, well-developed gravel layer which yielded a few rolled and abraded potsherds; and X is a yellowish bedded sand.

Wright concludes that these layers represent transgression on the land by the lake, which he thinks rose to levels now at an altitude of 590 feet above sea level, and that this transgression was greater than five feet, from something less than 585 to 590 feet above sea level. The transgression, while not of major proportion, since it did not greatly alter the topography and falls within the range of the secular changes mentioned in section 2.2.2, was nonetheless probably more than merely an exceptional storm beach, for it is thought to have been the cause of the deposition of dune sand over much of the ridge and it certainly at least coincides with (if it does not cause) marked reduction in intensity of occupation of the site.

These layers were found in only one area and are correlated by Wright with Layers XI through XIII on the rest of the site. The relationships are illustrated in Figure 8.

Layers XI through XIII. — These layers represent deposition of wind-blown sand in a number of forms: thin, flat deposits were laid over much of the site; in some areas scattered lenses of one layer occur, suggesting patches of herb-stabilized soil on an otherwise unstable land surface. In the central foreslope zone, dune formation occurred in such a way that slightly different-colored sands, often cross-bedded, alternated with darker layers that suggest temporary stabilization by plants. This dune is most impressive in the +700 profile shown in Plate IV and in Figure 7. The layers are telescoped into one stratum in the

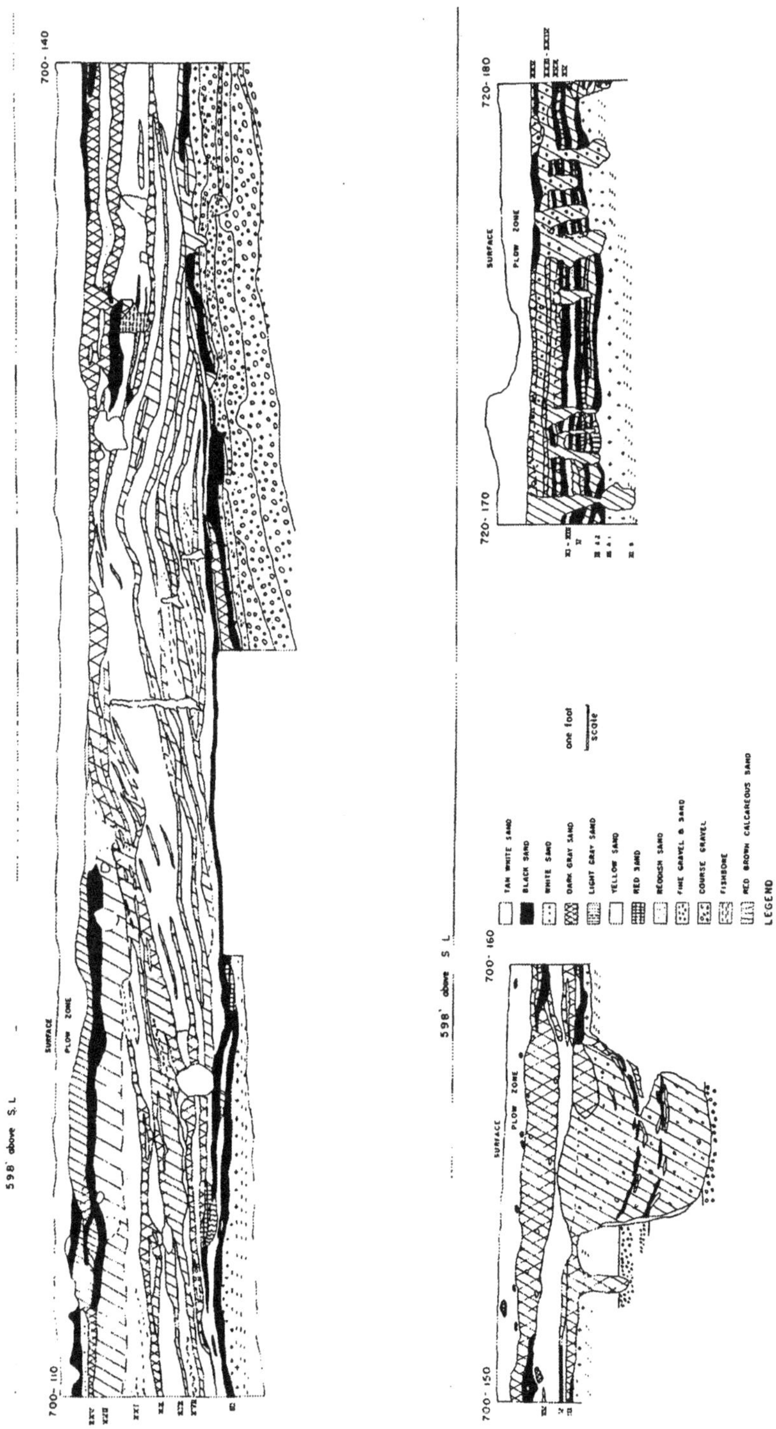

Fig. 7.—Cross section of central area of Juntunen site (Units 8-10 of Fig. 4). (Reproduced from H. Wright [1962]). Diagonal lines indicated mottled yellow and gray sand.

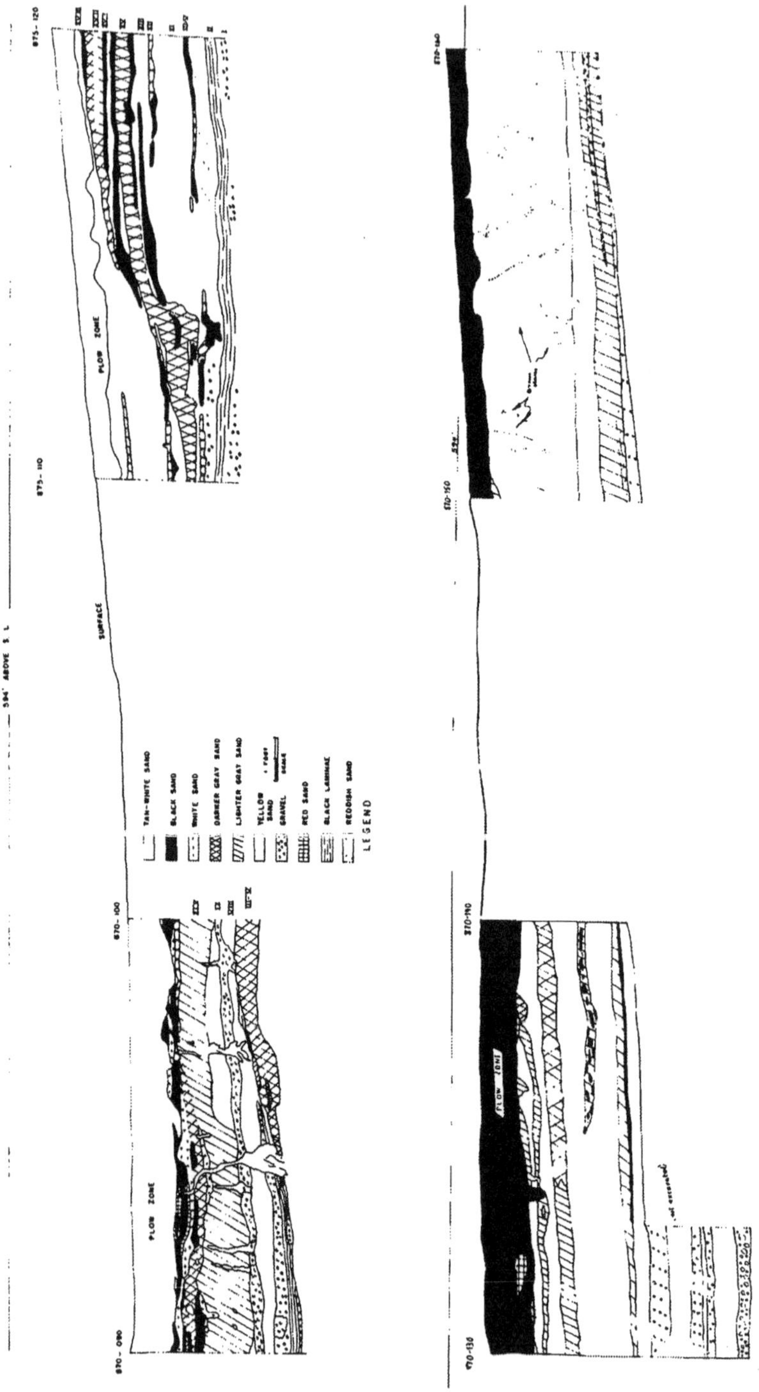

Fig. 8.—Cross section of Southwest Area (Units 25-28 of Fig. 4) (Reproduced from H. Wright [1962]).

topslope zone, as shown in Plate V, *a*.

Layer XV. — This variable layer of light- to dark-gray sand, shown in Plate V, *b*, owes its color to human occupation. There is some doubt whether it should not actually be assigned to XIII. Cessation in deposition is inferred.

Layer XVI. — A continuous layer throughout most of the site, this light-colored sand is the last unit to contribute to the growth of the dune in the central foreslope zone; the dune now reaches a thickness of 2.8 feet, an altitude of more than 596.3 feet above sea level (Fig. 7). Deposition is inferred to have outrun vegetation growth.

Layer XVII. — A major cessation of deposition followed by soil formation is seen in this layer, slightly darker than XVI but otherwise lithologically similar. Moderate podzolization in a few areas and the development of a meadow soil in many others indicates stabilization of the dune. Occupation D occurs in and on this layer, dated on charcoal at A.D. 1070 ± 75 (M-1141, Crane and Griffin 1961).

Layer XVIII. — Restricted to the former foreslope zone, this layer of yellowish-white sand forms a discontinuous layer that thickens to fill depressions in the surface of XVII and is cut off at its top in an angular unconformity. See Figures 6 (p. 32) and 7 (p. 36). Destruction of vegetation by human clearing and redeposition of high points of XVII is inferred.

Layers XIX through XXII. — Between XVII and XXV are a series of layers difficult to correlate and interpret. The sequence is believed to represent a period of erosion and deflation, accompanied and followed by deposition, meadow-soil formation, more deposition, gradual stabilization, and meadow-soil formation. The relatively brief Occupation E occurred during this period.

Layers XXIII through XXIV. — On the former topslope zone (now built up by Layers XI through XVII to about 596 feet above sea level) an unconformity was cut, planing the dune, and somewhat different deposits accumulated. Layer XXIII is a tan-gray sand with a few dolomite pebbles; XXIV is gray sand with a high frequency of pebbles (see Pl. V, *a*). The formation of these strata is inferred to involve deflation and redeposition of portions of XVII, growth of a soil, and — because of the occurrence of the pebbles — human activity, such as digging of pits into Layer I. Occupation E is inferred to represent the material culture of the people responsible for the spread of the pebbles. This interpretation of the course of events is open to the objection that the lithology of pebbles in Layer I and of those occurring in XXIII and XXIV is not identical; the frequency of dolomite is low in I, whereas it is the major lithic form in the later units under discussion. This problem cannot at present be solved.

Layer XXV. — Wherever this unit was not destroyed by deflation, erosion, land leveling, or plowing, it was seen as a relatively thick and roughly level layer of dark-gray to black sand, with grains showing a high frequency of complete overall polishing, suggesting much reworking by wind and subjection to prolonged chemical action. Major deposition of sand had ceased, which implies that the lake had by this time reached essentially its present level. A heavy grass cover formed, and an intensive occupation F, dated on charcoal at A.D. 1330 ± 100, took place (M-1140, Crane and Griffin 1961).

Subsequent Layers. — All subsequent depositional layers were destroyed by cultivation, deflation, and other causes in the nineteenth and twentieth centuries.

4.3 GEOMORPHOLOGICAL HISTORY

The following summary is quoted from H. Wright (1964:4):

> The core of the site ridge was an offshore gravel bar formed when the lake stood higher than 600 feet above sea level. . .As successively lower portions of the ridge were revealed coniferous forests spread over the ridge. By about A.D. 800 the water level had dropped to an altitude probably less than 585 feet above sea level and a developed podzolic soil had formed beneath the forest.
>
> At this time the site was briefly occupied, burned off, covered with lenses of sand, intensively occupied and burned off again. These occupations are grouped together as "occupation A."
>
> After this occupation the lake transgressed on the land rising to an altitude of 590 feet above sea level. It covered a portion of the "A" stratum and caused the deposition of sand dunes over much of the ridge. During this period of transgression two brief occupations, B and C, occurred on poorly developed herb stabilized soils. The latter occupation dates about A.D. 950.
>
> About A.D. 1050, most of the ridge seems to have been covered by a meadow soil. On this soil "occupation D" occurred. After occupation D a period of general erosion creating angular unconformities took place. In some places, however, the deposition of lenses of sand occurred. It was possible to isolate a brief "occupation E," believed to date around A.D. 1200 on a soil in one of these lenses.
>
> Following this period of erosion a thick meadow soil developed over most of the site ridge. The deposition of sand ceased, implying that the lake had now retreated to near its present level. An intensive "occupation F" believed to date around A.D. 1300 occurred on the meadow soil. All evidence of subsequent occupation within the area studied had been destroyed by plowing.

In view of the Arrowhead drive elevation and the occurrence of Arrowhead Drive materials on Juntunen, it seems clear that the lake level must have been below 595 feet by the time of that occupation (about A.D. 50).

4.4 ABORIGINAL OCCUPATIONS

The classification of provenience units into 25 stratigraphic layers permitted the postulation of six periods of occupation for the site as a whole. This alignment of the stratigraphy permitted a number of provenience units to be assigned to an occupation; the precise number is indicated in the third column of Table 2 (p. 34). On the basis of these assignable units (about 30 per cent of the total excavated) the work of Yarnell and Cleland was based. It was clearly unsatisfactory, however, that so many units should be in "limbo," —unassignable to one of the six occupations.

From the artifactual end, the great difficulty was that Occupations B, C, and E were poorly represented; in addition, positively assignable B and C units could not be distinguished by inspection from A, nor were their artifact content frequencies sufficient to permit statistical tests; nor could E units be distinguished from F, evidently because of both disturbance and lack of stylistic change.

Since such a small percentage of the provenience units of the site could be positively assigned to a unit of the sixfold series of occupations set up by H. Wright mostly on geological grounds and, further, since Occupations B and C contained extremely few artifacts and hence were not distinguishable culturally from A, it was decided to collapse A through C and likewise to group the last two occuaptions, E and F, resulting in three proposed phases of occupation, named "Mackinac," "Bois Blanc," and "Juntunen," respectively, as shown in Table 2 (p. 34). This grouping removed a great amount of uncertainty; many units whose differential assignment to A or B was not possible could nonetheless be clearly assigned to the Mackinac phase. Units whose assignment to one of the phases was uncertain but which occurred stratigraphically between assignable units were assigned to either one or the other of two intermediate groupings, Intermediates I and II. They were regarded as a class of mixed provenience units and excluded from certain statistical manipulations. Units now unassignable at all totaled 85, a considerable reduction from the 371 units unassignable in the sixfold system of "occupations." As will be shown in the sections describing the materials recovered, this tripartite division of the stratigraphy corresponds well to three culturally meaningful and separable divisions; thus the pottery wares (set up on archaeological grounds) bearing the phase names are highly correlated with their respective phases (set up largely on geological grounds).

In all that follows, use will be made of both systems, the A-through-F series of occupations and the threefold set of phases (plus the two intermediates), depending both on the stage of data reduction at which the particular study presented was performed and on the purpose in mind. Reference should be made to Table 2 (p. 34) for clarification.

PART II

DESCRIPTION AND ANALYSIS OF ARCHAEOLGICAL MATERIALS

INTRODUCTION

The sequence of geological events presented in the preceding part forms the matrix within which the occupations occurred; ultimately, the cultural and natural data will be combined in a depositional history. First, however, the formal analysis of archaeological materials, artifactual and non-artifactual, must be presented; their distribution in space and inferences with regard to temporal sequence and functional differences must then be discussed.

In the chapters that follow, the various classes of recovered materials and features will be treated first in purely formal terms; for example, pottery from all phases will be described and classified as one collection, regardless of provenience, then stratigraphic occurrence will be presented for each class, and, finally, the "behavior" of the different classes with respect to each other and to the provenience units will be discussed.

Description and analysis of materials are inseparable. Unless one is willing to present each artifact individually, stressing thereby the uniqueness of the individual, some information must be sacrificed in order to obtain "types" and some cases — artifacts, provenience units, strata — must be assigned to limbo because they fall between types and are thus indeterminate. In the chapters that follow, a disproportionately great amount of attention has been paid to pottery. This class of artifact, the most abundant on the site and containing more attributes than any other class, received particularly intense study. I have published a brief report on the ceramics (McPherron 1963a) and presented elsewhere the methodology that I used in an attempt to mechanize and evaluate classification procedures (McPherron 1963b); these matters will be discussed here in greater detail.

With the exception of copper artifacts, pottery types show the greatest variation through time and hence are of value in describing and explicating temporal and other change. Next after pottery in terms of abundance is the chipped-stone industry, which also displays change over time, particularly with respect to the unusual bipolar industry.

After discussion of the artifact classes, non-artifactual materials, and features, a distributional analysis will relate all of them to each other, permitting then correlation of formal, spatial, and temporal dimensions with the geomorphology, leading to a depositional history of the site. Based on these findings, the "anthropology of the Juntunen site" will be discussed in Part Three.

V

POTTERY

5.1 INTRODUCTION

The bulk of artifactual material recovered consisted mostly of potsherds. All that were held by the 1/4-inch screen through which all materials were sifted were collected, washed, and at least counted and weighed.

There were about 101,477 sherds in all. This mass of sherds was ultimately converted in the laboratory, by a procedure to be described (sec. 5.4), to an inferred total number of vessels represented by at least one sherd from the site; the 1,688 vessels thus identified still loom large when compared, say, with 245 scrapers, 152 projectile points, or 117 bone tools found. On the other hand, a vessel breaks into many pieces, which often get scattered over a surprisingly large area, both horizontally and vertically, so the probability of getting one sherd from a given vessel 20 feet from where it was initially dropped is much greater than that of getting a scraper dropped the same distance away, since it can be accepted that a scraper will not break into so many pieces. The total sherd sample analyzable for attributes numbered 4,750; thus a relatively small proportion of the whole could be used. Most of the 1,688 vessels are represented in the recovered sample by only one sherd. The accompanying table shows the

No. of Vessels	No. of Rim or Decorated Sherds Representing each Vessel	No. of Vessels	No. of Rim or Decorated Sherds Representing each Vessel
1316	1	13	9
143	2	2	10
68	3	13	11-20
29	4	5	21-30
27	5	8	31-40
18	6	2	41-50
16	7	9	51-100
15	8	4	101 and more

breakdown. Sherd weight distributions are shown in Tables 28 and 29 (p. 203). Thus, despite the great number of sherds collected and the attention devoted to them in this report, it does not appear that these Indians actually made unaccountably more pots than any other kind of artifact. Although it does not seem possible — given the kind of excavation done and the problem of variation in the number of pieces into which a vessel may break — to compare directly and numerically the frequencies of vessels with the frequencies of other artifacts from the site, there is still no reason to think that pottery-making assumed a disproportionate importance in aboriginal life at the site.

Another factor worth mentioning with respect to the quantity of sherds is that of size; since *all* sherds that could be detected in the sifters were kept, a great many were extremely small, useless for typological purposes, but of value when the question of average sherd weight in a given unit is at issue. (Uses of "average sherd weight" are dealt with in Ch. 14.) A distinction was made between sherds that were larger than a dime, which were normally fully processed, and those that were under that size ("microsherds"), which were counted and weighed but generally not numbered. A regression analysis of microsherd frequencies and weights in the first 100 provenience units containing more than 10 microsherds revealed that the weight of a lot of microsherds was an exceedingly good predictor of their number, suggesting that much tedious counting of these tiny sherds could have been eliminated. The mean microsherd weight turned out to be very close to 1.0 gram. (See Tables 28 and 29, p. 203).

In this report, ceramics assignable to the Late Woodland period will be considered in detail, while only brief mention will be made of the Middle Woodland sherds, which mostly pertain to an areally distinct Arrowhead Drive site.

5.2 JUNTUNEN POTTERY AS A WHOLE

5.2.1 INTRODUCTION

Preceding the analysis and description of pottery types, common characteristics of the ceramics considered as a single collection will be presented. When the Juntunen vessels are compared with those being made in the same period at other places in the Upper Great Lakes area, certain broad generalizations can be made. While considerable care was lavished on the decoration of Juntunen vessels, pastes and tempering materials were coarse, and sherds displayed a common tendency toward laminar splitting or exfoliating. Vessel sizes, as far as could be determined, varied over a fairly small range, but the decoration presented more variation than was seen in any other collection in the overall area that I was able to examine. A surprising number of instruments were employed in plastic decorating. They were used in a variety of ways, and the build-up into decorative designs exhibited great variability.

Two contrasts with many other of the similar wares may be seen in the amount and large size of the particles of granular temper and the vigor with which the formed vessel was paddled or fabric-impressed and then decorated. The various cords, sticks, and other apparatus were impressed into the clay with firm decision and a strong hand, in contrast with the somewhat similar wares of, for example, New York State or Ontario, where a lighter hand with the decorating tools was customary.

These vessels also saw hard use in cooking. Mending perforations were fairly frequent (though not tabulated during the processing of the data). Eight per cent of them had encrustations of carbonized cooking residues near the orifices, occurring both inside and out and generally fading out past the neck to the shoulder, giving way to an area oxidized by fire. The cooking residue was often so thick (up to 2 mm.) that it fully obscured the decorated area and was so tenacious that it could be removed only by vigorous use of a steel-wire scratch brush. This encrustation could well have resulted from the repeated cooking of fish in the vessel, with boiling-over and deposition of the gluey, nearly insoluble by-products of fish cookery, hard to remove from vessels even today. Had not other carbon been readily available for dating, this encrustation could have been processed for radiocarbon analysis, as was done by Mason (1964a) for Heins Creek (an ecologically similar site). Encrustations of this sort and magnitude were notably lacking from comparable vessels that I examined from sites in the Upper Great Lakes where subsistence activities involved major sources of food other than fish. Attempts at microscopic examination of the carbonized residues were made, but the results were inconclusive. Chemical analysis of possible remaining organic matter was contemplated but could not be arranged.

5.2.2 PHYSICAL ATTRIBUTES

Preliminary examination of the sherds indicated considerable homogeneity with respect to such attributes as paste, temper, hardness, and color. In view of the difficulties inherent in describing such characteristics on the basis of subjective impressions, and because of the apparent homogeneity throughout time, these attributes will be presented at the outset, while in the individual descriptions only significant departures from the norm will be mentioned.

5.2.2.1 Paste and Temper

Seventeen sherds, chosen in an attempt to represent various periods and types of pottery, were submitted to James Porter of the Lithic Laboratory, Southern Illinois University Museum, Carbondale, Illinois, for thin-section analysis. The results of the analysis strongly confirmed initial impressions; the report considered the sherds to be

> . . .a homogeneous series. All are grit tempered in a few paste types which, although most are sandy, appear to be the types one might expect from a source heavily glaciated. Little can be said for the grit except that it all appears quite fresh mineralogically (late Wisconsin) [Porter 1963].

One sherd examined in thin section, considered by Dr. James B. Griffin as being related to Ramey Incised, was not distinguished from the rest of the collection in terms of temper and paste, although it did contain some shell fragments. Porter found no trace of grog temper in the collection and, except for the shell temper in Ramey, a lack of any other type of temper as well. Porter did not, however, attempt to distinguish between glacial clays.

The grit of all specimens consisted mainly of crushed granitic rock; minerals that predominate, according to Porter, include green hornblende, quartz, plagioclase, feldspar, diorite, biotite, and muscovite. The sources of this material are not hard to find; scattered through the site — though with concentration in some layers that were regrettably not carefully observed and noted except in a few instances — were angular pieces of rock of this sort, commonly considered "firestones," although there is little direct evidence at Juntunen for this functional supposition. In many instances the rock was already disintegrating into its constituent mineral elements, suggesting that the comminution of rock for temper by Indians would not have been a difficult task: often rubbing between the fingers was sufficient to produce a handful of "temper." Such fire-disintegrated rocks have been observed on many other sites.

Within the sample of sherds submitted to him Porter was able to distinguish four paste types united in consisting of the poorly-sorted clays expectable in a freshly glaciated area. These are described by Porter (1963) as follows:

A — Very low silt content, low and very fine sand
B — No silt but much sand; chert is frequent in the sand
C — Like A, but with more fine and very-fine sand
D — Moderate amount silt-sized particles, low sand

"A" paste was found in one sherd from a conical-base incised-over-plain vessel in an obviously Middle Woodland context (F.45, dated A.D. 63) hence to be assigned to Arrowhead Drive or even earlier. It is comforting to find that this much earlier pot differs in paste, if not in temper, from the Late Woodland wares. Unfortunately, this does not hold true for all Arrowhead Drive sherds; one that might be regarded as close to Laurel Push and Pull (Stoltmann 1962) was assigned to the "D" paste category; this makes it indistinguishable from the latest vessels on the site. Fortunately, differentiating criteria exist in terms of style; but we can see in this situation an example of close continuity over time in functional, or non-stylistically-oriented, traits.

There is some tendency for "B" paste to be assciated with earlier pottery and for "D" paste to be associated with late, although this cannot be objectively tested and one is left with the impression that no consistent trends toward change in materials habitually chosen for pots can be detected. This seems to be the case as well for clearly "foreign" wares; thus the Ramey sherd plus a very distinctive-looking Oneota-like sherd could not be distinguished from the rest of the Juntunen vessels on the basis of paste and temper except for the definite presence of shell in the former and, in the latter, "some bar shaped cavities that well could represent leached shell" (Porter 1963).

5.2.2.2 Hardness

A popular variable often reported for new pottery types is hardness, measured with the usual mineral crayons on the Mohs scale. Most reports fail to provide the information that would render such hardness figures meaningful — sample size, range of variation, central tendencies, and the like. One is usually told that a certain type has a "hardness of about 2.5 to 3.0," for example, and one is then presumably supposed to be in a position to use such a measurement as an attribute when comparing other examples of pottery. To my mind, such attempts at presenting measurements in disregard of accepted statistical procedures are useless and a waste of time; in addition, my own experience with Juntunen vessels suggests, first, that the variability in hardness over one vessel may be greater than that reported for some whole types; second, that the "scratch test" with the crayons is so crude as to suggest that a "bounce test," listening to the sound produced by dropping the sherd on a hard surface, might yield equally valid results. I have no new measure of hardness to suggest at this juncture, and will let this matter rest, with the observation that vessels were well enough fired that no disintegration occurred when sherds were scrubbed in water and that they were sufficiently hard that a steel-wire brush did not usually damage vessel surfaces when it was vigorously employed to remove carbonized encrustations.

5.2.2.3 Color

Color is another attribute quickly eliminated from the list of those to be consistently measured in the study of the ceramics. This omission arose from the fact that color is obviously the product of a number of factors: clay constituents, firing conditions, use to which the pot was put, physical and chemical nature of the ground in which the sherds ultimately reposed. Decorated and rim sherds from the Juntunen site were most often stained with carbonized cooking residues, obscuring the original color; body sherds were usually oxidized from the fire. Firing in an open fire often resulted in vessels highly variegated in color. Differing soil conditions resulted in a number of sherds of the same vessel from different provenience units having extremes of color, yet capable of being glued together at the break. Thus sherds deposited in ashy soil or in a podzol "B" horizon became bleached to a very light-tan color; those lying in the greasy-feeling black midden deposits retained or possibly increased their blackish color. The value of recording color of sherds under these conditions seemed highly questionable. In general, it can be said that there is some tendency for a brick-red color in unbleached, unreduced, and unblackened sherds, although the range extends from a grayish-tan through various browns and grays. Color is one of the features in which Juntunen vessels exhibit marked variability, again contrasting with some other local traditions in the Upper Great Lakes.

5.2.3 MANUFACTURE

The method of manufacture of vessels is a factor that separates Juntunen from Arrowhead Drive (Middle Woodland) vessels. Whereas coil breaks can be seen in some of the Arrowhead Drive sherds, this is never the case with the late Woodland sherds, where breaks are always irregular and where the common splitting (totally absent from the Arrowhead Drive sherds) suggests something like laminated sheets not well knit together.

Most vessels were finished by pressing or paddling with boards wrapped with cord or fabric while support was supplied by the

the free hand on the vessel interior. A very few vessels — about 2 per cent of the total — showed no sign of such treatment, bearing wholly plain surfaces; these had a different appearance from the never perfect smoothing over of the corded surface that occasionally was performed on paddled vessels. The surface treatment included paddling or pressing with cord wrapped objects and impression with some sort of fabric. On some vessels (n = 129) the cord-marking was unmistakable, the cord being a fine twisted material closely wound around the paddling object. (See Plate XIX, *c*.) As to the rest, among those either cord-wrapped-stick or fabric impressed, uncertainty often exists as to the actual material used. Compare, for example, the bodies of the vessels shown in Plate XVIII, *a*, and XIX, *b*. As Quimby says, "I still cannot tell with certainty the difference between some kinds of cord marking and some kinds of fabric impressing" (1961:428). The number of vessels assigned to either of these categories, coarse cord-marking or fabric-impressing, is about equal, and I conclude that there was no strong preference for one type of finishing tool over the other.

5.3 TYPES OF VARIABILITY

There are a number of reasons for variability among vessels: no one can exactly duplicate, under primitive conditions, an earlier production; different individuals have different idiosyncratic habitual styles; cultural tradition specifies which techniques and processes are acceptable. Beyond these considerations, it is obvious that pots designed for different functions may well differ; when an extended family shares a common pot, that pot is likely to be bigger than one used by a nuclear family; storage vessels may have characteristics different from those of cooking-pots; and so on. The "roles" played by formal variation as a non-random phenomenon can, then, be dichotomized into (1) purely technological aspects — "functional" aspects proper — and (2) aspects serving primarily a non-technological function, which we may call sociological. It is necessary to make this distinction before entering the arena of argument over the problem of "types," which, like the question of the "ontological reality of culture," is a matter that can be discussed philosophically (if unprofitably) *ad infinitum*. I shall not here "revisit" the type concept more than is utterly necessary to state the assumptions upon which the analysis to follow will rest, and thus avoid a major diversion from the basic aims of this study.

It is my belief that the "nominalist" view, which states that types are constructs in the minds of the archaeologists, is not necessarily contradicted by the "realist" view as held by Spaulding, which contends that types are something in the real world which can be discovered by the archaeologist using suitable (usually statistical) techniques. To say that classifications are arbitrary and to say that they are inherent in the data may both be true; it is clear from the problems of taxonomy in biology, and specifically human evolution, that, as Simpson puts it, "Classification is not an exact science and is not likely soon to become one. . . . Complete agreement as to what is to be said is thus chimerical and indeed may not even be desirable. We can, however, agree as to *how to say what we mean*" (1963:18; emphasis mine). If pottery at a site falls into certain groupings with respect to formal attributes, the nature of these groupings can be studied and a classification scheme set up irrespective of whether it is "unique," in the sense that no other partitioning of the data would be satisfactory. Implicit in the use of the word "arbitrary" as criticism of taxonomies is the idea that the particular classificatory scheme of the archaeologist may not actually represent that of the makers of the vessels. Irrespective of whether or not this is true – and Frake (1962) shows how the use of the classifications of Western science in ethnography may lead to distortions – it is largely irrelevant with respect to the purposes for which taxonomies may be constructed in archaeology.

Traditionally, classifications of archaeological materials have been made to facilitate description, to identify what have been called "culture complexes," and to deal with problems of a historical nature. These aims are legitimate enough, although it can certainly be objected that archaeological "cultures" have often been inadequately defined as "a series of pottery types and other related artifacts" and that too often the job of analysis has been considered complete with the establishment of a chronological framework. This situation has done little to increase the popularity of archaeological reports among social anthropologists.

The pottery typology to be presented shortly was devised for purposes of description, to aid in temporal alignment of provenience units, to differentiate between stylistic and functional traits, and to facilitate comparison with other described pottery samples. When more sites are excavated, the typologies will need revision. For other problems, other typologies would no doubt be required. Several methods of analysis were used in the present study and their results compared, and certain experiments in typology were performed. The stages in analysis and their results will now be discussed.

5.4 PRELIMINARY STEPS IN ANALYSIS OF JUNTUNEN POTTERY

As mentioned earlier, initial sorting was into vessels. The rims, decorated body sherds, and undecorated bodies that clearly belonged to a classifiable vessel — numbering 4,750 — were laid out on a large table and sorted into groups of sherds that, beyond reasonable doubt, came from the same vessel. When sherds from one vessel came from more than one provenience unit, such information was encoded on a McBee edge-punched card so that, by selecting cards punched for a given provenience unit, one could see with what other provenience unit it shared sherds of the same vessels. Thus the unit of analysis was the inferred "vessel."

Since most of the pottery from the site consisted of previously unreported sorts, much time was devoted to attempts at establishing rough "types" by visual sorting into rough groupings, using the "gestalt" approach of overall similarity. This did permit breakdown of the collection into three or four large groupings, each of which shared a number of traits that separated it from the other groupings. Beyond this breakdown, subgroupings could be produced, but they seemed quite arbitrary and in fact varied according to who did the "gestalt" sorting; the reason was that the particular subgrouping produced depended on the criteria implicitly chosen or given greater weight by the sorter. No obvious way out of this difficulty seemed available, since there were no objective means for selecting criteria or weighting them differentially. Despite the dilemma, I believed that the variability present within some of the larger groupings was considerably greater than that customarily present within groupings that other archaeologists have been in the habit of defining as "types". The problem appeared to be one of locating attribute clusters, and accordingly I decided to prepare a list of the attributes or qualitités in which the vessels appeared to vary, to score the vessels on these attributes, and to use this set of objective variables in an attempt to achieve the finer subgroupings that I thought ought to be present in the pottery and that should assist in such problems as determining which provenience units were most alike.

There were other objectives for preparation and use of the attribute list. Sorting pottery by eye can lead to shifts in one's assessment of a particular type, owing to the finer discriminatory powers gained by practice as the analysis goes along. Thus consistency through use of written-down, hence unshifting, criteria was striven for. Another aim was an approach to the problem of variability within and among types: Is there (should there be) an equal amount of variability within each type? How can this variability best be described? Should types be mutually exclusive, or should overlap be present? I must hasten to point out that this present study will not attempt to attack all these problems.

Questions of this sort are common to problems of classification and selection; for example, the following set of conditions that a good classification may be expected to satisfy is offered by Parker-Rhodes and Needham:

1. There should not be any pairs of identical classes.
2. Objects which occur in exactly the same set of classes should have an extensive similarity of properties (otherwise the classification has "not gone far enough").
3. Every object should not be in a class to itself, nor should an appreciable proportion of the objects be thus separate (otherwise the classification has "gone too far").
4. In general, mutually exclusive sets of classes are not as useful as overlapping ones (though much better than nothing as for instance, the alphabetic separation of volumes of a dictionary).
5. In general, pairs of almost identical classes are less useful (though this requires qualification, since they _might_ form the only means of distinction between some objects).
6. The body of data constituting the classification should be presented as concisely as possible [1960:2].

The first and sixth of these conditions should be self-explanatory; the second and third have to do with the optimum number of groupings. The fourth is of interest in dealing with those cases which lie either on the fringes of a grouping or equidistant between two or more groupings (considered as mapped in a Euclidean space), when a decision cannot be made as to which of two or more groupings they should belong. The fifth is the general case of a problem that arose in dealing with the Juntunen pottery: some vessels were identical formally with established named types of Minnesota and Wisconsin yet could also be regarded as somewhat aberrant variants of a Juntunen type. In these cases, because of the taxonomic priority of the Minnesota and Wisconsin type designations, the separate classification was maintained despite the fact that it caused "pairs of almost identical classes" (one of which contained very few members, thus also approaching the objection made in the third point above).

5.5 POTTERY ATTRIBUTE LIST

Considerable time and effort were expended in selecting variables that would be of value in describing the vessels and to aid in finer partitioning of the whole assemblage. Attributes shared by all or nearly all vessels, such as paste and temper, were elminated in preliminary study; other (e.g., hardness, color) we dropped as being hard to observe in a consistent fashion.

The list finally decide upon and used for the study (as presented in the Appendix, p. 299) will now be discussed. It should be noted that an additional category, "Indeterminate" or "no decision possible," should be appended to the list of categories under nearly every attribute. It was found that this category was one frequently used in the analysis.

5.5.1 CONTINUOUS VARIABLES

Only three linear measurements — lip thickness, rim thickness, and diameter at lip — were taken, and of these the first is no doubt the most reliable, while the second, although the measurement was consistently taken 2-3 cm. below the lip for collarless vessels and 1-2 cm. below the collar for collared vessels, not only varies considerably for given vessel sizes and even on the same vessel, owing to method of manufacture, but also shows extremely low correlation with any other attribute or with any of the proposed types. Outside diameter at lip was measured using the usual concentric rings marked on paper; reliability of this measure was obviously lower, the less rim periphery was present, and it would probably have been desirable to include the length of periphery upon which estimate of diameter was based as an attribute, to be used in introducing a confidence factor to estimate of diameter.

5.5.2 DISCRETE ATTRIBUTES

All other observations were of a non-continuous nature. They fall into three major classes: predecoration vessel-surface finish, mode of manufacture and form of the rim area, and decoration.

5.5.2.1 Manufacture and Finish

There were many uncertainties as to exterior surface treatment (Appendix, p. 299, II. A.1), not only because it was hard to tell cord-wrapped stick from fabric but also because in many cases the finish had been largely obliterated on the neck and rim, where decoration was to be applied, either intentionally as a predecoration preparation or else incidentally as a result of the application of decoration.

The lip-rim complex (II.B) involved a number of attributes dealing with shape. Some of these were rather subjective and difficult to define, but it was believed that they were an advance over the way in which the cross-sectional shape of this area has frequently been dealt with, namely by drawing a number of "typical" cross sections, giving them code numbers, then assigning each subsequently studied vessel to one of the code varieties. This procedure actually combines a number of variables that, it was thought, might sort independently; for example, there is no a priori way to tell whether flattened lips are consistently found on vessels with flaring mouths, and rounded lips on straight-sided vessels. The study of this area of vessels was begun by looking at rim profiles, however, and the work did aid in suggesting suitable ways of analyzing rims into finer components. Some rim profiles that seemed "typical" are shown in Figure 9. The manner in which rim profiles were reproduced on paper might be commented on. I found that looking at the rough and irregular broken edge of a sherd led to distortions when one attempted to reproduce the profile by eye, and that taking measurements with ruler or calipers was clumsy and tedious. Consequently, I devise a simple device to enable the section of a sherd to be accurately traced. In Figure 10, *a-c*, various aspects of the gadget are shown. The principle is that of a device that slides on paper making a mark with a pencil directly below the point of a probe (stippled). I found it convenient to hold the sherds with a large office-style spring clip mounted to part of a goose-neck lamp. This permits the sherd to be easily positioned in such a way that the lip falls on a line perpendicular to the plane of the paper taped to the table, and the probe can trace the section without the wooden pencil-holding portion interfering by running into the sherd. Accurate profiles were quickly produced with this device.

The figure accompanying the Appendix illustrates the meaning of some terms used to describe vessels and show how some of the attributes were measured. Note that there is obvious correlation between some attributes; one would seldom find an everted lip (II.B.4) parallel to the plane of the vessel orifice (II.B.3.b) or of an even thickness (II.B.1.c). It is probable, however, that relatively little was gained, save in objectivity, by this fine analysis of lip and rim area.

"Collar" and "castellation" turned out to be of primary importance in terms of predictive power. The rare cases of "wavy-edged lip" castellation are shown in Plate X, *a-d*; all are from the earlier occupations. See "*e*" for an example of a "beaded" rim. A strip has clearly been added somewhat below the lip.

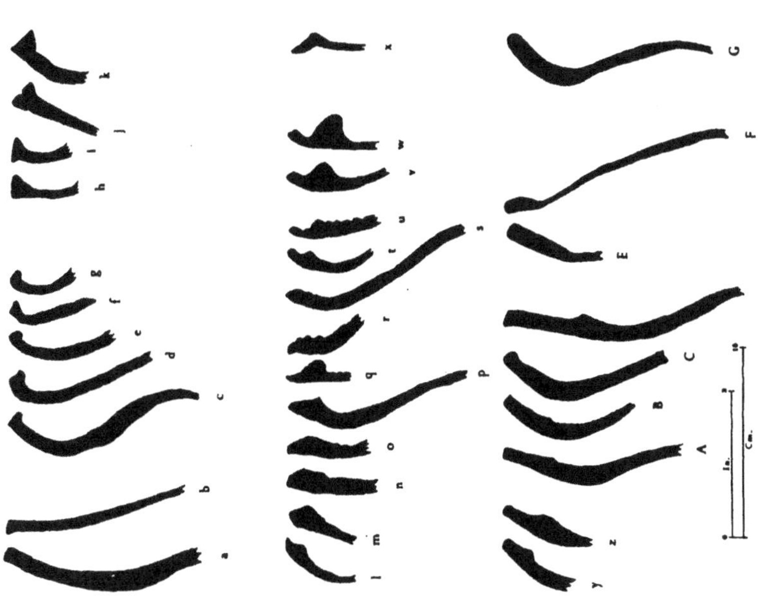

Fig. 9.—Typical rim profiles (exteriors to right)

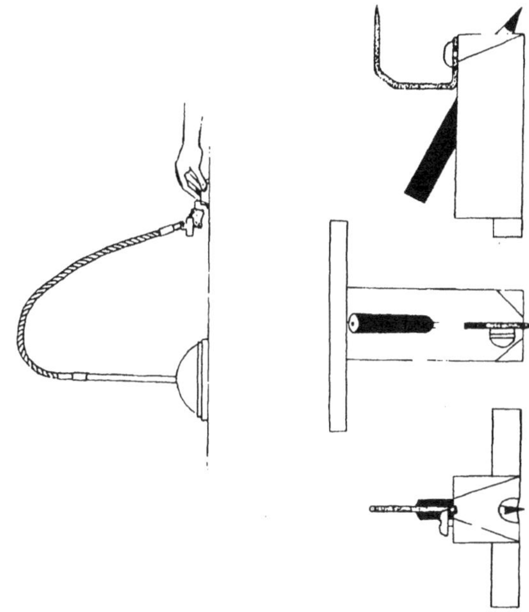

Fig. 10.—Sherd profile tracer

5.5.2.2 Decorative Techniques

The very minute breakdown of decorative techniques that was made is of significance in showing their considerable variety. To my knowledge, some of these techniques have never before been described.

A gradient extends from incising to punctating. Both use a sharp-ended tool, but in incising, the tool is pressed into the clay and drawn along evenly, with no intentional up-and down movements. Such incising gradates into linear punctation, in which a "dotted line" is produced, the drawing of the stylus through the clay being wholly replaced by up-and down movements. This observation is of course true only in so far as kinematics is concerned: the actual appearance of the lines produced is different, with drag-and-jab in some cases closely resembling dentate stamping or cord-wrapped-object impressions. Placing them in such a gradated series based on motor activity may be merely an imposition of Western categories upon a wholly different system, though this is considered irrelevant for the purposes of the analysis presented herein. With drag-and-jab, the tool is pressed into the clay, usually at an angle, then dragged for a short distance with decreasing depth of penetration but without loss of contact with the clay before the next stab or thrust is made. The distinction between "linear punctation" and regular punctation is one of spacing, and, although spacing of punctations was not included as an attribute (although it was considered), as a rough rule the linear variety consists of indentations with the space between not more than twice the width of the marks. Regular punctations, generally of no greater actual size, are spaced considerably farther apart, and the eye does not receive the impression of a "dotted line."

Among the objects used in producing punctations were knots or loops of cord; their use is most prominent in the earliest period. In Plate VI a latex cast, *a*, illustrates the technique. Evidently a two-strand twisted cord was held between the fingers and twisted until it kinked and formed a doubled cord; the area where the cord kinked and doubled on itself was pressed into the clay. Note that the edge of a cord-wrapped object (not shown in the latex) was used on the sherd, *a'*, above the double row of loop impressions. Another example is shown in *b*, a latex cast in which the loop is particularly clear. The technique is of interest as providing a stylistic link to some of the terminal Middle and earliest Late Woodland pottery of Wisconsin (cf. Keslin 1958), the only other area where this device is presently known.

The entry "cord-wound artifacts" is deliberately vague; a number of objects seem to have been wound and used to impress pottery. The thin edge of a paddle was a common core and was probably used in Plate VI, *a'*, and, more surely, in Plate VIII, *e* and *f*. In a number of instances, however, two-strand twisted cord was itself used as a core, with more twisted cord coiled about it, in the manner of bass piano or guitar strings; we may thus speak of "cord-wrapped cord." In Plate VII, latex casts are shown in which this technique is seen. In *a* through *e* the twisted underlying core is evident; *f* is unusual in that the core is very loosely twisted, and the cord that goes around it appears to bind it together. It is possible that the impressing tool in this case was actually the edge of a twined mat, for the infrequent appearance of the cord wrapping would be difficult to explain if it truly spiraled a single cord. In many cases the impressions of the "cord-wrapped cord" are closely spaced, and often it is hard to locate places where cord entered and left the vessel; it appears as if long pieces of the material had been wrapped around the rim and neck of the vessel, then pressed in.

It is not actually necessary to see the core directly to know that the tool was used around the concave inside surface of the vessel rim, as in Plate VIII, *a-a'*, and — particularly clearly — Plate IX, *d'*. There would seem to be no way in which a cord-wrapped *paddle* or other rigid core could produce such an effect on a concave surface. A core that appears to be neither twisted nor wrapped, thus perhaps a natural vegetable fiber or hide thong, is seen in Plate VII, *b-b'*.

The use of "cord-wrapped objects" is of interest and seems not to have been discussed in the literature since Hall's (1950) initial recognition of it. He used the term "pseudo-cord" and described the decoration as "impressions of cord-wrapped blades or paddle edges and of twigs" (1950:10). Hall states (1950:12) that it appears on Point Peninsula Corded pottery in New York; from my own examination of the late Point Peninsula and early Owasco pottery of New York, I would agree that this device was occasionally used. The technique is easy to recognize on the Juntunen site because these objects were pressed in firmly, often flush with the surface of the clay, as is apparent in Plate VIII, *b-b'*. Needless to say, the same *motifs* can be produced with the use of twisted cords.

In one vessel from the Juntunen site (Pl. XX, *c*), close inspection of a latex cast revealed what might be termed the "whipped end" of such a cord-wrapped cord. The pattern of alternating triangles on the vessel required that the impressions terminate abruptly, to give way to impressions laid on at an angle. Impressions that were identical indicated that they had been produced by the same cord-wrapped object and also that the end of it had been whipped, evidently to prevent uncoiling and fraying, by closer winding and some sort of knotting (the latter cannot be clearly seen).

The attention paid to these wound strings and thongs seems unusual, if indeed they all served solely to decorate pots. It would appear that ordinary twisted cord would have functioned just as well or that in many cases the edge of a cord-wrapped paddle — nearly universally used to prepare vessel surfaces and in fact very often used on lips or interiors even when cord-wrapped cords were used on the exterior — would have sufficed. On a site where so very few non-utilitarian objects were recovered, the inferred relative abundance of these highly specialized devices is rather surprising. I am inclined to speculate that they may have additionally served some other function, and one application where protection against fraying by a spiral wrapping would have useful is for bowstrings. Beyond suggesting this as a possibility, I can go no further. Hide thongs were the normally accepted material for bowstrings, but there is no indication that they were so wound. It does seem unlikely that two-ply, twisted cord, presumably of bast fiber, would have had the requisite strength for this application. But I can suggest no other function for these wrapped strings.

5.5.2.3 Decorative Motifs

Aside from size and shape (variables impossible to record for the majority of vessels), the most apparent differences among vessels were in modes of decoration. Most vessels were decorated by impressions on rim and neck, lip, and rim interior. Decoration was often complex and commonly called for several tools, most often cord-wrapped objects and punctating instruments, and the elaborateness of many of the designs indicated that there were many elements that would be of value in classifying, viewing change through time, and relating to other local traditions. Decoration was recorded only summarily for rim interior and lip; for rim exterior it was divided into what was considered the "basic" or "dominant" decorative motif and certain subsidiary elements. Such usage is roughly analogous to the use of "folktale motifs" in the study of folklore, or perhaps "themes" in music, and no doubt did not yield the most from the data, besides being somewhat subjective and arbitrary in that the analysis makes certain distinctions, but not others which might in fact be of importance.

After considerable preliminary study of the pottery, 15 "dominant motifs" were decided upon; it was expected that these should be adequate to describe about 95 per cent of the vessels. They are shown in Figure 11, and, since a reanalysis of the entire pottery sample would be required to improve upon them, we must content ourselves with them for the time being. As will be shown later, this one attribute was found to be the most sensitive of all in terms of efficiency in partitioning the vessels into groups.

One technique frequently employed on the periphery of or as an adjunct to the dominant motif was punctating, hence the occurrence of punctation — as the only element, as part of basic motifs, as superimposed over basic motifs or used below it — was separately recorded.

One some vessels, a second decorative motif was applied below the "major motif: (and thus below the rim of the vessel), usually in a pattern differing from those occurring on the rim; presence of such an additional motif was rare, however, and it was recorded as simple presence or absence (Pl. XVIII, *a*, and XXI, *a*, are good examples).

Lips were commonly decorated; impressions across the lip were most frequent (Plate VIII, *b*). When designs were produced by the drag-and-jab technique, a line of marks parallel to the edges of the lip was more common. A minority pattern, found in only a few early types, was the zigzag design shown in Plate VIII, *c-g*.

Rim interior decoration was present on slightly more than half the vessels and was generally a series of simple vertical impressions made with the edge of a cord-wrapped stick, or a horizontal band of cord or cord-wrapped-cord impressions. In Plate IX some of the variety in internal decoration is shown together with exterior motifs. Most internal decorative styles shown are fairly common except for *a'*, entirely unique in its imaginative combination of a number of elements. Decoration shown in IX, *c'*, was executed with cord-wrapped-paddle edge, contrasting thus with *d'*; *f'* and *g'* are good examples of simple twisted cord impressing. Note that *a-a'* are examples of drag-and-jab, whereas *b-b'*, executed with a rectangular-ended tool, verge on linear punctation. Example *c* has lip, and rim immediately below, decorated by impression of a rather sharp knife-like tool. It is hard to tell whether this ought to be regarded as "punctation"; no separate category for such impressions was set up.

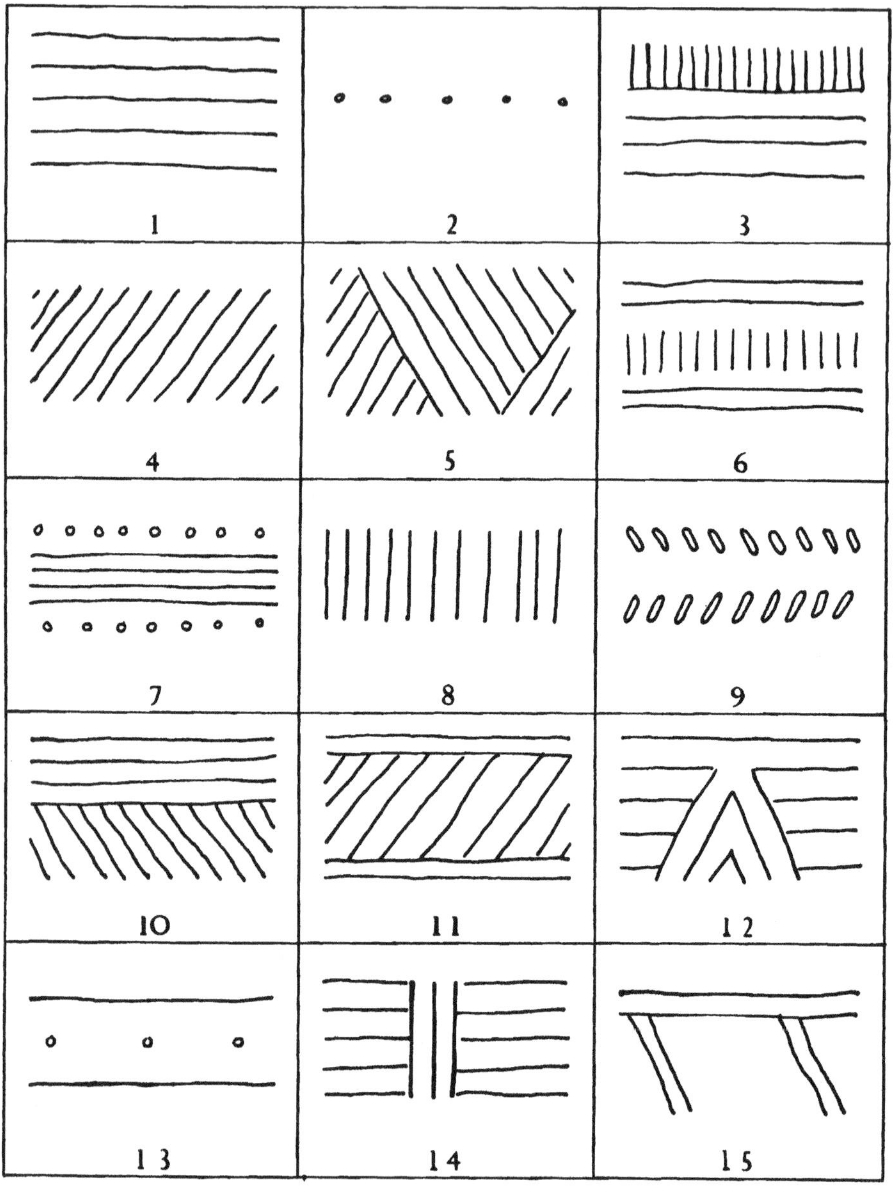

Fig. 11.—Dominant decorative motifs

5.6 EXPERIMENTS WITH THE ATTRIBUTE LIST

5.6.1 RESEARCH DESIGN

At an early stage in the study I decided to encode the information for each vessel in such a way as to permit rapid access. Both the key-sort edge-punched cards and the machine-punched IBM cards seemed suitable data-storing methods, and in fact I finished by using both types (though for different purposes). The process was begun using edge-punch cards to hold the data on the vessels, but, because of the time and labor involved in puching them by hand and because I began to envision the difficulties in handling around 2,000 such cards with the usual needles, I shifted to IBM cards.

Edge-punch cards do have the advantage that no machinery other than a hand punch and a couple of needles is needed. Also, various kinds of information that one may not find convenient to encode, such as drawings, can be put in the unpunched center portion of the card. These cards have been found very handy for the storing of information to be pulled out under various categories and for the solution of relatively small-scale problems using a desk calculator. However, the job of handling several thousand could be ponderous, and, furthermore, they do not lend themselves to multivariate statistical methods with computers. So, in the end, the data on the vessels were entered on coding sheets, from which IBM cards were punched. The deck of cards thus produced — one card for each vessel — was ready to be run through sorters and tabulating machines and could serve as data input to a computer.

The data on pottery were subjected to a number of procedures, which can be divided into two basically different kinds of operations: (1) descriptive statistic programs to explore distributions and summarize the data; (2) more specialized programs to investigate certain specific questions and test hypotheses.

The first kind of program produced nothing that could not be done by hand processes, such as sorting or plotting on graph paper, but did it very much faster and more accurately. An example may be seen in the frequencies of the pottery attributes over the whole site, included as part of the Appendix, which were obtained in less than two minutes of computer time. The saving of time, effort, and (indirectly) money, is obvious.

At a higher level, correlations, regression analysis, and chi-square and t tests were used to study the way the attributes and types were "behaving" with respect to each other, to detect those attributes which were most powerful in terms of distinguishing groups and discover those which could be eliminated without losing power of discrimination. This work and much of that to be discussed shortly was accomplished with the cooperation of Dr. James Lingoes of the University of Michigan Computing Center, who was at the time developing analytical techniques and computer programs for the IBM 7090 whose applications were close to the problems I wished to investigate. A number of separate programs were used, but basic to them all is a routine, included in a number of them as a subroutine, called "MAXPAC" (Lingoes 1963a). The usefulness of MAXPAC derives from the facts that data are often "nonlinear" and that the categories within each pottery attribute are on a purely nominal scale. That is, "gritty," which one might code as "2", is in no meaningful sense greater than "polished," code as "1". MAXPAC is designed to recode the data and compute "category weights," consisting of all possible scoring systems yielding linear regressions for variable pairs, each of which consists of a specified dependent variable and one of the independent variables.

5.6.2 INITIAL PROCESSING

Some "cleaning up" of the data was first necessary. The first step in this resulted from the presence of a considerable amount of "missing data" — vessels for which all attributes used in the study could not be recorded because of the small amount of the particular vessel actually recovered. In the case of continuous data, the program could have been directed to generate a mean value for each variable and substitute it in the empty slots. For the discontinuous or nonscalable attribute data (e.g., "cordmarked-punctated-incised"), however, this automatic method was unsuitable, so I chose instead to sort out the vessels, attribute by attribute, until I had a deck of cards representing 400-odd vessels for which information was available for all attributes. (Reduction of sample size was in any case required, since the initial number of vessels — 1,688 — exceeded the capacity of the program.)

The second step related to the distribution of categories within each attribute. Since one of the functions of MAXPAC is the production of ranked coded data from the raw input data, it is important that the category frequencies for each attribute be represented in a reasonable fashion in the sample. It was actually found that, in the reduced full-data sample of about 400 vessels, some categories ("interrupted linear," "decoration below major motif present") were not represented at all, while other variables consisted mainly of values toward one end of the scale plus one or two cases of extreme deviations from that majority. Since the recoding involves assignment of category interval values, the computer would tend to see the latter situation as a dichotomy, and the distinctions present within the tightly clustered majority would be masked. Thus, if vessel diameters ranged from 10 to 25 cm. except for one vessel whose diameter was 90 cm., the 10-to-25 cm. group would most likely be lumped together by the program and assigned a code number "1", while the 90-cm. vessel would be regarded as a second category and labeled "2", despite the interest one might have in the variation present within the 10-to-25 cm. group. In such a case, elimination of the 90-cm. case would be required. Sorting the Juntunen sample for situations such as the one described reduced the final sample to 388 vessels. It might be pointed out that MAXPAC is capable of handling the problem of missing or poorly represented categories, when the data are continuous, by collapsing poorly represented categories into one of the adjacent categories; but again this was unsuitable for the type of data involved, so it was done by hand, based on the frequency distribution tables printed out by the program.

The working sample thus consisted of 23 per cent of the vessels, but was obviously not drawn using random sampling procedures. The proportions of tentative types in the selected sample do not correspond to those for the site as a whole; for example, only classifiable vessels were included, and all examples of the "not classifiable" group were eliminated from the selected sample. The selecting procedure also affected attribute frequency; the ratios between attribute frequencies in the selected sample and in the parent group are indicated in the Appendix. In the accompanying table, actual frequencies of types (see Table 6, p. 78) in the selected sample are compared with what would be expected if the sample's type frequencies were proportional to those in the total collection from the site (omitting types not represented at all in the selected sample). A chi-square test for goodness of fit of sample to parent group was significant at the 1 per cent level, and it can be seen from the accompanying table that the differences are especially pronounced in the case of Mackinac Undecorated, Mackinac Banded, Bois Blanc Braced Rim, and Juntunen Drag-and-Jab. It should therefore be borne in mind that the discussion to follow is largely in terms of the selected sample, and may not accurately reflect the situation with respect to the overall collection from the site.

The purpose for my using MAXPAC was to produce suitably recoded data and category weights to serve as input to other

Type	No. in Selected Sample	No. Expected if Selected Sample were Proportionately Representative of the Parent Group
Mackinac Undecorated	74	47
" Punctate	45	44
" Cord Impressed	39	30
" Banded	71	51
" Zigzag Lip	4	4
Blackduck Banded	8	6
" Punctate	9	7
Bois Blanc Braced Rim	9	30
" Beaded	3	7
" Castellated Cord.	4	1
Point Sauble Collared	4	4
Juntunen Collared	4	4
" Linear Puncate	4	2
" Drag-and-Jab	34	79
Others	73	67
Totals	388	385

programs. The next step, and one of the most important operations of MAXPAC, was the process of linearization of the data. To understand what is meant by linearization, one may consider a contingency table representing the concurrences of the categories of one variable with those of another. (If one variable is picked as dependent variable, there would be as many of these tables as there are independent variables.) For a given table — say, "Decorative Motif" along one axis and "Internal Decoration" along the other — one can obtain a certain product moment formula, that is to say the correlation of one variable with another, but the regression line might well be curvilinear, in which case the real nature of the relationship would be distorted. The program generated a set of category weights, whose effect was to order the categories and scale the data in such a way that the relationship between any two variables was maximized by requiring linear regression of one on the other. With the aid of these category weights, one can obtain the maximum product moment correlation between each pair of variables. With the set of recoded data cards and the category weight cards from MAXPAC, one was then ready to move in several directions.

5.6.3 EXPERIMENTS IN CLASSIFICATION

5.6.3.1 Stepwise Multiple Regression

For the question of the relative worth of the different variables, a linear stepwise multiple regression program called "GUTREG" that utilizes the output from MAXPAC was used. At each step, that variable is added to the regression equation which contributes the most to the reduction of unexplained variability. Thus, in addition to other results, in essence one has his variables ranked as to importance.

With my own tentative type designations used as the dependent or grouping variable for MAXPAC and GUTREG, the regression program called in variables in steps, as seen in Table 3. The correlation coefficient between Intuitive Type and Collar is .764, and it will be observed that each additional variable increases the cumulative multiple correlation coefficient in a rapidly diminishing fashion; thus the inclusion of "Decorative Motif" brings an increase of .070, while "Lip Decoration" adds merely .002; despite its r of .31 with the dependent variable, it adds very little after the first eight variables have been called in because of its own correlation with the other variables.

Those variables listed in Table 3 that were not called into the regression equation are not ordered in any way, and their potential contributions to explanation of variability were not tested. They are included and numbered so that the correlation of the first two variables with some of them might be shown.

The 1 per cent level of significance was chosen as criterion for entering and removing variables; the ten variables called into regression thus meet this criterion, while the rest do not. There are a number of ways in which further information could have been extracted from this mode of analysis — by varying the significance level, deleting variables, forcing others into the prediction equation — but this extended analysis was not attempted, since both analysis and computer time were limited.

We may conclude from the work done, however, that for purposes of distinguishing among the "intuitive" types that I had postulated, attributes concerned with decorative techniques were of relatively little value, while certain variations of the lip and rim profiles plus "major decorative motif" were of considerable importance indeed. With these facts at hand, it might be desirable to concentrate on the significant attributes, perhaps dividing them more finely for greater discrimination, and redo the analysis of the vessels. Guidelines, at least, are now available which should aid in the study of similar pottery traditions.

TABLE 3

STEPWISE REGRESSION ANALYSIS OF POTTERY ATTRIBUTES ("TENTATIVE TYPE" AS GROUPING VARIABLE)

Step	Variable	Cumulative Multiple Correlation Coefficient	F Level	Correlation Coefficient with Dependent Variable	Correlation Coefficient with Other Variables
1	Collar	.764	540	.76	High* with 19, 4, 3; moderate with several others
2	Major decorative motif	.834	141	.51	Moderate with 21; low with several others
3	Castellations	.860	65	.66	High with 4; moderate with 24
4	Drag and jab	.870	28	.68	Low with 2 and 24
5	Lip form	.878	23	.37	Moderate with 1
6	Treatment of area to be decorated	.883	14	.39	Moderate with 2; low with 21
7	Interior surface finish	.890	11	.18	Low with several
8	Interior decoration	.893	9	.38	Low with 4 and 15
9	Lip decoration	.895	8	.31	High with 14; moderate with 2
10	Lip thickness	.899	4	.18	Low with 5 and 13

VARIABLES NOT CALLED INTO REGRESSION

Number	Name
11	Body thickness
12	Diameter at lip
13	Lip eversion
14	Incising
15	Cord impressing
16	Rectangular-ended stick impressing
17	Cord-wrapped stick
18	Cord-wrapped cord
19	Simulated fabric impression
20	Linear punctating
	Punctation:
21	occurrence
22	tool used
23	depth of impression
24	Decoration below major motif
25	Cooking residue, presence or absence

* High: ≥ 0.84; Moderate: 0.51—0.83; Low: ≤ 0.50

A continuation of the regression analysis work as outlined above would probably be of value, since those attributes chosen by GUTREG obviously function primarily to divide the vessels into two groups, "late ware" and "early ware," inasmuch as collars, castellations, and drag-and-jab appear on the former but not all all on the latter. Thus the problem of distinguishing subgroupings within the difficult-to-subdivide early vessels has only begun to be attacked; nevertheless, from the start described here it should be possible to pursue this problem further in a satisfactory fashion by analyzing "early ware" and "late ware" separately.

5.6.3.2 Evaluation of Tentative Types

Part of the output from GUTREG consists of a listing, for each vessel in the sample, of the predicted versus actual results from application of the regression formula. Thus it is possible to look at the vessels in terms of deviation between predicted and actual results. A summary of this information for the types that formed the dependent variable is shown in Table 4.

We can see from this table that Mackinac Undecorated and M. Punctate come out well, each having about 20 per cent of their cases with less than 10 per cent deviation. For M. Cord Impressed, 27 of the 29 cases with high deviation are from a subtype (variety *c* in Table 6, p. 32) much like Madison Cord Impressed. This subtype is therefore a poor taxon or else should not be included in this type. Notes made during the actual processing of the vessels indicate that the criteria for placing a vessel in this category were conflicting and unclear; the vessels assigned to it might well be re-examined with an eye to subdivision or incorporation in other categories. M. Banded is only fair; here, most deviation occurs in the Variety *I*. It is most likely that the major difficulty with both these subtypes lies in the typology of decorative motifs; both have rather complicated designs which were not well accounted for by the motifs as set up. This fact was recognized as the processing of sherds progressed, but at that stage little could be done to eliminate ambiguities unless one was willing to start afresh.

Juntunen Collared is apparently the type most poorly predicted by the regression equation, most of its members being predicted extremely poorly. It is not clear to me why this should be so; perhaps the vessels vary from the rest in attributes that were not recognized. Juntunen Drag-and-Jab, the late ware with large sample and small internal variation, holds up well, with 26 per cent under the 10 per cent level. The "Other" category, gratifyingly, is poor, nearly 90 per cent lying in the 100-999 per cent deviation slot, as should be expected for a residual category.

We may conclude from this investigation of the tentative pottery types that some are sound, without undue within-type variation, while others are very poor, suggesting the need for re-evaluation. Without the use of such a relatively sophisticated technique as regression analysis, it would have been very difficult to evaluate a typology in such an objective fashion.

5.6.3.3 Wares, Types, and Varieties

The " tentative" types mentioned above are those of the final stage of classification as shown in Table 6, (p. 32), where the

TABLE 4

DEVIATION OF POTTERY TYPES FROM ACTUAL RESULTS OF REGRESSION FORMULA, BASED ON GUTREG

Type	Number of Vessels with Percentage Deviation:				Total No. Vessels
	Under 10%	10-99%	100-999%	1,000% and Greater	
Mackinac Undecorated	17	57			74
Mackinac Puncate	9	35	1		45
Mackinac Cord Impressed		10	29		39
Mackinac Banded	8	38	25		71
Mackinac Zigzag Lip		4			4
Blackduck Banded		7	1		8
Blackduck Puncate		5	3		8
Bois Blanc Braced Rim		6	3		9
Point Sauble Collared	1	3			4
Bois Blanc Beaded Rim		2	1		3
Bois Blanc Castellated Corded		3	1		4
Juntunen Collared			1	7	8
Juntunen Linear Punctate	2	2			4
Juntunen Drag-and-Jab	8	26			34
"Other"		8	65		73
Total					388

"varieties" or "subtypes" represent preliminary types that were lumped together in later stages. The process by which the lumping was accomplished and the taxonomy hierarchically ordered into "wares," "types," and "varieties" needs still to be discussed.

The main purpose was to obtain types with approximately the same characteristics as those currently popular among archaeologists, in order to facilitate comparison. It should be emphasized that different problems require different taxonomies. For purposes of attacking a problem such as the setting-up of a taxonomy of excavation units (which itself should help elucidate the relationship between temporal and contemporary-functional differences) the pottery attributes themselves form a more sensitive set of predictors than would a set of vessel types based on the attributes. To illustrate this point, let us say that from any given provenience unit, sherds are excavated which can be referred to two vessels. If we describe the ceramic data in terms of types, we have two bits of information; two vessels of one or two types. If, however, we present the ceramic data in terms of the attributes observed on the two vessels, there is a great deal more we can say; if one is using 20 attributes, 10 times as many bits of information can theoretically be offered by using attributes rather than types. For practical purposes this number must be reduced somewhat because of correlations among the attributes: the 20 attributes do not constitute 20 independent statements, some being, in effect, restatements of others. It is still likely, however, that the sensitivity has been at least doubled. In addition, we are in a position to move beyond problems of description and classification into areas of more general anthropological concern, such as reasons why certain attributes were chosen at the expense of others. This subject has been tentatively broached by Deetz (1965; N.D.a.).

To return to the question of establishing satisfactory pottery types, it was mentioned that subjectively determined tentative types were established before the vessel information was encoded on cards. The approximately 35 types were included during the coding process as if they were categories of another attribute, so as a result the vessel cards contain both the attribute data and an entry representing a judgment as to which of the tentative types the vessel belonged. This was done to facilitate evaluation and validation of the initial types. I hoped to attack such problems as: Could a machine take the attributes and arrive at types, and what relation would these bear to my own? Were the attributes selected sufficient to permit determination of types, or, in making a judgment as to type, was I, without being aware of it, taking into account factors which I had not explicitly recognized, and about which a computer would therefore receive no information? Or, on the other hand, was I, while looking at the pottery, "seeing things" that were in fact not there; could a more consistent typology be arrived at by the use of the attributes than was possible by eye?

The original types on which the vessels were scored are seen as the lettered varieties of Table 6 (p. 78). At this early stage, an effort was made to "split" rather than "lump" wherever possible. Because of the lack of strong clustering among attributes in the earlier types, however, it was difficult to be consistent, and it became evident during the encoding process that criteria for assigning vessels to one "type" rather than another were shifting. This difficulty was ultimately eliminated by lumping together a number of the original types.

There are no established objective criteria for determining how much variability should be allowed within one type, beyond which a separation into two or more ought to be made, when one has data from only one site. Although multivariate methods of studying "distance" between groups exist, such as Mahalonobis' D^2 function and Fisher's discriminant function, they require quantitative data and are in any case designed for determining class membership of individuals where groups are known. Standard factor analysis, too, makes assumptions about the data to be factored which the largely qualitative pottery data would not satisfy. A number of "pattern analysis" and "cluster analysis" procedures exist: one of the former, devised by McQuitty, is discussed in Brook (1962) and subjected to critical analysis in Lingoes (1964). Most cluster analysis programs, however, require that data input be in terms of presence-absence of attributes or categories and are not able adequately to weight the variables.

5.6.3.4 Lingoes' "Taxonomic Optimization Procedure"

One procedure I employed was the "Taxonomic Optimization Procedure" (TOP), at that time being developed by James Lingoes of the University of Michigan Computing Center. Following is Lingoes' own description of the program.

> Given a set of variables, which may be quantitative or qualitative, the problem to be solved is that of finding the best single partitioning of the sample of subjects, such that the derived groups will be maximally separated on a dimension that accounts for the largest source of covariance among the variables. One need make no assumptions about the underlying measurement characteristics of the variables, since the computations are independent of the orginal units, be they nominal, ordinal, in-

terval, ratio, or mixtures thereof. The taxonomic optimization procedure (TOP) generates its own metric in the process of obtaining the best general single classificatory system for the given sample of subjects and variables.

TOP is useful primarily in those situations where the investigator does not know precisely which variables and what weights to use in arriving at a useful and reliable systematics of his data. The method can also be used for investigating various typological hypotheses by including them as grouping-variables in the analysis.

Briefly, the method involves coding the original data, producing contingency tables, calculating a matrix of chisquares, choosing a group classifier on the basis of the largest sum of chisquares, and solving for the orthogonal components of the chisquares for those tables generated from pairing each variable with the group selector [Lingoes1963b].

TOP was used to investigate the relationship between my tentative types and the attributes. When the numbered "tentative types" were included among the variables and TOP was asked to pick the "most pervasive" variable, it chose "tentative type" as the grouping variable. In successive passes, the program is capable of "trying out" different numbers of groupings; unfortunately, owing to the large number of categories in variables "tentative type" and "decorative motif," I was unable to make full use of this feature, hence had to forego one of the most interesting possibilities from the point of view of comparison of different classification.

The most significant results from TOP were obtained through use of different grouping variables. After satisfactory results were obtained from runs in which "tentative type" was included among the variables from which the grouping variable was to be selected, "tentative type" was deleted, requiring TOP to choose from the others; as might be expected, "decorative motif" turned out to be the next most pervasive factor. Based on the matrix of chi-square coefficients (a chi-square coefficient being defined as that number which when multiplied by the number of vessels yields chi-square), the probability of the significance of the association of the variables with each other can be determined, and those with strongest association are plotted as Figure 12. It can be seen why "decorative motif" was chosen by TOP as a group classifier; more variables are significantly associated with it than with any other variable. Some of the highest chi-square coefficients are between "decorative motif" and the three attributes describing punctation, and between "collar" and "castellation." After "decorative motif," the attributes with the most significant associations with other attributes are, in order, "castellation," "collar," and "treatment of area to be decorated."

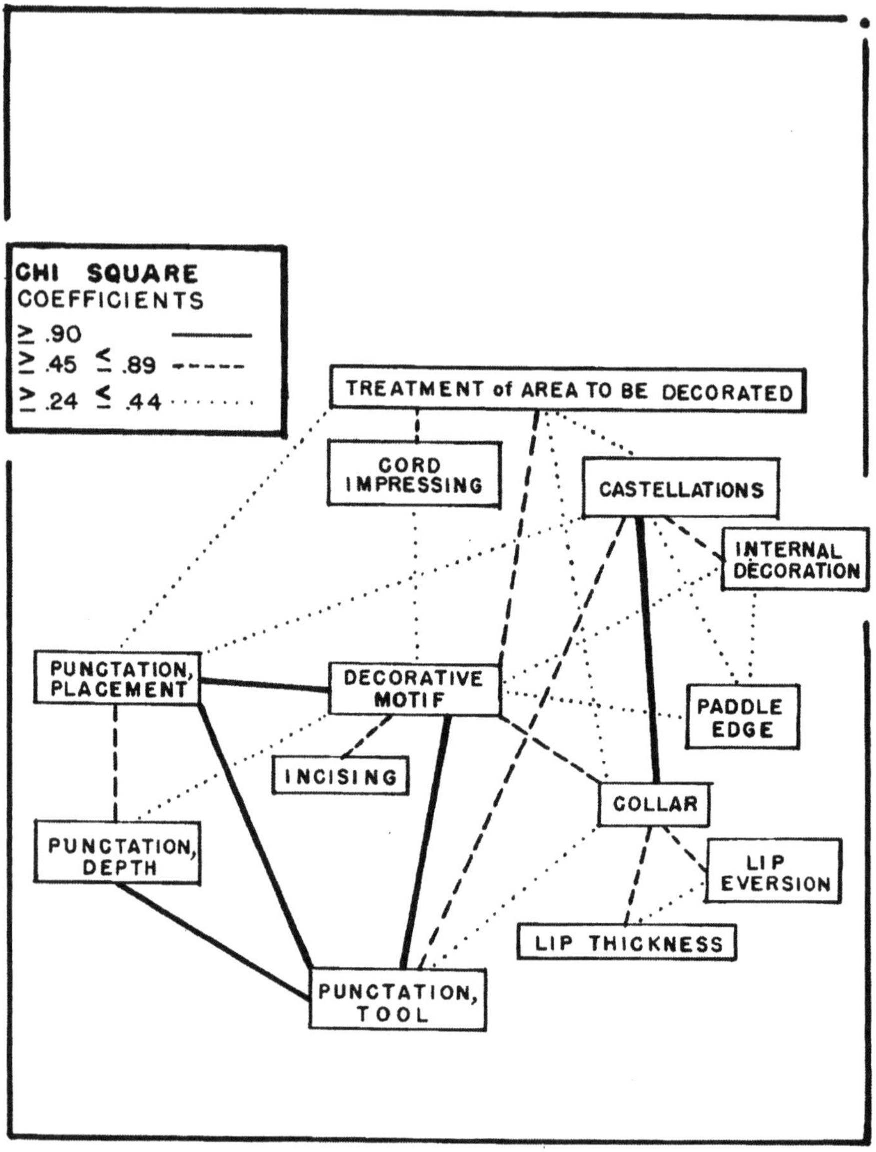

Fig. 12.—Interassociations of Pottery Attributes, based on TOP

TOP and GUTREG are based on quite different mathematical models and of course are attempting different things. It is thus of interest to compare the order in which attributes are called into the regression equation by GUTREG (Table 3 p. 67) with the ranking of attributes obtained through the sum of chi-squares from TOP. The latter are presented in Table 5.

TABLE 5

VARIABLES RANKED ACCORDING TO ASSOCIATION WITH ALL OTHER VARIABLES (BASED ON TOP, WITH "DECORATIVE MOTIF" AS GROUPING VARIABLE)

Attribute	Sum-of-chi-square Coefficients
Decorative motif	7.90
Punctation—occurrence	5.94
Punctation—tool used	5.80
Castellations	5.36
Collar	4.45
Treatment of area to be decorated	3.96
Punctation—depth	2.65
Cord impressing	2.31
Lip thickness	2.30
Cord-wrapped stick	2.21
Incising	2.20
Interior decoration	2.18
Lip eversion	2.11
Lip decoration	1.84
Body thickness	1.10
Rectangular-ended-tool impressing	1.09
Decoration below major motif	1.06
Rim flare	.96
Cord-wrapped cord	.91
Drag-and-jab	.72
Interior surface finish	.63
Simulated fabric impression	.54
Other decorative techniques	.49
Cooking residue (presence/absence)	.34

It may be noted that the punctation attributes, toward the top of Table 5, were not called up by GUTREG at all, which is probably to be explained by the fact that they do show a high degree of association with "decorative motif;" with the latter entered into the regression equation the punctation attributes then have little to contribute so far as the overall typology is concerned. "Drag-and-Jab," on the other hand, showed very small degree of association with other attributes, yet was called into regression by GUTREG at the fourth step. "Drag-and-Jab's" low sum of chi-squares would presumably mean that it would never be selected as a grouping variable by TOP, yet my experience indicates that it is one of the best indicators of late (Juntunen phase) pottery. Since it does have a few significant associations with other variables, it presumably is not replicated by other attributes, hence is of value for that reason.

Further experiments with TOP and GUTREG might include forcing into the prediction equation variables with high sums of chi-squares, and causing TOP to choose as grouping variables attributes with high ranking according to GUTREG.

5.6.3.5 Graphic Representation of Typological Distance

The questions as to the relation of the types to each other, the relative "distance" between them, and the amount (if any) of overlap, were approached with a procedure that permitted plotting of types as points on graph paper. Category weights were factored then the two sets of factor loadings with largest etas were processed to produce two independent sets of "new category weights," which were then used as Cartesian coordinates. This procedure, described in Lingoes (1963d), was followed twice, using as the dependent variable, first, my own tentative types and, second, the next variable selected by TOP ("decorative motif.)" These plottings are presented as Figures 13 and 14, respectively. It will be realized, of course, that these are reductions of types considered as points in an n-dimensional space to 2-dimensional representations, hence a number of different factors are not being considered at all. Nevertheless, the results are worth discussing.

The first plot is shown (Figs. 13 and 15) in two forms; the circled numbers of Figure 13 represent the pottery types of the "intermediate" stage of analysis (cf. Table 6, p. 78); they consist of combinations of the originally posited types. Figure 15 shows essentially the same plot as Figure 13 but adjusted in terms of the wares and types of the final stage of analysis by collapsing into one type some of the separate types of Figure 13 and by

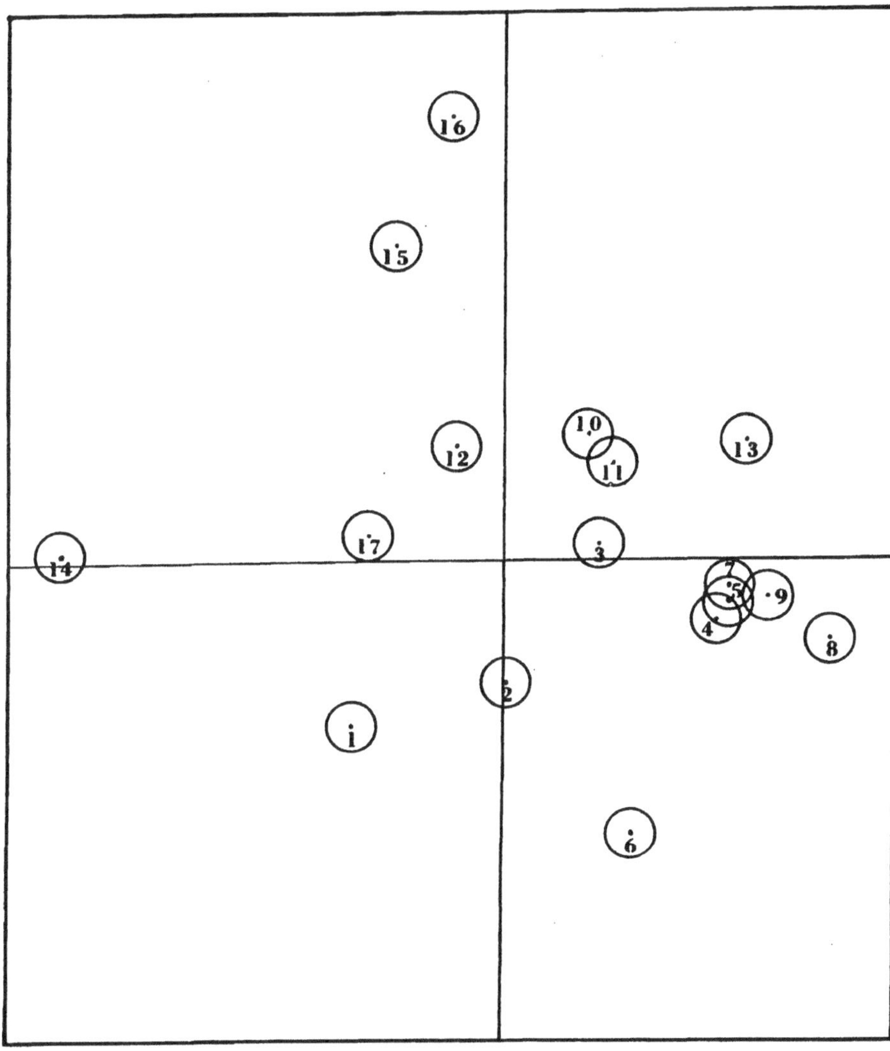

Fig. 13—Plotting of Intermediate Types (Table 6) with type numbers as grouping variable (Lingoes technique).

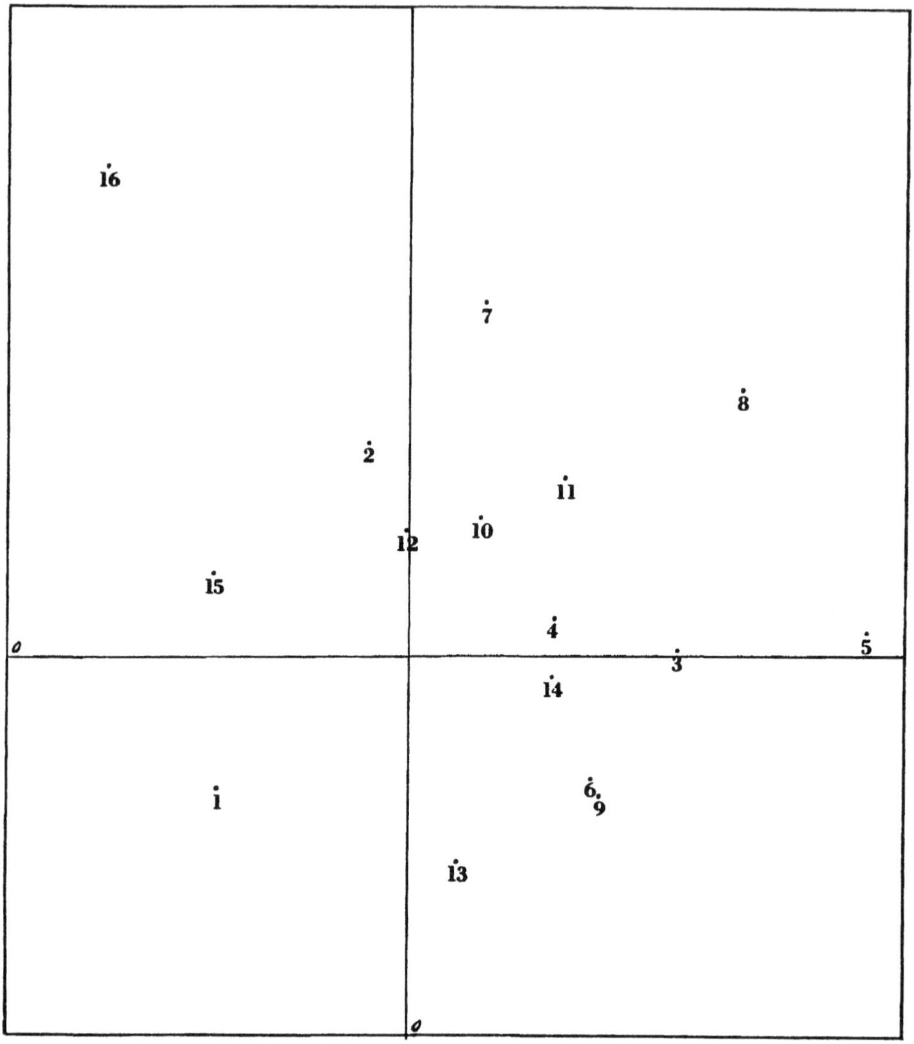

Fig. 14.—Plotting of computer-generated types, "Decorative Motif" as grouping variable (Lingoes technique).

TABLE 6

JUNTUNEN POTTERY TYPOLOGY

Ware	Type Name	Sample Size	Intermediate Type No.	Variety Name	Variety Letter
MACKINAC	MACKINAC UNDECORATED	169	1	*	A
	MACKINAC PUNCTATE	157	2	*	B
	MACKINAC CORD IMPRESSED	108	3	Horizontal Bands	C
			3	Diagonal Bands	D
	MACKINAC BANDED	182	4	Sharp-edged Tool Impressed	E
			4	Herringbone Lip	F
			5	Horizontal Bands	G
			5	Diagonal Bands	H
			7	Squared Bands	I
	MACKINAC ZIG ZAG LIP	15	6	*	J
BLACKDUCK	BLACKDUCK BANDED	20	8	*	K
	BLACKDUCK PUNCTATE	25	9	*	L
BOIS BLANC	BOIS BLANC BRACED RIM	108	10	Castellated, Simulated-Fabric Dec.	M
			10	Corded Collar	N
			10	Blackduck-like Decoration	O
			10	Bulging Lip	P
	BOIS BLANC BEADED RIM	25	12	Thin Beading	Q
			12	Thick Beading	R
	BOIS BLANC CASTELLATED CORDED	5	13	*	S
POINT SAUBLE	*	15	11	*	T
JUNTUNEN	JUNTUNEN COLLARED	22	14	*	U
	JUNTUNEN LINEAR PUNCTATE	6	15	*	V
	JUNTUNEN DRAG AND JAB	281	16	*	W
ONEOTA	*	42	--	Grit Tempered Variety	X
			--	Shell Tempered Variety	Y
RAMEY	RAMEY INCISED	15	--	*	Z
SPRING CREEK	*	2	--	*	AA
IROQUOIS	IROQUOIS LINEAR	2	--	*	BB
ARROWHEAD DRIVE	*	5	--	*	CC
Juveniles' Vessels	*	21	--	*	DD
"Others"	*	242	--	*	--
"Not Classifiable"	*	221	--	*	--

* Not subdivided at this level

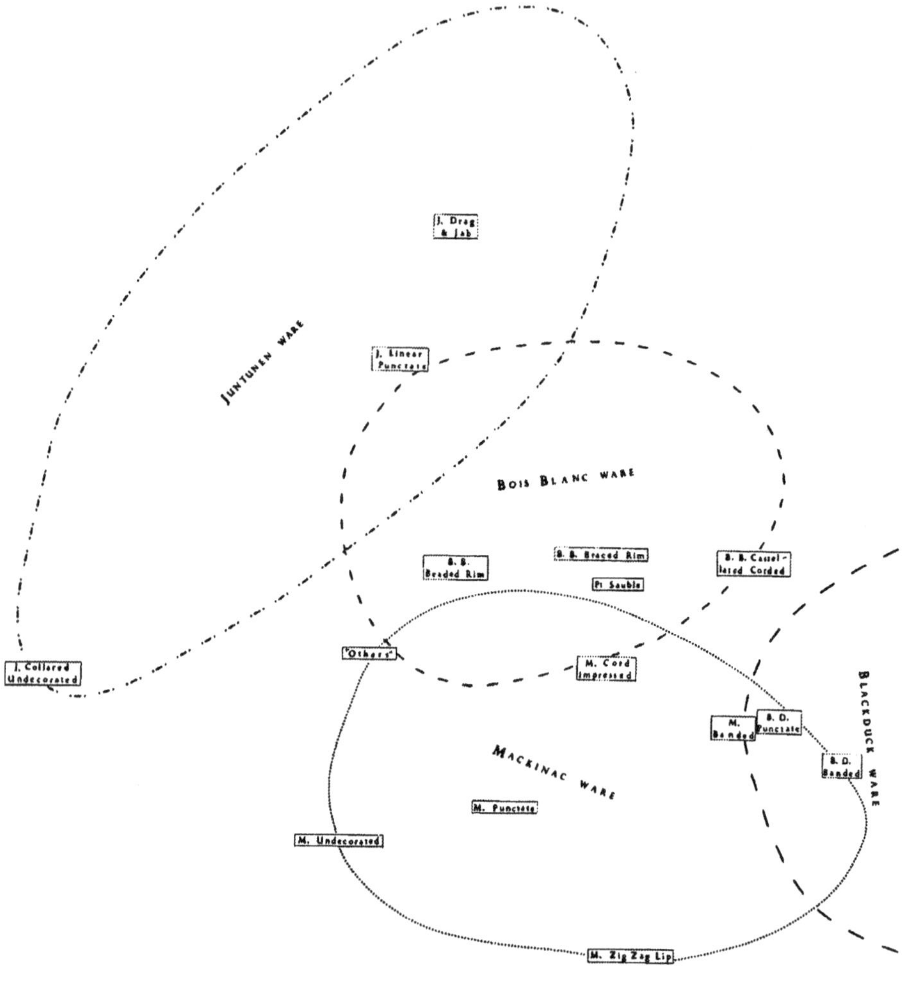

Fig. 15.—Relationships among the final pottery types, based on the plot of Figure 13.

circling what were decided upon as wares. The rationale for this treatment will be discussed in the sections describing the types. It is apparent from Figure 15 that, while the attribute or variable of stratigraphic provenience on the site was not supplied by me to the computer, yet the vertical axis (representing the factor with the highest lambda) does in fact provide a fair indication of the actual stratification of pottery types. Thus Mackinac ware (the wares and types will be defined and discussed shortly), typical of the lowest occupation levels hence one of the earliest wares from the site, appears at the bottom of the chart, while Juntunen ware, restricted to the uppermost occupation levels and typologically similar to wares from other regions at the same time period, is at the top of the chart. Bois Blanc ware, appearing in the middle occupation levels, is placed on the plot in the same relative position with respect to the other wares, and one observes that Bois Blanc ware is considerably nearer to Mackinac ware than it is to Juntunen ware, a situation that can be corroborated by inspection of the pottery. Juntunen ware thus appears as a typological intrusion on the site.

The position of Blackduck ware was difficult to determine archaeologically because it occurred mostly in highly disturbed deposits. Its position on the plot, however, is eminently reasonable, in terms of both the time of its occurrence at other sites and its stylistic similarity to the Mackinac ware; as seen here, Blackduck Punctate in fact is "closer" typologically to Mackinac Banded than it is to the other Blackduck type, B. Banded.

When the pottery was being studied, there was a question of relating Juntunen Linear Punctate to other types. It is shown in Figure 15 almost equidistant between Juntunen Drag-and-Jab and Bois Blanc Beaded, a reasonable indication of its stylistic relations to these other types. In terms of time, it is also probable (though it cannot be demonstrated) that it occurs between the time of popularity of the Bois Blanc ware and that of Juntunen Drag-and-Jab. If so, then we have a time marker for the period between the middle, or Bois Blanc, phase (*ca.* A.D. 1100), and the late, or Juntunen, phase (*ca.* A.D. 1300). On the other hand, J. Linear Punctate's high vertical postion on the chart may be a function of its mode of decoration (linear punctations only). It could be argued on stylistic grounds that J. Linear Punctate should be assigned to a ware other than Drag-and-Jab; in terms of the "distance" between types of the same ware seen on Figure 15, however, inclusion within the Juntunen ware does not seem unreasonable.

Although Juntunen Collared, a type lacking decoration, lies well apart from the other Juntunen-ware types on the plot, it was included in the Juntunen ware on the basis of vessel shape similarity and because of the likelihood that its position on the plot is erroneous; this was the type predicted most poorly by the regression equation of GUTREG; in all probability it should be shifted upward to a position parallel to Juntunen Drag-and-Jab.

The horizontal dispersion of types in Figure 15 is not so easily explained but appears to have to do mainly with simplicity versus complexity of decoration (left to right, respectively). Thus Juntunen Collared has collars, lips bearing finger-impressions, but no castellation or other decoration; it is the most "undecorated" type from the site, in fact, and thus its leftward position is not unreasonable. Mackinac Undecorated has a plain exterior but usually has decorated lip and interior, hence is second in terms of "undecoratedness," and thus its position fits this explanation of the horizontal axis.

On the far right, representing "complexity" of design, lies the Blackduck Banded type. Blackduck ware is renowned in the Upper Great Lakes area for richness of design, and vessels of this type have a great number of combinations of techniques and design elements.

It would be of interest to generate other plots using other factors; judging from the success achieved from the use of the first two, more information could be obtained. It can of course be argued that the computer did nothing but corroborate what I knew already and, in fact, did not perform as well as I did myself, since some types seem a bit out of place. The surprising thing to my mind is that it did as well as it did; it seems to me that programs of this sort might well be particularly useful in sorting out collections with mixed stratigraphy. At any rate, it is surely of significance that the two types most poorly predicted by the regression equation were also those most far-flung on the chart. Information of this sort, if received in time, should send the archaeologist back to his sherds to see what he might have overlooked.

The second plotting of machine-derived types (Fig. 14), with "Decorative Motif" as grouping variable and "Tentative Types" deleted, is much less easy to interpret. We are dealing here with "types" based on the decorative motifs of Figure 11 (p. 61) — the tentative types were left out of consideration. The first question is what the relation of these types is to those of the first plotting. Time is evidently again represented vertically;

the motifs placed on the bottom two-thirds of the chart are most frequently associated with early types, while those of the top third occur most commonly on later types. Bois-Blanc phase types are not well shown, largely because these types are distinctive mainly in features other than decorative motif. Their placement, as far as can be seen, is not out of line vertically; the motif most associated with middle occupation types is 5.

Interpretation of the horizontal component in this chart is not intuitively clear. It appears that motifs most found on vessels assigned to the "Other" type occur here as horizontal outliers; hence this dimension may refer in some degree to typological "normalcy" (in the center) versus "deviancy."

5.6.4 TYPES OF THE FINAL STAGE OF ANALYSIS

The first chart (Fig. 13, p. 76) was used as a basis for further collapsing of types. Such collapsing was regarded as necessary because of my lack of confidence in the reality of the distinctions between some of the original types. Since the new category weights have means of zero and a variance of $1/2N \times 10^3$, three standard deviations are approximately 3; the 3 s.d. figure was used to determine the radii of the circles in Figure 13. Thus 3 scale units on the figure may be taken as a critical distance, such that when points are closer than this distance they should be merged. In practice, I merged them liberally and united Intermediate Types 4, 5, and 7, as seen in Figure 13, into one type, M. Banded (Fig. 15).

If bivariate techniques had been sufficient to reveal significant differences in clusterings of attributes among the pottery types, it would have been possible to present the probabilities that the types finally arrived at were in fact separate entities; although multivariate varieties of variance analysis exist, this statistical method has not thus far been applied to the sample at hand, and the final types decided upon are those of Figure 13 but lumping 4,5, and 7 as in Figure 15, and with the addition of a number of other types that were not included in the statistical procedures.

Descriptive data on the types will shortly be presented, followed by more detailed discussion of the occurrence of them on the site and elsewhere. The format of presentation will be along lines currently popular (e.g., Griffin [ed.] 1950, Stephenson and Ferguson 1963), with exception that those attributes for which more than 95 per cent of the pottery did not vary will not be repeated for each successive type unless there are special reasons to do so. Paste, temper, and color were discussed earlier (sec. 3.2.2); one may generalize for the collection with regard to method of manufacture by saying that sherd breaks were irregular and that there were no signs of coil breaks. The marked proclivity to splitting, generally close to the mid-plane between exterior and interior, indicates that little cohesiveness in sherd cross section was achieved, which is presumably related to manufacturing techniques.

Although the continuous measurements—lip thickness, body thickness, outside diameter at lip—were ranked low by GUTREG for their ability to separate types, it seemed worthwhile to investigate whether any types did in fact differ significantly in these attributes. The measurements were recorded during processing of vessels in two different ways. All pottery was measured when possible, but for the bulk of the sample the measurements were recorded in coded intervals; of these, in addition, only lip thickness was included as an attribute in the statistical procedures previously described; body thickness and rim diameter were omitted. Toward the end of the recording of measurements and attributes for the pottery sample, I decided to commence recording the measurements both in the coded form and in direct, uncoded form. Thus there was a relatively small sample of vessels for which one could investigate differences among the types in means and variances of these measurements. Student's *t* and the variance ratio (F) tests were employed, utilizing Bendig's "*t*-test for independent groups" program in the University of Pittsburgh's IBM 7070. Results of analysis are presented as Table 7, and it is clear that there are pronounced similarities as well as differences in between-type means. They will be referred to in the discussions of the relevant types.

In the final stage of analysis, 20 pottery types were decided upon as providing a reasonable partitioning of the ceramics from the Juntunen site. Summary data on wares, types, and varieties are provided in Table 6. (p. 78). Two categories were established for vessels that could not be assigned to any of the 20 types. "Other" was used for vessels represented fully enough to be otherwise assignable but not falling into any of the types established; that they are in fact intermediate is suggested by their central position in Figure 13 (p. 76). "Not classifiable" was the category for vessels represented by such small fragments as to preclude judgment as to type, although they could be scored for at least a few attributes. Both these classes were fairly numerous, totaling 463 vessels or 27 per cent of the entire pottery collection from the site. Here is another reason why classification of provenience units in terms of attributes would be considerably more sensitive than a classification in terms of

TABLE 7

TESTS OF SIGNIFICANCE (t, F) FOR DIFFERENCES AMONG SOME JUNTUNEN POTTERY TYPES IN CONTINUOUS VARIABLES

Types Compared (See Key, below)		Hypothesis of Interest concerning Group-I Types	Statistics								t: Probability (1-tailed test)
			Group I			Group II					
Group I	Group II		n_1	$\bar{X}_1$	s_1	n_2	$\bar{X}_2$	s_2	t[a]	F	
Lip Thickness											
1	2 - 4	1 thinner	27	9.04	2.24	46	8.80	1.84	0.45	1.50	.30
5	2 - 7	5 thicker	5	13.00	2.10	37	8.43	1.79	5.10	1.66	Less than .005
14	2 - 4	14 thinner	10	7.20	1.47	11	9.55	1.92	2.96	1.70	Less than .005
Body Thickness											
1	2 - 4	1 thinner	27	5.74	1.38	46	6.26	1.36	1.55	1.04	Less than .05
14	1-13, 15, 20, 21	14 thinner	11	5.00	3.28	50	5.94	2.13	1.17	2.55	Greater than .20
8 - 9	2-7, 12-15, 20, 21	8-9 thinner	10	5.30	2.10	46	5.65	2.67	0.38	1.49	.30
Outside Diameter at Lip											
1	2 - 4	1 smaller	6	21.33	3.25	11	24.73	2.77	2.13	1.50[b]	Between .02—.05
1	2 - 15, 20-21	1 smaller	6	21.33	3.25	56	25.36	6.87	2.34[c]	3.79[b]	See Footnote [e]
5	1 - 4	5 larger	4	28.00	4.53	17	23.53	3.36	2.12	2.27	Between .02—.05
8 - 9	2-7, 12-15, 20, 21	8-9 larger	10	26.30	7.24	46	25.15	6.77	0.44	1.24	.30
14	2 - 4	14 larger	10	27.30	4.82	11	24.73	2.77	1.41[c]	3.06[d]	Greater than .05
14	1-12, 15, 20, 21	14 larger	11	27.18	4.61	50	24.26	6.87	1.32	2.06	Greater than .05

Key to Pottery Type Numbers

1. Mackinac Undecorated
2. M. Punctate
3. M. Cord Impressed
4. M. Banded
5. M. Zigzag Lip
6. Blackduck Banded
7. Blackduck Punctate
8. Bois Blanc Braced Rim
9. B. B. Beaded
10. Pt. Sauble Collared
11. B. B. Castellated-Corded
12. Juntunen Linear Punctate
13. Juntunen Collared
14. J. Drag-and-Jab
15. Oneota
20. Others
21. Not Classified

a: $$t = \frac{|\bar{X}_1 - \bar{X}_2|}{\sqrt{\left(\frac{n_1 s_1^2 + n_2 s_2^2}{n_1 + n_2 - 2}\right)\left(\frac{1}{n_1} + \frac{1}{n_2}\right)}}$$

(except where otherwise noted)

b: Probability slightly greater than .05

c: $$t = \frac{|\bar{X}_1 - \bar{X}_2|}{\sqrt{\frac{s_1^2}{n_1 - 1} + \frac{s_2^2}{n_2 - 1}}}$$

d: Probability less than .05

e: P of .10 if variances are assumed equal, otherwise between 2 and 5 per cent pottery types: using the latter, more than a quarter of the data would be thrown away, unless, of course, one were willing to regard "other" and "not classifiable" as valid "types"!

Formal taxonomic description will now follow; note that summarized data on occurrence of the more important attributes are presented in graphic and tabular form in Tables 7 and 8. Note further that these type definitions are based upon restorable vessels where available, otherwise upon rim and decorated sherds grouped into "vessels" as described earlier. Undecorated body sherds were used in definition of types only when they could with reasonable certainty be assigned to a particular vessel. Thus the definitions are "vessel types" and not "sherd types."

5.7 JUNTUNEN POTTERY TYPES

5.7.1 MACKINAC WARE

Mackinac ware is defined on the basis of 1,713 sherds representing 631 vessels. The ware is formally very close to the "Lake Michigan Ware" defined for early Late Woodland pottery of Wisconsin by McKern (1931), which however is still formally a *nomen nudum* in that no types have been assigned to it. Unlike Lake Michigan ware, however, Mackinac ware has designs executed with both twisted cords and cord-wrapped objects, the "pseudo-cord" of Hall (1950). Mackinac ware is characterized by absence of collars or castellations, presence of thickened lips, inferior raw materials or manufacture or both, with large grains of grit temper, and a strong tendency for sherds to exfoliate or split into an inside and an outside portion. Surface finish is by cord-wrapped paddle or fabric; few unambiguous cases of the latter were found. Vessels are fairly squat in form, with height about equal to maximum diameter; bases are semi-conoidal. Decoration was executed with cord-wrapped objects, twisted cords, and pointed or flat-ended tools.

Mackinac ware is one of a series of generically similar wares that enjoyed an enormous geographic distribution in early Late Woodland times—roughly from A.D. 700 to 1100—from tidewater Virginia to the northern Plains (cf. Hall 1950). There is no published general discussion of this class of wares, but such a study of stylistic variation in space, taking into consideration ecological and other differences, would be useful and should help elucidate the changing patterns of between-group interaction (cf. Binford 1962, 1964). Besides the close similarity to Lake Michigan ware, there are marked similarities to the Blackduck ware of Minnesota and Manitoba (Wilford 1955; Evans 1961; MacNeish 1958), and fairly close similarities to some of the late Point Peninsula and

TABLE 8

SUMMARIZED DATA ON POTTERY ATTRIBUTE FREQUFNCIFS

Type	Sample Size	Decorative Motifs: None	1	2	3	4	5	6	7	8	9	10	11	12	13	14	15	Other	Indeterminate
Mackinac Undecorated	169	155	1	1															12
M. Punctate	157	4	3	117		2		1			6								24
M. Cord Impressed	108	5	35	1	11	26	8	2	4		1	4	5	1		1		3	4
M. Banded	182	11	43	8	32	9		24	16	3		3	6					1	26
M. Zig Zag Lip	15	8																	7
Blackduck Banded	20	3	3	1			1				2				2	7	1		
B. Punctate	25	3	4	1	8	1				1					3				4
Bois Blanc Braced Rim	108	16	18	2	20	13	3	1		4	1	3	1				1	3	22
B. B. Beaded Rim	25	4	1	8		2				2	2		1					1	4
B. B. Castellated Corded	5						4												1
Point Sauble Collared	15		3		3		2					3						3	1
Juntunen Linear Punctate	6		5	1															
Juntunen Collared	22	8		8		3					1								2
Juntunen Drag and Jab	281	48	120	3		10	5	3		2			1	11	1	3		16	57
Oneota	42	36																	6
Children's Vessels	21	10	2	3		1	1			1								1	2
"Others"	242	60	39	39	4	17	1	3		9	1	1	1		1	3	1	12	50
Not Classifiable	221	102	10	7	1	3											1	1	95

Type	Rim-thickening Element: Beading	Bracing	Collar	Castellations	Smoothing of area to be Decorated	Interior Brushing	Rim-lip Form: V-shape	Rectang.	Splayed	Rolled	Other	Indeterminate	Interior Decoration	Lip Decoration	Decoration below Dominant Motif	Decorative Techniques: Cord-wr. Stick	Cord-wr. Cord	Linear Cord	Punctations: Oblong	Round	Drag & Jab	Incising/trailing	Others
Mackinac Undecorated			1	1	42	94		24	104	39	1		76	115	1	58	6	14	27	3	2		
M. Punctate					50	54		31	105	17	2	2	85	142		62	4	8	114	21			12
M. Cord Impressed	5			2	88	37	1	36	46	8	8	12	77	103		25	7	79	35	14		2	
M. Banded				1	153	77	1	49	123	4	1	4	122	175		69	44	46	133	10	1	1	
M. Zig Zag Lip					3	9		1	13		1		7	15		12	1	1	1				
Blackduck Banded					15	7		5	12	2		1	11	19		17	2	1	3	10			
B. Punctate				1	15	8		12	7	1	2	3	17	24		19	2	2	9	12	1		1
Bois Blanc Braced Rim		68	9	53	79	11	62	26	8		8	4	78	83	1	56	14	9	25	21		3	8
B. B. Beaded Rim	18	4	1	1	6	4	11	5	3		5	1	14	13	1	9		2	13	1	1	1	
B. B. Castellated Corded			1	4	5	2		4	1				5	5		2	2	1	3	1			
Point Sauble Collared	2	12		1	11	3	2	10	1		2		9	12	1	2	1	6	4	3	1		2
Juntunen Linear Punctate			5		5	5		4	2				5	6					6				2
Juntunen Collared			19		6	6		19	2			1	6	17		3		1	12		2		
Juntunen Drag and Jab		6	169	88	270	31	5	155	30	1		90	226	243	15	17	4	7	79	5	232	1	
Oneota					36	2	2	27	1	1	3	19	2	43		2			2			2	2
Children's Vessels				1	8	1	1	11	6			3	3	15		3	1	1	6			1	
"Others"	3	7	57	28	132	84	7	139	55	8	24	9	132	193		51	6	30	111	23	42	14	4
Not Classifiable			18	8	126	20	1	59	99	8	8	46	149	197		91	14	13	78	15	28	4	

early Owasco types of New York State (Ritchie and MacNeish 1949). I have seen no pottery from southern Ontario that is as similar to Mackinac as is early New York Owasco, which merits consideration.

5.7.1.1 Mackinac Undecorated

A. Summary Definition

The proposed type Mackinac Undecorated consists of vessels like the other types of this ware in shape but consistently smaller in size. Decoration is absent except for lips and interiors. See Plates XI *a, c, d*.

B. Type Description

(1) Sample size

299 rim sherds representing 169 nonrestorable vessels.

(2) Formal Attributes

(a) Vessel Shape and Size.—Smallest vessels from the site as judged from measurements of diameter at the lip and wall thickness (cf. Table 7, p. 84); lips commonly splayed or out-rolled. Overall shape unknown, but most likely conforms to other types of this ware.

(b) Surface Treatment.—Most commonly treated with paddle wrapped with coarse twisted cord or some sort of fabric. Some interiors were "brushed" with a coarse scratchy material, producing a striated appearance parallel to the lip.

(c) Decoration.—Absent below lip edge; lips commonly dedecorated transverse to the lip, using a cord-wrapped object (cf. Pl. XI, *a*) or sharp-edged tool (Pl. XI, *c*). A high frequency (50%) of rim interiors are undecorated; when present here, decoration is generally with same tool as on lip, in vertical impressions.

(3) Spatial-Temporal Distribution

(a) Geographical Range.—Unknown

(b) Temporal Range.—Mackinac phase

C. Relationships

In absence of decoration and roughness of surface finish, this type somewhat resembles some of the early Late Woodland pottery from the Spring Creek site, Muskegon County, Michigan. The lack of distinguishing features makes comparisons difficult.

5.7.1.2 Mackinac Punctate

A. Summary Definition

Vessels of this proposed type have outflaring rims and semiconoidal bases. On sub-lip exteriors, punctation is sole decorative technique, hence motifs are restricted to single or double rows of punctations. A rather high frequency of undecorated interiors is found. See Plates XI, *b*, *e-h*; XII; XIII, *a*.

B. Type Description

(1) Sample size

392 rim sherds comprising 2 restorable and 155 nonrestorable vessels.

(2) Formal Attributes

(a) Vessel Shape and Size.—Common shapes are as Plate XII, *a*, *b*; rims are generally flared outward, and lips are almost invariably thickened and splayed or outrolled. Vessels usually have a rounded shoulder, with only moderate curvature below the shoulder (compared, for example, with Mackinac Banded, below), and semiconoidal bases. The restorable vessels indicate a fairly squat form; the shape of Plate XII, *a*, is thus regarded as typical, while XII, *b*, is rather more elongated than usual. A few vessels with straight sides (e.g., Pl. XIII, *a*) were assigned to this type.

(b) Surface Treatment.—Cord-wrapped stick (Pl. XII, *a*, *b*) or Fabric (Pl. XI, *f*; Pl. XIII, *a*).

(c) Decoration.—(i) Exterior: punctation, most often with rectangular-ended object (Pl. XI, *f-h*), round-ended object being the only other variant and somewhat rare (Pl. XII, *b*, *c*). Spacing between punctations varies from "wide" (*ca.* 3/4 inch; Pl. XII, *b*) to "close" (Pl. XI, *f*; *ca.* 1/4 inch). No clustering of the closeness of spacing with other attributes was observed. Depth of punctation varied from very shallow (Pl. XI, *g*) to very deep, with bosses produced on the interior, often with fingerprints in the clay showing how support had been supplied during the impressing process (see Pl. XI, *f*). Deep punctating, yet without the marked interior bossing, was most common.
(ii) Lip and interior: M. Punctate shares with M. Undecorated a high frequency of undecorated rim interiors (45% of the cases for each). Lips and interiors were most often decorated with cord-wrapped object; Plate XII, *a*, shows an exception, with impressions produced by a sharp edged tool.

(3) Spatial-temporal Distribution

(a) Geographical Range.—Vessels resembling this type in many respects have been found in Wisconsin and other parts of Michigan. Mason (1966) reports sherds representing 4 or 5 vessels from the Heins Creek site on the Door Peninsula of Wisconsin, with punctation as the exclusive decorative technique "in amazingly heterogeneous forms" (24).

(b) Temporal Range.—Mackinac phase, especially occupation A.

C. Relationships

On the Juntunen site this type occurs most frequently in association with Undecorated, M. Corded, and somewhat less frequently with M. Cord Impressed. Stylistic similarities of this group of types are greatest with eastern Wisconsin; on the Door Peninsula, Mason's (1966) type Heins Creek Corded Stamped shares many attributes with M. Punctate.

5.7.1.3 Mackinac Cord Impressed

A. Summary Definition

Decoration is with twisted cords or (rarely) cord-wrapped stick; motifs begin directly below lip, without the "introductory" row of vertical impressions seen on many other types. Similar to Madison Cord Impressed of Wisconsin. See Plate XIII, *b*, *e*, *e'*, *h*, *h'*.

B. Type Description

(1) Sample Size

275 rim and decorated body sherds comprising 1 restorable and 107 nonrestorable vessels.

(2) Formal Attributes

(a) Vessels Shape and Size.—Overall shape unknown; probably conforms to other types of this ware. Lips are often straight rather than thickened or splayed, are often not everted, and rims show less flare than do other types of this ware.

(b) Surface Treatment.—Cord-wrapped stick; no suggestion of fabric impressing was observed.

(c) Decoration.—(i) Exterior: two varieties or subtypes may be distinguished in terms of decorative motif: one with horizontal bands, often running up to the lip, and another with diagonal bands, more often set off top and bottom by rows of punctates. On exteriors, motifs are executed with twisted cord, motifs 1, 2, and 4 being most common. (Motif 4 is rare on many other types.) Cord-wrapped object is used rarely, on lips only. Punctation, when present, is characteristically executed by loops or knots of twisted cord (Pl. VI; XIII, *e*). Motifs often run right up to the lip, without the band of vertical impressions starting at the lip edge and extending for 1-3 cm. below and meeting the motif, often seen on other types. (See Pl. XIII, *b*, *e*.) (ii) Interior: commonly decorated in bands parallel to the lip, using twisted cord.

(3) Spatial-temporal Distributions

(a) Geographical Range.—Unknown

(b) Temporal Range.—Seems confined to Occupation A.

C. Relationships

Of all Juntunen types, some vessels of M. Cord Impressed are closest to Madison Cord Impressed (Baerreis [1953], Keslin [1958], and Wittry [1959]), although the Juntunen pottery is not identical to these vessels. At the Heins Creek site, however, vessels assigned by Mason (1966) to Madison Cord Impressed are very nearly identical with Juntunen Cord Impressed. Elements in which these vessels are similar to each other but different from the Madison Cord Impressed of central and western Wisconsin, as described by Baerreis, include flattening and thickening of lips, lip decoration, use of punctation, and sherd thickness. Mason (1966:22) observes the close similarity between Madison Cord Impressed at the Heins Creek site and Point Sauble Collared (described below). This similarity is certainly borne out at the Juntunen site for Juntunen Cord Impressed and Point Sauble; in the revised computer-produced plot of the types shown in Figure 15 (p. 79) it will be noticed that, of all types included within the Mackinac ware, M. Cord Impressed is typologically closest to Point Sauble.

Pottery like M. Cord Impressed may occur in southeastern Michigan, judging from some of the sherds from the Younge site (Greenman 1937; cf. especially Pl. XVII, *c*). I know of no occurrences, however, in the interior of the state.

Occurrences of M. Cord Impressed with types showing connections with Minnesota and Manitoba certainly illustrate the "crossroads" nature of the Juntunen site; it is unfortunate that more is not known of the early Late Woodland pottery of areas in Ontario to the north and east of the Straits of Mackinac; at present, other than sporadic undated occurrences of Blackduck pottery, the only well-placed occupation temporally is at the Pic River site on the north shore of Lake Superior (J. Wright 1966a). Dated A.D. 950±80 and described as "a pure component of the Blackduck focus" (GSC-85, Dyck and Fyles 1963), this component should correspond temporally to late Occupation C at Juntunen, so appears not to extend as far back in time as Heins Creek or earliest Juntunen. The Frank Bay "Primary Transitional" level immediately above Point Peninsula, (Ridley 1954) is placed around A.D. 1050, again too late for the Mackinac phases at Juntunen.

At both Heins Creek and Juntunen, the cord-impressed pottery is seen associated with other types that are not seen in central and western Wisconsin. In the light of suggestions that Madison

Cord Impressed occupies a terminal Middle Woodland to early Late Woodland position in places in Wisconsin and Iowa, its association (or at least the association of pottery showing most of its attributes) at two places at the northern end of Lake Michigan with unquestionable Late Woodland pottery is of interest, particularly since there are otherwise indications of some sort of hiatus, however interpreted, between Middle and Late Woodland occupations in certain places in the Upper Great Lakes. We would seem to have, here at least, a bridge across the stylistic portion of the hiatus. It should be noted that C-14 dates on Heins Creek and Juntunen Occupation A suggest contemporaneity.

5.7.1.4 Mackinac Banded

A. Summary Definition

Mackinac Banded vessels have fairly complex designs in horizontal or diagonal bands, often bordered by rows of punctations at top and bottom. A band of short vertical impressions is common between edge of lip and top of decorative motif. This type looks stylistically intermediate between Mackinac (and Madison) Cord Impressed and Blackduck ware and is of major importance in Mackinac phase occupations at Juntunen. See Plates XIII, *c-c'*, *d-d'*, *f-f'*, *g-g'*; XIV, XV, XVI.

B. Type Description

(1) Sample Size

722 rim and decorated body sherds comprising 4 restorable and 178 nonrestorable vessels.

(2) Formal Attributes

(a) Vessel Shape and Size.—As seen in Plate XIV, *a-b*, shape is closely similar to Mackinac Punctate. Vessels are squat, being about 1.3 times as wide (at the shoulders) as they are high. Plate XV, *e*, is exceptional in having a straight neck; most have pronounced constriction at the orifice and considerable rim flare above that. Lips are commonly thickened.

(b) Surface Treatment.—Cord-wrapped-stick impressed (clearly seen in Plate XIV, *b*) with occasional possible use of fabric impressing.

(c) Decoration.—Five varieties may be distinguished within this type (see Table 6 p. 78). (i) Sharp-edged-tool impressed: A sharp tool such as a knife blade is impressed in the same patterns as those produced with cord-wrapped-paddle edge; usually restricted to lip and immediately sub-lip rim. Plate XIV, *b*. Frequency on site: 37. (ii) Herringbone Lip: A variety with exceedingly thick lips, and a combination of tool impressions on and at each edge of the lip such as to produce, when looking at the lip, the effect shown here. Generally abberrant designs on exterior. Not illustrated. Frequency on site: 9. (iii) Horizontal Bands: Bands on rim exterior and neck, usually produced by cord-wrapped cords. The variety closest to Heins Creek Cord-wrapped-Stick Impressed (Mason 1966). Lips ordinarily decorated diagonally with cord-wrapped paddle edge. Plate XVI. Frequency on site: 46. (iv) Diagonal Bands: As iii, but with diagonal bands set off top and bottom by horizontal bands. Frequency on site:13. (v) Squared Bands: Horizontal bands alternating with rows of elongate punctates or cord-wrapped-stick-edge impression. Plate XV, *c*, *e*; Motif 6, Figure 11 (p. 61). Frequency on site: 77.

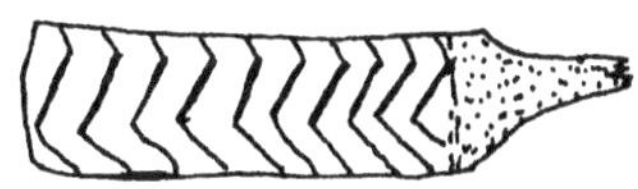

The bands of exterior decoration may be produced with either twisted cord or cord-wrapped object (Pl. XIV, *a* and *b*, respectively), and these two sorts of devices appear to be—here as at Heins Creek (Mason 1966)—in free variation, whereas in other areas one or the other device appears alone. When twisted cord is used to produce the "major decorative motif," the other areas decorated—lip and interior—are still most commonly decorated by means of cord-wrapped object, which suggests that the use of twisted cord was, for some reason, being reserved for display in the most prominent position, while the seemingly more mundane cord-wrapped object was relegated to subsidiary usages. This situation is evident in Plates XIII, *a*, and XIV, *a*, *c*, and *e*. Of all types in the early occupations at Juntunen, this is in many ways the most aesthetically satisfying.

Punctation is an extremely common adjunct element to decoration, as can be seen in the plates, and often borders the horizontal bands of design or fills the space between lip and beginning of motif. Horizontal bands of decoration—the "major motifs" themselves—extend only rarely up to the lip.

Sharp-edged tool impression seems in free variation with punctation and short corded-paddle-edge impression and is virtually restricted to this type on the Juntunen site. It may be seen on lip and immediate sub-lip in Plate XIV, *b*. This is very definitely not incision. Hasty and rather crude crosshatched incising occurs on the vessel shown in Plate XIV, *a*, exceedingly unusual at this time on the site both for the technique of incising itself and for its placement: a second decorative motif below the one on the neck is very rare. It certainly looks like an afterthought in this case. Lips are invariably decorated, usually across the lip, and interiors are commonly decorated.

(3) Spatial-temporal Distribution

(a) Geographical Range.—Eastern Wisconsin to Straits of Mackinac.

(b) Temporal Range.—Mackinac phase.

C. Relationships

As with M. Cord Impressed, closest relationships are with Wisconsin. Some of the vessels from the Kletzien and Nitschke mounds (McKern 1931) are very similar in shape and decoration. A number of the vessels included by Mason (1966) in Heins Creek Cord-wrapped-stick Impressed would clearly fall in the Juntunen Mackinac Banded type; Mason's examination of the Juntunen material indicated that the opposite was likewise true; yet to collapse these types would not, in my opinion, do justice to the range of the material. What we are dealing with, I think, is two populations, which overlap but whose "means and variances" are significantly different. It would be exceedingly interesting to measure and study this overlap.

Excavations of Late Woodland sites in Michigan have hitherto been concentrated in the lower portions of the state, and it can be said that nothing very similar to the Mackinac ware has been located. A few sherds from the Younge Site (Greenman 1937) are similar, but even here the closeness to Mackinac is not as great as the typological closeness of pottery from some Wisconsin sites to Mackinac.

Mackinac Banded *may* appear in the Upper Great Lakes at the same time as the Blackduck ware but at the present this cannot be demonstrated, and it would be as well to suppose that Mackinac ware had some temporal priority and that it may represent some of the attributes later incorporated into Blackduck. It seems as reasonable to posit this as to think that the similarities between Mackinac and Blackduck are the result of "influence" of the latter on the former.

5.7.1.5 Mackinac Zigzag Lip

A. Summary Definition

Mackinac Zigzag Lip is known only from rim sherds which are highly distinctive in a number of features. Exterior decoration is lacking; interiors are often roughened or "brushed"; very thick lips—carefully smoothed, almost polished—are decorated in zigzag pattern executed by cord-wrapped object. Plate VIII, *c-g*.

B. Type Description

(1) Sample Size

25 rim sherds comprising 15 nonrestorable vessels.

(2) Formal Attributes

(a) Vessel Shape and Size.—Unknown; conforms to rest of Mackinac ware in terms of rim profile (Fig. 9, p. 56, *h-i*). Lips are significantly thicker than those of other types of this ware, and outside diameters at lip, as inferred from the small sections of rim preserved, are significantly larger (see *t*-test results, Table 7, p. 84). It cannot be determined whether the larger rim implies greater vessel size or simply wider and perhaps more prominent orifices. About half the vessels lacked signs of cooking residue; it is possible that this fact, coupled with the suggestions of different size or shape, may indicate that the type served a function different from that of the others of this ware. The proportion of these vessels lacking cooking residues was the second highest on the site; it could not, however, be shown that this difference was statistically significant.

(b) Paste and Temper.—Based on subjective impressions, there is some contrast with the other types here in that the tendency to split was not so marked and the texture of the paste and temper was not as coarse.

(c) Surface Treatment.—Conformable to rest of ware except for lip finish.

(d) Decoration.—Exterior decoration wholly lacking in all 15 cases; interior decoration lacking in 10; decorative efforts confined to lips, which were carefully prepared by smoothing, apparently by rubbing a wet finger over the partially hardened clay. In contrast with these unusually smooth lips are the roughened exteriors and unsmoothed interiors; coarse brushing around the interior was fairly common. Cord-wrapped object was the only decorative device observed. In a few cases, alternating triangles produced by the zigzagging were filled in with cord-wrapped object impressions (Pl. VIII, *f-g*).

(3) Spatial-temporal distribution

(a) Geographic Range.—Unknown

(b) Temporal Range.—Probably restricted to Occupation C (late Mackinac phase).

C. Relationships

Zigzag lips appear occasionally on Blackduck pottery and other pottery in the Mackinac ware, but this combination of attributes makes the type almost unique at Juntunen. It will be noted on Figure 15 (p. 79) that it lies at the far end of the cluster of types, noticeably apart even from the other types of the Mackinac ware.

At this point it might be pointed out that Mackinac Ware can be lumped together for comparison with pottery of other areas. In general, the similarities with Wisconsin, particularly the Door Peninsula, are most striking. Similarities with Blackduck pottery, while of a "generic" nature, are still more marked than those with areas to the east of the Straits of Mackinac. Southern Ontario—if Pickering represents the contemporary pottery there—seems entirely different (cf. J. Wright [1966b]). There are no close similarities with the pottery of New York State, and what similarities there are seem roughly divided between late Point Peninsula and early Owasco. Ritchie (personal communication) considers that Mackinac ware resembles pottery of the Kipp Island phase of late Point Peninsula more than it resembles any Owasco pottery. From my own observations of New York State pottery, in Rochester and Albany, the vessel shapes throughout are unlike Mackinac ware shapes, and both Point Peninsula and Owasco are characteristically lightly paddled and impressed, in contrast with the heavy, bold impressing of most Juntunen pottery. Of the Point Peninsula series, some vessels of Wickham Corded and Point Peninsula Corded (but not any of those illustrated in Ritchie and MacNeish [1949]) are reminiscent of some Mackinac Banded decorative motifs and techniques. A major difference is the total lack of rocker and dentate stamping in Mackinac ware, which still persists in late Point Peninsula. Of the Owasco series, some of the Carpenter Brook Cord-on-Cord sherds (see esp. Ritchie and MacNeish [1949] Fig. 39, *c*) are close to Mackinac Punctate and Mackinac Banded, although there are many significant differences. Some Wickham Corded Punctate sherds I saw in the Rochester Museum come as close to Mackinac Banded and Blackduck vessels as any I have seen from New York State. One rim from Bell-Philhower (Rochester Museum Cat. No. AR40653), probably Owasco Corded Horizontal, and four rims from Wickham (Cat. No's. 39538, 39554, 39669, 39703), in a drawer labeled Wickham Corded Punctate, fall within range of Mackinac Banded. The New York sherds were excavated by William A. Ritchie and examined by me at the Rochester Museum of Arts and Sciences through the courtesy of Charles F.

Hayes III; most of the ones I refer to here are not illustrated or specially discussed in Ritchie and MacNeish (1949).

One marked feature of Mackinac ware (also noted for the Door Peninsula by Mason) is the variety of decorative devices and motifs used on rim exteriors and interiors. Some of this variety is shown in Plate XVI, where interiors and exteriors of the same sherds are illustrated.

The foregoing remarks regarding stylistic similarities would suggest that in the Mackinac phase, the Juntunen site was located toward the eastern edge of an overlapping pair of interaction spheres, one with sites mostly east central Wisconsin, the other with sites in Minnesota, Ontario, and southern Manitoba. The implications of this in terms of cultural ecology and "style zones" will be considered later.

5.7.2 BLACKDUCK WARE

Blackduck pottery of Wilford's (1955) Blackduck Focus, classified by Evans (1961) and generally considered indentical with the "Manitoba ware" of MacNeish's classification (1958), seems to be a fairly homogeneous category with a wide geographic distribution—from Saskatchewan to eastern Ontario, but more limited in a north-south direction—and presents a number of problems, some purely archaeological and some perhaps "culturological." Among archaeological puzzles, the temporal range, if data and dates be accepted at face value, is extraordinary. Radiocarbon dates on Blackduck sites range from shortly after A.D. 900 up to 1500 and J. Wright (1966a) indicates that modified Blackduck pottery was found with French gunflints at the Pic River and five other sites. Although he can see some stylistic change in the pottery over this 800-year period, the pottery is considered still recognizably Blackduck; the situation is peculiar in terms of change in pottery elsewhere in the Upper Great Lakes over this period. It would be a convenience if the Juntunen data could help clarify this matter.

Blackduck sherds occurred at Juntunen in habitation deposits ranging from relatively undisturbed to obviously very mixed and ranging in time from Occupation A of the Mackinac phase to the plow zone. The frequency at different times is shown in Figure 16. It was noted that neither Bois Blanc nor Blackduck pottery occurred in pure and undisturbed units of the earliest phase, which suggests that Mackinac ware has some temporal priority on the site; unfortunately, Blackduck's first appearance on the site cannot be definitely pinned down. It seems highly unlikely that it was being made in Juntunen component times, for, although sherds of all periods appear in the Juntunen component because of the disturbance in prehistoric times as well as in the recent past, the trend as shown in Figure 16 certainly indicates it to be a matter of mechanical disturbance rather than persistence of an older tradition.

It may be asked whether the cumulative percentage curves of Figure 16 represent actual differences or whether, because of the small number of Blackduck sherds recovered, the curve for Blackduck might not in fact correspond to that of either Bois Blanc or Mackinac wares. To test these hypotheses, chi-squares were calculated, and the results are shown as Table 9. We see

TABLE 9

CHI-SQUARE
TESTS FOR INDEPENDENCE OF POTTERY TYPE FREQUENCIES THROUGH TIME

	Pottery Ware or Type								
	a. Mackinac vs. Blackduck Wares			*b.* Blackduck vs. Bois Blanc Wares			*c.* Mackinac Cord Impressed vs. Mackinac Banded		
	Mack.	Blackd.	Totals	Blackd.	B.B.	Totals	M.C.I.	M. Ban.	Totals
Juntunen	30	4	34	4	12	16	6	10	16
Interm. II	149	13	162	13	48	61	22	62	84
Bois Blanc	56	11	67	11	42	53	15	21	36
Interm. I	89	12	101	12	22	34	29	34	63
Mackinac	259	14	273	14	26	40	53	74	127
Totals	583	54	637	54	150	204	125	201	326
χ^2 (4 d.f)	11.4			38.5			7.6		
p	< .05			<< .01			> .10		

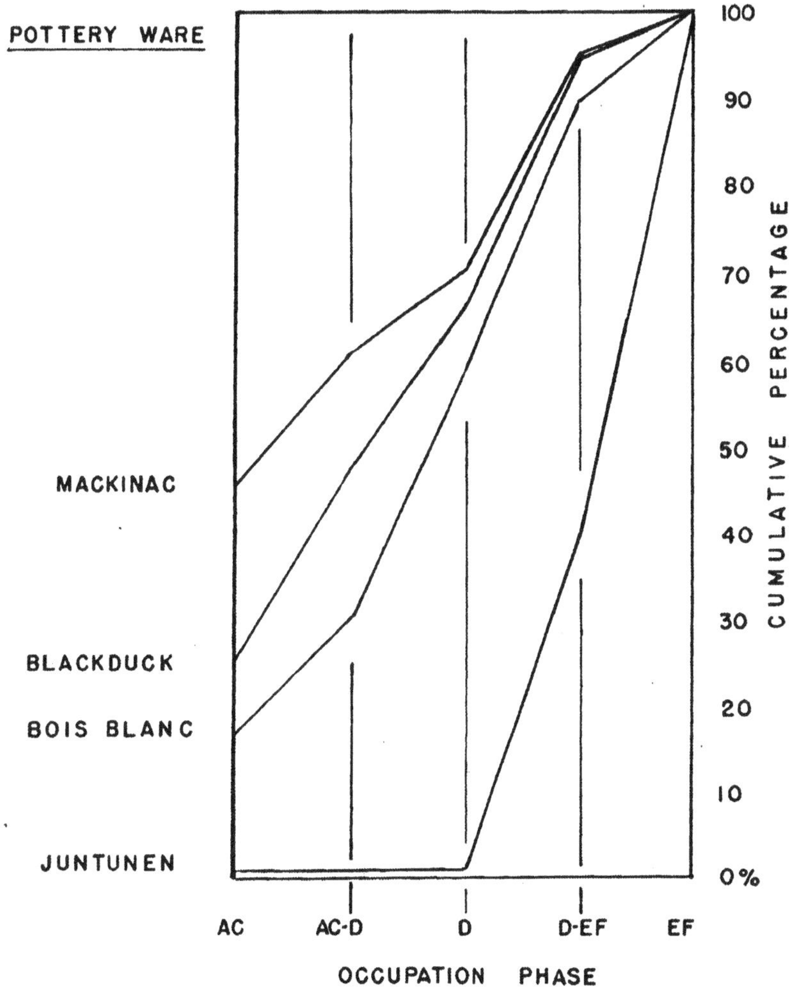

Fig. 16.—Cumulative percentages of pottery wares through time.

from column *a* that it is unlikely that the rise and fall in popularity of Blackduck parallels that of Mackinac; the low frequencies of the former compared with the latter in the Mackinac component can be regarded as a real difference. It is *exceedingly* unlikely that Blackduck parallels Bois Blanc ware (Table 9, column *b*), and these two situations certainly suggest that Blackduck enjoyed its greatest popularity at the Juntunen site between the times of florescence of Mackinac and Bois Blanc wares, that is, between A.D. 800 and 1100. Its decline in popularity after the latter date, and the fact that it occurs henceforth only in deposits suspect for disturbance, does not argue directly against its continued popularity elsewhere. The Hungry Hall carbon estimate A.D. 1200 ± 60 (S-109) dates a horizon with mixed Blackduck and Selkirk Focus pottery. The dates from Minnesota mounds spread between the eighth and the fifteenth centuries A.D. and in any case were obtained from materials excavated in the 1930's and kept in open storage ever since, for which reason contamination may be suspected.

As a check on the chi-square tests of Blackduck versus other wares, two types in the Mackinac ware were similarly tested for independence, and the results are reported as column *c* in Table 9. We see that there is no good reason to believe that they behave differently through time.

It should be explained why the cell entries differ from frequencies reported elsewhere herein: for these tests, a vessel was counted each time it occurred in a different provenience unit. Thus, if the vessel was represented by two sherds from the site and these were in the same provenience unit, the vessel was counted once; but, if the two were in different units, it was counted twice. This procedure was used in order to avoid biasing the situation when a decision would otherwise have had to be made as to which occurrence of a given vessel should be counted, to the exclusion of all others.

While, on the basis of stylistic traits, 45 vessels from the site were judged to be assignable to the Blackduck ware, it has to be admitted that, on other criteria, there are differences between Juntunen Blackduck and the Blackduck pottery of Minnesota, southern Saskatchewan, Manitoba, and Ontario. If the latter pottery were compared with the Juntunen pottery of the Mackinac and Blackduck wares and "mapped" in the manner by which the Juntunen types were compared with each other (cf. Figs. 13, 15, pp. 76, 79), we would no doubt see that Juntunen Blackduck lies closer to Mackinac ware than to the more northerly Blackduck ware. The Juntunen Blackduck pottery, then, presents a problem in classification because of its intermediate status; but there *are* differences from Mackinac ware, and the assignment to the established Blackduck ware does emphasize the close stylistic similarities with the northern ware.

Perhaps the most striking difference between Juntunen and "classic" Blackduck lies in attributes of paste and temper; most genuine Blackduck sherds are of fine paste, rather well fired, hard, dense, and show little tendency to exfoliate and split—all this in marked contrast with the poorer-quality Juntunen pottery.

Juntunen Blackduck pottery has not been sorted into the categories of either MacNeish (1958) or Evans (1961); rather, two broad categories were tentatively established to facilitate analysis; each of them encompasses a number of MacNeish's and Evans' "types." The significance of some of the distinctions made by these authors seems difficult to justify; both have set up separate types on the basis of what are surely nondistinctive variations. Thus the sole difference between MacNeish's "Manitoba Horizontal" and "Manitoba Herringbone" lies in the addition of a single row of indentations; some of his "Sturgeon Falls Fabric-Impressed" would be "Manitoba Horizontal" had he not judged that the former had surfaces roughened by fabric rather than by cord-wrapped paddle, again a case of free variation, if real, but in fact possibly a case of overestimate of ability to discriminate. I was often unable to distinguish fabric from cord-wrapped paddle with Juntunen and other northern Great Lakes ceramics, as was Quimby (1961). In any case, various surface treatments are described for the Blackduck ceramics of Minnesota (Evans 1961:40). Thus assignment of "Sturgeon Falls Fabric-Impressed" to the Selkirk Focus (MacNeish 1958:167) is probably not justified. With regard to Evans' (1961) types, they are admittedly often only subtypes at best and are mostly cases of free variation of one decorative element, so no "emic" difference is involved.

The data thus far recovered from the Juntunen site will unfortunately not clarify the dating of Blackduck pottery. This report will in fact further complicate the picture by subdividing Blackduck pottery a different way and introducing new names, which are probably as little likely to become part of the common parlance among Great Lakes archaeologists as are the terminologies of MacNeish and Evans. A description of the variation occurring through space and time will be possible only by study of *all* occurrences of Blackduck (or "Manitoba") ware utilizing a comprehensive and minutely partitioned framework sufficient to describe and define the manifold and multiform variations in style present within this widely spread ceramic tradition. A major difficulty in this undertaking will be the preparation of an attribute list adequate to describe stylistic variation. Rather than encoded decorative motifs (as used in the present report), such a scheme should be capable of taking into account, for example, a range of variation in application of punctation, such as seen in Plate XVII, *a-c*. In *a*, punctation is rectangular, shallow, and placed below all other elements. In *c*, it is round, deep, and placed above all sublip design elements. Again, with respect to the first sublip design element, in *a* it is diagonal cord-wrapped object impressions; in *b*, horizontal cord-wrapped-object bands plus the superimposed punctations; in *c*, solely punctations. Isolating elements of design and defining their placement with respect to others presents several problems if the aim is exploration of similarities and differences utilizing automatic data-processing equipment. I suggest that the literature concerning programs for handling natural languages would be a suitable place to begin looking for ideas; there, too, problems involve units of various lengths (words), comparable to the decorative pattern on a vessel. Within these units one may be interested in both presence or absence and order of occurrence of smaller units (morphemes=decorative elements); beyond this one may search for minimal distinctive units: phonemes in the case of words, some undefined "emic" units in the case of decorative designs.

For the purposes of the present report, however, two easily distinguished classes of Blackduck ware were isolated and named, and these classes will now be discussed.

5.7.2.1 Blackduck Banded

A. Summary Definition

Blackduck Banded is a category that includes such types as MacNeish's (1958) Manitoba Horizontal and Manitoba Herringbone, plus possibly Sturgeon Falls Fabric-Impressed, and all of Evans' (1961) "types" that have horizontal bands of cord-wrapped-object impression. It is characterized by horizontal bands, applied to areas usually smoothed, and by punctations often subsequently applied on top of other design elements. Illustrations: Plate XVII, *a-d*.

B. Type Description

(1) Sample Size

46 rim sherds comprising 20 nonrestorable vessels.

(2) Formal Attributes

(a) Vessel Shape and Size.—Vessel shape unknown; no shoulder or base sherds could be associated with rims, so one cannot state whether bases were rounded, as at the Schocker site (cf. Evans 1961, Fig. 1), or semiconoidal, as with Mackinac ware. There is at any rate no evidence that the variety of vessel sizes noted by Evans for Minnesota is present on the Juntunen site; sizes conformed to the Mackinac ware as far as can be judged from rim diameters.

(b) Surface Treatment.—No significant departures from Mackinac ware were observed. The vertical brushing characteristic of northern Blackduck was seen in only three cases (cf. Pl. XVII, *d*).

(c) Decoration.—(i) Techniques: cord-wrapped objects and punctating tools with round and rectangular or chisel-shaped ends were the only device used; twisted-cord impressing was wholly absent. (ii) Exterior: whereas rectangular punctates were most common in the Mackinac ware, round punctates predominated in the two Blackduck types and were often used in a peculiar way common to Blackduck and the Bois Blanc ware (to be described below) but absent from, or found only rarely in, other Late Woodland wares from the Juntunen site or elsewhere. This mode of application consists of a "superimposing" of rather widely spaced punctations on top of another design element. This superimposed decoration is clearly seen in Plate XVII, *b* and *d*. Here both punctating modes are seen: that just described, and that generally used in other wares, namely, a row of punctations above and/or below the other elements of design.

Design elements prominently feature horizontal bands executed in cord-wrapped object. Except for short impressions immediately sub-lip, bands of diagonally applied impressions do not occur. (iii) Lip and interior decoration: conform closely to Mackinac Banded, except that horizontal bands around the interior are lacking.

(3) Spatial-temporal Distribution

Discussed under "Blackduck Ware."

C. Relationships

The types set up by Evans (1961) for Minnesota and named Osufsen Cord and Punctate, Nett Lake Cord and Punctate, Schocker Cord Impressed (cord-wrapped object is the actual tool), and Schocker Horizontal Cord would be included; for southeast Manitoba, McNeish's (1958) Manitoba Corded, Manitoba Horizontal, Manitoba Herringbone, Blackduck Brushed, and Sturgeon Falls Fabric-Impressed would be included in the type here being discussed, since evidence seems to be lacking sufficient to separate them typologically.

5.7.2.2 Blackduck Punctate

A. Summary Definition

Blackduck Punctate is like Blackduck Banded except that decoration on exterior is restricted to patterns produced by punctations. Not illustrated.

B. Type Description

(1) Sample Size

98 rim sherds comprising 25 nonrestorable vessels.

(2) Formal Attributes

Same as Blackduck Banded except for exterior decoration which is restricted to patterns of punctations produced by rectangular-ended tools, except for vertical cord-wrapped-object impressions on rim immediately below lip. A few sherds had the vertical brushing characteristic of northern Blackduck.

(3) Spatial-temporal Distribution

See under "Blackduck Ware."

C. Relationships

Evans' (1961) Waskish Vertical Cord and Punctate, Nett Lake Vertical Cord, and Mud Lake Punctate would fall into this category. Mackinac Punctate shared the exterior decoration but was usually distinguishable in terms of lip decoration, rim profile, surface finish, and interior decoration.

5.7.3 BOIS BLANC WARE

The name Bois Blanc ware is proposed for 793 sherds representing 5 restorable and 133 nonrestorable vessels. The ware is characterized by (1) rims thickened by folding over or by addition of a strip, (2) castellations, and (3) cord-wrapped-object decoration. It is the ware characteristic of the Bois Blanc phase (Occupation D), and in many respects bears strong stylistic similarities to Point Sauble Collared of Wisconsin (Baerreis and Freeman 1958). However, it also retains Mackinac and Blackduck traits that are not shared with Point Sauble and is thus stylistically intermediate. Point Sauble and Bois Blanc together share changes from the earlier Lake Michigan and Mackinac wares with their T-section rims, to braced-rim sections with pointed lips. The former are shown in Figure 9 as *h-k*, the latter as *l-s* (p. 56).

Many of the decorative elements characteristic of Blackduck as against other early Late Woodland wares are also found on Bois Blanc ware; an example is the practice of superimposing a row of small punctations upon a band of corded decoration.

Baerreis and Freeman (1958) indicate that, at Aztalan and Point Sauble, the most common decorative device was twisted cord, with cord-wrapped-stick decoration considerably less frequent. Bois Blanc ware shows the opposite situation; cord-wrapped object appears on 80 per cent of the vessels, while twisted cord is seen on only 16 per cent. This again shows the stylistic similarity of Bois Blanc ware to Blackduck, which wholly lacks cord-impressed decoration.

5.7.3.1 Bois Blanc Braced Rim

A. Summary Definition

Braced rims ("incipient collars") with sections most like Figure 9, *p*. (p. 56); castellations; decoration on thickened rim immediately below lip in closely spaced cord-wrapped-stick impressions and below that in techniques and styles similar to Blackduck; gently sloping vessel sides. Plates XVII, *e-f*, XVIII-XIX.

B. Type Description

(1) Sample Size

496 rim and decorated sherds comprising 3 restorable and 105 nonrestorable vessels.

(2) Formal Attributes

(a) Vessel shape and size.—In several cases, sufficient material was recovered to indicate that vessels lacked the relatively pronounced shoulders of some Mackinac ware (see Pl. XVIII, *a*, and XIX, *a* and *c*; cf. Pl. XIV). Basal sherds of two restorable vessels indicated round rather than conoidal bottoms. Rim profiles are characteristically like Figure 9, *l*, *m*, *o*, *p* (p. 56). Rim interiors are thus straight and unchanneled, hence unlike Figure 9, *w*. The "braced rim" seems to have been achieved either by addition of a separate rim strip or by molding of the lip and rim. One can observe a gradient between extremely everted cases of T-section lips and braced rims (cf. Fig. 9, *j* and *p*, p. 56). In Plate XVII, *f*, the "bracing" is absent, but this vessel conforms to the type description in other respects. Plate XIX, *b*, illustrates a vessel atypical in both rim form and decoration, yet like Bois Blanc in some other respects; it was considered outside the range and put in the "Others" category. The style of decoration was observed on some Blackduck sherds from Minnesota, however. Plate XIX, *c*, is a vessel unique in a number of attributes: rim interior is channeled (Fig. 9, *w*, p. 56);

decoration is likewise aberrant. It was nonetheless included in the type.

Fifty-three of the 108 vessels bore castellations, 22 lacked castellations, while the remainder were indeterminate. In diameter, the type cannot be distinguished from Mackinac ware.

(b) Surface Treatment.—As Mackinac ware. Note that the body of the vessel in Plate XVIII, *a*, was treated in random directions with a paddle wrapped fairly loosely with coarse cord. Plate XIX, *c*, is also paddled, but the cord is much finer and tightly wound around the paddle, and care was taken to make all impressions vertical. Plate XIX, *a*, may be a case of fabric impression.

(c) Decoration.—Four varieties were recognized within this type: (i) Castellated, Simulated Fabric Decoration: Vertical or diagonal rows of closely spaced impressions on thickened portion of rim, using edge of cord-wrapped paddle. Such decoration is seen in Plate XVIII, *a*; the impressions immediately below the thickest part of the rim show that a solid rather than flexible core was involved, in contrast with the horizontal rows below, where continuity in the impressions indicates that the core around which the cord was wound was both flexible and long. In some cases, the impressions immediately below the lip were placed in such a way as to suggest that the intention was to simulate fabric impression, as seen in Plate XVIII, *b-d*. Frequency on site: 57.

(ii) Corded Collar: No castellations; profile *l* in Figure 9. Decoration generally restricted to corded-paddle impressions on the thickened portions of rims, which themselves were generally thinner than in the foregoing variety. Not illustrated. Frequency on site: 6.

(iii) Blackduck-like Decoration: The "bracing" of this variety is intermediate between that of the foregoing two varieties and some extreme examples of Mackinac ware with T-section lips. Decoration is in horizontal bands, usually of cord-wrapped cord, with widely spaced punctations amid the motif, as in Plates XVII, *f*, and XIX, *a*. Frequency on site: 27.

(iv) Bulging Lip: Rim profile *r* (Fig. 9, p.56); the appearance is as if the lip were rounded so as to form no sharp junction with rim, with pressure applied from inside the rim. Decoration is usually in horizontal twisted-cord-impressed bands around the bulging lip, with a row of punctations at the base of that. Not illustrated. Frequency on site: 18.

Plate XVIII, *a*, is vessel with an exceedingly rare decoration for the site at this time period: a second motif was placed below the motif on the rim-neck area. The second motif itself is complex and highly unusual, but even more striking is the technique, the earliest known occurrence of the drag-and-jab technique on the site, of interest here because it occurs in combination with a number of other decorative modes. Provenience is Occupation D, and the vessel is securely linked stratigraphically to the level with a carbon date of A.D. 1070 ± 75.

The V-shaped lips are generally decorated with cord-wrapped stick, and interior decoration conforms in style and frequency to the Mackinac ware.

(3) Spatial-temporal Distribution

(a) Geographic range.—Sherds that could be included within this type are in the Golson collection of pottery in the Museum of Anthropology, University of Michigan. The sherds came from the area of the Schultz site, Saginaw County, Michigan. In addition, four of the nine identifiable vessels from the Scott Point site on the northern shore of Lake Michigan (described in Binford and Quimby 1963: 284) were of this type.

It is of interest that Bois Blanc Braced Rim occurs over a relatively great distance, with very little stylistic variation, at least from the north end of Lake Michigan to the Saginaw Bay area, and always in places readily accessible by water transport.

(b) Temporal Range.—Chiefly occupation D, but may well commence in C and last into E.

C. Relationships

Stylistic similarities to both Blackduck and Point Sauble have been mentioned; Bois Blanc Braced Rim is typologically intermediate in many respects. Of other Wisconsin pottery, Hahn Cord Impressed (Keslin 1958), very similar to Point Sauble, also resembles Bois Blanc Braced Rim. Of other types on the Juntunen site, the latter seems closest to Point Sauble Collared, Mackinac Cord Impressed, and Bois Blanc Beaded (to be discussed next); this impression is borne out by the position of Bois Blanc Braced Rim on Figure 15. Ridley illustrates a sherd of my iii variety from his "Frank Bay Transitional" level of the Frank Bay site, Ontario (Ridley 1954:46— Fig. 21 *i*).

5.7.3.2 Bois Blanc Beaded

A. Summary Definition

Bois Blanc Beaded is characterized by a strip of beading that thickens the rim below the lip, usually by the addition of a rim fillet. Typical profiles are shown in Figure 9, *q-w* (p. 56). Vessels appear to have had nearly straight sides and no flaring of the rim; overall shape is unknown. Castellations are absent. Decoration is by cord, cord-wrapped stick, and punctations, in about the same proportions as seen on Bois Blanc Braced Rim. The most closely related type seems to be Hahn Cord Impressed of Wisconsin.

B. Type Description

(1) Sample Size

239 rim and decorated body sherds representing 2 restorable and 23 nonrestorable vessels.

(2) Formal Attributes

(a) Vessel Shape and Size.—Vessel form is unknown, but there was a very low incidence of lip eversion and rim outflare, indicating that vessels had fairly straight sides. Size, as reflected in diameter at lip, was about average for the site.

(b) Color.—Compared with most other types, this one exhibits a high frequency of a pronounced brick-red color.

(c) Surface Treatment.—Cord-wrapped paddle or fabric was used, as with the types previously described; one difference is the low frequency of smoothing-over of the cord at the neck. Smoothing was observed in only 3 out of 17 vessels.

(d) Decoration.—Two varieties could be recognized: one with rather thin "beading," with profiles as *t* and *u* in Figure 9, (p. 56) and one with extremely heavy beading, with profiles as *v* and *w*. (i) Thin Beaded: Exterior decoration mainly with twisted cords, generally in horizontal bands, except on the beaded area, where vertical rows of short corded-paddle edge impressions are common. Plate XX, *a*. Frequency on site: 22. (ii) Thick Beaded: Exterior decoration most often in cordloop punctations. Beaded area is treated with corded paddle in the same fashion as body of vessel, and with no smoothing-over. Juncture of the applied fillet or "beading" and rim of vessel is generally obvious. Plate X, *e*. Frequency on site: 3.

Interiors, as mentioned, were more often undecorated than with other types from the site.

(3) Spatial-temporal Distribution

(a) Geographic Range.—Unknown

(b) Temporal Distribution.—Chiefly occupation D; the Thick Beaded variety may possibly be somewhat later in time, although this could not be demonstrated.

C. Relationships

The closest similarities are to pottery from the Hahn and Horicon sites, Dodge County, Wisconsin; Plate 4, no. 5, of Keslin's (1958) report shows a sherd very close to the variety here called Thick Beaded. No. 12 of the same plate is similar to Thin Beaded. (The sherds illustrated in the present report are unfortunately not as representative as might be desired.)

It is interesting that the sherds assigned to Hahn Cord Impressed and illustrated by Keslin (1958) on the top row of Plate 5 are rather unlike the others he illustrates. They are in fact almost identical with sherds of a vessel which Ritchie and MacNeish (1949:105) assign to a Point Peninsula type, Wickham Punctate, illustrated in their paper as Figure 38, *f*. The identity extends to the folded-over, corded, ragged-bottom-edged collar, and the rather large, widely spaced punctations. There is nothing like the modal variety of Hahn Cord Impressed, to my knowledge, in New York collections, and I would suggest that in both the Wisconsin and New York cases, this sort of pottery ought to be re-examined in an attempt to explain the remarkable similarity. My misgivings with regard to the typological unity of Hahn Cord Impressed are also sounded by Mason, who could assign four sherds from the Mero site to Keslin's type, but considers that "it is likely that several pottery types have been subsumed in Keslin's proposed type. . ." (1966:140).

5.7.3.3 Bois Blanc Castellated Corded

A. Summary Definition

Bois Blanc Castellated Corded is characterized by thick bodies and rims but unthickened lips, little rim outflare, no lip eversion, decoration with cords, cord-wrapped objects, and interrupted-linear punctations frequently in patterns forming opposed triangles (Fig. 11, motif 5, p. 61). Temporal placement is difficult because most sherds came from highly disturbed deposits; earliest occurrences are from Intermediate I layers, hence assignment to C or D is probably reasonable.

Plate XX, *b*-*c*.

B. Type Description

(1) Sample Size

58 sherds comprising 5 nonrestorable vessels.

(2) Formal Attributes

(a) Vessel Shape and Size.—Unknown, other than that rims exhibit moderate outflare. Two vessels were castellated, two were probably not, and one was indeterminate.

(b) Decoration.—One vessel had simple cord, two bore impressions of turtle-suture near the lip (Pl. XX, *b*), two had interrupted linear punctation decoration (Pl. XX, *c*), and two displayed punctations. Four of the five had opposed triangles as decorative motif, and all had decoration from the lip extending downward farther than most decoration from the site. The use of cord-wrapped cord on the sherd in Plate XX, *c*, was discussed previously, section 3.5.2.

(3) Spatial-temporal Distribution

Because of the small size and the fact that all but one sherd came from archaeologically mixed and geologically unassignable units, temporal placement is difficult. The type may appear in Occupation C and may persist until E.

C. Relationships

Unknown.

5.7.4 POINT SAUBLE COLLARED

Forty sherds representing 15 vessels from the Juntunen site were assigned to the ware and type named and defined by Baerreis and Freeman (1958) for eastern Wisconsin. The type site is located just north of Green Bay in northeastern Brown County. Similar pottery is reported from Aztalan, but proper taxonomic designation and description is lacking. It is said to differ from Point Sauble in 14 attributes (Baerreis and Freeman 1958), notably in a distinction between round and angular orifices, the latter occurring only at Aztalan. Keslin (1958) in his report on the Hahn and Horicon sites reports similar pottery but fails to discuss the similarities of his pottery with that described by Baerreis and Freeman. In my opinion, leaving aside the question of heterogeneity in Keslin's types, his and Baerreis and Freeman's might be considered closely related types in a common ware. If this could be demonstrated to be the case they would parallel Bois Blanc Braced Rim and Beaded Rim from the Juntunen site, and relationships between eastern Wisconsin and the Straits of Mackinac might be clarified.

The Juntunen Point Sauble material is formally identical with that from Heins Creek and Mero in Wisconsin (Mason 1966). Whether the vessels were imported or made locally is difficult to tell in the absence of pottery thin-section analysis directed to this problem. Macroscopically, paste and temper of Juntunen's Point Sauble could support either alternative. In terms of formal attributes, however, the correspondences can be listed: decoration is with twisted cord, the faint internal textile impressions mentioned by Baerreis and Freeman are present, braced rims (true "collars" appear at Aztalan and the type site, but not elsewhere) and cross sections are identical, and—more surprisingly—two vessels from the Juntunen site have the angular orifices reported from Aztalan. None has any sign of castellations.

The appearance of this Wisconsin pottery at the Juntunen site strengthens the already strong indications of interaction with areas along the northern and western shore of Lake Michigan during the earlier half of the occupation of the site. These indications will be discussed in detail later, in chapter XV.

5.7.5 JUNTUNEN WARE

Juntunen ware is defined on the basis of 1,031 rim and decorated body sherds representing 309 vessels, of which 5 were restorable. Similar pottery was also collected from Arrowhead Drive and the Round Island site, but only that from Juntunen will be considered here.

The ware is characterized by nearly universal presence of true collars (Fig. 9, *x-F*, p. 56) and decoration produced by linear punctations and drag-and-jab techniques; cords and cord-wrapped sticks have declined markedly in popularity by this time, but incising is not yet used. Whereas all pottery previously discussed forms part of a spatial-temporal continuum with marked traditional features, Juntunen ware represents a sharp stylistic break with previous pottery traditions as seen at the Juntunen site; primary participation in a broad area of stylistic interaction extending into Wisconsin and Minnesota is replaced by a narrower style-area extending into Lake Superior and with stronger stylistic similarities to the Ontario peninsula and western New York State than was true for earlier periods. The late appearance of the ware on the Juntunen site (around A.D. 1300) is seen in its concentration in Occupation E and even greater predominance in F.

5.7.5.1 Juntunen Linear Punctate

A. Summary Definition

Juntunen Linear Punctate is characterized by smoothed surfaces, presence of true collars, absence of castellations, rounded body shape, and decoration solely by closely spaced but separate punctations. It is restricted to late occupation phases. See Plate XX, *d*.

B. Type Description

(1) Sample Size

96 sherds representing 1 restorable and 5 nonrestorable vessels.

(2) Formal Attributes

(a) Vessel Shape and Size.—Rim profile is typically as *E* of Figure 9 (p. 56); bodies are evenly curved with no suggestion of sharp shoulder. Bottoms are rounded. Although all measurable vessels had a rim diameter very close to 25 cm., the orifices appear larger compared with the bodies, and their capacities may have been slightly less than those of the types discussed hitherto. Collar height ranges from 3-5 cm. Lips are mostly flat and unthickened.

(b) Surface Treatment.—After beating with cord-wrapped paddles, the entire surface was at least partially smoothed over. Traces of the previous paddling can be seen on the body of the vessel in Plate XX, *d*. Interior surfaces near the lip are striated or brushed.

(c) Decoration.—All had bands of linear punctations on the collar, the motif being number 1 (Fig. 11, p. 61), produced by an instrument having an end shaped like a screwdriver. Lips and interiors were similarly treated. At the base of the collar where it thins to the thickness of the vessel body, another row of punctates was applied, spaced more widely than those on the collar, hence evidently not intended to form merely the bottom row of the motif. This trait is very common on Juntunen ware.

(3) Spatial-temporal Distribution

(a) Geographic Range.—Unknown

(b) Temporal Range.—All sherds came from either D-EF (Intermediate II or Juntunen phase) units, but they always occurred below pure F phase levels, hence assignment to E, between A.D. 1070 and 1330, seems indicated.

C. Relationships

No closely similar ceramics are known from other areas; such similarities as do exist are of a very general nature. Smoothed surfaces, collars, and punctated designs appear on some of the earliest pottery that has been called "Iroquois" in Ontario and New York state.

5.7.5.2 Juntunen Collared

A. Summary Definition

Juntunen Collared is distinguished from the other types of this ware by its coarse paste and large temper particles; by absence of cord-wrapped paddle malleation; by presence of collars, absence of castellations, and meagerness or absence of decoration. Most occurrences were from Intermediate II provenience units. No illustrations.

B. Type Description

(1) Sample Size

35 sherds representing 22 nonrestorable vessels.

(2) Formal Attributes

(a) Vessel Shape and Size.—Vessel shape is unknown; typical rim profiles are as in Figure 9, *y-D,F*. (p. 56). There was no rim flare or lip eversion. Most vessels had collars 2 to 4 cm. high; no vessel was castellated.

(b) Surface Treatment.—Surfaces were rough and granular, and there were no signs of malleation with any object.

(c) Decoration.—Six vessels had rim-interior decoration; all but five had decorated lips; eight lacked rim-exterior decoration.

(3) Spatial-temporal Distribution

(a) Geographic Range.—Unknown

(b) Temporal Range.—The highest frequency of occurrence is Intermediate II levels, hence temporal position between Bois Blanc and Juntunen phases is inferred.

5.7.5.3 Juntunen Drag-and-Jab

A. Summary Definition

Juntunen Drag-and-Jab is characterized by cord-wrapped-paddle finished vessel bodies without sharp shoulders and with rounded bases, by well-defined collars and castellations, and by decoration in a variety of techniques but especially featuring "drag-and-jab" (also called "stab and drag," "push-and-pull," "interrupted linear"). Incising is absent; secondary decorative motifs placed below collar occur oftener than on any other Juntunen-site type. This type is characteristic of and virtually restricted to Occupation F, dated around A.D. 1300. See Plates XXI, XXII.

B. Type Description

(1) Sample Size

893 sherds representing 4 restorable and 277 nonrestorable vessels.

(2) Formal Attributes

(a) Vessel Shape and Size.—Typical rim profiles are Figure 9, *y*, *D*, *F* (p. 56). Out of the 281 vessels, 118 had collars 2-4 cm. high; 29 lacked true collars but conformed to the type in all other respects. Most lips were unthickened; the mean lip thickness was 7.20 mm., and as seen from Table 7, (p. 84), the difference in mean lip thickness from Mackinac ware ($\bar{X}$=9.55 mm.) is significant. There is no significant difference in vessel wall thickness. Most vessels lacked flaring of the rim and lip eversion.

Of 138 vessels with enough rim section recovered to provide the information, 96 bore castellations. While castellations on Bois Blanc ware were often merely small peaks on an otherwise uniform and circular rim, with no correlation in placement between the peaks and exterior decorative motif, the lips on Juntunen Drag-and-Jab vessels generally curved evenly between peaks, and the castellations were visually reinforced by elements in the design motif, as seen in Plate XXI, *a*, XXII, *a*, *h*, *h'*. Orifices were circular: even at the peaks there was very little tendency toward angularity, looking down from the top.

No significant difference in outside diameter at lip could be demonstrated to exist between Juntunen Drag and Jab and other wares (Table 7, p. 84), so, to the extent this variable estimates volumetric capacity, there appears to be no major change in vessel size during the occupation of the site. No type, incidentally, showed a bimodal distribution from which the existence of different size-classes within a type could be inferred.

(c) Decoration.—The predominant technique was "drag-and-jab," which appeared on 232 out of 281 vessels. Although this is the modal technique, it does grade at one end into separated punctations in which "dragging" is absent (Pl. XXI, *c*), and at the other extreme into interrupted linear—a form of incising in which the bottom of the groove varies in depth (Pl. XXII, *e*). Cords and cord-wrapped objects were used on only 28 vessels. A row of separate punctates or drag-and-jab impressions was placed at the base of the collar in nearly all cases.

Decorative motif was most often simply three or four lines of drag-and-jab impressions circling the collar; sometimes this was broken at the castellations with vertical lines or inverted triangles, as in Plate XXI, *a-b*, XXII, *a,h*.

Lips and interiors were commonly decorated; some external and internal patterns are seen in Plate XXII, *b-i*, *b'-i'*.

Seventeen vessels had decoration below the collar; this may be seen in all three cases shown in Plate XXI. Although the sample is small, in the cases at hand the designs were rather different from those used on the collar; zoned decoration in bands with intervening spaces left undecorated was common.

(3) Spatial-temporal Distribution

(a) Geographic Range.—Sherds falling within the range of this type as found at Juntunen were recovered from a few sites in the Upper Great Lakes. Some of the sherds excavated under the direction of Tyler Bastian from sites in and near copper pits on Isle Royale, Lake Superior, can be included; these are of particular interest in view of the prominence of the copper industry in both places. A few sherds in the National Museum of Canada excavated by James V. Wright from the Pic River site in Ontario (J. Wright 1966a) fall within range; this site also has projectile points identical to the Juntunen points that will be described in the next chapter. One sherd from a mainly historic-period site three miles from Blind River near the mouth of the Mississaugi River, on the North Channel, Ontario, is in the Juntunen range. These occurrences give some indication of the geographic spread of the type. Notable is the absence of this type from the sites along the north shore of Lake Michigan from the Straits of Mackinac into Wisconsin (see Binford and Quimby [1963] and Mason [1966]).

(b) Temporal Range.—While there is some uncertainty as to the time of first appearance of some types from the site, there is none whatever with regard to this one. It is unquestionably restricted to the E occupation (in which its presence may be the result of mixing of layers) and F. The carbon date of A.D. 1300 for a pure F-occupation feature (F.20) containing only this type (one vessel shown in Pl. XXI, *a*) probably represents the time of greatest popularity.

C. Relationships

Other than the sherds from Isle Royale, nothing resembling this type has been reported for the area to the west of the Straits of Mackinac. At this time, quite different pottery was being produced in Wisconsin, Minnesota and Southeastern Manitoba. The closest relationships—and they are not really very close—of J. Drag-and-Jab are with the Barrie-Uren horizon of southwestern Ontario and the early Iroquois pottery of western New

York State. Most pottery from the Pic River and Michipicoten sites which I examined through the courtesy of James Wright of the National Museum of Canada (J. Wright 1963, 1966a) did not, in my opinion, resemble Juntunen ware to any striking degree, although Figure 7 of Plate II in Wright (1966a) is within the range of variation.

The Barrie Site, Simcoe County, Ontario (Ridley 1958), assigned by James Wright (1966) to the Pickering Branch of the Ontario Iroquois Tradition, has yielded ceramics some of which closely resemble Juntunen in many respects. Plates 3 and 4 of Ridley's (1958) report show sherds with collars, horizontal bands of drag-and-jab decoration, and castellations; most of these sherds probably fall into MacNeish's (1952) Iroquois Linear. As described by MacNeish (1952), this type has decoration in drag-and-jab ("overlapping linear punches" [19]) but is otherwise much like Ontario Horizontal. Both are considered very early in the Iroquois series, and (a point of divergence from Juntunen) are rarely castellated.

Marian White (1961), describing the earliest Iroquois-tradition pottery in the Niagara Frontier area of New York State, notes that, at the Oakfield site (the earliest known site of this tradition), decoration by cord-wrapped stick and interrupted linear occurs on a total of 30% of the vessels, the decoration being placed most commonly in horizontal lines, and that both techniques decrease after this phase in favor of incising. Interrupted linear and drag-and-jab is rarer than at Barrie, but the latter site has no cord-wrapped-stick impression, so in this respect Juntunen appears to share characteristics of both sites. My own examination of the Oakfield materials showed a number of ceramic and other similarities with Juntunen which the latter does not share with the subsequent phase, Kienuka.

In summary, a contrast at Juntunen with earlier phases is seen in the greater stylistic similarities of Juntunen Drag-and-Jab to pottery of the Iroquois area at around A.D. 1300; similarities with Wisconsin and Minnesota seem much attenuated by this time.

5.7.6 RAMEY INCISED-LIKE

Ramey Incised, a Cahokia Old Village type, was described by Griffin (1949); a derived variety is represented at the Juntunen site by 11 sherds, probably all from one vessel. Eight sherds are decorated and are illustrated in Plate XXIII, *a-c*. This vessel is the farthest northeast occurrence of a distinctive Middle Mississippian type that also occurs in Wisconsin, as at the Carcajou

Point site (Hall 1962).

(1) Formal Attributes

(a) Vessel Shape and Size.—The vessel is a bowl with rolled lip and probably a sharp shoulder, thus conforming to the similar bowl illustrated from the Carcajou Point site (Hall 1962, vol. 2, Pl. 45, *a*). Rolled lips are characteristic, but the walls—ca. 2 mm. thick—are considerably thinner than most vessels of this type.

(b) Manufacturing Details.—Shell temper is visible on the surface and at breaks, but as Porter's (1963) report on thin-section analysis indicates, shell constitutes only about 20% of the vessel's total temper, the greater proportion consisting of grit similar to that found in most other vessels from the site but smaller in grain size (0.08—0.80 mm. dia.). The paste conforms to one of the four rather similar paste categories Porter set up for the entire Juntunen pottery collection. Thus the likelihood is small that this vessel was imported from outside the drift area. The surface is plain and was fairly well burnished.

(c) Decoration.—Curvilinear designs, not uncommon for the type, were executed by smooth trailing. There was no interior or lip decoration.

(2) Spatial-temporal Distribution

(a) Spatial.—Nine sherds came from units intermediate between Bois Blanc and Juntunen phase levels. This group of sherds includes all those illustrated in Plate XXIII, *a-c*. One sherd, probably of this same vessel, came from a unit assigned to the Mackinac Phase, while another, definitely of this vessel, came from an undisturbed yellow sand underlying a brown layer, also assigned to the Mackinac Phase. The problem is whether the last-mentioned sherd's position dates the vessel, or whether the majority of the sherds, from units much later in time, date it. All the sherds came from one 10 x 10-ft. square (700-180), hence the probability is high that their vertical distribution reflects disturbance.

From my experience with the massive disturbance in the soft sand of this site, and especially in view of the numerous post-holes, root channels, small pits, and animal burrows, I would suggest that the single sherd from Mackinac Phase levels is suspect, for all the other sherds of this vessel came from Bois Blanc and Juntunen Phase levels, and it would seem unlikely that ten sherds should have been disturbed and only one left in its original position.

(b) Temporal Placement.—Uncertain in view of the foregoing, but in light of the fact that Ramey Incised has been reported for a number of locations in Wisconsin, including Carcajou Point (see Hall 1962:115-121) and the Mero site on the Door Peninsula (Mason 1966) it seems probable that the vessel was brought to or made on the Juntunen site at the time when most pottery shows clear affinities with Wisconsin, i.e. in the Mackinac or Bois Blanc Phase. It seems unlikely that the vessel is contemporary with the Oneota style pottery (to be discussed next), because the latter occurred almost exclusively in the plow zone, whereas the Ramey sherds came mostly from units below the plow zone.

5.7.7 UPPER MISSISSIPPIAN POTTERY

232 sherds representing about 53 vessels with crushed-rock and shell temper, mostly too fragmentary to identify other than by reference to surface finish and/or temper, can be assigned to Upper Mississippi Oneota wares.

5.7.7.1 Shell Tempered Sherds

One vessel, represented by six smooth-surfaced sherds with shell temper visible at the area of fracture, had a slight collar as in Figure 9, *n* (p. 56) and trailed decoration as in Plate XXIII, *d-e*. I can assign this to no published category, but it most likely belongs to the Oneota group.

Fourteen other shell tempered body sherds were found. All were undecorated, had smooth surfaces, and ranged from 3 to 5 mm. thick. Those assignable to a level were all from the Juntunen Phase.

5.7.7.2 Grit Tempered Oneota Pottery

212 rim and body sherds representing about 35 vessels were recovered. Resemblances are closest to Mason's Oneota-like pottery from Mero.

(1) Formal Attributes

(a) Vessel Shape and Size.—All vessels with the relevant portion preserved show a sharp angle at the neck, forming a broadly flaring rim, which sets them off from other wares at the site. Profiles are as *G* in Figure 9 (p.56); features of vessel shape are visible in the sherds illustrated in Plate XXIII, *f-h*. No handles or other appendages were recovered.

(b) Manufacturing Details.—Porter's 1963 thin-section studies of Juntunen pottery included sherds from three vessels of this category. Two sherds were of his "D" paste variety, found only in vessels of the latest occupation phase. Significant paste and temper differences between Oneota and other Juntunen pottery cannot be demonstrated, but Porter's study does bear out gross observation, which suggests that paste was better and temper particles of finer grain than with other Juntunen pottery. It was also observed that the Oneota pottery lacked the notable propensity of other Juntunen sherds to split.

(c) Surface Treatment.—No traces of corded-paddle application were detected. Surfaces fell into two categories: one with a fully smooth and rather "silty" feeling surface, neither polished nor gritty, and one with surfaces malleated with a plain paddle and distinctly gritty in appearance and feel. In Plate XXIII, *g* and *j* are sherds of the first category, while *f* and *h* are examples of the second. The sample size was too small for these observations to be more than suggestive of real differences.

(d) Decoration.—Only one vessel was decorated elsewhere than on the lip. It had coarse trailing on body sherds in a pattern that could not be reconstructed. No associated rims were recovered. Lips of most vessels, on the other hand, were most commonly decorated by scalloping or finger pinching and indenting, as seen in Plate XXIII, *f-j*. The relative frequency of decoration except on lips and the rarity of handles was also noted by Hall (1962:55) for Carcajou Point Oneota.

(2) Spatial-temporal Distribution

With few exceptions, the Oneota-like pottery occurs in the plow zone or, if in undisturbed contexts, then as the uppermost occupation level, as in Feature 1, which was apparently intact but found only a few inches below the surface. Thus Oneota's vertical distribution on the site differs from that of the Juntunen ware, the pottery characteristic of the latest known sizeable occupation phase, so it is suggested that Oneota first appeared on the site toward the end of the Juntunen Phase. Oneota was found associated with Juntunen ware in an unmixed context only in Feature 1—more evidence suggesting that Juntunen ware was being made for some time on the site before the appearance of Oneota. Because of the small Oneota sample recovered and the compression and telescoping of layers in the later periods due to cessation of deposition of aeolian-borne sand and/or increase in processes of erosion, the precise situation cannot at present be determined.

Dates between A.D. 1200 and 1400 have been suggested, for example, by Mason (1966:186) for this sort of Oneota pottery in Wisconsin; for the Juntunen Oneota, a date toward the later end of this range would be reasonable.

One other vessel—one of the two intact pots recovered—belongs to the Oneota category; it is illustrated in Plate XXIV, *c*. This miniature pot was deposited as grave goods in an ossuary (Feature 11). It had been placed upright with the quite different Woodland-looking pot of Plate XXIV, *a-b*, inverted over it. The Oneota-like miniature, 4.8 cm. in diameter and 3.3 cm. high., has a typical shape, but rather than being perfectly round viewed from the top, the shoulder has an octagonal form. It has a rolled lip, no internal or lip decoration, and exterior decoration consisting of a double wavy line bordered by bands, all executed with linear punctates. Except for the octagonal shoulder as viewed from above and the decoration technique, the vessel is formally similar to Oneota pottery. The ossuary—dug in an area apart from the contemporary settlement, for all sherds in the fill were of earlier periods—has been dated A.D. 1320 ± 75 (M-1188, Crane and Griffin 1963). This vessel is not unique; a very similar miniature pot from an Oneota intrusive burial in the High Island Mound, Minnesota, is in the collections of the Department of Anthropology, University of Minnesota. Its diameter at the shoulder of 10.2 cm. makes it about twice as big as the Juntunen specimen, and its shoulder instead of being located near the top as with the Juntunen pot, occurs near the bottom. Other than these differences, the vessel is nearly identical to the Juntunen miniature, and we may fairly speak of a class of Oneota miniature mortuary vessels. The feature of one pot inverted over another is, however, unique to the Juntunen site, and the association of Oneota with a Mackinac-like vessel is hard to explain.

5.7.7.3 Relationships of the Mississippian Pottery

The pottery related to Ramey Incised and Oneota is an indication of continued stylistic closeness to contemporary cultures in Wisconsin; because of the rareness of these sherds relative to the other pottery on the site, they should probably be considered evidence of trade or sporadic stopovers of small groups of people from regions to the west of the Straits. The association of the miniature Oneotoid and Woodland vessels in the ossuary indicates the continuation of a Mackinac-like tradition into the Juntunen phase. The Woodland minature is not a replica of any Mackinac-ware type, however, and its presence is frankly a puzzle.

The shell and grit tempered Upper Mississippian pottery seems most similar to the Oneota component of the Mero site on the Door Peninsula, Wisconsin (Mason 1966) where, as at Juntunen, it forms the latest prehistoric component on the site. Unlike most other Oneota pottery but like Juntunen in this respect, Mero Oneota has an unusually high proportion (40 per cent) of grit tempered vessels; only 15 grit tempered sherds, for instance, were found at Carcajou Point (cf. Mason 1966:171 and Hall 1962:53). The small size of temper particles in comparison to Late Woodland wares, the low frequency of decoration elsewhere than on lips, and the virtual absence of handles, are other traits held in common between Mero and Juntunen (Mason 1966: 179).

5.7.8 SPRING CREEK POTTERY

Two sherds of undecorated cord-marked pottery lacking the flaring orifice, thickened and everted lip, and lip decoration of Mackinac ware were recovered. One sherd came from a Mackinac phase level. The closest similarities seem to be with pottery from the unpublished Spring Creek site in Muskegon County, eastern Michigan, dated A.D. 967±75; (Crane and Griffin 1958: M-512). Typological similarities are with Mackinac ware.

5.7.9 IROQUOIS LINEAR

Two sherds—in paste and temper quite unlike other pottery from the site—were assigned to Iroquois Linear (MacNeish 1952:19) and should date around A.D. 1300. One sherd came from the bottom of a postmold whose top was lost in the plow zone; it is illustrated in Plate XXV, *a*. The other sherd came from the plow zone. Decoration on the collar is by the interrupted linear technique; lip was not decorated.

5.7.10 ONTARIO OBLIQUE

The single sherd tentatively assigned to MacNeish's (1952) Ontario Oblique (Pl. XXV, *b*) came from Feature 1, the hearth which also yielded many fragments of a grit tempered Oneota vessel, a Juntunen ware sherd (Pl. XXI, *c*), as well as several sherds more characteristic of earlier occupation phases. Its provenience here is quite reasonable.

5.7.11 LALONDE HIGH COLLAR

Four sherds from a single vessel were identified by Mr. Frank Ridley of Islington, Ontario (personal communication), as Lalonde High Collar. All came from the plow zone. They are shown in Plate XXV, *c*.

5.7.12 OTHER LATE TYPES

Three other unique sherds may be discussed. All came from the plow zone. Plate XXV, *d*, is the castellated portion of a rim lacking both true collar and decoration. The rim was thickened by addition of a strip. Plate XXV, *e*, shows a thick rimsherd with a low collar, decorated solely on rim exterior with impressions of a knife-like tool and large punctates. Plate XXV, *f*, is from a vessel with a broadly flaring orifice, unlike most Juntunen pottery but somewhat like Oneota; it was coarsely finished and decorated solely with an irregular row of punctates on the rim.

5.7.13 JUVENILES' POTS

91 sherds representing 21 vessels that are clearly the handiwork of small children were recovered. They are characteristically very uneven in thickness and symmetry, and technically imperfect in finish and decoration (in which respects they contrast with the miniature pots). They have usually less than one-half the average orifice diameter of full-size pots, but reflect the stylistic traditions of the periods in which they were made, although decoration tends to be much simpler. Two such vessels from Mackinac Phase layers are shown in Plate XXIV, *e*-*f*.

5.7.14 ARROWHEAD DRIVE POTTERY (MIDDLE WOODLAND)

Little horizontal overlap between Juntunen and Arrowhead Drive was observed. Except for Feature 45, only eight Arrowhead Drive sherds(representing two vessels) were recovered from the whole area of Juntunen, and all of these came from only two provenience units.

The pottery characteristic of the Arrowhead Drive site is to be the subject of separate report, but may be briefly characterized here as follows:

(a) Vessel Shape and Size.—While sizes are unknown, shapes are clearly different from Juntunen wares in the absence of any sharp curvature, as in shoulders, flaring rims, everted lips. Lips are not thickened, nor are collars found.

(b) Manufacturing Details.—Coil fractures are common, indicating the coil method; in contrast these are never found with Juntunen pottery. All pottery is of a uniform light tan color with no firing clouds visible. Temper seemed on macroscopic examination to be of finer granitic particles than the Late Woodland wares.

(c) Surface Treatment.—No signs of cordmarking as on most Juntunen pottery was observed; sufaces were either smooth or (more characteristically) finished with what appears to be some sort of dentate stamping. Internal surfaces often looked scraped.

(d) Decoration.—Almost no overlap with the Late Woodland decorative technique was observed. Commonest techniques consisted of linear and curvilinear stamping, usually with a dentate tool, and a drag-and-jab technique that differed considerably from the Late Woodland practice. The few rims recovered were not thickened or decorated.

In terms of formal similarities with other pottery, generic resemblances are highest to the Laurel pottery of the Bruce Peninsula, Ontario (Wright and Anderson 1963), and to some of the Point Peninsula types of New York State (Ritchie and MacNeish 1949). None of the pottery could be fitted into any existing type, however.

The occurrences of Arrowhead Drive pottery on the Juntunen site cannot be *in situ* (except for F. 45); they are in association with Late Woodland pottery and do not even come from the lowest levels in the squares in which they occur. Hence they are useless for purposes of establishing a stratigraphic sequence, but their occurrence on the area of the Late Woodland site at all is worthy of note.

5.7.15 "OTHERS"

The 390 sherds considered typologically intermediate between the postulated categories or outside the range of any category were put in the "Others" bracket. They represent 242 vessels, about 15 per cent of all vessels.

5.7.16 "NOT CLASSIFIABLE"

This category represents all decorated or rim sherds too small or too poorly preserved to permit a judgment. There were 264 of them, representing probably 221 vessels.

VI

STONE INDUSTRY

6.1 CHIPPED STONE

6.1.1 MATERIALS

The large assortment of chert varieties utilized in all periods of occupation may be broken down initially into raw materials: those obtainable locally from outcroppings and those of non-local origin. The former, called "Bois Blanc Chert" (Landes *et al.* 1945:82 Harrison 1963) is described as white to bluish-gray chert interbedded with light-gray to buff-gray dolomite. It has a coarse texture and a poor conchoidal fracture, is non-shiny and opaque, and may have various cherty inclusions. Often slight banding may be evident as the result of weathering and replacement. This material occurs as bedrock and as outcrops over the entire island, except for a thin band of St. Ignace dolomite along the north shore, an area including the Juntunen site. Outcrops of Bois Blanc chert also occur on the tip of the southern peninsula of Michigan around Cheboygan and on most of the other islands in the Straits area. The material is of importance, since it is the major outcrop form of chert immediately available to aboriginal inhabitants of the Straits area, is visually distinguishable from most other cherts used at the Juntunen site, and is the material of about a quarter of the artifacts at the site.

Non-Bois Blanc cherts may in turn be dichotomized into "Eastport" chert, representing nearly a third of the Juntunen stone industry, and "Others." The gray or tan banded material called "Eastport" (Binford and Papworth 1963) was further studied by Harrison (1963), who concluded that it was largely derived from Traverse Limestone outcrops along the lake margin near Eastport, Antrim County, Michigan. Harrison offered 10 per cent as a conservative estimate of the proportion of Eastport in the Juntunen sample and prepared the following description: "Specimens from Juntunen are light tan to gray, sometimes with a rosy tint, and generally have thin brown, gray, or red-brown banding" (Harrison 1963:8). Compared with Bois Blanc chert, Eastport is considerably more homogeneous; displays fewer irregularities, joints, and fracture planes; and has finer texture. It may be noted that finished tools of Bois Blanc chert are almost entirely restricted to larger bifaces, while bifaces as well as some projectile points and scrapers were made of Eastport.

"Others" includes all remaining non-Bois Blanc chert varieties, most of which occurred in low frequency or else were so variable as to preclude the establishment of "types." An attempt at typing was tentatively made however; it resulted in about 35 "types," with great difficulty being experienced in assigning new specimens to the established categories.

In general, "others" are characterized by smooth to "waxy" and shiny appearance and by high quality from the standpoint of flaking properties. Nearly all scrapers, most small projectile points, and nearly all the bipolar or small core industry were made of these materials. Harrison's (1963) description of some of the varieties may be summarized:

"Tan-gray to Black." Excellent conchoidal fracture, sharp edges; tendency for ripple formation when struck. High surface luster; often translucent around the edges.

"Greenalite." One fragment (UMMA Cat. No. 40919).

"Pale Blue." Numerous impurities and inclusions.

"Gray Chalcedony." Translucent, finely textured, no luster.

"Jasper and Carnelian." A few pieces widely varying in color and texture.

"Agate." Only 6 specimens in entire Juntunen collection.

"Quartz, Quartzite." Large range in color and diaphaneity.

"Green Chert." One mid-section of large projectile point (UMMA Cat. No. 62783) bears remarkable resemblance to material from Coxsackie Flint Quarry, Green County, New York.

In summary, three sorts of chert were utilized: (1) Bois Blanc chert, easily obtained locally from outcrops but generally tabular and of rather poor quality and evidently not suitable for such tools as scrapers, whose cutting edge had to bear stress—about 30 per cent of collection; (2) Eastport chert, of better quality, available in large format from outcrops at somewhat greater distances (about 60 miles)—about 20 per cent; and (3) fine-quality cherts ranging into the semiprecious, whose source is largely undetermined but which evidently occurred principally in the form of small waterworn and presumably glacially deposited pebbles usually not greater than about 5 cm. in diameter—about 50 per cent.

The ratio of Bois Blanc to non-Bois Blanc cherts changes over time, as shown in Table 10. The relative preference for good quality cherts ("Non-Bois Blanc") increases with time, being especially pronounced in the last (Juntunen) phase. Figure 17 illustrates the changes graphically in terms of frequency per cubic foot. We observe that Occupations B and C of the Mackinac

TABLE 10

FREQUENCIES OF BOIS BLANC AND NON-BOIS BLANC CHERTS IN THE DIFFERENT OCCUPATION PHASES, TOGETHER WITH RATIOS

Phase	Number of Pieces		Ratio
	B.B.	Non B.B.	
Juntunen	433	3,177	0.14
Bois Blanc	471	1,586	0.30
Mackinac	1,777	2,326	0.76

phase are exceedingly sparse in artifact density, that the greatest density occurs in the Bois Blanc phase, and that the dropoff in density in the Juntunen phase is most marked in terms of Bois Blanc chert. The density of non-B.B. relative to B.B. chert in the Bois Blanc phase is of interest, since it is at this time that the use of high-quality cherts in a bipolar technique of chipping appears to occur in other places in the upper Lake Michigan area (cf. Binford and Quimby 1963).

Investigation as to whether the patterns of chert working and utilization on the site reflected the change in preference of chert type was made by studying the number of provenience units of the site that yielded the two fundamental types of chert. In Mackinac and Bois Blanc phase units and in those not assignable to a phase, there are only slight differences in the respective number of units. In the Juntunen phase, however, the difference is marked, with considerably fewer units containing B.B. chert. This is consistent with the ratios as seen in Table 10; the surprising fact is that in the earlier phases there were not more units containing B.B. than are observed. To test whether the observed difference in number of units containing the two types could be explained solely on the basis of sampling error, a test of independence was performed, as shown in Table 11, from which we conclude that the difference cannot be explained on the basis of sampling error alone and that there do therefore appear to be differences between Juntunen and the other phases in the patterns of horizontal distribution of the two chert types on the site. The greater evenness of distribution in the earlier phases contrasts with the irregularity in the Juntunen phase and suggests sharper differentiation in the last phase with regard to loci of specialized activities on the site.

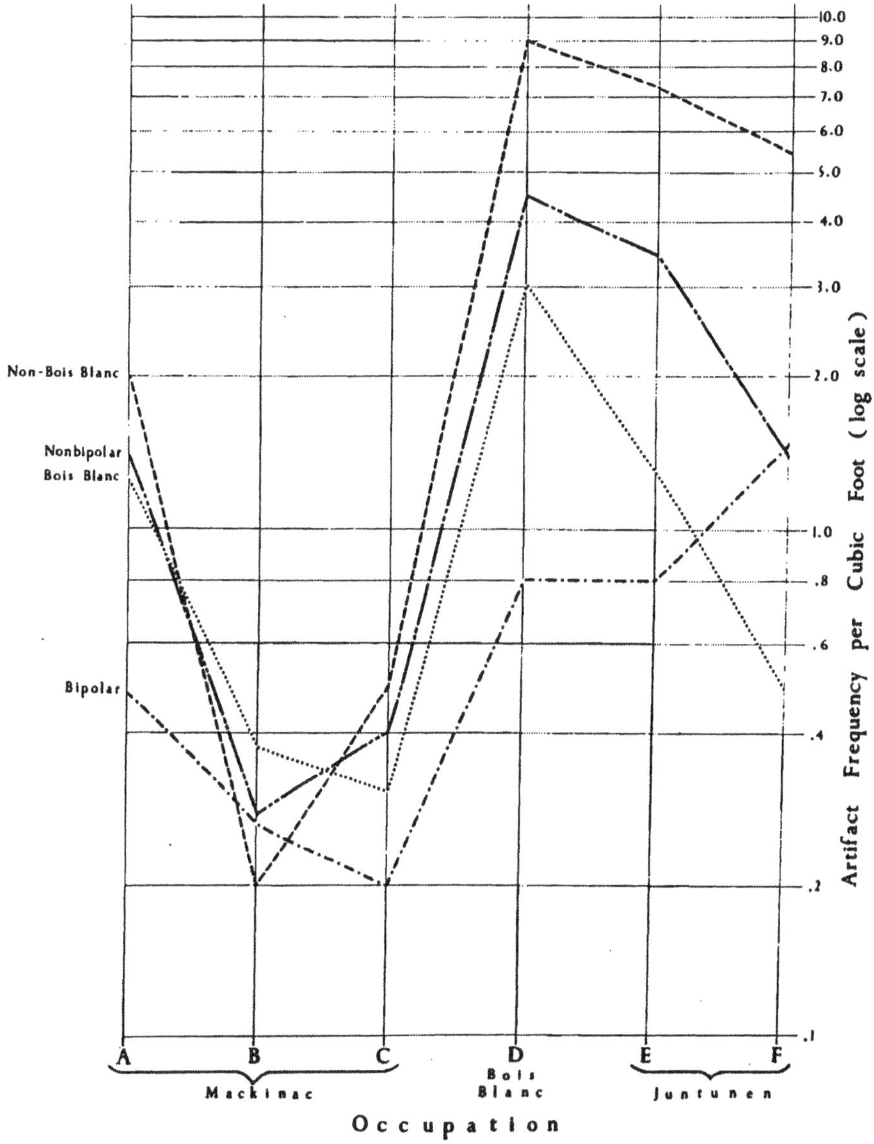

Fig. 17—Density (frequency per cubic foot) of chert types and flaking techniques, by occupation.

TABLE 11

CHI SQUARE TEST OF INDEPENDENCE OF CHERT TYPE ON PHASE

Phase	Units Containing		Totals
	B.B	Non-B.B.	
Juntunen	26	60	86
All others	280	325	605
Totals	306	385	691

$x^2 = 7.22$ $p < .01$

At all periods of Late Woodland occupation, the desired end-product of stone-toolmaking strongly influenced choice of chert variety. Thus almost no scrapers were made of Bois Blanc chert, which tends to crumble under pressure; relatively few were made on Eastport chert; and the great majority were made on high-quality cherts with good conchoidal fracture and smooth, shiny cleavage faces with few imperfections. On the other hand, the relatively infrequent large bifaces were made of Bois Blanc and Eastport cherts and never of the high-quality cherts, either because high-quality cherts did not occur in nodules or pebbles large enough to permit the manufacture of the larger bifaces or because such cherts were sufficiently rare and prized as to be reserved for scrapers, which call for cutting edges resistant to crumbling under pressure. Probably both these considerations were involved.

6.1.2 TECHNIQUES OF BLANK PRODUCTION

Besides the variable involving choice of different materials for their chipping properties, at least two different technological patterns were employed in processing the raw materials. One involved the production of fairly large and thick flakes, in plan often expanding, in section often wedge-shaped. A fair amount of flat striking platform was detached along with the flake, and prominent bulbs of percussion were produced. This technique seems identical with that termed "free flaking" by Witthoft (1957). The other pattern is described by Binford and Quimby as "bipolar," which "refers to the fact that on each core there are two opposed striking platforms or zones of percussion" (1963:289-91). Based on my own experience with 3,630 items produced with this technique, a large number do bear scars on the basal portions that appear to result from their having been supported against a hard anvil during the flaking procedure. The term "bipolar" seems to have originated with Teilhard and Pei, who used it to describe the mode of manufacture of some of the artifacts at Choukoutien. They observe:

> Many times the flakes were obtained by an ordinary sideflaking of the core; a single bulb or star marks the point of percussion. But very often also (chiefly in the case of the smaller quartz fragments) the original stone has been crushed between two boulders [emphasis in original], the result being the production of elongated laminae or cores, split and cracked at two diametrically opposite points. We shall call such specimens 'bipolar flakes' or 'bipolar fragments' ('outils écaillés doubles' of Prof. Breuil?) [1932:352].

Certain of the artifacts illustrated in the publication quoted bear a strong resemblance to Juntunen bipolar artifacts, the chief difference being the absence from Juntunen of the "star" of percussion, that is, lines radiating out from the point at which the blow hit the core, representing internal cracking of the core that did not result in splitting off portions of chert. Artifacts of this sort are described in the European literature as *pièces écaillées*.

"Free flaking" is described by Witthoft as the most common chipping pattern generally encountered archaeologically, one in which, it is inferred, the "vector of the hammer blow forms an acute angle with the plane of the face of the core" (1957:17), resulting in wedge-shaped flakes. As the vector of force moves toward a position parallel to the face of the core, the detached flakes are described as becoming flatter and thinner until, when the vector is directed inward toward the body of the core, a flake may be thickest and widest at the end opposite the area of percussion. The technique with vector parallel to face of core is termed "flat flaking" by Witthoff; that with vector directed inward toward body of core "resolved flaking" (1957:17-18). Witthoff points out also that the latter two techniques are frequently associated with hinge fractures, that resolved flaking cannot be done except with "high quality, glassy and homogeneous flints," and, further, that "many industries which emphasize expert flat or resolved flaking show very conspicuous bruising of striking platforms. . . .the result. . .of contact between large areas of the hammer-face and the striking platform. . ."[p. 18].

On the Juntunen site, chert debitage was easily sorted into two large classes, based on the presence or absence respectively of the attributes of free flaking and the bipolar technique. The partitioning was even further simplified by the striking fact that nearly all pieces on non-bipolar debitage were considerably larger than bipolar pieces, and were, in addition, produced on Bois Blanc or Eastport cherts (which appear to have occurred in nature in tabular form) whereas nearly all bipolar debitage was manufactured on rolled and weathered pebbles of high-quality cherts ranging in diameter from about 2.5 to 5 cm., as estimated from large fragments with cortex preserved.

In the process of analysis, the chert from the site was sorted by provenience unit into categories, as shown in Table 12. A formal description of the two basic industrial processes inferred to have been prevalent follows, attention being directed particularly to the "formal modifications. . .made in the raw material during

TABLE 12

CHERT DEBITAGE CATEGORY FREQUENCIES AND PERCENTAGES BY CHERT VARIETY AND FORMAL CLASS

	Category	Frequency	Per Cent
1. By chert variety:	Bois Blanc Chert	4,334	25
	Non-Bois Blanc Chert	12,927	75
	Total	17,261	100
2. By formal class:	Shatter	1,157	7
	Decortication flakes	1,244	7
	Non-bipolar flakes	6,452	37
	Non-bipolar cores	339	2
	Bipolar flakes	2,885	17
	Bipolar cores	744	4
	Other	156	1
	Utilized flakes	217	1
	Chips	17	Negligible
	Unclassified	4,050	28
	Total	17,261	100
	Total Weight	38.407 kg.	

the process of manufacturing artifacts" (Binford and Papworth 1963:79).

6.1.2.1 Non-Bipolar Technique

No quarry site or other source of materials worked by non-bipolar techniques was located, and materials encountered at the Juntunen site suggest that Bois Blanc and Eastport cherts were initially modified elsewhere after being quarried and then brought to the site in the form of "cores," a term referring to "any block of raw material prepared so that flakes could be removed in a systematic manner for later use as blanks for artifacts" (Binford and Papworth 1963:83). Chert debitage classifiable as "shatter"—fragments with "angular and irregular cleavage planes" (Binford and Quimby 1963:286) and lacking bulbs and waves of percussion and striking platforms, considered to be the by-product of initial stages of working the raw material—occurred as a relatively low proportion of the total chert collection from the site (6.6%) and consisted mostly of Bois Blanc chert, with a small amount of exotic chert shatter, and almost no Eastport at all.

Blocks of Bois Blanc or Eastport chert showing signs of utilization as cores are characteristically about twice or three times larger than cores used in the other technique, usually have a number of relatively flat faces from which flakes were removed, and are thus formally similar to the "block cores" of Binford and Papworth (1963). There are no signs that the cores were held on anvils for flaking. There is a total absence of the crushing, nibbling, and multiple-hinge fracturing characteristic of the bipolar technique.

Flakes drawn from such cores, by what is inferred to be a "free-flaking" technique, usually have fairly sizable flat striking platforms and well-developed bulbs of percussion and are two to three times larger, on the average, than flakes drawn by the other process. There are a number of types: irregular thick wedges, evidently the result of trimming cores to shape; fairly thick rectangular flakes with flake scars and ridges on the external face running parallel to the long axis of the flake; and a variety of shapes of minor occurrence. In general, cores of Eastport chert show more careful preparation and handling than do those of Bois Blanc chert, on which the difficulties of achieving the desired cleavage are generally apparent.

As shown in Figure 17 (p. 126), the popularity of non-Bois Blanc cherts increases with time—there is a striking increase in the ratio of non-Bois Blanc to Bois Blanc cherts in the Juntunen phase. A parallel change in the popularity of the two flaking techniques can also be seen. Thus the non-bipolar frequency line approximates closely the Bois Blanc chert frequency line, and the shift to popularity of non-Bois Blanc chert in the Juntunen phase is reflected in a marked increase in production of bipolar products.

6.1.2.2 Bipolar Technique

The other flint-working technique prevalent at the Juntunen site is one clearly adapted to the exploitation of high-quality cherts occurring in nature in small pebbles rounded and deposited by glacial action in till and on beaches. The precise locations from which the materials appearing on the site were obtained are unknown; no suitable deposits yielding pebbles of this sort were encountered on the island, and on the beaches most pebbles and cobbles are of basalt, granite, and dolomite, with chert being exceptionally rare. That sources of fine chert in even larger format were actually somewhere available, however, is demonstrated by the fact that most scrapers were made of large, thick flakes struck off cores that must have been considerably larger than any recovered from the site.

It is perhaps possible that the bipolar cores from the site represent spent cores originally much larger in size, but it is somewhat surprising that from the entire site not a single larger core was recovered of size suitable for producing flakes for scrapers. An inference is that production of blanks for scrapers, and perhaps of most of the scrapers themselves, was done elsewhere than at the site. There is considerable overlap in chert varieties between scrapers and products of the bipolar technique, but the range in varieties is much greater for the bipolar, with numerous varieties that do not also appear as scrapers, suggesting that sources of chert used for scrapers and for the bipolar technique were not identical.

The "free flaking" or "non-bipolar" technique was used to produce fairly thick flakes ranging in length from 2.5 to 7.0 cm. from block cores of various rather irregular but basically rectanguloid shapes derived from raw-material sources that were mainly outcrops. The flakes themselves were secondarily elaborated into a variety of tool forms, especially large bifacially worked implements commonly interpreted as projectile points and knives.

The "small core" or bipolar technique, on the other hand, was adapted to the utilization of entirely different cherts, so there is a situation of nearly complete mutual exclusiveness between technique and chert types used. The bipolar technique is highly correlated with exotic cherts and chalcedonies, which yield sharp cutting edges but were apparently available mainly as small pebbles in the range of 2 — 4 cm. High-quality chert *could* evidently be obtained in larger sizes, as seen from the scrapers, but, as far as can be determined, the manufacture of scrapers seems to have take place elsewhere than at the Juntunen site, whereas the entire sequence of steps of reduction of the smaller pebbles is present *in situ.*

Although the various bladelet and microblade industries of the Old and New Worlds demonstrate that tiny cores—formally similar to full-sized blade cores except much smaller—could be handled so as to yield perfect bladelets, at Juntunen and other sites in the northern Lake Michigan area a rather peculiar and seemingly clumsy technique was used, and the resultant products are in part like and in part quite unlike those of other industries based on small cores.

A peculiarity of the industry is the presence, on the ends of the majority of pieces, of a marked battering and crushing, leading in many cases to multiple step-fracturing in the adjacent areas. This appears to be at least partly the result of resting cores on stone anvils for support during percussion flaking. Other aspects of this phenomenon, however, lead me to believe that this is not the whole story, and further elaboration will come later (p. 140). As for anvil stones, a number of pitted stones were recovered, whose pitting could have been produced by their having been used in such a way.

There is considerable uniformity in the size of pieces resulting from this technique, with a mean length of 2.5 cm., a range of 1.5 to 3.9 cm., and a rather low degree of dispersion (s.d. of 0.7 cm.). The sample from which these data were obtained consisted of 57 cores selected (subjectively) as "typical" during the process of analysis. To what extent they represent the entire sample from the site is unknown, but it is interesting to note that this s.d. is very close to a pooled s.d. for lengths of Binford and Quimby's (1963:292) six varieities of "bipolar cores:" s.d. = 0.82. On the other hand, a pooled mean for these lengths is 3.17, rather larger than the mean of 2.5 cm. for the sample of Juntunen bipolar cores. It seemed worthwhile to test whether the difference between these mean values indicated a real difference between the parent sources, and the results of the t-test are shown in Table 13. The obtained value of t, 7.1, is very much greater than one would expect if the Binford and Quimby sample and the Juntunen sample had been drawn from a common population; hence if the former sample has qualities of randomness one can apparently regard the differences as real. As a hypothesis to explain these findings, difference in available form of raw materials is suggested. It is clear, nevertheless, that, given these differences, the way of handling the material at the site discussed was very similar indeed.

TABLE 13

TEST OF SIGNIFICANCE FOR DIFFERENCE IN SIZE OF BIPOLAR CORES BETWEEN JUNTUNEN SITE AND OTHER SITES

$$\left(t = \frac{\text{difference in means}}{\text{standard error of difference}}\right)$$

	n	s(Pooled)	s^2(Pooled data)
Binford and Quimby's data:	49	0.84	0.67
Juntunen site:	57	0.70	0.49

Difference in means = 0.67

Standard error of difference = 0.10

t = 7.1

6.1.2.3 Steps in Processing Raw Material

A. Shatter

Of the total chert debitage, 1,157 pieces (7 per cent of the whole) were classified as shatter, defined as the unplanned random breakage resulting from the heavy blows of the first phases of working the raw material. No breakdown of shatter by chert variety or other attribute was made, but it was observed that about 80 per cent consisted of Bois Blanc chert. Of shatter in exotic high-quality cherts, some consistency was noted in that a frequent form (its proportion of all shatter was not noted) consisted of pieces that looked like segments of an orange, having one rounded surface (which on an orange would be the surface under the peel) consisting of the original cortical surface of the pebble and with the other two faces perfectly flat, lacking striking platforms or bulbar complex. The possible significance of this form is discussed below under Bipolar Cores.

B. Decortication Flakes

Binford and Quimby, discussing a nearly identical stoneworking technique from sites at the northern end of Lake Michigan, set up a category of decortication flakes as follows: "(1) the external face of the flake is the unmodified cortex. . .; (2) the internal face shows scarring from heavy percussion. . ." (1963:287). From the Juntunen site, 1,244 pieces, or 7 per cent of the total, were classed as "decortication flakes." Of these, the ones of high quality chert (hence *inferred* to pertain to the bipolar industry) were somewhat different from those described by Binford and Quimby, probably because of the non-tabular form of most of the Juntunen original raw material in distinction to the tabular form seen by Binford and Quimby. Most exhibit *not* "strong *negative* bulbs of percussion" (Binford and Quimby 1963:287) but normal positive ones, and the irregular scarring described by these authors does not usually appear. In fact, a separate class of "decortication flakes" on the Juntunen site is not a valid category at all if the category is thought of as a wish on the part of the Indian to remove cortex as a distinct preliminary step, for such a step does not seem to have existed, and most of the flakes so classified should probably be relegated to a subcategory of the general trim flakes detached in the initial shaping of a core, to which category they belong on the basis of most attributes. "Decortication flakes" on the Juntunen site are generally as thin and well-formed as any others and further, need not be treated as a separate class both because cortex is present on many artifacts and because it does not appear to have been regarded, for work-a-day tools, as an inferior surface that must be removed. A number of scrapers have, as upper faces, unmodified cortex; similarly, several projectile points were made by edge-trimming fairly thin cortical flakes. Thus, if of suitable shape, flakes with cortex were utilized in the same fashion as non-cortical flakes and, if thick enough, were often even used as cores, the flaking occurring from the primary plane of cleavage.

C. Bipolar Cores

A number of forms have been tentatively classified as "bipolar cores." Because they are an exceedingly important part of this flint-chipping technique, particular attention will be paid to them. Since the industry is closely related to that described in some detail by Binford and Quimby (1963), the points of comparison will be stressed.

Of a total of 17,250 pieces of chert debitage, 744 pieces, or 4 per cent of the total chert, were classed as bipolar cores. All the six core types established by Binford and Quimby (1963:289-96) are also present on the Juntunen site; however, in the analysis of the Juntunen chert, these categories were not used. My impression, based on a study of all the chert from the site, is that there are two fundamental kinds of bipolar cores: (1) polyhedral ("cylindrical" or "radially symmetrical"); and (2) flat, or "back and front," as illustrated in Figure 18.

Three terms serve to define the geometry of a cylindrical core: "top," that portion against which the majority of blows to detach flakes were directed; "bottom," opposite of top; and "faces," referring to the roughly parallel flake scars forming

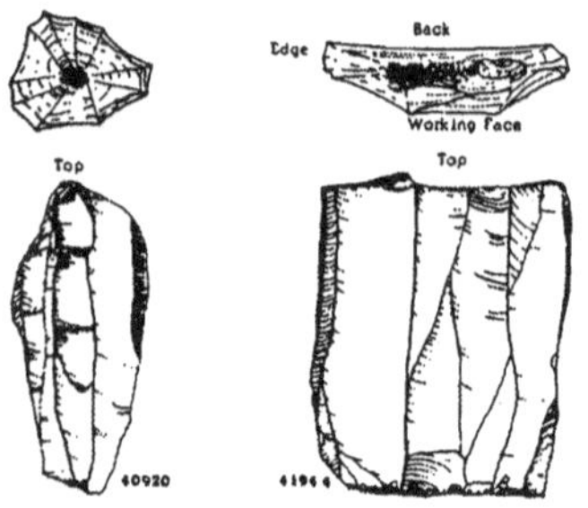

a b
Fig. 18—Two basic bipolar core types.

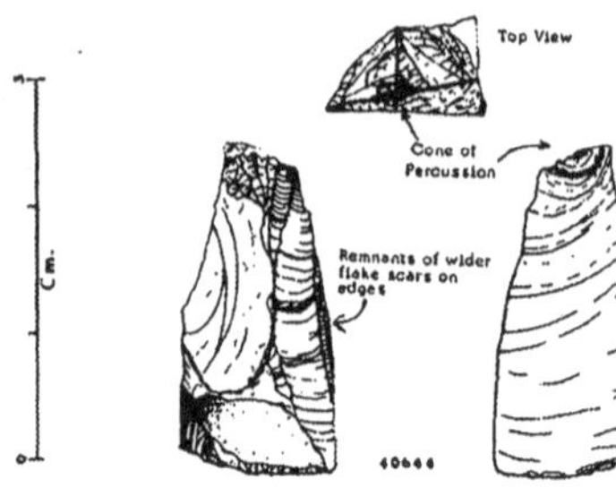

Fig. 19.—Split bipolar core.

the periphery of the core. For flat cores, in addition to "top" and "bottom," the terms "working face," or "front," "back," and "edge" (whose usage is illustrated in Figure 18) are employed in this report. Both faces may of course be "working faces," in which case the core has no "back," a situation suggesting the possibility of intergrades from "flat" to "polyhedral." Such intergrades are in fact not very common, and so the two categories, from my observations, do represent genuine modes. Polyhedral cores are shown in Plate XXVII, in which *h-j* are somewhat unusual specimens, whereas *a-g* may be regarded as typical.

One peculiar feature of the small cylindrical bipolar cores calls for particular attention. About a quarter of them, with parallel flake scars all around the periphery, and pointed at both ends, fail to show bulbar complexes, ripples, or any other indications of the knapping process. It was difficult, in fact, to see how they had been produced at all. A possible solution to this problem was obtained through experiments performed on a few of the unaltered chert pebbles recovered from the site, in an effort to reproduce the supposed fashion of working the material. A pebble was simply laid on a concrete floor, to simulate the anvil stone, and struck a smart blow from a hammerstone directed straight down. The results were variable. In three cases nothing remained but a collection of primary shatter, some of it with the "scarring from heavy percussion" and "internal cleavage faces of an unsystematic angular and cubical nature" described by Binford and Quimby (1963) as characteristic of primary shatter and decortication flakes. In one instance, however, a particularly flawfree pebble of good quality chert broke into eight pieces, classifiable as follows:

Category	No.	Description
Shatter:	1	"split pebble"
	2	"orange segments (mentioned earlier)
Decortication flakes:		
	1	fairly thin flake
Cores:		
	1	perfect cylindrical "core"
Core fragments:		
	2	"split cores"
Unclassifiable:		
	1	flake

It thus appears that the "orange segment" pieces with cortex described earlier and the bulbless "cores" are related and are evidence that pebbles were, at least sometimes, broken open in the very simple fashion described and that some of the objects classed as "cores" should possibly be reclassed as some form of shatter. (Unfortunately, this discovery was made virtually at the end of the process of analysis of the stone industry from the site; therefore, what proportion of artifacts classed as "bipolar cores" should be reassigned is not known.)

The majority of cylindrical cores, however, are not perfectly symmetrical radially and bear signs of battering at both ends as well as flake scars indicative of intentional detachment of flakes by separate successive blows. The ones in which top and bottom have been reduced to little more than battered points may, of course, be nothing more than the end-product—exhausted nuclei—of cylindrical cores, or even of flat cores if blows had been directed so as to remove flakes from the ends rather than from the faces—which did in fact occur, as witnessed by the presence of a number of flakes with an almost semicylindrical or equilateral-triangular cross section, evidently drawn from the edges of cores such as that illustrated in Figure 18, *b* (p. 135). These are the "variety E" or "end" flakes of Binford and Quimby (1963:298, Fig. 133).

Flat cores constitute the majority of the bipolar sample and occur in greater variety of shapes and sizes than do cylindrical ones. A common subcategory had battered ridges top and bottom, the areas bearing the blows of percussion having been reduced to mere edges, with flaking from one or both sides. In some cases it appears as if a thick flake had been used as core; in other cases the presence of a flat or even concave back of the core, together with only narrow traces of flakes along the ends, indicates that the piece is actually a split core, derived either by accident or by design. Split cores may, of course, result from the splitting along the long axis of either cylindrical or flat cores. They also overlap formally with "end-flakes," and because of the overlap, sorting them into the proper category was not possible in many cases. One recurrent feature of split cores, however, that appears to mark them off from the usually thinner flakes, is the frequent presence on the broad face of cleavage, first, of parts of a genuine cone of percussion toward the top, leaving no doubt from which direction the force was applied; second, marked concentric ripples, evidencing heavy force. In all probablility, then, split cores were merely one of the unplanned results of a poorly controlled flaking procedure and were not a sought-after product. In any case, no formal artifact class on the site is based on split cores, although an occasional one may have an edge modified with scraper retouch.

The sample of cores mentioned above, selected for "typicalness" during analysis of the chert, contained 16 cylindrical cores. There were 30 flat cores with opposed ridges in the sample, and it appeared that there was greater variation in length within the latter class than within the former. Accordingly, alternate flat cores were selected to make both categories equal 16 in number, and an analysis of variance was done to test the hypothesis that the two samples were drawn from identical normally distributed populations. The results are presented in Table 14, and for this sample, then, the difference in variance between the two categories may be considered real. There seems no obvious reason why the cylindrical cores in the sample should be distributed so closely about the mean; it may be noted that the situation at the Juntunen site is the opposite of that recorded by Binford and Quimby (1963) for their surface collections on the northern shore of Lake Michigan, although their sample of only three "opposing point" (cylindrical) and four "opposing ridge" (flat) cores makes it seem highly likely that sampling error suffices for an explanation.

A number of cores appear to be merely hemispherical split pebbles utilized directly as cores. They could be regarded as "flat cores inasmuch as flakes are drawn mainly from one face, the cortical back of the pebble being left unaltered. One of these cores is illustrated in Figure 20.

TABLE 14

ANALYSIS OF VARIANCE IN LENGTH BETWEEN TWO TYPES OF BI-POLAR CORES

	Cylindrical Cores (Opposed Point)	Flat Cores (Opposed Ridges)
SX	34.60	38.80
SX^2	75.92	98.26
n	16	16
$\overline{X}$	2.16	2.42
s	0.26	0.51

F = 3.130
(Significant at 1% level)

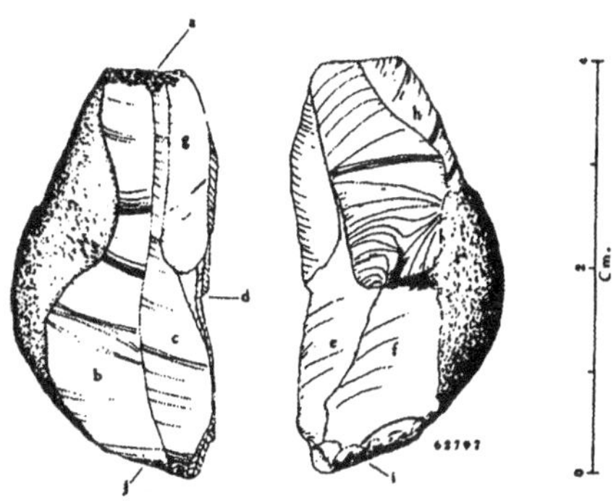

Fig. 20.—Bipolar core with cortex on back.

Several attributes common to bipolar cores may be pointed out with reference to this illustrated specimen. The top of the core was reduced to a ridge; on one side only, the ridge was subjected to considerable battering, resulting in the multiple step or hinge-fracturing seen near the top at *a*. It looks as if many blows had been directed to this area, perhaps in an effort to detach another long flake from the faceted face of the core; why this should, and how it could, have been restricted to only one side of the ridge, under this hypothesis, is anything but clear. The situation is reminiscent of one described for cores from Shan-Koba by Semenov:

> Splintering is a normal occurrence on almost all cores, but what is noteworthy is the persistence of the craftsman, who after one unsuccessful attempt to detach the flake, repeated it numerous times, still without result. When the edge was splintered and broken he moved the end of the presser back and exerted it several times in the center, before he finally threw the core away [1964:50].

Again, for the Kostenki I site, Semenov finds that

> the operator using the core repeatedly exerted pressure before producing a successful detachment, in order to find a favourable spot to apply his strength. Only in rare instances did he detach a blade at the first exertion [1964:53].

Much of the earlier flaking on the core of Figure 20 had been done in an adroit fashion, resulting in three or four flakes that ran the length of the core (Fig. 20, *b*, *c*, *d*, and probably *e*). One flake *(f)* originated at the bottom of the core and ended in a hinge fracture about halfway up. Flake *g*, ending in a hinge fracture, started at the top. Flake *h*, with heavy rippling, was an early flake perhaps associated with initial opening of the pebble. Thus the discrepancy between the evidences of competent flaking and the crushing or battering, with apparent failure to produce satisfactory flakes, is difficult to understand. The fact that this battering is of such frequent occurrence, is so often found on cores from which good flakes had previously been derived, and differs so much from the flaking designed to remove long flakes, suggests that it may perhaps represent a deliberately taken measure on the part of the worker—perhaps to alter the shape of the striking zone, along the lines of the faceting performed on Levallois cores to alter the angle between striking platform and outer face of the core, permitting the removal of a flat, thin, sheetlike flake. An argument against this supposition in the Juntunen case is the fact that the battering most frequently is seen, not on the side of the ridge opposite to that from which flakes are being drawn, as was the case with Semenov's material, but on the same side, so it would not have served to alter the angle of striking platform.

At the bottom of the core shown in Figure 20 may be seen another battered ridge *(i)*, again with the battering on only one side of the ridge. It might be supposed that this crushing was the result of the core's having rested on an anvil stone for flaking. However, the ridge is concave, not flat or convex (this is not apparent in Fig. 20), and again the peculiar battering is on one side only *(i* but not *j)*.

D. "Gouged-End Artifacts"

The presence of pronounced battering and crushing of a particular kind at the ends of otherwise distinctive pieces makes it desirable to place them in a separate artifact class, to which the name "gouged-end artifacts" is tentatively assigned. These pieces, clearly products of the bipolar technique, show the following properties. Most have a convex outer face, with an average of three to four parallel flake scars, and a flat or concave inner face generally with one long and broad flake scar, showing that these pieces themselves may be regarded either as rather thick flakes or as rather thin longitudinally-split segments of a cylindrical or flat core. At one or both ends a kind of chipping in fine, abrupt multiple hinge-fractures has produced a hollowed-out or dished area on the flat face of the piece, so that the ridge forming the end of the piece presents a formal similarity to the cutting edge of a wood gouge.

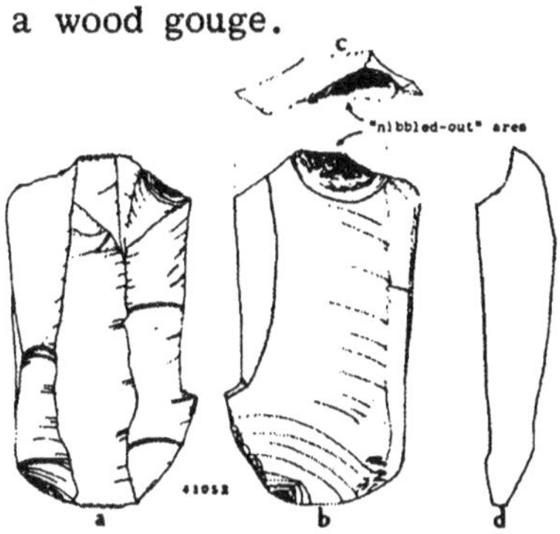

Fig. 21—"Gouged-end" artifact.

Figure 21 shows a typical gouged-end artifact. In *a*, the convex outer face has a number of facets indicating flakes removed, with both ends of the piece being used as striking platforms. The inner face is hown in *b*; here the broad flake scar and remaining portions of bulbar complex at the bottom indicate that the whole piece was detached from a larger core, with only one flake (along the right margin in *b*) having been removed from the surface of cleavage subsequent to the initial detachment of the piece. The gouged-out area, produced apparently as the last step, is seen in *b* and *c*, and the cross-sectional shape of the artifact is shown in *d*.

Other similar artifacts are illustrated in Plate XXVIII where *a* is the only quartz artifact of this type; in the others of this plate, battering both top and bottom is evident. The drawing of the end-view of *e* illustrates the very common feature of curved ridge as seen looking at the end. Plate XXVIII, 6, shows an artifact rather like a scraper in such details as outline, size, and steep retouch, but with inner face flaked (rare for scrapers) and with the working edge "gouged out"—whether intentionally or through heavy use is not clear—to form the curved edge seen in the top view.

In the discussion of flakes and bladelets produced from bipolar cores presented in the next section, it will be pointed out that no formal artifact class based on them could be identified, nor did most of them reveal signs of reworking or consistent use. It almost appears that flakes and bladelets were merely wastage in the process of preparing cores for use as artifacts or at least that cores, when they had reached a certain minimum size, were often altered or utilized in a particular way, with the peculiar nibbling or step flaking on the flattest surface, to produce objects whose end or ends resemble modern steel wood gouges. Only one artifact produced by a non-bipolar technique at all resembled "gouged-end artifacts." As seen in Plate XXXI *a-c*, the concave edge at negative bulb of percussion of a fairly thick flake shows removal of small flakes. Whether this was a preparation for or a result of use cannot be determined. It cannot at present be demonstrated that this *formal* class (in the sense of a clustering of attributes) also constitues a *functional* class. Neither is it clear at the present stage of analysis whether these objects were the result of a deliberate intention on the part of the makers to produce them; whether they were only the natural result of a particular flaking technique, some products of which were then incidentally used as a kind of tool; or whether they were merely spent cores and core segments. Nevertheless, the gouged-end artifacts do constitute a valid formal class and are capable of being described and studied as to mode of manufacture, as presented herein and in Binford and Quimby (1963).

E. <u>Bipolar Flakes</u>

As seen in Table 12 (p. 129), 2,885 flakes inferred to have been struck off bipolar cores were tabulated for the site as a whole. The ratio of bipolar flakes to cores is 4:1, against 20:1 for the free flaking technique. The 4:1 ratio seems somewhat less than might be expected for such an industry but is perhaps not unreasonable considering the small size of most raw-material pebbles. One wonders, however, why such a small quantity of shatter and cortical flakes referable to both techniques appears in the assemblage. Perhaps most initial flint-working stages took place elsewhere.

If derived from the edges of flat cores, flakes generally are fairly thick and have quadrangular or triangular cross sections. If derived from the working faces of either cylindrical or flat cores, flakes are usually long, flat, and thin, with multiple parallel flake scars on the outer surface and with a curved inner surface indicating that the cores from which they were derived had a spindle-shaped or at least convex surface. These flakes are formally similar to other bladelets, such as, for example, Dorset, Poverty Point, and Cahokia. Most Juntunen bladelets are narrower than 11 mm., thus fulfilling in this respect W. E. Taylor's (1962) criterion for Arctic microblades. Unlike most other bladelet industries, however, the thickness of the Juntunen specimens ranges from about 2 mm. up through items that are about "half a core" in thickness or about 7 mm., making a dichotomy between "bladelet" and "split core" impossible.

Representative bladelets are illustrated in Plate XXIX (orientation has most-used striking zones up). Here we observe, especially in *a, c, f, g, i,* a common feature of the bladelets: the striking platforms are extremely small—generally narrower than 1 mm.—and commonly consist solely of a bruised and battered area or point, conforming to similar areas observed on cores. In Plate XXIX, items *a* through *e* are thin flakes, while *f* through *i* represent the opposite ("split core") end of the thickness range. The longest flakes inferred to have been produced by the bipolar technique are shown on Plate XXX. Here *a* is triangular in cross section and thus appears to have been removed from an edge rather than from a face of a flat core; its maximum thickness is 0.6 cm. Example *d* shows the unusual feature of slight scraper retouch at the top. Drawings of some flakes, to clarify details, are presented in Plate XXXI, *d-g'*.

Unlike such bladelet industries as those from Poverty Point (Ford and Webb 1956) and Cahokia (Perino 1960, Mason and Perino 1961), the Juntunen bladelets were not ordinarily blanks or an intermediate step in the manufacture of a formal class of artifact, such as the Cahokia drills. Instead, the majority of them show no sign of subsequent reworking or use, and where it does occur (usually in the form of scraper retouch), the area of the flake chosen for the retouch seems quite random—retouch may thus be found anywhere on a flake and may originate on either face of the flake. It appears then that these bladelets were utilized (if at all) in the same casual way that other irregular flakes were occasionally picked up, retouched, and used (see below, sec. 7.1.3.2).

6.1.2.4 Other Techniques

The materials selected for manufacture of projectile points and scrapers were mainly the fine-grained, glassy, high-quality cherts also used in the Juntunen site bipolar technique, yet the small physical size of all classes of the products of the bipolar technique as found on the site seems to eliminate them as the source of blanks for the projectile points and scrapers. The relatively few large points, well outside the size range of the majority of points, are also made of different material (Bois Blanc or Eastport chert), and these two facts suggest that the large points may have been produced locally, utilizing a non-bipolar technique on local materials.

Since cores, flakes, and other debitage, of high-quality chert and of a size suitable for making into points and scrapers, are not known from the Juntunen site, it must be inferred that the stages of manufacture of these artifacts, at least as far as the production of blanks, were conducted elsewhere than at the site, suggesting that blank production might be a specialized activity at some other location. Such a supposition is supported by the specialized nature of the activities inferred by Binford and Quimby (1963:303) for the Point Detour Bay site in southeastern Delta County, Michigan Upper Peninsula, about one hundred miles west of the Juntunen site, evidently on the Bois Blanc phase time level. According to Binford and Quimby,

> . . . Raw materials were gathered and collected at the site and initially modified on the spot into nuclei from which were struck flakes for future use as blanks for tool production. The residual nuclei (cores) as well as all the debris associated with the working were left at the site while the flake blanks were removed for future processing into tools. The absence of finished tools, chips, pottery, and other artifacts at this site suggests that any single occupation was of very short duration and that dwelling place activities were not performed there [1963:303-4].

The industry represented at the Point Detour Bay site utilized the same bipolar technique and appears to demonstrate the existence of functionally specific sites of this nature. Point Detour and Juntunen would then be complementary as to kind of artifacts. I infer that either blanks or the points and scrapers themselves were produced where high-quality raw materials were available in sizes larger than the pieces being worked at the Juntunen site.

6.1.3 FINISHED PRODUCTS

6.1.3.1 Projectile Points and Bifacially Worked Artifacts

As a generalization about the Juntunen projectile points, it can be said that most are small, triangular, of a minimal standard of workmanship, and that virtually no change occurred in these respects during the period of occupation of the site. There is some variety represented at the site—at least six types of pointed implements can be recognized—but, as seen in Table 15, the great majority (133 out of 198, or about 67 per cent) fall into the single category "small triangular projectile point."

TABLE 15

FREQUENCY DISTRIBUTION OF PROJECTILE POINTS AND BIFACIALLY WORKED ARTIFACTS BY TYPE AND PHASE

	Phase						
Type	Mackinac (A-C)	Intermediate I	Bois Blanc (D)	Intermediate II	Juntunen (E-F)	Unassigned	Total
Juntunen Triangular	21	6	4	23	6	32	
Juntunen Notched	7	1	4	3	5	21	133
Medium-sized notched and stemmed	2	1	1	4	1	3	12
Large notched and stemmed			1		1	2	4
Bifacial ovates	3				1	3	7
"Cache points"	1			1	1	2	5
Large bifacial fragments	4	1	1	2	2	12	22
Other	1	3	1	3	2	5	15
Total	39	12	12	36	19	80	198

The projectile points from the first summer's excavations were initially studied by David Taggart, who prepared a report on them (Taggart 1962) including attribute lists for the several types he recognized. When the remainder of the points were available for study, I added them to Taggart's list while re-examining those studied by Taggart in order add a few further attributes, such as weight and some attributes from the list published by Binford (1963). The final list is seen in Table 16. Each bifacial artifact and projectile point was studied

TABLE 16

ATTRIBUTE LIST FOR PROJECTILE POINTS

I. Discrete attributes

A. Chert type

1. Bois Blanc
2. Gray banded (Eastport)
3. Other

B. Cortex

1. Present
2. Absent

C. Flaking

1. Striking-platform and bulbar complex, location
   a. Tip
   b. Base
   c. Corner
   d. Side

2. Extent of bifacial chipping
   a. Bifacial
   b. Less than 1/3 primary flaking surface remaining on one side
   c. Equal to or greater than 1/3 primary flaking surface remaining on one side
   d. Unretouched on one side
   e. Only edge trim; retouch absent

3. Tertiary retouch
   a. Lacking
   b. Present

D. Condition

1. Whole

2. Broken
   a. Base only preserved
   b. Tip only preserved

E. Transverse section*

1. Missing data
2. Plano-convex

*Illustrated in Binford 1963;203

3. Plano-triangular
4. Biplano
5. Biconvex
6. Bitriangular
7. Asymmetrically biconvex
8. Asymmetrically bitriangular
9. Convexo-triangular

F. Longitudinal section*

1. Missing data
2. Plano-convex
3. Biplano
4. Biconvex
5. Asymmetrically biconvex
6. Concavo-convex
7. Excurvate
8. Ovate or triangular
9. Assymetrically ovate
10. Assymetrically excurvate
11. Asymmetrically concavo-convex

G. Sides

1. Straight
2. Convex

H. Base

1. Markedly concave
2. Slightly concave
3. Flat
4. Convex
5. Missing

I. Shoulder

1. Prominent
2. Non-prominent
3. Basally projecting barbs

J. Haft element

1. Absent
2. Side-notched
3. Corner-notched
4. Stemmed
5. Missing data

*Illustrated in Binford 1963:203

II. Continuous variables

A. Length
B. Width
C. Length/width
D. Thickness
E. Width/thickness
F. Notch width
G. Weight

III. Provenience

A. Level
B. Catalogue number

IV. "Type"

---

for all attributes on the list, though of course breakage and other factors resulted in much "missing data." The designation "projectile points and bifacial artifacts" is used because, while most share certain general attributes, such as the presence of a point at one end, many projectile points are unifacial, and many bifacially worked implements can hardly be termed projectile points. Thus perhaps "pointed chipped stone tools" would have been preferable—such a term would emphasize the fact that we are really dealing with a formal rather than a functional class. These artifacts will now be discussed by types, in the order of Table 15.

A. Juntunen Points

The term "Juntunen point" is here assigned to a class of points forming a variant on the general style of triangular Late Woodland points. They constitute the overwhelming majority of points from the site at all periods (total of 133) and while they show variability in a number of attributes, they are united with other Late Prehistoric points as against points of other time periods. Thus their shape in outline is characteristically triangular, and they are commonly small in size. About half (67 cases) are of exotic cherts; Bois Blanc chert was particularly avoided. Nine showed remnants of cortex, and in a few of these cases outright "decortication flakes" had been used as blanks, with no attempt made to remove it. Striking platforms and/or bulbar complexes, where observable, were located at tip (18), base (20), or corner (11). Primary chipping (in the sense employed by Binford 1963:206)—namely, chipping other than mere trimming of edges to shape—ranged from a total obliteration of the orginal flaking surfaces (full bifacial working), through items retouched on one face but with no retouch at all on the other, hence "unifacial" artifacts, to points with both original surfaces of cleavage completely intact, the items having been brought to shape solely by edge-trim. Points were scattered in frequency fairly evenly through this range of variation. Secondary retouch (cf. Binford 1963:206) was noted for only four of these points.

As might be expected, size and thickness of the flake-blank from which the point was made governed the extent of facial retouch; the mean weight of points with edge-trim only was nearly 1 gm. lower than those with full bifacial retouch. The mean weight of all the small unnotched projectile points was 2.0 gm., with s.d. of 1.1, so this difference in weight is probably not statistically significant; but if mean weights are plotted for points falling into each of the five retouch categories, ranging from bifacial to edge-trim only, a trend toward lightness is observed moving through this range of categories. It is also worth noting that the edge-trim-only points are highly correlated with very high-quality cherts, while some of the bifacially worked points were made of somewhat less perfect materials. Unfortunately, adequate evidence is lacking as to the technique by which flake-blanks for points were produced, since the essential differentiating attributes—striking platform and bulbar complex—were usually obscured by chipping. Where they were observable, however, and judging from the relatively short, broad, and thick nature of the flakes, it does appear that the bipolar technique was not normally used to produce blanks for projectile points or scrapers. As also in the case of scrapers, evidence of on-site production of blanks for these implements in the form of cores or raw blanks of suitable size was singularly lacking from the site. Thus the projectile points add to the impression that initial stages of manufacture of many stone tools took place elsewhere than at the site.

Of the 133 points classified as Juntunen points, 92 were more or less triangular; some are shown in Plates XXXII and XXXIII. The relative indifference to bifacial symmetry is well illustrated by Plate XXXII, *b*, *n*, *p-s;* by Figure 22, *a*, *e*, *d;* and by Plate XLVI, *l*, *m*. The last two are edge-trim-only cases of which *m* was also left with its unaltered cortical face. It and its neighbor, *l*, were the two points included in the "personal kit" buried with an individual in an ossuary (Feature 11).

Illustrating range in weight from Plate XXXII, one of the smallest points from the site, weighing 0.55 gm. and apparently

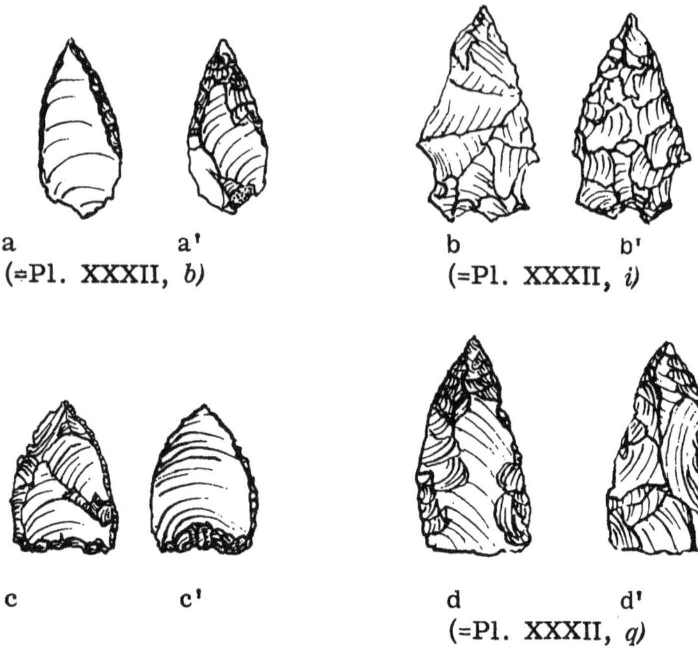

Fig. 22.—Varieties of flaking done on Juntunen points

unbroken, is seen in *n*; the heaviest is *l*, 4.60 gm. Plate XXXII, *m*, unique for thickness and deeply concave base, lies outside the weight range for Juntunen points (see Table 17) with 6.40 gm. and should be classed as a Levanna point (Ritchie 1961).

Haft elements—usually shallow side notches or stems—were found on 41 Juntunen points, a selection of which is shown in Plates XXXII, *i*, *u*-*y*, *A*-*C*, *E*-*H*, and Plate XXXIII, *j*. The question may be asked whether haft elements are a free variant within one type of Juntunen points, or whether the presence or absence of haft element is associated with other differences, justifying their recognition as a distinct type using Spaulding's (1953) argument. Accordingly, *t* and F tests were employed to compare these two groups of points on every attribute for which they had been measured. The results are summarized in Table 18. We see that there is less than 1 chance in 100 that the mean lengths of these two groups of points are in fact the same, and less than 1 in 20 that their relative frequencies of chert types represent a common parent population. It further

TABLE 17

SUMMARY STATISTICS ON PROJECTILE POINTS AND BIFACES

Attribute	Juntunen Points				Medium Notched/Stemmed				Large Broken Fragments				Large Notched/Stemmed			
	Range	$\bar{X}$	s	n	Range	$\bar{X}$	s	n	Range	$\bar{X}$	s	n	Range	$\bar{X}$	s	n
Length (mm)	14 - 42	28	6	112	36 - 57	42	6	8	48	--	--	1	58 - 69	63	5	4
Width (mm)	9 - 29	16	3	114	13 - 24	18	3	10	19 - 47	29	9	6	25 - 32	28	3	4
Thickness (mm)	2 - 9	4	1	131	3 - 6	5	1	11	3 - 10	7	2	22	9 - 11	10	1	4
Length/width Ratio	1.0 - 3.4	1.7	.3	110	1.7 - 3.2	2.5	.5	8	- - -	--	--	--	1.8 - 2.6	2.2	.4	4
Notch Width (mm)	4 - 17	10	3	41	7 - 13	10	2	12	- - -	--	--	--	13 - 18	15	2	4
Weight (gm)	0.4- 4.6	2.0	1.1	111	2.3 - 5.0	3.9	1.1	8	- - -	--	--	--	98	--	--	1

Attribute	Bifacial Ovates				"Cache Points"				Others			
	Range	$\bar{X}$	s	n	Range	$\bar{X}$	s	n	Range	$\bar{X}$	s	n
Length (mm)	41 - 55	48	3	7	58 - 69	64	4	5	32 - 64	47	11	4
Width (mm)	23 - 37	27	5	7	27 - 29	28	1	5	15 - 39	29	9	6
Thickness (mm)	6 - 13	9	1	6	6 - 8	7	1	5	4 - 10	8	1	7
Length/width Ratio	1.4-2.3	1.7	2.4	7	2.0-2.5	2.2	.2	5	1.6-3.4	2.1	.5	4
Notch Width (mm)	---	--	--	--	---	--	--	--	---	--	--	–
Weight (gm)	5.7-14.0	9.4	1.2	7	7.3-14.0	10.9	2.6	5	2.6-5.0	5.4	2.0	3

Attribute	Juntunen Points	Medium Notched/Stemmed	Large Broken Fragments	Large Notched/Stemmed	Bifacial Ovates	"Cache Points"	Others
Condition	Whole / Broken	Whole / Broken	Whole / Broken	Whole / Broken	Whole / Broken	Whole / Broken	Whole / Broken
Total	111 / 22	8 / 4	-- / 22	8 / --	7 / --	5 / --	4 / 11
Chert Type	BB[1] EP O n	BB EP O n	BB EP O n	BB EP O n	BB EP O n	BB EP O n	BB EP O n
Total	4 15 67 86	-- 3 5 8	1 1 11 13	-- 1 2 3	3 1 1 5	-- 1 1 2	4 2 4 10
Base	M[2] S F C n	M S F C n	M S F C n	M S F C n	M S F C n	M S F C n	M S F C n
Total	2 16 19 35 72	-- -- 2 6 8	1 1 1 0 3	-- 1 -- 2 3	-- -- -- 5 5	-- -- 2 -- 2	-- -- -- 3 3

[1] BB = Bois Blanc
EP = Eastport
O = Others
n = sample size

[2] M = Markedly concave base
S = Slightly " "
F = Flat base
C = Concave base
n = sample size

TABLE 18

ATTRIBUTES IN WHICH JUNTUNEN TRIANGULAR (GROUP 1) AND JUNTUNEN NOTCHED (GROUP 2) POINTS WERE FOUND TO DIFFER SIGNIFICANTLY

Attribute	Mean (group 1)	Mean (group 2)	s.d. (group 1)	s.d. (group 2)	*t*	F
Length (mm.)	27	29	12	7	3.35	2.94
Width (mm.)	17	16	7	4	1.32	3.75
Chert type (see attribute list)	2.9	2.7	.3	.6	2.47	3.66

t value needed for significance for 2-tailed test with
∞df {at 1% level = 2.58
at 5% level = 1.96
F ratio value needed for significance
with $\frac{40}{100}$ df {at 1% level = 1.79
at 5% level = 1.51
N (group 1) = 92
N (group 2) = 41

appears that, for all three attributes, the two groups do not come from parent populations with the same variance. I conclude, then, that we may regard these two groups of points as of separate type status, and accordingly they are here named "Juntunen Triangular" and "Juntunen Notched" points respectively. (The use of the term "notched" is not to be regarded as failure to recognize the fact that some of them are actually "stemmed," in current norms of terminology.) Further (although the difference is not quite significant at the 5 per cent level) it may be noted that Juntunen Notched points had a greater frequency of convex than straight sides and that more broken points were classed as Juntunen Triangular than as Juntunen Notched.

It may be asked whether the relative frequency of these very similar projectile points varies with time. Whereas in the Mackinac Phase 27 points possess and 11 lack haft element, in the Juntunen Phase the frequencies are identical, 12 and 12. The chi square value for a test of independence between level and haftedness was 2.106 or 1 chance in 10 of the association's being due to chance, so, while the data are suggestive, we are hardly in a strong position to make a conclusion in this respect.

Twenty-two broken Juntunen points were found, suggesting recovery from game and removal from arrow shafts. More broken points came from deep levels than from superficial ones, indicating that the breakage cannot easily be explained away by disturbance subsequent to deposition. Seventeen of the 22 had the tip broken off; isolated tips were thus rare, to be expected if arrows with broken points were brought back for repointing. There was a sharp dip in proportion of broken points to whole ones in the Bois Blanc Phase and, while it is probably too much to see improved marksmanship in this, it does add one more to the series of differences in relative frequencies of artifacts and attributes unique to the Bois Blanc Phase.

Summary statistics on some attributes are presented in Table 17. Comparing Juntunen points with the other types in this class, the mean dimensions are all seen to be smaller than for any of the other types, while the variability in size, summarized as weight, is much greater—0.4 to 2.0 gm. This comparison confirms the general visual impression of informality, poor workmanship, and variety in shape presented by Juntunen points. The length-to-width ratio indicates a rather short point in relation to width, as compared with similar points from other areas, for example New York State and Wisconsin. Thus the mean length-to-width ratio for 200 points from Aztalan is only 1.37 (Maher and Baerreis 1958). There seems to be a pronounced avoidance of concave bases and a slight preference for convex ones. Convex sides (an attribute not shown in Table 17) are found about twice as frequently as straight sides; concave ones do not occur.

B. Medium-Sized Notched and Stemmed Points

A heterogeneous grouping made largely on the basis of size, "medium-sized notched and stemmed points" can hardly be regarded as a "type" except as a means of differentiating from other points the 12 specimens placed in this group. Some are illustrated on Plate XXXII, *f*, and XXXIII, *a-d*, *f-i*. Note that *e*, closely resembling a Snyders point, did not come from the Juntunen site but was the sole finished artifact recovered, with a few flakes, from a locality about one mile from the site, on an elevated point probably exposed even in Nipissing times, where Bois Blanc chert outcrops. This area (mentioned in sec. 2.3.2) was examined (with negative results) for evidence of chert quarrying. Note also that *d* came from Arrowhead Drive, a Middle Woodland site slightly overlapping horizontally with the Late Woodland Juntunen site. Neither point was included in the statistics of Table 17, but both are illustrated here for comparative purposes. Note finally that XXXIII, *j*, is another Juntunen point.

With regard to the points under consideration, it is probable that no true category is represented at all. Points shown in Plate XXXIII, *a*, and *g-i*, for example, exhibit a certain consistency in their rather vague notching and indifferent workmanship and suggest that larger points were occasionally made for certain purposes. On the other hand, *b* and *c* suggest Late Archaic items; *b* in particular is closely similar to the Hunt points of the Hodges site (Binford 1963:130) and the point shown in Plate II of the Brock Street Burial report (Kenyon and Cameron 1961). No Late Archaic site on the island is known; nevertheless, these two points, as well as the "cache points," discussed below, certainly do not suggest Late Woodland styles, although they may pertain to the Middle Woodland (Arrowhead Drive) occupation. The two illustrated items discussed stand out by virtue of craftsmanship; *c* in particular, though highly asymmetrical in transverse section, is exceptionally finely made on excellent translucent chert of a sort unique to the site. Unfortunatley, like *b*, it came from a mixed-provenience unit.

Vertical distribution of these points, as seen in Table 15, (p. 144) yields no further information.

C. Large Notched and Stemmed Points

Of the four large notched and stemmed points recovered, illustrated as Plate XXXIII, one *(k)* comes from the Arrowhead Drive site. The other three come from the Juntunen Phase but vary in a number of attributes; *n* alone has secondary retouch; *m* is made of an odd and unique coarse pinkish chert and is stemmed, while the others might better be described as notched.

D. Bifacial Ovates

The seven objects from the site classified as bifacial ovates may represent finished artifacts or stages in manufacture, but their crude appearance, coupled with the fact that four were made of Bois Blanc chert—a higher proportion than that found in any other type—suggests that they were tools in their own right, functioning perhaps as knives. No evidences of usage were observed.

All but one are illustrated in Plate XXXIV, *a-f*. By exception, *f* is finely made; *e*, on the other hand, is very crude. No clustering with respect to level could be discerned.

E. "Cache Points"

Three of the five items classified as "cache points" bear a striking formal resemblance to Dimondale points in Michigan and some Meadowood points (Ritchie, 1965:183). These three are illustrated in Plate XXXIV, *g-i*, where lighting brings out details of chipping and contrasts them with the ovates. They are shown again, this time with the other two added, in *j-n*, where the chert materials are better seen. In this series, *j* is of Bois Blanc chert, *l* is a good example of a gray-banded Eastport chert, and the other three are made of "other" cherts unrepresentative of the majority of artifacts from the site. With the possible exception of *j*, it is suspected that these artifacts are not the product of Late Woodland industry. The two that can be assigned to H. Wright's levels are from late levels. For some reason artifacts not representative of their period seem to cluster in the later occuaptions. On the other hand, it may be observed that Plate XXXIV, *k*, with its straight sides and roughly triangular outline, is unlike Late Archaic points and that *l-n* are somewhat asymmetric, with a greater amount of secondary retouch along the more convex side. All lack edge grinding. In these respects they resemble two artifacts (not illustrated) relegated to the "Other" category, crudely made bifaces of Bois Blanc chert, one 64 mm. and the other 39 mm. in length, with pronounced asymmetrical outlines, which would be conventionally regarded as "knives." It may well be that resemblances to artifacts of earlier periods are purely fortuitous and that all these bifaces, plus perhaps the ovates as well, should be grouped together under some such rubric as "large bifaces." If this were done, then we could perhaps add to this grouping the 22 fragmentary bifaces, none of which revealed haft element, that are grouped together here as "large bifacial fragments." None is illustrated herein. In their original form, some of these bifaces must have been considerably larger than any hitherto described. One was 4.7 cm. wide at the base and may have been 11 cm. long. In another, that may have been almost as big, the surfaces present a banded appearance reminiscent of Eastport chert; this banding, however, is revealed to be purely a superficial modification or patina attendant upon weathering by the fact that the banding is totally lacking at the surface where the object had been broken, where the material is a uniform gray and obviously not anything like Eastport. Thus between manufacture of the artifact and its being broken enough time had intervened to allow the formation of this marked patination on its flaked surfaces, while such patina did not have time to develop between breakage and recovery via excavation, all of which suggests the possibility that the artifact was picked up intact, long after its manufacture, by Late Woodland Indians, then reused and broken. Such reuse can be positively attested for the broken base of a large bifacial fragment—the sharp edges where it had snapped formed a natural scraper, and it was so used until one edge was markedly and smoothly worn away. The other edge seems not to have been used at all. Such extreme wear was seen on only one other scraper from the site.

F. "Others"

The residual category for pointed artifacts, "Others," contains the two knives previously mentioned, a number of enigmatic bifacially chipped items, and the five gravers from the side. The gravers are shown in Plate XXXV. Specimen *b-b'* may well be a reworked point, *c-c'* is otherwise very similar to many scrapers from the site; all the rest have some scraper retouch. Only *c-c'* shows signs of wear.

6.1.3.2 Scrapers

Artifacts with steep retouch in one direction on one or more edges are conventionally classed as "scrapers," and although this term is objectionable because it imposes a function a priori on a formal class of artifacts whose mode of utilization has not been demonstrated, it is embedded in tradition and will be retained here. Scrapers, then, are divisible on the Juntunen site into two major categories. There are, first, the small "thumbnail" scrapers, all very much alike in most respects, usually with steep-angle working eges made on the distal end of thick flakes, with relatively marked "corners" or junctions between edges giving roughly rectanguloid appearance. Then there is a series of what might be called "casual" or "unplanned" scrapers—large, thin, wholly irregular flakes, usually of high-quality smooth and shiny chert, with a centimeter or two along one or more edges retouched steeply. In these scrapers placement of retouched area tends to fall on long, straight edges or on concave edges, and there seems to have been no preference for thick, well-supported edges, the retouch being actually most often on a rather thin edge. In most cases it is difficult to decide whether the "retouch" was deliberate or merely the result of use, but the evenness and nature of the chipping make intentional retouch seem more likely. It is not the kind of chipping resulting from use as knife or saw. This category obviously grades off into "utilized flakes," in which no deliberate preparation is discernible. In terms of what has hitherto been said about flintworking on the site, these artifacts certainly are evidence of the availability of pieces of high-quality raw material larger than were utilized in the bipolar technique, and they were very obviously not produced by a bipolar technique. Since it is hard to see why such essentially scrap material should have been brought onto the site, its existence does not support the hypothesis that scrapers and projectile points, or blanks for them, were produced exclusively off the site. But then they are also relatively infrequent: 245 formal scrapers were recovered as against a total of only 217 other pieces that were "utilized"—this includes the casual scrapers and all other flakes with signs of use.

Some attention will now be devoted to the 245 formally consistent scrapers. A mean length of 2.3 cm. and mean width of 2.0 cm. suggest generally equidimensional outline; thickness has a mean value of 0.5 cm. Weight seemed an appropriate overall measure of size; a histogram and summary statistics are presented as Figure 23, where we see that the modal scraper falls

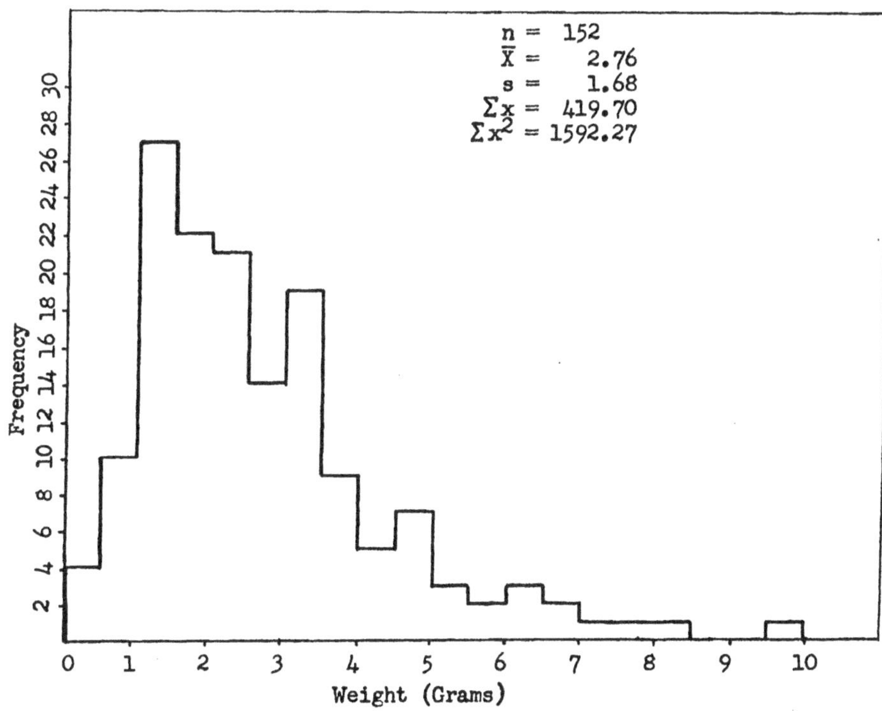

Fig. 23.—Weight distribution and summary statistics for unbroken scrapers

in the 1.1 to 1.5 gm. range, while the mean is nearly 3 gm. Scrapers can clearly be of any size above a certain minimum, but there was a surprising preponderance of small ones, and the fact that they were mostly rather thick, indicating reduction in outline from a much larger flake, indicates that the small size was a matter of preference or end result of resharpening. Only one showed any signs of alteration for hafting, and the generally small size is hard to understand unless most scrapers recovered were items discarded as being too small after repeated sharpening. Regrettably, any scraper resharpening flakes would have passed through the 1/4-inch screen used in excavation.

If the bulbar element is regarded as the proximal end, the overwhelming majority (96) had the distal end retouched; 24, in addition, were retouched on one side, and 19 on distal end and both sides; 27 showed signs of use on an unretouched side.

Scrapers were most often widest at the distal end, and because faces were almost never retouched (except for thinning—10 cases, or obliteration of bulbar complex—18 cases) it may be seen that the flaking scars present before the flake was detached from the core are most often perpendicular to the distal end, or parallel to the long axis of the scraper. Thus they could be described as "end scrapers," but such a description has little meaning, since the mean length-to-width ratio is only 1.1 and a number are broader than they are long, and since evidence is lacking for reduction in length by resharpening.

The main working edge (distal end) is usually straight to gently convex, with very few (5 cases) truly rounded ends. The junction of main working edge with sides ("distal-lateral junction") is generally pronounced, with often a slight suggestion of ears.

Many of these features can be seen in Plate XXXVI, where *a-c* illustrate a typical range of shapes, the most common working ends, and the "ears" mentioned above. Specimens *d-f* are departures from this common pattern: *d* is retouched nearly all around, *e* on two edges plus the special rounded area at upper right, and *f* is retouched on three edges.

Cortex was present on 40 items, roughly one-fourth of the total scraper collection—again evidence not supporting selection against this category of flake for toolmaking purposes. Plate XXXVI, *e*, is basically a "decortication flake."

Every tenth scraper was examined under a low-powered microscope in an effort to determine the way it had been used through traces of wear. Whereas only a few showed no wear or use at all, only two had rounded edges as if used on abrasive but soft materials. The rest displayed minute step-flaking at the working edges, suggesting that these artifacts were used on hard materials and discarded (or resharpened) after only relatively minor wear. This coupled with the already mentioned strong selection for dense shiny cherts, suggests an application for which scrapers had to be very sharp; making bone tools was apparently a major use for them, judging from the many striations, scratches, and chatter-marks on bone artifacts. If scrapers were in fact being used to prepare animal skins at the site, either my examination of them failed to detect it or else other tools were used. No explanation is available for the small size of most scrapers; they would appear to have been inconvenient to hold, yet all indications are to a deliberate reduction in size. Further study along the lines of Semenov's (1964) work may provide solutions to these problems.

Inferences from vertical distribution of scrapers will be considered in chapter 14.

6.2 PECKED AND GROUND STONE

In view of the great quantities of other materials recovered, the paucity of pecked or ground stone artifacts is rather surprising. Only 11 such items were found, and each of them seemed a bit peculiar. These objects will now be described individually.

In Plate XXXVI, *g* is an unfinished celt from F-23, so pertaining to the "A" occupation. It has two flat surfaces, apparently natural, with signs of both chipping and pecking around the edges. Measurements are 10.5 cm. long, 7.3 cm. maximum width, 4.5 cm. minimum width and 2.5 cm. thick. Material is a fairly fine-grained greenish-gray stone.

Plate XXVI, *h*, is a finished adze, broken cleanly across. It is 6.1 cm. wide, and 3.3 cm. thick at its widest point and is of a slightly coarser-grained stone than *g*. No signs of pecking remain. Found in plow zone.

Plate XXXVI, *i*, is the broken end of a crudely bifacially worked object of an iridescent material with some laminar properties. It was worked to size by chipping with no definite sings of pecking or grinding, and is included here largely on the basis of general shape and the non-flinty material of which it is made. Dimensions are 7.5 x 6.7 x 1.7 cm., and it probably pertains to the "A" occupation.

Plate XXXVI, *j*, is an apparently unbroken artifact of roughly quadrangular cross section, with signs of batter or pecking on sides and ends. It is either an unfinished tool or one blunted through use. Dimensions, 6.2 x 3.0 x 2.2 cm.; material, a rather coarse green stone. Found in plow zone.

Plate XXXVI, *k*, is a broken, crudely bifacially-worked tool of a black laminar slatey material, chipped to shape, if that term may be used. Dimensions, 7.3 x 4.7 x 1.3 cm. Not assignable to phase.

Plate XXXVII, *a*, is a red palette from the "personal kit" of Feature 11. It bears stains from the decayed pyrites strike-a-light. It is unclear whether it occurred naturally in this shape or was ground; the only signs of grinding are on one edge. It may have been broken at the left edge but was certainly used afterward, as evidenced by the rounded edges at the break area. Dimensions are 7.4 x 4.1 x 1.2 cm.

The three remaining pecked and ground objects to be described are roughly cigar-shaped, bi-pointed artifacts of approximately quadrangular cross section; two are illustrated in Plate XXXVII, *b-c*. It is tempting to interpret them as net-sinkers, but there is no support for this view. All came from Juntunen Phase contexts. In the same plate, *d-g* are artifacts in the possession of Mrs. John Bible, Bois Blanc Island, collected by her late husband reportedly from the area of their farm, about a mile inland at the west end. Items *d-e*, *g* are pecked and ground cigar-shaped objects very similar to the two just mentioned, while *f* is an adze.

Plate XXXVII, *b*, is of a finer-grained stone than *c*, although both are blue-gray in color. There are signs of pecking on all four surfaces, mostly ground away. Both these artifacts came from the "personal kit" of Feature 11, which contained a mixture of utilitarian and ideological goods.

Plate XXXVII, *c*, has portions of original stone cortex on at least two opposed sides and was pecked, then ground, on three sides. The ends are blunt and do not at all come to an ax-like ridge; there are also no signs of utilization. Dimensions, 8.2 x 2.6 x 2.3 cm.

The third such object from the site (not illustrated) is of a fine-grained reddish stone, with one side still rough but with other sides ground smooth and flat. It came from an unassignable level within Feature 22, so is either "E" or "F" in occupation level.

6.3 HAMMER AND ANVIL STONES

The 20 items in the hammer and anvil stones category do not represent an unbiased sample, since most that were collected during excavation were not recorded; thus correlation with other artifact classes is not possible and statistics are suspect. All can, at any rate, be characterized as being non-spherical, generally with two opposed flat faces. Anvil stones have elongated marks in the center of one or both flat faces; these marks are often discrete, and it is hard to see what other kind of service would have produced them. None of the 20 was solely an anvil stone; all, in addition, had diffuse bruising marks at some spots or areas or all around the periphery indicating use as hammers. About half the collection had signs of use in both ways.

Range in weights of those saved was from 85 to 920 gm. with a mean of 420 gm. There is a hint of a bimodal distribution, with peaks at 100 and 400 gm.

6.4 OTHER USES OF STONE

Other than the deliberately fashioned artifacts just described, stone appears in two other situations that should be mentioned. The first is the frequent occurrence of granite cobbles, invariably split and cracked along planes a right angles to each other. Insufficient attention was paid to them during excavations, perhaps because they almost never occurred in concentrations sufficient to cause comment or in association with other features. While such stones are commonly interpreted as "firestones," the cracking and splitting being considered the result of the heat, it is notable that the "hearths" from the site (themselves rather peculiar) were never filled with or ringed by such stones. Nevertheless, the angularly cracked granite cobbles were not uniformly distributed on the site and certainly were brought to the site by man, hence reflect cultural activity. Specific inferences, however, cannot be drawn from their distribution and abundance on the site.

The other stone occurrence reflecting some sort of activities at the site is the concentration in certain layers—especially XXIV (see sec. 6.2 and Pl. V, *a)*—of dolomite pebbles, ranging in size from about 0.5 to 2.0 cm. The gravels underlying the site contain dolomite pebbles of this size range, but dolomite is of minority occurrence, whereas in the layers under discussion pebbles of dolomite but not of the other stone types occur in a matrix of apparently wind-deposited sand containing artifacts. It is hard to see how the pebbles could have been deposited by natural agency, but no explanation why they should have been brought there by the occupants is available.

6.5 SUMMARY

Two different techniques of stone-chipping can be distinguished. One featured large, flat striking platforms on fairly thick flakes with prominent bulbs of percussion, and removal from block shaped cores. The technique was used at the Juntunen site mostly on Bois Blanc and Eastport cherts, though off the site it was apparently also used to produce, on cores of shiny, high quality chert, blanks to be taken back to the site for making projectile points and scrapers. The other technique is inferred to be one adapted to the utilization of very small glacially rolled pebbles—most not more than three cm. in diameter—that could not be successfully handled by the first technique mentioned. This, the bipolar technique, has a known distribution along the north shore of Lake Michigan between the Straits of Mackinac and Green Bay, places where large pieces of high-quality cherts may have been scarce. The products of the bipolar technique include "gouged-end artifacts" and bladelets; many of the latter may have been used as they came off the core, though my examination failed to yield evidence of such use.

Finished products from the site include notched and unnotched triangular points in shapes much like Late Woodland triangular points in other areas, but characterized especially by the minimal nature of the chipping, which may perhaps be correlated more with the kind of initial blank from which the point was made than with esthetics. Two types were recognized: Juntunen Triangular and Juntunen Notched, there being slightly more than twice as many of the former as of the latter. The only site known to me whose points duplicate those from Juntunen is Pic River (Wright 1966a). The 21 points I examined in the National Museum collections are all fully within the Juntunen-point range in every respect; 13 are Juntunen Triangular and 8 are Juntunen Notched. The unifacial working noted for Juntunen points is also seen in the Pic River ones; only 3 were fully bifacially worked, and 1 partly so. The chert from which they were made included a variety of high quality sorts, with some brown cortex present indicating the cores were derived from rolled cobbles, as were the Juntunen points.

Other point types at Juntunen—most considerably larger than Juntunen points—were present in very minor quantities, and contamination from the partly-overlapping Arrowhead Drive site may be suspected.

Scrapers—nearly all of fine-quality dense and shiny cherts—differed from those found on many Late Woodland sites in their nearly equidimensional outline; they are thus "thumbnail" rather than "end" scrapers. None showed any element to facilitate hafting. Again, the most similar scrapers are those from the Pic River site, although the Pic River scrapers do not duplicate the Juntunen ones as closely as in the case of the projectile points. Whereas almost no Juntunen scrapers were reworked on the broadest or ventral face (the plane of detachment from the core), many of the Pic River scrapers are flaked on both faces, a trait they share with a number of other sites. Again, while Juntunen scrapers cluster fairly tightly about a norm, my impression was that the Pic River ones showed a considerably greater variability.

Pecked and ground stone artifacts were exceedingly rare. There was one object representing the initial stages of making a celt, one tip of a broken adze, several other fragments, and three cigar-shaped pecked and ground objects of unknown function. The latter have not, to my knowledge, been previously reported in literature.

VII

COPPER

7.1 INTRODUCTION

The Juntunen site is the only known Late Woodland station with a fully represented copper manufacturing industry analogous in some respects to the Archaic "Old Copper Culture." A total of 776 pieces of copper were recovered, ranging from virtually unaltered raw material to completed implements, thus constituting the largest collection for any period from any site in the United States, and one certainly unique for its period. No other Late Woodland workshop site has been found to date, and indeed the number of other Late Woodland copper finds is not great, most occurring in the Michigan-Wisconsin area. Copper is virtually nonexistent in New York State in the late period. We may suppose then that the working of copper at Juntunen is a function of proximity to deposits.

Analysis of the copper was performed by Barry Kent and Ronald Vanderwal of the Museum of Anthropology, University of Michigan, who prepared a report (Kent and Vanderwal 1962) that forms the basis of the account given here. Their procedure was as follows:

> The lab work involved both cleaning and the cataloguing of items. Some amount of time was spent on attempting to decide upon categories into which the various types could be placed. There are no previously documented descriptions of Woodland copper upon which the present categories could be based. Thus, the artifacts from the Juntunen site were arbitrarily assigned types on the basis of similarity of appearance and of, at a later date, inferred function. The artifacts were then separated into these various groupings. Frequent dividing, or in some cases lumping, was necessary in order to attain relatively satisfactory groups to work with. . . . This number of types was gradually reduced. . .to a final set of 8 types, which is now believed to be the most parsimonious with meaning, even though in four of these categories, fewer than 6 artifacts are represented [Kent and Vanderwal 1962].

In comparison with the "Old Copper Culture," a prominent feature of the Juntunen copper industry ("New Copper Culture"?) is the diminutive size of both raw material and finished objects. In view of the fact that, disregarding size differences, some of the artifacts formally resemble those of the "Old Copper Culture," an attempt to explain this peculiarity is desirable, particularly since those sources available to the Late Archaic populations and yielding pieces of raw material permitting the fabrication of fairly sizable implements were presumably also available to the Indians of Late Woodland times. Two answers may be suggested: either differences in the source of supply are indicated or else cultural norms, emphasizing small tools, directed the quest for raw materials to a selection of pieces of smaller initial size.

It is evident that copper tools of the Late Archaic duplicate, in many respects, those made of other materials in regions where copper is not available. Thus close analogies with respect to both form and size may be observed between the rubbed slate Laurentian lanceheads and the copper objects of similar form found in Ontario, Michigan, and Wisconsin. Stone objects were large, compared to later times, and copper objects of similar formal description followed suit. A characteristic of late prehistoric cultures in the eastern United States, on the other hand, is a reduction in size of many artifacts. Thus projectile points over a wide area are characteristically small and triangular, and a reduction in size of cores and flakes can also be observed. I suggest that this, and not so much differences in loci of availability of raw material, accounts for the pronounced size difference between Late Archaic and Late Woodland copper industries; corroboratory evidence for this hypothesis is provided by the close stylistic ties seen between Juntunen and Isle Royale in terms of ceramics. Of all areas in the Upper Great Lakes I have examined, the Isle Royale Late Woodland ceramics are certainly closest to those of the Juntunen site at the time the copper-working industry was enjoying its heyday there. Thus there appears to have been no cultural barrier preventing occupants of the Juntunen site from obtaining materials from Isle Royale and forcing them to rely on other sources of supply, such as the small nuggets that are occasionally encountered in glacial drift. That is not to say, of course, that Isle Royale was *the* or even *a* source of supply; Kent and Vanderwal suggest the Keweenaw Peninsula, limited sources east of Lake Superior, and drift or float copper. It should further be pointed out that, as Kent and Vanderwal (1962 n.p.) put it, "there is no genetic continuity between the 'Old Copper Culture' and the Juntunen and other late sites; in fact, there is a 1300 to 2300-year hiatus between the 'Old Copper Culture' and the later tradition."

Why, then, were no large pieces of raw material encountered at the Juntunen site? Why were all fragments, both those derived from working process and the essentially unaltered raw pieces, smaller than any artifact, and why did most artifacts look as if they had been made up of several pieces of copper? I believed a clue may be contained in the work of Tyler Bastian, who found evidence of occupation on Isle Royale from Late Archaic through the historic period but no evidence that pottery-making peoples continued the working of the copper mines opened up by earlier people. Late Woodland people appear to have contented themselves with collecting their copper from places on the island where it could easily be had without laborious mining operations, but subject to the limitation that only small pieces could thus be obtained—no drawback, since the object was not to fabricate large heavy tools anyway.

7.2 TEMPORAL CHANGE

Aside from the stylistic variations in pottery seen to occur through time, perhaps the most striking temporal change during the occupation of the Juntunen site is the fact that copper-working is totally absent from the earliest period and flourishes only in the latest. Again, correlation can be made with the situation on Isle Royale, where the pottery is predominantly of the late end of the Woodland period, corresponding with the Juntunen phase at the Juntunen site. No explanation at all is available for the lack of copper-working in the earlier portion of the Late Woodland period (from about A.D. 750 to 1200) but it is notable that copper-working does appear at the same time that maize became important, ossuary burials appear, settlement patterns changed, and zones of stylistic similarity in pottery underwent realignment. It might be suggested, then, that copper became an item in a trading network that had undergone some rather radical shifting; little evidence is available, however, and the meager evidence from the Late Woodland period in the area does not strongly support the idea of the Juntunen site as the source of manufacture and trade in copper artifacts. Thus at the Dumaw Creek site in Oceana County, Michigan, about 44 beads, 48 hair-pipes, and an ornamental plaque composed of tubular beads were recovered (Quimby, personal communication). This site is 300-400 years later than the Juntunen site. At the Johnson site on Isle Royale, where pottery indicates a date between around A.D. 1300 and A.D. 1650, two smaller copper knives were found (Bastian, personal communication). The Pic River site on the north coast of Lake Superior (J. Wright 1966a) yielded a copper knife similar to one of the Isle Royale finds. The Seul Chois site in Schoolcraft County, Michigan, a site (with Bois Blanc-ware pottery) described by Binford and Quimby (1963) as containing a bipolar industry, also yielded a fragment of a copper knife similar to specimens from Juntunen. Copper awls like those from Juntunen have been found on Summer Island in Delta County, Michigan, again associated with very late Woodland pottery and Oneota-like pottery fragments.

It seems likely, then, that the use of copper in the western Upper Great Lakes area was extensive in Late Archaic times, was in operation, as inferred from occurrence in other areas, in Middle Woodland times (though this is not attested by the meager evidence from Upper Great Lakes sites of this period), and continued sporadically, apparently without the long-distance trading of earlier times, in Late Woodland. The changes in the ways copper functioned in Eastern United States societies throughout the stone-age continuum should be an apt subject for study after better control of the data has been achieved.

7.3 MANUFACTURING TECHNIQUES

At no time is there evidence that copper was reduced from ores, cast, or melted; manipulation involved pounding and, it may be inferred, annealing lumps of native copper. When copper is hammered, it loses ductility, becoming hard and brittle. The temperatures provided by campfires would have been sufficient to restore the metal to the exceedingly ductile dead-soft condition in which copper-working is easiest (almost never encountered in modern commercial copper, such as tubing). On the Juntunen site, occurrences of copper are highly correlated with places where fires had been built, further supporting the theory that the occupants were familiar with annealing.

The basic techniques used in forming artifacts were (1) hammering into shape from solid lumps and (2) rolling into shape from previously formed sheets. The relative frequencies of these two processes are not known, because no artifacts were sectioned for study, and surface inspection was not always adequate for differentiation. From my examination, however, it appears that most artifacts were formed by folding over the material on itself at least once.

The question came up whether artifacts were on occasion made by hammering together discrete pieces of copper. Experiments conducted at my suggestion failed to produce "welding" of copper, even when the pieces were red hot when the attempt to fuse them was made. All these trials were made with industrial copper without using flux, although the surfaces were well cleaned before an attempt was made to join them. It does appear that oxides will prevent at least the kind of copper we used from joining (i.e. in the way that iron can be welded by forging at white heat), at the temperatures available without bellows or other specialized equipment. Occasional small pieces were encountered that had obviously flaked off of finished tools, but here again we probably have the ends of rolled copper sheets.

A nearly complete range in stages of manufacture was recovered. The least finished form was represented by irregular lumps with very rough surfaces and many pits and fissures, lacking surfaces rubbed by contact with other rocks and sand, and with only irregular signs of pounding, so evidently representing occurrences of copper in a rock matrix, pounded only to dislodge the unwanted pieces of rock. Examples of this stage may be seen in Plate XXXVIII, *a, b, c, j*, with *b* being the least finished of the three. No lump recovered was greater than 5 cm. in any dimension.

Pounding and annealing of such lumps, if directed toward the solid-tool process, might result in reject fragments such as shown in Plate XXXVIII, *f, g, h;* if directed toward production of sheet material, *d* provides a good example of success: a fairly flat piece without serious splitting, which after annealing might have been rolled up into some desired tool. Although the welding hypothesis must be rejected, it does seem likely that, in the rolling process, sheets might have been overlapped in the same fashion in which one wraps up a package using several sheets of paper, and if carefully done and well pounded afterward such a "sheet-metal joint" might well prove serviceable. Such in fact seems to have been done; there are a number of broken copper awls that appear to have severed at a joint, where the principle of joining was solely the interlocking of the two sheets during rolling, reinforced by pounding. Plate XXXVIII, *i*, is another example of a fragment of a sheet, probably broken off a larger sheet while being hammered.

The utilization of several sheets to produce a thick object may be clearly seen in Plate XXXVIII, *k*, in which a sheet had been folded over on itself, another slipped in between and the whole pounded flat. Then, beginning at the edges, blows had been directed toward rolling the thickened mass. At the right or pointed end, this pounding had been carried further, and the piece as we have it gives the impression of a failure which had then been subjected to some not empirically useful pounding at one end. This situation is not uncommon with the copper pieces—often the purpose of some of the pounding and shaping is difficult to divine. This is the case with Plate XXXVIII, *f*, a convex coiled object that could not have been designed as a bead yet does not resemble any other known artifact. Here the pounding seems to have been to no useful purpose, but suggests a fit of pique, the play of children with discarded pieces, or perhaps a "whittling" activity. Plate XXXIX, *a*, shows another thick piece composed of one or more sheets rolled and pounded. Here too, intended function is obscure.

A final step in manufacture was frequently grinding, and the resulting striations are visible on a number of flat surfaces. It was often incomplete, so that irregular surfaces remained in areas, as in Plate XXXVIII, *e*, showing a bar made of thickish sheet stock rolled, pounded to shape, and ground. The center portion reveals a pitted appearance, probably the result of hammering with and on stones.

What kinds of tools were used to fabricate the copper objects? For that question no answer whatever is currently available. We were cognizant of the problem during excavation and searched all stones for traces of copper or other unusual indications. While many stones bearing marks of having been used as hammerstones or anvils in flint-chipping were recovered, none of suitable size and material for hammering yet lacking these marks or bearing other marks suggesting use on copper were found, forcing us to the conclusion that either we did not recognize the tools used in copper technology or else the same stones were used for it that were used—concurrently or subsequently—for flint-chipping. No signs of specialized instruments—pounders, grinders, or anything else—were recovered, and indeed there were rather few hearths yielding both copper fragments and hammerstones. So this problem remains unsolved, a situation reminiscent of other lacunae in the archaeological data (i.e. tools for blade-making; pressure-flakers) discussed by Semenov (1964).

7.4 COPPER ARTIFACT TYPES

Kent and Vanderwal decided upon a division of the copper objects into 8 categories, and these are presented with their frequencies in Table 19. All the forms discussed and illustrated so far fall into the "Wastage and Raw Materials" category, of which those in the plates are fairly representative. It can be seen that this category is very much greater in frequency than all the others combined, so there can be no doubt that copper was actually being processed on the site.

Among the identifiable artifacts, the model category consists of pointed objects characteristically square or rectangular in cross section and in some cases pointed at both ends. These, the "awls" of Kent and Vanderwal, range from exquisite and

TABLE 19

COPPER ARTIFACT CATEGORIES AND FREQUENCIES

Categories	Frequencies for All Units
Awls	57
Knives	8
Beads	25
Pendants	2
Triangular points	1
Conical points	1
Other	12
Wastage and raw materials	670
Total	776

perfect specimens up to 13 cm. in length, down to broken, irregular, or bluntly pointed examples, as illustrated in Plate XXIX, *c-h*. In *d-f* the laminated appearance resulting from the sheet method of manufacture is evident. Note that in no cases are such hammer marks visible as could be seen in XXXVIII, *k*; the roughness can probably be best explained as weathering, and any burring or upsetting or the material resulting from hammering was ground off, leaving sharp, right-" angle edges.

No evidence of use was observed on any of the awls. With the blunt-ended ones, it might be supposed that the bluntness resulted from use, but if so no signs could be detected. The size distribution of copper awls, however, is very close to that of bone awls, and it is logical to suppose that the former, possibly hafted, were used as piercers, particularly in the working of skin garments. If they were so used, their sharp edges would certainly have been a useful adjunct to the sharp point in producing holes for lacing. It has also been suggested that they may have been used as fish gorges, but in view of their difficulty of manufacture, such usage seems somewhat improbable.

The eight knives—resembling contemporary "butter knives" and with distinct haft elements—were all similar and like the specimen shown in Plate XXXIX, *b*. The tang end of this specimen was folded back to produce a hooked effect, presumably to prevent its falling out of the hafting arrangement. The edge was ground to a point. All knives lack laminations, hence were made of single sheets. Cautious attempts at bending seemed to indicate that they had been left in the hammered, unannealed, or work-hardened state. Of all copper artifacts, quadrangular awls and the little "butter knives" are closest to the copper tools of 1,500 years earlier. The eight Juntunen knives ranged from 3.5 to 4.0 cm. in length.

The next most common copper artifacts were beads, which occurred in a variety of shapes and sizes, from short and ring-shaped to cylindrical and elongated. There were only two of the former, each less than 5 mm. in length, diameter about 1 cm. There were 22 cylindrical ones, ranging from 1.0 to 4.3 cm. in length. In one case three were found *in situ*, with the thong on which they had been strung preserved by the copper salts. One bead, shown as Plate XXXVIII, *l-l'*, the largest in the collection, might be described as cigar-shaped. All beads were formed by rolling sheets or strips of copper.

Both objects defined as "pendants" by Kent and Vanderwal came from a grave of uncertain date, of the Juntunen phase (Feature 21). They are roughly oval in outline, and each has a small expanding projection. The larger appeared to have had a small cord around its projection. Measurements were 2.7 x 2.2 cm. for the larger, and 2.3 x 1.7 for the smaller. Both were made of thin sheet copper.

The two objects classed as "points" consist of an isoceles triangle 1.8 cm. at base, 3.9 cm. from base to apex, and a conical point 4.8 cm. in length.

The "other" category contained such objects as that illustrated in Plate XXIX, *i*, which is hollow, broken off at the larger end, with a strip twisted back, and folded and bent in at the smaller end as if by pressure. Whether it is a stage of manufacture, a reject during manufacture, the result of individual caprice, or a broken functional artifact cannot be ascertained. The same holds true for the other 11 items in this category.

7.5 DISTRIBUTION ON SITE

The copper industry having been formally described, it remains to discuss its vertical and horizontal distribution. A total of 133 provenience units yielded copper, and for study of distribution artifacts were divided into two classes, "finished" (Kent and Vanderwal's categories 1-7) and "unfinished" (category 8). Analysis by levels, using H. Wright's (1962) scheme, yielded results presented in Tables 20-22.

TABLE 20

DISTRIBUTION OF COPPER-BEARING PROVENIENCE UNITS, BY PHASE

Phase	No. of Provenience Units Containing Copper		
	Finished	Unfinished	Total
Juntunen	8	16	24
Bois Blanc	4	5	9
Mackinac	1	6	7
Unassigned	39	54	93
Total	52	81	133

TABLE 21

DISTRIBUTION OF COPPER PIECES, BY PHASE

Phases	No. of Pieces		
	Finished	Unfinished	Total
Juntunen	22	240	262
Bois Blanc	7	20	27
Mackinac	1	6	7
Unassigned	62	362	424
Total	92	628	720

We see from Table 20 that of the 133 provenience units, 40 could be assigned to levels, and much the greatest frequency (24) belonged to the Juntunen phase. Only seven units from the Mackinac phase contained copper, and each of these units, as seen in Table 21, contained only one piece, which suggests that disturbance of stratification might be a plausible explanation and that in fact no copper at all was being worked in the earliest Late Woodland phases. It is my opinion that the use of copper commenced no earlier than the Bois Blanc phase.

If in the latest or Juntunen phase there are twice as many *units* with "unfinished" as with "finished," there are nearly seven times as many unfinished *pieces* as finished, as seen in Table 21. Both these tables show that a significant rise in production occurred in the latest phase; if four times as much copper appear in Bois Blanc as in Mackinac, the increase, going from Bois Blanc to Juntunen, is by a factor of 10; in addition, the occurrences in Bois Blanc may be partially explained by contamination from later occupations.

The fact that the increase in the Juntunen phase is predominantly in "unworked" is striking. There is a three fold increase in "worked" but a more than ten fold increase in "unworked," going from Bois Blanc to Juntunen, which certainly seems more than a chance phenomenon and suggests either that, as more copper-working was done, the ratio of scrap to finished products increased or else that more finished products were being produced and then shipped out in the latest periods, only the scrap remaining.

TABLE 22

RELATION BETWEEN FREQUENCY OF COPPER AND FREQUENCY OF COPPER-BEARING UNITS, BY PHASE

Phase	(a) No. of Copper bearing Units	(b) No. of Copper Pieces	Column _b_ Divided by _a_
Juntunen	24	262	10.9
Bois Blanc	9	27	3.0
Mackinac	7	7	1.0
Unassigned	93	424	4.6
Total	133	720	(Mean) 5.4

Table 22 summarizes Tables 20 and 21 and presents, in the right-hand column, the ratio of pieces to units for each level. The overall ratio for the site (5.4) is shown in the lower right corner; this is reasonably close to that for the unassigned units (4.6). The most important variations are seen in Mackinac and Juntunen. In Juntunen, more pieces of copper occur in fewer units—that is, units that are not rising in numbers from earlier levels at a rate commensurate with the number of pieces. This phenomenon will be further discussed in Part III, where it will be shown that certain other artifact classes exhibit similar behavior, while others do not. The number of vessels per unit, for example, does not change over time. But copper does, and the conclusion is inescapable that we are viewing an activity reaching a peak at the later levels of occupation, and in particular in the latest occupation, F.

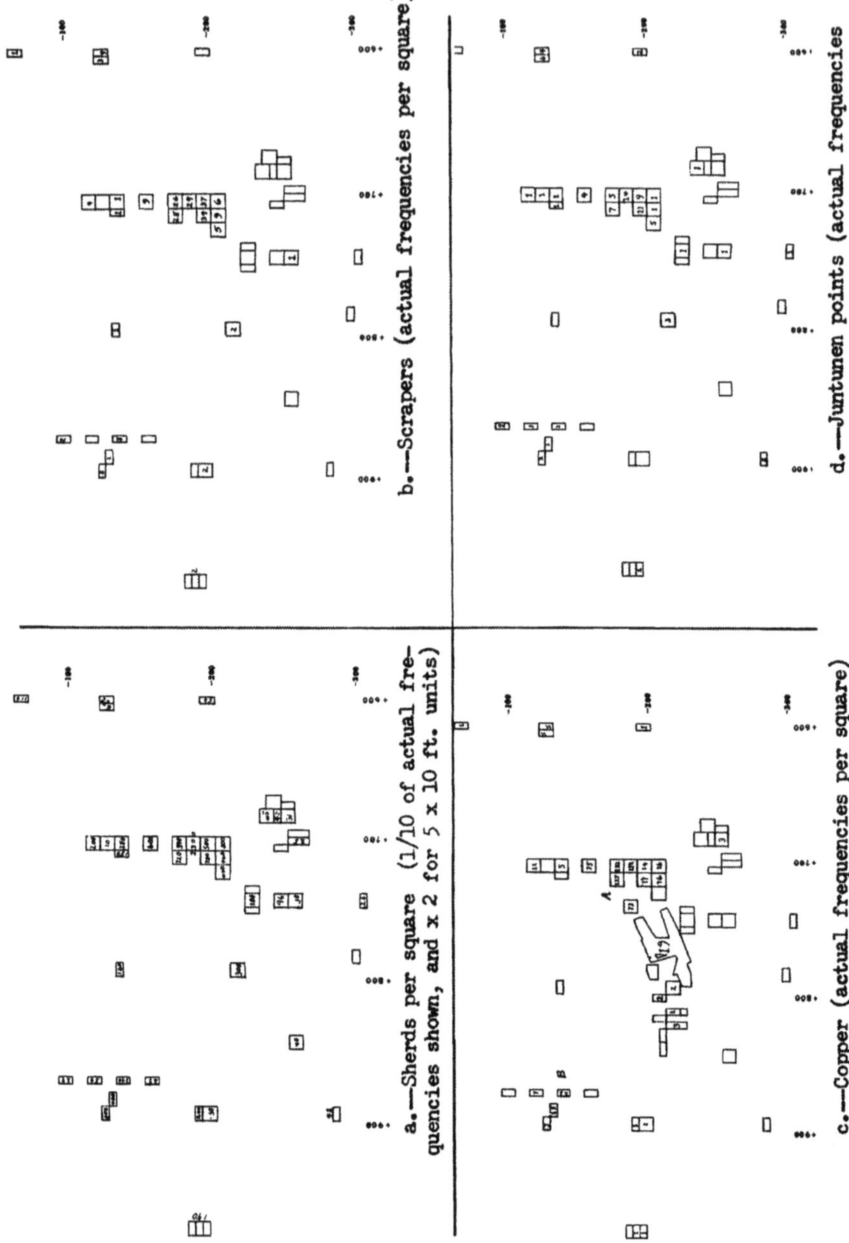

Fig. 24.—Horizontal artifact distributions

The horizontal distribution of copper on the site is shown in Figure 24, *c*, p. 174, where we see two areas of copper concentration, labeled A and B.

Of the two areas, A, an area of immense concentration of all classes of artifact and occupation residues, is much denser in copper, with one square (700-180) containing 232 pieces, almost twice as many as the next densest square (710-180). These facts will be referred to again in the discussion of settlement patterns.

VIII

WORKED BONE

8.1 AWLS

Of the 120 whole or partial artifacts of bone, antler, and tooth recovered, over half (69) were long pointed objects here termed "awls", although they may not all have been used for piercing. These 69 implements can further be divided in half according to material; bird and mammal bones were used in nearly equal proportions. Cleland found that the only identifiable birds and mammals were loon and moose. Plate XL illustrates a fair sample of the awls. In the bottom row, the first two from the left are made of moose bone, while the next two are of loon.

Most items shown in the top two rows of this plate are broken tips, so the impression of an even gradient in size from items only 20 mm. long is inaccurate. The 32 fully preserved awls range in length from 50 to 140 mm. and there is the suggestion of a bimodal distribution with peaks at about 85 and 125 mm. Lengths of unbroken and broken awls are graphed in the accompanying figure. Unbroken awls show a bimodal distribution. The third row in Plate XL contains items of the first modal

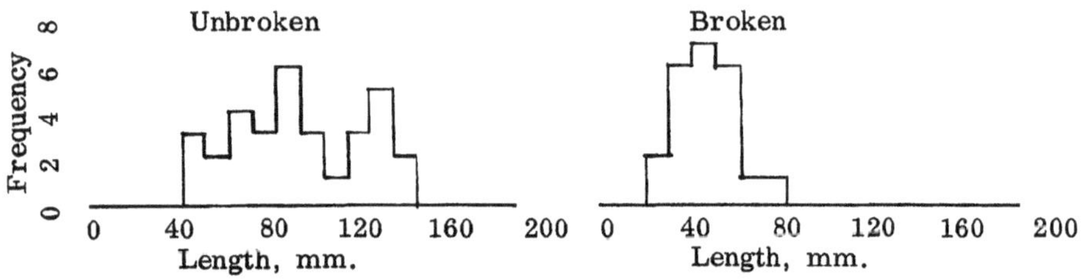

Size Distribution of Bone Awls

category; the bottom row contains most of the items of the second category. The awl on the far left in this row is 176 mm. long, and, because there were three other bone items from this size up to 200 mm. (not classed as "awls" because they were unfinished), the possible existence of a third mode in length is suggested, giving us "small," "medium," and "large" awls, not unreasonable inasmuch as there were probably a number of different operations requiring tools of this sort—piercing skins, sewing, weaving, mat-making, and possibly use as fish gorges. The fact that awls with finished ends ranged down to about 50 mm. (thus well below the first posited mode), while there were few immediately above each mode, might best be explained as indicating resharpening of broken-tipped awls.

Awls of animal bone were often simple splinters ground to a point. In some cases, the shafts were scraped with a hard, sharp tool, either to remove adhering soft tissues or to thin them. Scraping is evidenced by long facets and by "skip" or "chatter" marks normal to the facets, where the scraping tool did not cut smoothly but bounced up and down. If any of the formally defined scrapers were being so used, they must usually have been held with ventral face against the work and pushed, rather than being pulled with distal edge against the work, for most facets on awls were smooth and lacked signs that would have been left by the juncture of flake scars in the form of striations parallel to the long axis, an unavoidable feature of "scraper retouch."

8.2 HARPOON HEADS

The nine partial and entire harpoon heads recovered are shown in Plate XLI, *a-i*. All are unilaterally barbed, thus suggesting more of a link with cultures to the west of Juntunen, such as Arvilla, than with cultures to the east, as New York Owasco (if uni- vs bilateral barbing are functions of style and not utility). All are made of bone from large unidentified mammals, probably moose. In every case, both tip and barb were sharpened. Where the shaft end is sufficiently preserved, a drilled line hole is seen. Notch barbs were produced by a combination of cutting and grinding. The incompleted harpoon head of Plate XLI, *h*, shows that sufficient force was sometimes exerted during the notching process to split the entire shaft. Heads were probably made reusable by sharpening after breakage, as suggested by Plate XLI, *i*.

In view of the indications from faunal remains that fish were a major food item, it is rather surprising that so few fishing implements were recovered. The 134 projectile points contrast in a puzzling fashion with the small total of nine whole or partial harpoon heads recovered at this fishing station, particularly in the absence of evidence of other means of fishing.

8.3 OTHER WORKED BONE

A beaver incisor hafted in the tine of a deer antler was recovered from Feature 45 (Arrowhead Drive phase). Twenty-six other beaver incisors were excavated from Late Woodland phases; most were thinned on the lingual aspect at the proximal end by scraping and/or grinding, presumably to facilitate hafting, although no evidence of hafting was in fact found.

Seven tubes made of bird longbone were recovered. They were open, smoothed, polished at both ends, and had outside diameters between 0.5 and 0.9 cm. An unknown number of others may have gone unrecognized and been classed as "bone fragments."

One bone needle was found. It was made of a rounded piece of mammal bone, 80 mm. from the fairly sharp point to the eye with rounded polished edges, and had broken off at the eye. It is possible, although perhaps not highly probable, that some of the broken "awls" may in fact be broken needles. If so, it is surprising that no other evidence of eyes was found. In addition, most broken awls increase in thickness too rapidly to suggest that they are broken-off needle tips.

There was one antler tine, 104 mm. long; it came from the "personal kit" found with Burial 3, F. 11. A dark material that might be pitch was found at the blunt end, suggesting that the antler may have been hafted, perhaps as a projectile point.

Four pieces had a chisel-like sharpened end and a blunt opposite end with some evidence of pounding. They may have been used as chisels or wedges.

One broken pointed object, 95 mm. long, is shown as Plate XLI, *j*. Its function is uncertain, but its surface illustrates well the mode of working bone: the parallel ridges representing scraping and the "chatter marks" are clearly seen. This object may have been a harpoon-head blank or a matting tool.

Three pieces of bone about 50 mm. long had edges notched at regular intervals, resembling a type of noisemaker. If a stick had been rubbed along the notched edge, a rattle would have resulted, which would have been effective if amplified through attachment of the bone to a resonating membrane.

Two pieces of turtle carapace bore signs of engraving in a pattern that could not be determined. One turtle scute was perforated. These pieces suggest decorated turtle-shell rattles.

Aside from the frankly unidentifiable bone objects bearing signs of working, two of the occurrences of dog and one of eagle may be mentioned. One day (Feature 39) had clearly been butchered; four vertebrae were cut down the middle from the ventral side, after which the vertebrae were broken outward. The head of the femur was cut and split from the shaft; the distal end of a radius also shows numerous knife cuts. A tibia of another dog (40737) bore a number of notches cut or sawed with a stone knife. Some marks may be evidence of removal of soft tissues; a ring of "sawing marks" at about the center of the shaft probably indicates attempts to cut through the bone or weaken it in order to snap it in two. A left eagle humerus (65149), cut 80 mm. from the head, bore similar signs of "sawing marks." The consequent break in this case was a clean one.

In general, nothing unexpected was found in the worked-bone collection, and vertical distribution does not suggest significant variation over time in bone-tool utilization. Perhaps the most difficult fact to explain is the paucity of harpoon heads. The good preservation of many items enables inferences to be made with regard to method of tool manufacture.

IX

ABORIGINAL POTTERY PIPES

9.1 FREQUENCY DISTRIBUTION

A total of 77 pottery pipe fragments were recovered, representing 65 pipes. They were distributed by levels as in the accompanying table.

VERTICAL DISTRIBUTION OF ABORIGINAL POTTERY PIPES

Phase	Number
Mackinac (A-C)	10
Intermediate I (AC-D)	7
Bois Blanc (D)	7
Intermediate II (D-EF)	4
Juntunen (E-F)	9
Not assignable to phase	28
Total	65

I conclude from the table that there is no significant variation in frequency as a function of time.

9.2 FORMAL ANALYSIS

There were no complete pipes and only a few were represented well enough to enable an estimate of over-all shape and size to be made. Most were represented by only one small fragment, so no attempt was made to set up "types".

9.2.1 MACKINAC PHASE PIPES

Seven of the 10 pipes from Mackinac phase levels were represented by stem fragments. Three were rectangular in cross section. Two (41626, 62964) were broken at juncture of stem and bowl, and lengths from end of bit to this point of breakage were 5.5 and 8.5 cm. These two were undecorated, but the third (41404), a 5.5-cm. length of stem with no sign of bowl, was decorated with four parallel incised lines, two on top of the stem and one on each side. In addition, this specimen bore remnants of red pigment, which had apparently been applied not over the entire surface but in lines paralleling the incising. This pigmentation was unique for any ceramic object on the site, although such color was found on some shell beads in Feature 11.

Three stems had an approximately ovoid cross section and were undecorated; the other had two flattened surfaces on top and was rounded on sides and bottom, like the section shown in Plate XXVI, *b*, and the flattened surfaces had criss-cross decoration executed by impression of a sharp-edged tool.

There were three bowl fragments; two are shown in Plate XXVI, *c* and *f*. Note that *c* has decoration with linear cord; *f* is undecorated but has a thickened bowl rim. The third fragment was undecorated.

9.2.2 FIRST-INTERMEDIATE LEVEL PIPES

Levels intermediate between Mackinac and Bois Blanc phase levels and not clearly assignable to either yielded several fragments, two of which are worth discussion.

One stem (41402) was complete to the point where it joined the bowl, a joint evidently poorly made. The bowl should have formed an angle of about 45 with the stem, and the angle was produced in the stem, which curved upward over much of its length. There was no decoration, and the stem was roughly round in section.

The only human effigy from the site was a fragmentary pipe bowl (40818, Pl. XXVI, *a)* recovered in three pieces from three separate provenience units. The well-modeled face, with prominent nose, nostrils produced by punctations, and eyes produced by gashes, is surrounded by a border consisting of an incised line and a row of punctations. The bowl was probably almost square; on the sides are preserved portions of a design with curvilinear elements, produced by incising. The lip of the bowl is decorated with punctates and an incised band.

9.2.3 BOIS BLANC PHASE PIPES

Only two stems from the Bois Blanc phase were sufficiently preserved to warrant description: both were roughly ovoid in section and undecorated. One bowl, illustrated in Plate XXVI, *e*, had bands of cord-wrapped-object decoration. Another bowl fragment, which appears to have been nearly spherical, was decorated by punctates applied in no apparent pattern.

9.2.4 JUNTUNEN PHASE PIPES

Four fragments from the Juntunen phase could be studied. One, a square-bowl "Huron style" pipe drawn in Plate XXVI, *b*, and almost identical with the specimen from the Buffam Street site in New York State illustrated by White (1961, Pl. V, Fig. 4), was decorated by incising on the sides of the bowl and incised nicks on the stem, as well as by deep punctations at the four corners of the bowl. The paste of this specimen was unusually fine compared with the other pipes, and its manufacture and finish were of very high quality.

The second specimen consisted of a bowl and part of the stem. The bowl was undecorated, moderately flaring but not trumpet-shaped, and formed a right-angle to stem, which had a diamond-shaped section with incised nicks along the sides.

The third was a portion of stem with a round section, and the fourth—if it is a fragment of pipe and not a child's pot—is castellated and decorated with punctates in a pattern that could not be reconstructed.

9.2.5 OTHER PIPES

Of the considerable number that could not be assigned to a phase, three bowl fragments are shown in Plate XXVI, *d*, *g*, *h*. The first (65120) has bands of decoration in exceedingly fine cord-wrapped object; the second (40866) has cord-wrapped object plus punctations; the third (41532) has three incised lines.

9.3 TEMPORAL INFERENCES

It appears that a change in popularity of stem cross section from rectangular to oval or ovoid with two flattened surfaces can be seen; beyond this, the sequence of pipe forms corresponds well with that of the Owasco-Iroquois sequence in New York State. It is notable that, whereas incising is almost wholly absent from all pottery at the site, it appears freely on pipes of all periods.

X

POSTCONTACT ARTIFACTS

Materials of Euro-American manufacture are of particular importance in placing postcontact occupations on the site spatially and temporally and in indicating the extent of disturbance of aboriginal deposits. They will be considered first by material, then by distribution on the site.

Pieces of window glass were by far the most frequent material found, followed by metal objects other than nails, as shown in the accompanying table. Some of the metal pieces were quite heavy

FREQUENCIES OF POSTCONTACT ARTIFACTS

Artifact	Number
Window and bottle glass	623
Wire nails (round)	96
Cut nails (square)	91
Ceramics	247
Cartridge cases	6
Clay pipes	17
Metal Buttons	4
Other metal objects	107

and obviously pertained to the logging-camp operations. Of the cartridge cases, one was a ".50-70 U.S. Government," a type introduced in the late 1860's and rapidly superseded; the others were purely modern types.

The clay pipestem fragments were all of the nineteenth century, some stamped "Montreal."

Four metal buttons were sent to Mr. S.J. Olsen for study. He most kindly provided identifications, as follows (the unit numbers are those of excavation units, as in Fig. 4 p. 20):

Unit 32: U.S. Army, Artillery Corps enlisted man's button, 1814-21 period

Unit 32: U.S. Army, Infantry, enlisted man's button, 1816-21

Unit 34: U.S. Army, Artillery Corps enlisted man's button, 1814-21

Unit 33: Sportsman's button made by the Waterville Mfg. Co., in operation in the 1840's.

Unit 32 also yielded one broken gunflint, the only one recovered from the site; Unit 33 yielded two unglazed, fired clay marbles. These data, plus the fact that all but one of the kaolin pipestem fragments came from Units 32, 33, and 34, indicate the presence of an early nineteenth-century occupation at the southwest edge of the site. That this residence should have involved the military is in accord with the known existence of a "U.S. House" on the west end of the island, roughly indicated on the 1839 map (Karpinsky [1931]; see sec. 2.4). A low mound just off the site at the southwest edge, visible in Figure 4 (p. 20) as the farthest left 596-foot contour, may be related to this histori occupation, but it was not investigated during excavations. Material pertaining to somewhat later times, such as most of the glazed ceramics, glass, and iron, do not have this highly localized horizontal distribution but are more or less evenly distributed over the site.

Historic material is naturally heaviest in the plow zone; where it occurs at any depth, it usually corroborates other evidence of disturbance and mixing, The high correlation between presence of historic material in a provenience unit and inability to assign it to a specific phase on the site is indicated in the accompanying table, where the paucity of historic artifacts in assignable provenience units supports the "purity" of units assigned to these phases. Those few "out of place" historic artifacts in otherwise ostensibly undisturbed layers suggest the activities of burrowing animals, a process taking place on the site even at the present time.

DISTRIBUTION OF POSTCONTACT MATERIALS

Phase	No. of Provenience Units Containing One or More Pieces	Total No. of Pieces
Unassigned and Intermediate	71	1,173
Juntunen	5	12
Bois Blanc	2	3
Mackinac	3	3

Further work could be done with the historic materials, especially pipes and glazed ceramics; but it would be of still greater value if done in conjunction with efforts to locate and excavate historic occupations on the west end of the island.

XI

PLANT AND ANIMAL REMAINS

11.1 GENERAL

The study of organic habitation residues is of very great importance in reconstructing cultural activities. It provides information that can be gained in no other way about the technology, including what is generally called "subsistence economy," as well as clues with regard to population size, ecologic and climatologic changes through time, and even beliefs, values, and other ideological elements of culture reflected in differential selection and subsequent treatment of plants and animals. The Juntunen site is of importance in providing "by far the greatest amount of information about prehistoric plant foods in the Midwest" (Yarnell 1964:143).

The utilization of natural resources at the Juntunen site can be regarded as an example of the "inland fishing complex" of Rostlund (1952). The soils and climate of the Canadian biotic province are not well suited for large-scale agriculture. The heavy forests did not support a large big-game population, and the major food resource under these conditions in a land rich in lakes had to be fish. Given the requisite skills and knowledge, fish could be an abundant resource most of the year.

The contemporary plants and animals of the Upper Great Lakes were discussed earlier (secs. 2.1.2, 2.3.3); it may be reiterated that the extensive deforestation caused by lumbering and fire has greatly changed the ecology since prehistoric times; thus for example some animals encountered in the area today, such as deer, coyote, and wolf, are seen archaeologically rarely or not at all.

There is no preserved evidence that any wild plant ever contributed a really important amount of calories to the Juntunen diet. Plant foods were at all times mainly a supplement, although the Juntunen evidence certainly suggests that what was available was eaten. At the edges of the clearing in which the site is located, Yarnell located a number of berry-producing plants growing that were also represented archaeologically; they include bearberry, Juneberry, fire cherry, bunchberry, elderberry, and partridge berry (Yarnell 1964:30). They and other economic plants growing on the island indicate continuity with the archaeological past. Of the plants growing on the site itself, differences were observed between the southwestern and the northeastern halves; on the former, the common milkweed grew abundantly, while the grass cover was short and rather thin, so that "blow-outs" occurred in a number of places. On the northeastern half of the site, milkweed did not occur at all, while the grasses grew more thickly, reaching waist height by the middle of summer. It is difficult to account fully for this difference in terms of observed subsurface features; the grass was thick both in areas with heavy concentrations of habitation residues and on thinly-occupied portions of the backslope zone. It seems possible that variations in the elevation of the water table may at least partially account for the observed marked difference in vegetation.

Perhaps because of the dolomite bedrock deposits and the good drainage in the sand, preservation of bone was good; even fish ribs and scales (at least in the Juntunen phase) were often intact. Efforts were made to collect all occurrences of vegetal and animal remains. Most of the collecting was done either by watching closely while sifting or by bagging unsifted lenses and the contents of pits. Very much material was obviously lost in this fashion. Small seeds either fell through the sifters or else got ground up by the rocks and sherds as the sifters were shaken; it was also easy to overlook small charred particles in black soil. Perhaps the surprising thing is that so much small and fragile material was actually recovered.

11.2 BOTANICAL EVIDENCE

Although samples of palynological analysis were collected from all parts of the site, preparation and study of a few samples by Meredith Black revealed no preserved pollen; further preparation of samples was abandoned. A core sample from a bog about two miles inland from the site was studied by Ronald Vanderwal, but this pollen series cannot be satisfactorily demonstrated to correlate temporally with the sequence at the Juntunen site. In general, the core showed constancy in coniferous elements and a decrease in deciduous elements through time, with a sharp increase in swamp-and-bog elements at the top of the sequence. If this floating sequence is in fact temporally synchronous with the period of Late Woodland occupation, then it would provide independent support for the inferred sequence of ecological changes at the site.

The laborious jobs of analyzing the floral and faunal evidence were performed by Richard Yarnell and Charles Cleland respectively, both then of the Museum of Anthropology, University of Michigan. Yarnell's methodology may be quoted:

Most of the larger plant remains were found by low-power microscopic examination of samples of charcoal remaining after gross sifting in the field. Most of the smaller seeds were located by low-power microscopic examination of the mixed detritus that remained after fine sifting of cultural deposits in the laboratory. Altogether, about 80 lots of identifiable plant remains were located (excluding wood charcoal, etc.) and about 20 lots that included nothing which could be definitely identified or apparently consisted of intrusive materials. Identifications were accomplished by direct microscopic comparisons with check materials which in most cases were taken from living plants, but in many cases archeological remains previously identified by Volney H. Jones were especially helpful.

Of the identified plant remains, 15 are apparently food materials, 2 are weed seeds, and 1 is birchbark which occurred here and there throughout the site. The food remains included kernels of corn, fire cherry pits, pits of one or more other cherries (sand cherry, black cherry, or chokecherry), pits of Canada plum, hazel nuts, bearberries, chenopod seeds (apparently mostly *Chenopodium album*, but one collection appears to be *C. hybridum* var. *gigantospermum* Rouleau), seeds of blackberry, raspberry, etc., blueberries or cranberries, grape seed, elderberry seeds, beechnut fragments, acorn fragments, sumac seeds (probably *Rhus typhina* or *R. glabra*), and pepperroot tubers. The weed seeds are of the genus *Galium* (bedstraw, cleavers), perhaps *G. triflorum* Michx. and a *Rumex* species (dock, sorrel), perhaps *R. verticillatus* L. or *R. orbiculatus* Gray. Altogether there were 153 significant finds of plant remains [Yarnell 1964:34].

Data on plant occurrences are summarized in Table 23. It should be noted that, at the time Yarnell's study of the plants and Cleland's study of the bone were made, relatively few provenience units could be assigned to an occupation level (as can be seen in the totals of Table 2, p. 34), hence the conclusions drawn from the vertical distribution of these residues must be considered tentative. A critical question, the time of introduction of maize on the site, could not be definitively answered at that time. Maize is of particular interest at Juntunen because it represents the northernmost archaeological occurrence, except for relatively late sites in North Dakota. Only kernels but no cobs were found at Juntunen, identified as "early generalized Eastern Complex" by Yarnell (1964:110).

With the completion of the analysis of artifacts and the reduction of the six "occupations" posited by H. Wright to three phases, it became possible to assign many more provenience units. Only in the case of maize have the biotic data been re-examined in the light of these reassignments. From the table on page 189

TABLE 23

PLANT REMAINS IDENTIFIED BY YARNELL*

Plant Remains	Carboniza-tion[1]	Occurrence Number	Occu-pation
Birchbark *(Betula papyrifera)*	N,C	27	A-F
Hazel nut *(Corylus rostrata)*[2]	C	25	A-F
Corn *(Zea mays)*	C	19	A-F
Fire Cherry *(Prunus pennsylvanica)*[3]	N,C	14	F
Blackberry, etc *(Rubus* spp.)	N,C	10	F
Cleavers *(Galium* sp.)	C	7	F
Elderberry *(Sambucus pubens)*	N,C	7	F
Unidentified tuber	C	7	D
Unidentified "large seed"	C	7	F
Chenopod *(Chenopodium* spp.)	N,C	6	F
Bearberry *(Arctostaphylos) uva-ursi).*	C	4	F
Sumac berry *(Rhus typhina?)*	N,C	4	F
Beechnut *(Fagus grandifolia)*	C	4	F
Acorn *(Quercus* sp.)	C	4	F
Pepperroot *(Dentaria laciniata)*[2]	C	3	F?
Cherry *(Prunus* sp.)	C	3	E?
Canada plum *(Prunus nigra)*[2]	C	2	E
Grape *(Vitis* sp.)[2]	C	1	F
Blueberry *(Vaccinium* sp.)	C	1	E
Dock *(Rumex* sp.)	C	1	F?
Total		153	

[1]C=Carbonized; N=Noncarbonized.

[2]Not observed by Yarnell among the contemporary plants of island.

[3]Exclusive of those from rodent burrows.

* based on Yarnell (1964, Table VII).

it may be seen that maize occurs most often, in fact, in the Juntunen phase but that there is one occurrence in the Bois Blanc phase and two in Mackinac. One of the latter is from materials between square sheets 8 and 9 in excavation unit 870-100 (Unit 25 in Fig. p. 20); the other is from Feature 9. There was no sign of later disturbance in either case, and the associated artifacts are solely of the Mackinac Phase. So while maize no doubt first became of consequence on the site only in the last

DISTRIBUTION OF MAIZE KERNELS BY PHASE

Phase	Occurrences
Unassigned	4
Juntunen	11
Intermediate II	1
Bois Blanc	1
Intermediate I	0
Mackinac	2
Total	19

phase, it does appear to have been present from the first.

Some chenopod seeds were found in the residues analyzed, but no grasses and no wild rice. From Table 23 we see that some plant materials, notably maize, hazel nut, and birchbark, occurred throughout the occupations. Birchbark was often found in small squares about 1 x 1 cm., perhaps suggesting plaited baskets. Many other plants occurred only in late occupations—this includes most of the berries and the tuber—which may represent increase in the number of these plants growing around and on the site, differential utilization through time, or differences in the seasons at which the site was occupied. The presence of weed seeds in Juntunen phase units as well as conclusions by H. Wright (1962) indicates that the site was well cleared of trees by this time. No plants occurred solely in early phases, a contrast with the faunal situation.

Yarnell concludes from study of the plant remains that the site was occupied at least from May to October:

> With only four exceptions, the known plant foods represented are available for collection in August. Pepperroot tubers may be collected in April to May, elderberries. . .ripen from June to July, beechnuts ripen from October to November, and chenopod seeds ripen from early autumn to early winter. The indication is that most of the plant remains were deposited during the period of July to September and perhaps from May to October or a little longer. *Galium* seeds are mature during approximately the period of May to October, whereas *Rumex* seeds mature from June to September. . . . It may be that the pepperroot tubers were collected later or that they were stored and used in late summer, but there is nothing to indicate that the Indians were not present on the site as early as May. . . .
>
> An occupation lasting at least from May to October is supported also by climatic data. . . . The average date of the latest spring frost is about May 18 while the average date of the first autumn frost is about October 6. This gives the Juntunen site an average frostless season of at least 140 days [Yarnell 1964:39-40].

11.3 FAUNAL EVIDENCE

Charles Cleland's analysis of a large fraction of the nearly 48,000 (mostly fragmentary) bone remains enabled him to identify 53 species. Table 24 (derived from Cleland [1966, Table 31]) lists these in relative order of abundance and includes estimates of the numbers of individuals represented by the totals shown. Cleland's comments on these estimates may be quoted:

> The number of individual mammals is quite accurate while that of the birds is accurate in most cases. The estimate of numbers of fish are usually very conservative. Although general conditions for the preservation of bone material were quite good at the Juntunen site, the actual number of identified specimens is quite small relative to the total amount of bone. This condition is thought to be a function of both the intensity of occupation and the nature of the bone material. In areas of intense occupation, the bone material was apparently subjected to much trampling under foot. The skull plates of sturgeon, for example, though fairly strong, were fragmentary, seldom being recovered intact. Since most of the bone from the site is fragile fish bone, much of it was fragmented beyond identification. In addition, most mammal bone was probably intentionally broken. . . .
>
> Fish remains make up over 85 per cent of all of the bone material. Of the fish remains, 62 per cent were vertebrae, none of which were identified because they were so abundant that their identification would have taken many months. To these are added the large amount of extremely fragmentary fish bone so that the actual percentage of identifiable bone is very small [Cleland 1966:187].

It will be recognized that the plant and animal remains recovered reflect, not unbiassed samples of the species and their frequencies actually present in the area, but cultural selection on the part of the inhabitants, plus of course the vagaries of preservation, recognition, and collection. Despite these uncontrolled factors, considerable information on habitat and ecology may be derived, and Cleland's (1966) observations and conclusions in these respects will serve as the basis of the following discussion.

11.3.1 MAMMALS

The mammalian fauna is typical of the Canadian biotic province, a zone of transition between the Hudsonian to the north and the Carolinian to the south. Some species typical of the Canadian are nevertheless absent from Juntunen: these are the medium to large carnivores—fisher, wolverine, skunk, red fox, wolf, lynx, bobcat. They were surely present in the area, and in fact are found in other Late Woodland sites; Cleland concludes

TABLE 24

THE RELATIVE REQUENCY OF IDENTIFIED ANIMAL SPECIES FROM THE JUNTUNEN SITE

Scientific Name	Common Name	No. of Bones	% of Total Identified Bones	Minimum No. of Indiv.
Acipenser fulvescens	Sturgeon	888	36.0	350(?)
Coregonus cluplea-formis	Whitefish	262	11.0	119(?)
Castor canadensis	Beaver	245	10.0	46(?)
Haliaeetus leuco-cephalus	Bald Eagle	240*	10.0	12
Canis familiaris	Dog	196	8.0	31
Gavia immer	Loon	75	3.0	20
Stizostedion vitreum	Walleye	61	2.5	14
Ectopistes migra-torius	Passenger Pigeon	57	2.3	17(?)
Lepus americanus	Snowshoe Hare	37	1.5	18
Salvelinus namay-cush	Lake Trout	36	1.5	24
Lepisosteus osseus	Longnose gar	29	1.2	7
Catostomus catos-tomus	Longnose Sucker	28	1.1	7
Tamias striatus	Chipmunk	26*	1.1	8
Peromyscus mani-culatus gracilis	Deer mouse	23*	..9	5
Catostomus commersoni	White sucker	18	.7	5
Perca flavescens	Yellow perch	16	.6	5
Chrysemys picta	Painted turtle	16(?)	.6	6(?)
Corvus corax	Raven	15	.6	10
Cervidae	....	13	.5	..
Micropterus salmoides	Largemouth Bass	12	.5	4
Lutra canadensis	Otter	11	.4	7
Alces alces	Moose	10	.4	7
Erethizon dorsatum	Porcupine	10	.4	5
Meleagris gallopavo	Turkey	10	.4	6(?)
Rangifer caribou	Caribou	8	.3	3
Ursus americanus	Black Bear	7	.3	6
Aplodinotus grun-niens	Drum	7	.3	4
Moxostoma	Sucker	7	.3	..
Micropterus dolomieu	Smallmouth Bass	7	.3	3
Moxostoma anisurum	Silver Redhorse	6	.2	1
Larus delawarensis	Ringbilled Gull	6	.2	3
Branta canadensis	Canda goose	6	.2	4
Anas	Duck	6	.2	..
Clethrionomys gap-peri	Redbacked Vole	5	.2	5
Corvus brachy-rhynchos	Crow	4	.2	2

TABLE 24

THE RELATIVE FREQUENCY OF IDENTIFIED ANIMAL SPECIES FROM THE JUNTUNEN SITE

(Continued)

Scientific Name	Common Name	No. of Bones	% of Total Indentified Bones	Minimum No. of Indiv.
Odocoileus virgin-		4	.2	4
ianus	Deer	4	.2	2
Synaptomys cooperi	Bog Lemming	4	.2	1
Moxostoma aureolum	Northern Redhorse	3	.1	3?
Emus blandingi	Blanding's Turtle	3	.1	2
Ictalurus punctatus	Channel Catfish	3	.1	2
Esox lucius	Northern pike	2	.1	2
Cyanocitta cristata	Blue jay	2	.1	1
Bucephala clangula	Golden Eye	2	.1	2
Passeriformes	Passerine birds	2	.1	2
Bonasa umbellus	Ruffled Grouse	2	.1	2
Tamiasciurus hud-sonicus	Red Squirrel	2	.1	1
Chelydra serpentina	Snapping Turtle	2	.1	1
Ictalurus nebulosus	Brown Bullhead	2	.1	1
Salmo	Salmon-trout	2	.1	2
Hydroprogne caspia	Caspian Tern	2	.1	1
Strix varia	Barred Owl	1	..	1
Accipiter gentilis	Goshawk	1	..	1
Aegolius acadicus	Saw-Whet Owl	1	..	1
Buteo lineatus	Red-Shouldered Hawk	1	..	1
Martes americana	Marten	1	..	1
Ondatra zibethica	Muskrat	1	..	1
Mustela vison	Mink	1	..	1
Ambloplites rup-estris	Rock Bass	1	..	1
Cyprinidae	Minnow Family	1	..	1
Stizostedion can-adense	Sauger	1	..	1
Gallus gallus	Chicken	9	.4	3
Bos taurus	Cow	8	.3	4
		2,469		

*High total bone count due to articulated skeletons of buried or intrusive remains.

that their absence from Juntunen indicates a culturally determined avoidance. The mammalian fauna does not offer much help with respect to the problem of the months during which the site was occupied.

11.3.2 DOGS

Domestic dogs were fifth in frequency among the animal remains from the site both in terms of bones recovered and the estimated number of individuals (31). Dog bones were encountered in all occupation phases of the site, but in only one instance (Feature 5) was there enough bone from one individual for Cleland to reconstruct a complete skull. This was a young animal, intentionally buried.

Haag (1948) found a size gradient in aboriginal dogs, with increase in size from south to north. The Juntunen dogs are larger than either their temporal or geographic position in Haag's study would indicate. They can be considered a very large variety of his Woodland-Mississippian dog, and it is suggested that their unusual size may possibly be accounted for by their diet, which was probably rich in fish offal.

Dogs were commonly eaten by the Juntunen inhabitants. Bones were usually as fragmentary and scattered as those of other food animals, and there is evidence of butchering. Four cervical vertebrae and a femur of a young dog found in a large refuse pit (Feature 39) show knife cuts. The vertebrae were cut longitudinally along the midline of the centrum from the ventral surface, then the rib cage was forced outward to break the vertebrae along the midline of their dorsal surface. The femur shows cuts just below the head suggesting removal of the hind leg.

That dogs were of some ceremonial significance is indicated by the previously mentioned entire dog burial of Feature 5. Other elements in this feature include the articulated burials of a snowshoe hare and a bald eagle. Another instance of the use of the dog in ceremonial activity was the inclusion of the right and left legs minus feet of a dog in the medicine bundle associated with Burial 3 of Feature 11.

11.3.3 BIRDS

The avian fauna is unusual, first, in that for a heavily water-oriented site very few ducks appear—yet they are usually abundant at sites, even those with primary reliance on agriculture. Second, the commonest avian species was the loon, an ordinarily extremely wary aquatic bird. An explanation for these facts will be offered in section 11.3.6.

Many of the other birds are carrion eaters, understandable if the site was, as one may well picture it, usually littered with decaying fish offal and guts.

Clues as to seasons in which the site was occupied are offered by passenger pigeon and Canada goose: juveniles are absent, showing that collection took place in summer and/or fall, but not in spring. The wild turkey here has its farthest northern occurrence, suggesting a warmer climatic period during the Bois Blanc Phase.

11.3.4 EAGLE BURIALS

Cleland's analysis of the eagle remains will be quoted in full.

> Other than the dog and snowshoe hare burial in Feature #5, the only species interred deliberately was the bald eagle. . . .(Feature 5) contained 133 eagle bone fragments from one individual; nearby square 970-200 contained a burial of 24 eagle bones. . . . Feature 28 contained a burial of over 100 eagle bone fragments; in the same square, Feature 13 contained a few eagle remains. Feature 16. . . .also contained an eagle burial which was not recognized as such during excavation. All of these features seem to be associated with cultural material dating no earlier than occupation level C, but most of them seem to be associated with occupation levels E and F. A few eagle bones were apparently not given this special treatment since they appear in the village refuse. The bald eagle does not occur in occupations earlier than level D indicating that peoples of the late occupations made a conscious effort to take eagles and that these birds received preferential burial no doubt in connection with some unrecognized ideological concept. The burial of Feature 28 was that of an adult. The skeletal elements recovered included all the bones of both legs and the wings including the clavicle, scapula, and part of the sternum on the right side, the vertebrae of the cervical region and a few of the distal lumbar vertebrae. The pelvis, rib cage, almost all of the sternum, and the cranium were absent. The differential inclusion of various elements is quite puzzling. The most likely explanation seems to be that an entire eagle was not buried but only the skin containing the more distal elements of the skeleton. This seems to be confirmed by the eagle remains of Feature 5 which contained only fragments of limb elements. All the limb bones of the eagle of Feature 28 were broken and in such a regular manner that it seemed purposeful. These breaks may have been the result of the manipulation of the skin. Another interesting aspect of this skeleton is a partially healed fracture of the distal end of the right radius. This bone was either purposely broken to keep the bird a captive or it was in the process of healing when the bird was captured. Both explanations seem equally plausible.
>
> The other eagle burials contain a few assorted skeletal elements and most of these are far from complete. The general rule seems to have been that eagle reamins were buried. The practice of burying animals other than dogs is quite rare in the northeastern United States. The only other occurrence of an eagle burial in this area was reported by Ritchie (1945) from the late archaic Frontenac Island site. This burial

(Trench 3, Section 1) appears to represent the entire eagle with the exception of the skull. The absence of the skull was perhaps the result of later disturbances.

In square 700-200, the site of the eagle burials of Features 28 and 13, there was small pit at the level of square sheet 10 which contained the proximal end of an eagle humerus which had been neatly cut from the shaft 80 mm. below the head. The object of this cut was probably to obtain the shaft as a bone tube, and the left over end was simply buried. Numerous bone tubes from the site were made of bird bones about the diameter of eagle long bones.

It is interesting to note that there seems to be a special clustering of eagle burials. At least two were recovered in the vicinity of square 970-185 and at least three from square 700-200. The significance of this pattern is open to speculation, but it appears that specific areas were designated for the burial of eagle bones [Cleland 1966:207-08].

11.3.5 REPTILES

Reptiles are represented by three turtle species, again indicating a summer occupation. Turtles were probably collected primarily for their bony carapaces, useful as containers and for making rattles. Some turtle shell fragments were engraved.

11.3.6 FISH

The fish—85 per cent of all bone material—provide good indicators of the seasons of the site's occupation. Sturgeon (the most abundant fish) shows occupation by at least late spring, probably soon after the ice had gone out. Sturgeon is a spring spawner. Whitefish and lake trout indicate occupation to late November or early December (when they spawn); they are available in quantity in shallow waters only in the spawning season.

Some absences from the archaeological record may be noted: bowfin, repugnant, at least to our taste; burbot, spawning January—March; muskellunge, generally rare on prehistoric sites. Many smaller species, and small individuals of the larger species, are absent. This may offer a clue as to fishing techniques. It does not argue for the use of nets: if they had been used, a more representative sample of the total fish fauna should be present. Further, primitive nets might have been impractical for the large strong fish such as lake trout and sturgeon. Finally, no "net sinkers"—grooved stones—were encountered on the site. There is, however, evidence for fish spearing in the harpoon heads from the site. This would account for the large fish. On the other hand, only a few harpoons were found in the excavations; whitefish are very abundant yet not easily speared; large set gill nets are mentioned in most early historic accounts, and the dipnets on poles operated from canoes mentioned for the Sault Ste

Marie region obviously would have left no imperishable evidence. In addition, there seems no reason to assume that all net sinkers must have been specially prepared; a cord can be secured to any stone, so despite the stereotype of the grooved "net sinker" (whose major occurrences by the way are, as Rostlund points out, not in areas notable for either lakes or fishing) the absence of what are commonly interpreted as "net sinkers" need not preclude the use of set gill-nets with floats and weights. Further evidence supporting the use of nets is seen in the observation by Rogers concerning Mistassini fishing practices. After stating that "there appears to be a larger catch of whitefish when three-inch stretched mesh is used, numbers decreasing with all other mesh sizes," he notes that "the longer the net is left untended, the greater is the amount of predation on the captured fish by loons, lake trout, and burbot" (Rogers 1958:141). Thus there may be a causal connection between the unusually high proportion of loons among the avian fauna mentioned earlier and the use of nets, if ways were known to take loons concentrated at nets (and if nets were in fact used).

11.3.7 MOLLUSCS

The molluscs recovered from the site were identified by Barry Miller of the Museum of Paleontolgoy, University of Michigan. They are listed in Table 25 (based on Cleland [1966, Table 36]). Very few came from actual habitation deposits in contexts suggesting use as food, so they were evidently of very little importance as a subsistence item. This is consistent with their rarity on the contemporary beach. Most of the aquatic species came from waterlaid deposits such as the pre-occupation layer I (Table 2, p. 34); most terrestrial species came from the disturbed and redeposited gravels and sands in the vicinity of ossuaries, where they were evidently attracted by decaying organic matter. Nearly all occurrences of the commonest of the terrestrial forms, the tiny *Helicodiscus parallelus*, were recovered amidst the skeletal remains of the ossuaries, particulary Feature 11. Possible causes of their occurrence outside the forest, their natural habitat, will be discussed when the ossuaries are being described.

Cleland comments:

> Most of the molluscs of the Juntunen site are rather common species which thrive under a wide variety of habitats. . . . There are, however, two interesting species both of which are extensively southern. The pelecypod *Elliptio dilatatus* is not common in the northern Lower Peninsula of Michigan, and the most northern record of this species in the extensive files of the Mollusc Division of the University of Michigan

Museum is from Alpena at least 50 miles southeast of Bois Blanc Island. The same situation is true of *Pleurocera acuta*, and the appearance of these species on Bois Blanc seems to constitute or approximate the northern limits of their range. Perhaps, at least in the case of *E. dilatatus*, the Juntunen samples may represent a northward extension during warmer times or relict populations from previous warm periods [Cleland 1966:203].

TABLE 25

MOLLUSCS OF THE JUNTUNEN SITE

Species	No. of Individuals	Per cent of Total Non-exotic species
TERRESTRIAL GASTROPODS		
Helicodiscus parallelus	79	33
Anguispira alternata	32	13
Zonitoides arboreus	25	10
Triodopsis albolabris	19	8
Polygyra	7	3
Stenotrema fraterna	3	-
Polygra albolabris	2	-
Retinella electrina	1	-
Zonitoides nitidus	1	-
Discus cronkhitei	1	-
AQUATIC GASTROPODS AND PELECYPODS		
Unionidae	15	6
Pleurocera acuta	14	6
Goniobasis livescens	13	5
Elliptio dilatatus	11	5
Pleurocera (sp.)	10	4
Ligumia recta	3	-
Ligumia nasuta	2	-
Ligumia (sp.)	2	-
Strophitus (sp.)	1	-
EXOTIC SPECIES		
Anculosa	2	
Prunum apicinum (formerly Marginella)	762	

Shells of two species exotic to the Great Lakes but native to the southeastern states were recovered as beads. Two beads of the freshwater gastropod *Anculosa* and a great number of "marginella" beads (formerly *Marginella apicina,* now assigned to *Prunum apicinum* [Menke]) were found, some of the only evidence from the site suggesting participation in long-distance trade networks toward the south. The molluscs were not analyzed by levels except for the two exotic species; these all came from the Juntunen phase.

11.4 EXPLOITIVE PATTERN

We may conclude that, while many kinds of edible plants were recovered and maize kernels were relatively abundant among the plant remains, animal food and above all else fish was the primary food source. A large variety of species of both plants and animals was exploited as they became locally abundant between spring and late fall. While the site may well have been abandoned in the dead of winter, there is no good reason to believe that it could not have been occupied for the rest of the year. The two fish spawning periods are of crucial importance for hunting and gathering populations in this zone; the early spring sturgeon spawning occurs when other plant and animal resources are most scarce, and the late fall whitefish spawning should have permitted a fish store to be laid in for winter, by drying, smoking, or perhaps freezing.

11.5 HABITAT ANALYSIS

The accompanying table is a résumé of the biotic evidence,

SUMMARIZED DATA ON PLANTS AND ANIMALS

Occupation	Species
F	First appearance of 13 plants (Table 23) and of red-shouldered hawk, bluejay, crow, northern redhorse sucker. Habitat preference is like occupation A.
E	Only appearance of snapping turtle, Canada plum.
D	Only appearance of northern pike, Blanding's turtle, turkey, goshawk, bear, blueberry, "large tuber." First appearance of chipmunk, bald eagle. Rare occurrences: loon, raven, porcupine, red-backed vole.
C	Only appearance of ruffed grouse, deer mouse, cherry. Increase in number of mammal species.
B	Only appearance of freshwater drum. First appearance of deer.
A	Birchbark, hazelnut, maize. Animal species confined to this occupation: channel catfish, saw-whet owl, ring-billed gull, otter, red squirrel. High proportion of fish to mammal species.

showing first appearance of different species. The habitat analysis of the bone from the whole site done by Cleland indicates almost equal numbers of species preferring the Hudsonian, Canadian, and Carolinian biotic provinces, which fits the concept of the area as an ecotone or zone of transition. With regard to local habitats, there is a balance between deciduous and coniferous-preferers, but a strong predominance of species that inhabit either swampy or aquatic environments, which fits the picture of the island, low and swampy over much of its area.

PERCENTAGE OF SPECIES OCCURRING IN EACH HABITAT TYPE CALCULATED BY OCCUPATION LEVEL

	A. Biotic Province				B. Habitat Type					
Occupations	Hudsonian	Canadian	Carolinian	Cosmopolitan	Aquatic	Swamp and Bog	Coniferous	Deciduous	Transitional	Cosmopolitan
E and F	30	26	21	21	17	40	17	4.4	4.4	2
D	25	28	25	20	19	31	16	9.5	4.7	2
B and C	29	26	22	22	22	26	18	18	14	--
A	40	25	15	20	17	48	25	8.5	--	--
All occupations	22	25	22	29	20	33	18	15	7.8	4

Change in faunal frequencies over time is suggested by Cleland. The accompanying table of species percentage, reproduced from Table 29 of Cleland (1966), shows the species grouped by occupation, biotic province, and habitat preference. Figure 25 (p. 200) shows the changes graphically (with the "levels" of Cleland's original Figure 4 adjusted to the "phases" of this report). All changes are rather minor; the biggest change in species-frequency reflecting biotic province occurred between the Mackinac and Bois Blanc phases—the former has more Hudsonian and less Carolinian. Bois Blanc shows an increase in Carolinian, a drop in Hudsonian, and—referring to Figure 25, *b*—a drop in the swamp-and-bog lovers. The Juntunen phase shows a return to the biotic-province conditions of Mackinac, with an even more marked increase in swamp-and-bog at the expense of deciduous habitat preferers. A minor period of increased warmth may be reflected in the Bois Blanc phase; this evidence will be further considered in Part III in connection with artifact frequency changes.

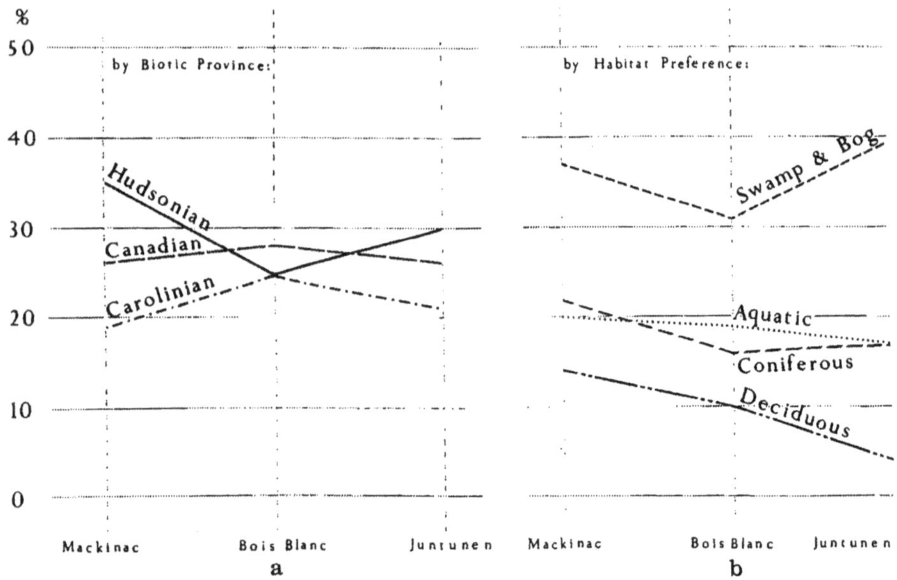

Fig. 25—Percentage of animal species in the three cultural phases (based on Cleland [1966, Fig. 4])

XII

BURIALS

12.1 INTRODUCTION

The burials recovered from the Juntunen site are of particular interest for their information on mortuary practices and religion, for the grave goods, including miniature vessels and a man's personal-effects kit, and for the number of well-preserved skeletons permitting detailed study of human biology.

Sixty-five (and possibly a few more) burials were recovered from seven features* (F. 8, 11, 18, 21, 34, 43, and 45). Most of these were "ossuaries" containing reburials of individuals in various stages of decomposition. Five features with 56 individuals are of the Juntunen phase; one with 8 individuals is of the Middle Woodland Arrowhead Drive component; one is not assigned but probably pertains to the Juntunen phase. Bones representing an uncertain number of individuals, dug by untrained persons at various times prior to the University of Michigan excavations, were also available for study.

Physical anthropological study of the human remains (omitting F. 8 and 21) was done by Charles Eyman and Robert Bettarel (Eyman 1964; Eyman and Bettarel 1965), and their conclusions will be referred to herein.

12.2 OSSUARIES

The survey report by Braidwood (1932) defined what we call the Juntunen site as a mound. He described it as being 25 by 45 feet in plan and 2 feet in height, as having evidences of pothunters' pits in three places, and with sherds and fragments of human bones lying on the surface. From his report, it is clear that the mound he describes is the one indicated in Figure 26.

Excavations were conducted in the mound area during three summers, revealing the mound to contain a number of separate ossuaries. The excavated portions are shown in several figures. All excavated areas appear as Unit 6 in Figure 4 (p. 19); in Figure 26, dashed lines represent Unit 6, and the shaded portions indicate features. Figure 27 presents a more detailed plan of the mound area. Burial features other than those in the mound area are shown in Figure 5 (p. 23).

It appears that the mound no longer has the height of two feet noted by Braidwood but is now lower by one-half to one foot. Its original height cannot be estimated, but it seems unlikely that it was ever of monumental proportions.

* Abbreviation, both singular and plural: F

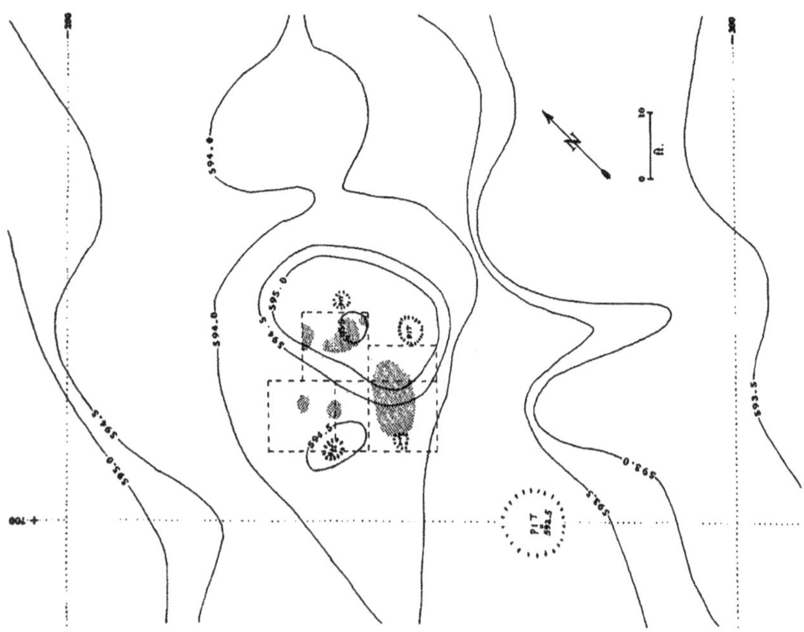

Fig. 26—Topography of mound area (The dashed lines enclose the area shown in Fig. 27.)

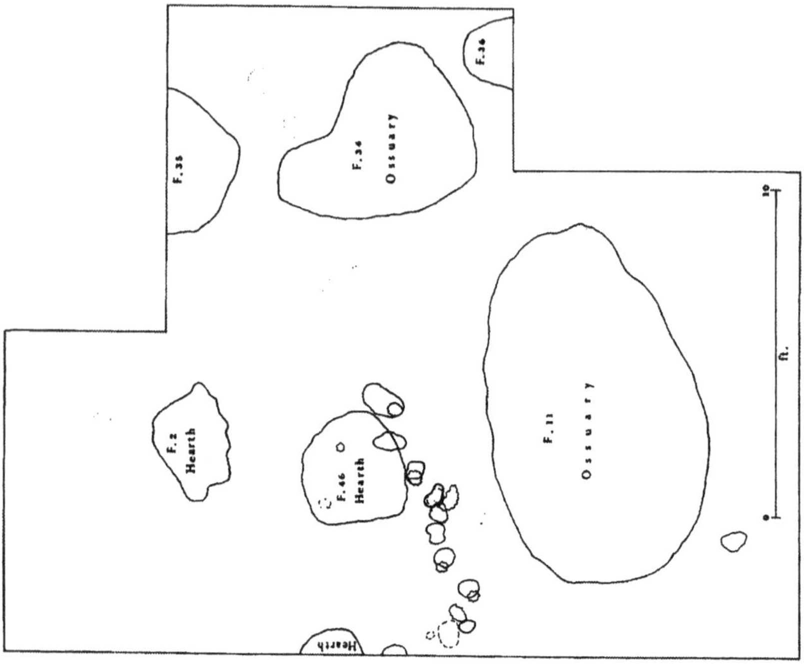

Fig. 27.—Features in mound area

12.2.1 FEATURE 11

Feature 11, excavated at the end of the 1960 field season, was the largest ossuary encountered. It yielded remains of 35 partial or complete individuals, classified as 21 adults and 14 subadults, with three occurrences of grave goods. Excavation and recording were conducted by A.T. Steegman and S. Srikrishen.

A cross section of Feature 11 and nearby areas is shown in Figure 28, from which it can be seen that a pit was scooped out through habitation levels and water-laid strata of sand and gravels, the material removed being deposited nearby, possibly accounting for the tilted lenses of assorted redeposited sands and gravels seen at the left portion of Figure 28 and in Plate XLII, *a*. The black sand immediately overlying sterile sands and gravels pertains to the Mackinac phase by reason of both stratigraphy and artifact content, while the higher lens of black sand with a high frequency of dolomite pebbles seen toward the left of the vertical profile is inferred to pertain to the Bois Blanc phase. The ossuary itself pertains to the Juntunen phase on the basis of stratigraphy, similarity to other ossuaries on the site, and the carbon date of A.D. 1320 ± 75 (M-1188; Crane and Griffin 1963) obtained on charred-bark pit lining. The absence from the ossuary of sherds characteristic of the Juntunen phase, as well as their rareness in the vicinity of the ossuary, suggests that this area was not occupied in Juntunen-phase times. One might suppose it to have been covered by heavy vegetation. On the other hand, the evidence that the mound area was subjected to leveling in historic times may mean that an existing Juntunen-phase occupation layer was simply removed. On the whole, the total absence of Juntunen sherds from the ossuary fill (that yielded 60 sherds representing all other occupation phases) argues for the first hypothesis.

The manner in which the ossuary was constructed was as follows. A pit was scooped out, about 3.5 feet deep and about 3 by 6 feet in plan, and lined with bark fiber (bast?). Eleven highly disarticulated bundle burials were then placed in the bottom, mostly as compact units separated from adjacent bundles, indicating that perhaps each was inclosed in a skin or textile bag or robe. Few were complete skeletons; some lacked the skull, and a few bundles included extra long bones. Articulated elements usually included vertebrae and ribs, feet, and tibia and fibula. A plan of the bottom layer of bones in the ossuary is seen in Figure 29.

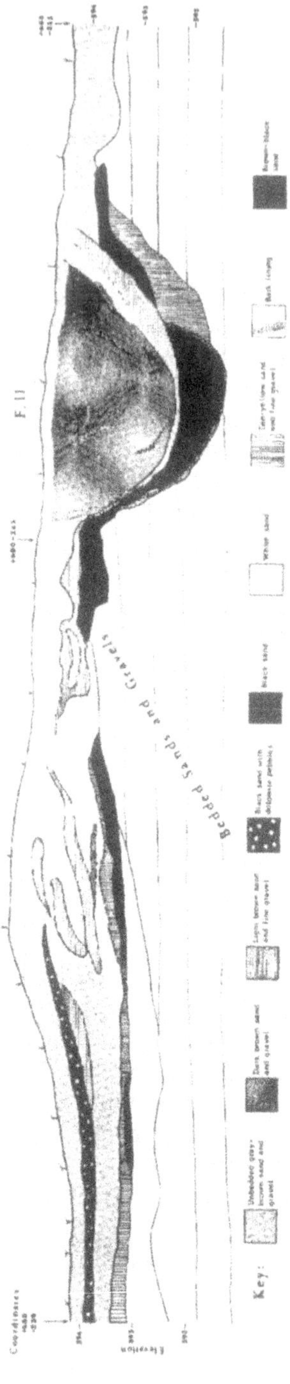

Fig. 28 — Section of mound and Feature 11 along +680 axis

Fig. 29 — Plan of bottom section (Level 3) of Feature 11

After organic matter of some sort had been placed over the bundles (represented by the brown-black sand of Fig. 28), the pit was enlarged somewhat—the walls above the bottom layer become less steep—and some sand was deposited on the burials already in the pit, giving it dimensions in plan of about 5 by 11 feet. Twenty-four more burials were then put in place. There is no indication that appreciable time intervened between deposition of the first set of burials and the remainder, but the two layers are clearly separable on the basis not only of condition of the burials but also the change from brown-black sand to a less dark brown-sand matrix, and there is an intervening sterile layer of light-brown sand and fine gravel—perhaps incidental to the enlargement of the pit.

The 24 burials in the top part of the pit were laid upon, partly separated by, and sometimes covered by, additional bark lining. The last individuals were the least disarticulated. What was then done to finish the ossuary cannot be precisely determined because of subsequent leveling, but it does not appear that anything other than heaping up of backdirt took place. There was a striking localization of odd bits of bone very near the surface (Pl. XLII, *b*); whether this is of archaeological context or the result of subsequent disturbance is hard to say. A pothunter's pit narrowly missed the ossuary at the south end (see Fig. 26). Note that the bone close to the surface, as seen in Plate XLII, *b*, contrasts strongly with the first real burials (Pl. XLIII, *d*) in being a wholly disorganized jumble. Such loose pieces of bone were not recovered from the ossuary fill, and it looks as if the odd contents of sacks and bags had been emptied as the backfill was being replaced. From Plate XLIII, *a*, it may be seen that the bark sheeting began to appear less than a foot below the surface and that it was more than just a pit lining, since such sheets apparently underlay a number of individual burials. This sheeting averaged slightly more than an inch in thickness, and where carbonization preserved the material sufficiently to permit such observation, its fibers were seen to run parallel, showing that it was not a woven textile. Whether the carbonization occurred before the bark was deposited cannot be determined. Where such charring did not take place, the material was reduced to a brown-black humus-like condition. Note in Plate XLIII, *a*, and *d*, that the soil contents of the ossuary at one level range from yellow sand (rare) to a predominant dark-brown sand with gravel. The skulls in *d*, from right to left, are of B. 1, 2, and 3.* Their uppermost

*Burials (abbr.: B.) were numbered consecutively starting with 1 for each ossuary.

point had an elevation of 594.2 feet. Figure 30 is a plan drawing of the top level of undisturbed burials. Plate XLIII, *b*, shows B. 1-3 at the same stage of excavation as *d*, but taken with the photographer to the northwest of the ossuary, permitting the row of postmolds shown in plan in Figure 27 to be seen. Burial 4 appears at the far left. The dark area just to the right of the nameboard is a kit of personal items included with B. 3, making this individual one of the most important items encountered.

12.2.1.1 BURIAL 3 AND FEATURE 10 (PERSONAL KIT)

Burial 3, one of the last to be placed in the pit, was lying on and covered with several layers of bark separated from each other by the sand and gravel pit fill. It was a middle-aged male buried or reburied at such time after death that the extremities had become detached, but those parts with strong ligamentous attachemnt, such as spinal column, legs, and feet, were still held in position. A fairly large plaque of bone had been removed post mortem from the right parietal and squamous region and wás missing from the ossuary; see Plates XLIII, *c;* XLV, *a* (taken after "personal kit" had been removed), LI, and Figure 30. When placed in the pit, the femora were reversed laterally, and the left femur was pushed up into the rib cage, as seen in Plate XLV, *a*, and Figure 30; the pectoral assemblages (minus manubrium, the only missing skeletal part) lay between the feet. Eyman (1964) noted a fair amount of pathology, which in its totality suggested to him aberrant or premature aging.

Directly beside the right ilium (and overlying the displaced left knee joint) lay a tightly grouped collection of items, designated as Feature 10, of which some were utilitarian and some evidently related to religious beliefs and practices. An over-all plan is seen in Figure 31. Plate XLIII, *c* and *d*, show the kit in association with B. 3; Plate XLIV shows two stages in dissection of the feature. Plate XLV, *a*, was taken after the kit had been completely removed. From the close juxtaposition of most of the items, it can be inferred that the collection had been held together by a container and deposited as a unit with the individual. It presumably represents his personal kit of tools and "medicine" items.

An inventory of included objects is provided in Table 26; most of them are also pointed out in Figure 31, reconstructed from photographs and the (unfortunately inadequate) field sketches.

Most prominent at the top of the kit was a brown iron oxide mass. The presence of a piece of spongy-looking stone (Pl. XLVI, *k*),

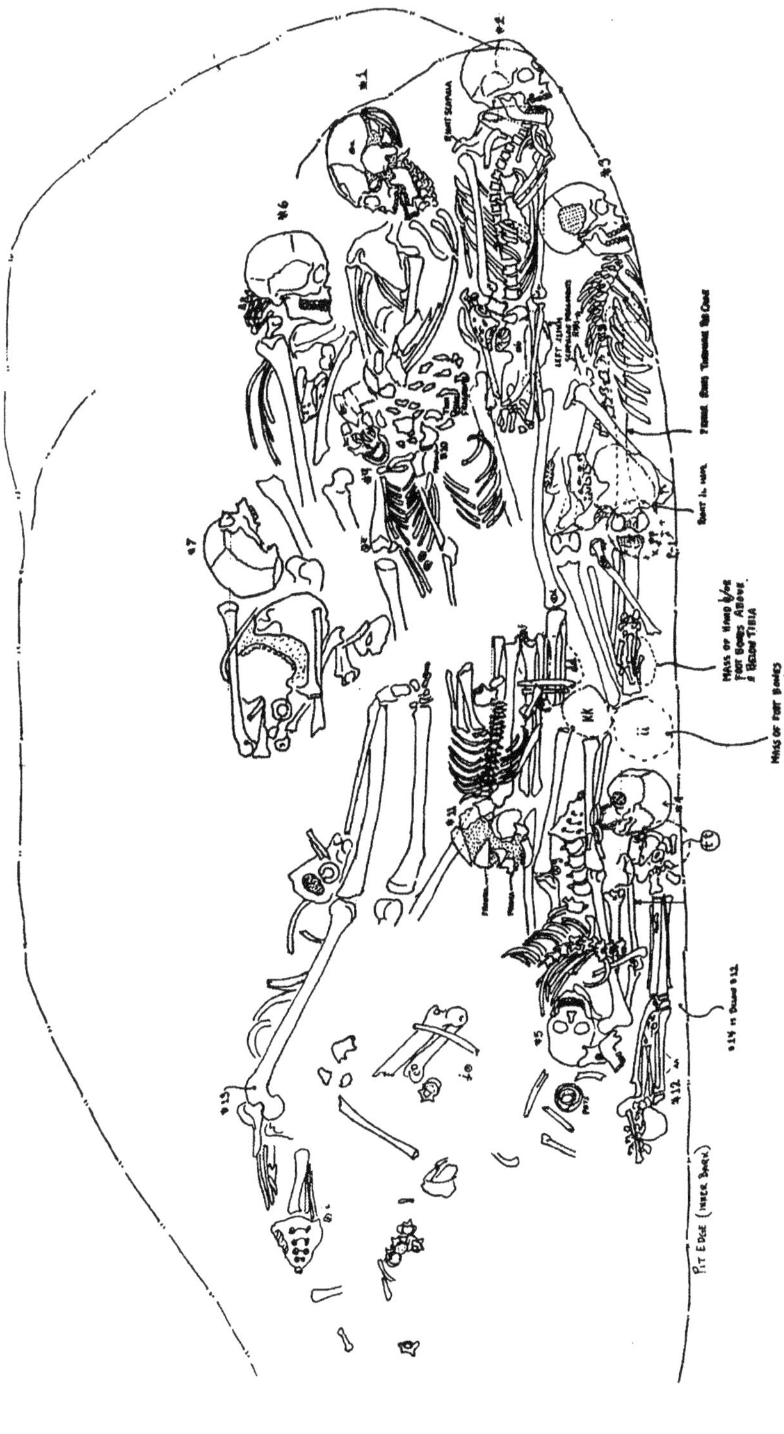

Fig. 30— Plan of upper level of burials in Feature 11
(Scale: 7/8 inch = 1 foot)

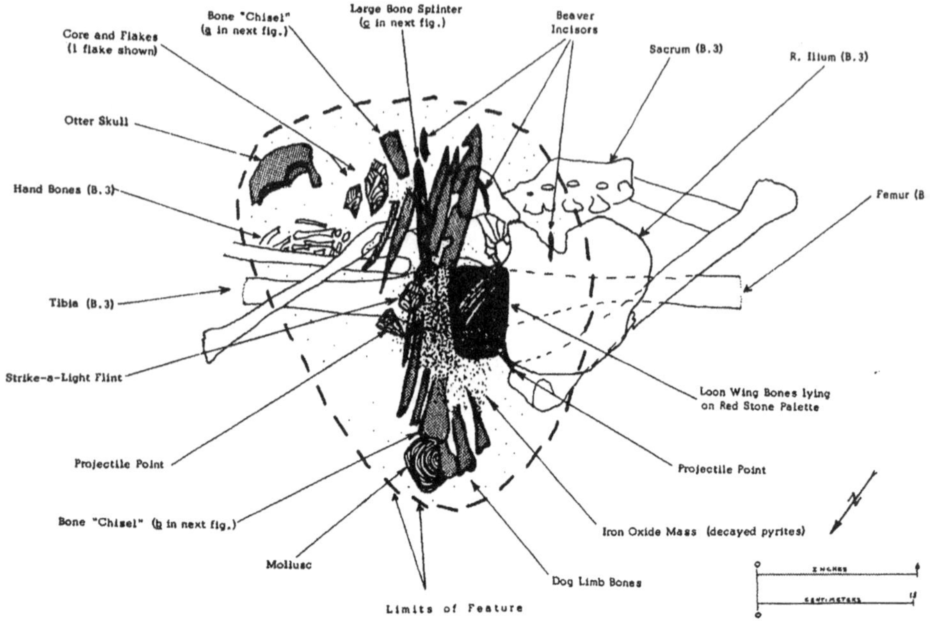

Fig. 31— Feature 10, personal kit associated with B. 3, F. 11

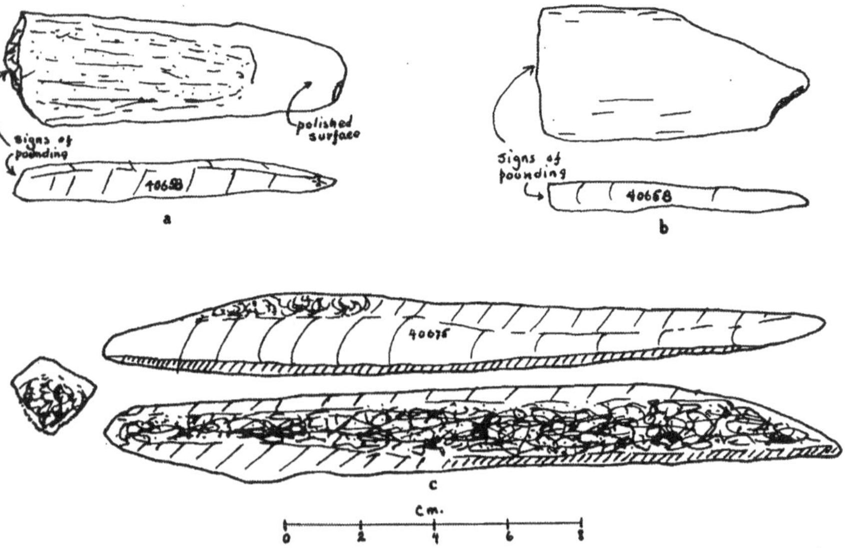

Fig. 32— Some bone artifacts from F. 10

constituting the remnant from within whose interstices something had disintegrated, and the presence of a heavy flint flake with abraded edges (Pl. XLVI, *j*), amid the mass of "rust", indicates that this set was an iron pyrites/flint strike-a-light. Similar fire-making equipment has been recovered from other sites, notably from New York Owasco stations.

TABLE 26

FEATURE 10: PERSONAL KIT INVENTORY

Strike-a-light oufit, iron pyrites and flint (40664)
Red stone tablet or palette (40654; Pl. XXXVI, *l*; described in sec. 6.2.)
Two Juntunen points, unnotched (40653; Pl. XLVI, *l-m*)
Two cigar-shaped ground-stone objects (40655; Pl. XXXVII, *a-b*; described in sec. 6.2)
Three cores and 13 flakes (40656, 40657)
Copper awl (40663)
Pair of shells of a lake mollusc (*Elliptio Dilatatus*)
Otter skull and baculum (40662)
Three harpoon heads (40659; Pl. XLVI, *a-c*)
Two large bone awls (40661) and two small awls (40660, Pl. XLVI, *f-g*)
Two flat wedge-shaped bone pieces (chisels?) (40658; Pl. XLVI, *i*; Fig. 32, *a-b*)
Large bone splinter with polished tips (40675; Fig. 32, *c*)
Antler tine (Pl. LV, *h*)
Six beaver incisors (Pl. XLVI, *d-e*)
Two pairs of loon wings
Four legs minus feet of a dog
Tibia of a snowshoe hare
Parasphenoid of an extremely large sturgeon
Twined fabric (Pl. XLVI, *o*)
Mole skin with fur (Pl. XLVI, *n*)
Misc. pieces mammal and fish bone

The red stone tablet (pl. XXVII, *a*), previously described in the stoneworking section (6.2) bore no signs of use but would have been suitable for grinding and polishing bone tools and was even thin enough to have been used in finishing the notches in harpoon heads. On top of it and generally underlying the strike-a-light were the loon-wing bones. From their articulated position it can be inferred that the wings included skin and thus probably feathers when deposited.

It is notable that the majority of objects lie approximately parallel to each other, indicating that the container for the kit was oblong.

The three harpoon heads (Pl. XLVI, *a-c*) make up a third of the total recovered from the whole site. All are in rather poor shape, in contrast with most bone from the site. The high frequency of harpoons here plus the fact that a number of items—the red stone tablet, strike-a-light, bone "chisels," otter skull, cigar-shaped ground-stone objects—are unique or nearly so for the site suggest that, while some of these items may have been in every man's kit, they were essentially "unexpendables" or items carefully preserved against loss or damage.

Uniqueness cannot be attributed to the chert cores and flakes (none showing bipolar technique), which could have come from anywhere on the site. Their presence seems to indicate that irregular flakes were frequently needed and were ordinarily carried about. These were fishing folk, and perhaps the kit included items needed in a boat, so such "scrap" had to be in one's kit.

The pair of mollusc shells may have been utilitarian—perhaps used as tweezers—or ideological, but the dog legs, loon wings, otter skull and baculum, and gigantic sturgeon parasphenoid can hardly have been anything but "medicine." It is notable that the dog, while a food animal, was also buried, apparently in a ceremonial fashion. Feature 5 consisted of burials of a dog, a snowshoe hare (note the tibia of a snowshoe hare in F. 10), and an eagle. One might almost ask why no eagle remains were present in the personal kit!

Notable artifact absences from the kit include pottery and scrapers. This suggests that scrapers might have been used primarily by women. The four awls—two short and two long—plus the large bone splinter (Pl. XLVI, *i*) with polished tips, the antler tine, and the copper awl, on the other hand, suggest that, assuming that garments were made by women, these pointed tools were also used by men, and the making and repairing of nets immediately comes to mind. It is of course also possible that the pointed-end items (apart from the large single-ended awls) were used as fish gorges.

Evidence as to the nature of the container of all these items was provided by materials preserved through contact with metallic salts. Plate XLVI, *n-o*, shows the preserved fragments of twined fabric made of twisted fibers (though quite unlike the twisted fibers seen in cord-impressed pottery) lying next to the skin and fur of what microscopic examination of the hair revealed to be a mole (an animal not otherwise recorded archaeologically from the site). It appears, then, that a twined bag at least partly lined with moleskin was the container for the kit.

If such personal kits were possessed by all men, then the question arises why this adult male was the only individual buried with his. None of the included items in the kit suggests a status symbol or ornament, nor does any of the "nonfunctional" items suggest an unusual concern with the supernatural, hence there is no evidence that the individual was of different status (e.g., shaman) from the others. His manner of burial, also, did not depart from that of the others. On the other hand, the pathologies suggesting "aberrant or premature aging" to Eyman (1964) and making this individual almost unique might be construed as indicating qualities sought for in shamans. The question simply cannot be definitely answered.

12.2.1.2 BURIALS 1, 2, 6, 7, 9, and 10 (Top Layer, SW 1/2)

Burials 1 through 3 and 6 were oriented similarly at the same level with heads against the south end of the pit; the first three were also among the best preserved in the feature. All were classed as males.

Burial 1, a young adult male, was the only complete and fully articulated individual, hence perhaps a primary burial. The skull is seen in Plate LX. His health at death was good except for dental pathologies. As shown in Figure 30 (p. 207) and Plate XLVII, across the lower part of his body were laid two children, B. 9-10. The sex of the children, as with all children from the site, could not be determined.

Burial 9 (under five years) was missing a few bones, although not the ones expectable through disintegration, and, as evident in the plate, there was little disorientation of the limbs. Burial 10 (under three years) lacked a number of bones, and most of those preserved were badly fragmented, but the indications again are of a primary interment. The positioning of these two children on top of B. 1 certainly suggests close kinship.

Burial 2 was a middle-aged male in nearly complete articulation (Pl. XLV, *b*). There was evidence of bark at the pit edge above and below the skull and below the postcranial skeleton. The part of the body above the pelvis rested on the left side of its back. The right scapula was situated under the neck in such a way that it cut through the inferior angle region of the left scapula, perhaps the result of tight binding of the arms to the body before burial. There was post-mortem plaque removal from the left temporal (Pl. LI). Pathology is present in the form of spondylolisthesis of many vertebrae.

Burial 6 (at the top of Pl. XLVII, *a*) was an elderly male, perhaps the oldest individual from the ossuary, with plaque removal from the left parietal and squamous region (Pl. LI). Although complete except for patellae (missing in almost all individuals), the burial was deposited in a considerably disintegrated form, as evident from Plate XLVII and Figure 30 (p. 207). He had lost only one tooth ante mortem, and exhibited no significant pathology.

Burial 7 (next to B. 6), a young adult male, was again a confused mass of bones, with mandible, left scapula, sternum, patellae, and most ribs missing. The cranium is shown in Plate LI and can be seen in Plate XLVII, at top left in *a* and at the top in *b*.

12.2.1.3 BURIALS 4-5, 11-14

The burials discussed so far formed the top layer in the right half of the pit as viewed in Figure 30 (p. 207). They occurred in substantially one level, suggesting that, before they were deposited, a separate layer of fill and bark had been prepared for them. In the other half of the pit, however (the left half as seen in Fig. 30, Pl. XLVII, *b*, and Pl. XLIX; the right half as seen in Pl. XLVIII, *a*), the burials do not appear to have been laid on a prepared floor but rise toward the end of the pit. The appearance of this other half at the time the first burials were being uncovered is seen in Plate XLVIII, *a*, while XLVII, *b*, and Figure 30 show the uppermost set of burials. Plate XLIX shows a slightly later state of excavation than XLVIII, with B. 2, 3, and 6 removed.

Burial 4 (Fig. 30 and the face-down cranium at bottom right in Pl. XLVII, *b*,) was a middle-aged male with extensive dental abscesses and a "fracture-like oval depression just above the lambdoid suture at about the midpoint on the left side of the skull" (Eyman 1964; cf. Pl. LI). Missing parts were the right scapula, the innominate, fibulae, patellae, sternum, and sacrum. Immediately to the left of this skull is the top of a bundle of bones (B. 27; marked at *tt* on Fig. 30, p. 207) extending to the bottom of the pit, evidence that the filling of the ossuary occurred as a single operation.

Burial 5 was classed by Eyman as a young adult female. A plaque had been removed from the right squamous and parietal region of the cranium. Other than that, the individual was complete except for the patellae. Eyman observed fungoid excrescences on very many bones and suggested subperiosteal osteomyelitis as cause. On the left side of the skull, on the zygomatic arch at about the zygion and just left of the external auditory meatus, and again on the temporal bone, were observed several roughly parallel and mostly vertical cuts. They suggest slashing of the left side of the face; if post mortem, perhaps this was to detach the mandible. It is notable that such marks are wholly absent from the right side—the side from which the plaque was removed. (The marks do not show up well in Pl. LI.)

About 6 inches to the northeast of the skull were found two miniature vessels, seen *in situ* in Plate XLVIII, *b*, and after repairs in Plate XXIV, *b-c*. The smaller of the two, made in an Oneota pattern, was strikingly similar to a vessel from an Oneota intrusive burial in the High Island Mound, Minnesota, that I saw in the collections of the Department of Anthropology, University of Minnesota. It was upright and contained nothing but fill identical with that in the surrounding area. The somewhat larger second vessel, of a "Woodland" style and certainly showing nothing of the Juntunen-ware tradition, had been inverted over the first.

Burial 11, marked with a small tag on the shattered skull in the center of Plate XLVII, *b*, was a child ten to twelve years old. The trunk, pelvis, and femora were in articulation. A number of parts were missing: scapulae, clavicles, left radius and ulna, the tibiae and fibulae, sacrum, and patellae. Although most children were found placed in direct contact with an adult in the pit, the association of this child with any other burial is unclear.

Burial 12, shown in Figure 30 (p. 207) between B. 5 and the edge of the pit, actually lay somewhat lower than B. 5. It was highly disarticulated and lacked skull, scapulae, right clavicle, left humerus, right radius and ulna, sternum, sacrum, and patellae. Immediately below B. 12 lay B. 14 (cited as "13a" by Eyman and Bettarel [1965]), classed as a middle-aged individual of indeterminate sex. This was a fairly incomplete burial, lacking mandible, left scapula, right clavicle, left humerus, radii, right ulna, right innominate, left femur, most lower leg and foot bones, hands, ribs, sternum, sacrum, and patellae. Despite this incomplete condition, the spinal column and remaining pelvic parts were in articulation, as were the right femur, tibia, and fibula.

Burial 13, a middle-aged individual of indeterminate sex, is partly visible in Figure 30 (p. 207) and Plate XLVII, *b*, and was articulated except for joints of limbs to trunk. Only the sternum and patellae were missing. Considerable pathology was observed.

12.2.1.4 BURIALS 15-23

The interments just considered were from the left half of the pit as seen in Figure 30 (p. 207) and were the uppermost in that part of the pit. To regard those now to be presented as occurring in a separate "layer" is an oversimplification resulting from the necessity of recording the burials in two-dimensional form on paper. In fact, however, the only genuine stratification in the pit was between the burials in the black sand at the bottom and those in brown sand and gravel above, with a layer devoid of skeletal material intervening. It should be understood that what we are dealing with in the portion of the pit above the sterile layer is a continuous and non-stratified deposition of burials, with each burial (or a group of them) separated from the rest only by what is inferred to have been sheets of bark fibers. Recording such a three-dimensional feature was a continously vexing problem, particularly since the first burials encountered were not the very uppermost and there was often no clear separation between individuals. Making drawings of the skeletons as they appeared, including elevations, was extremely tedious and time-consuming, yet the photographic techniques at our disposal and known to us seemed inadequate to record everything that needed to be recorded. Much was learned from this ossuary, and in the second year field techniques were improved as the result of experience both in the field and in the laboratory. The second year, each bone was numbered in ink as it appeared, and both drawings and photographs were made with these numbers included so that later the position of any bone could be verified. The successful use of this technique is illustrated by Plate LIII, particularly *c*.

Burial 15 (Pl. LI) was a young adult male whose third molars were but recently erupted. Pathological conditions noted by Eyman indicate an aplastic right hip. A plaque had been removed from the left frontal and parietal region. The individual had been placed extended and supine, although a number of skeletal parts were missing—left scapula, clavicles, five cervical vertebrae, some ribs—and most vertebrae were displaced. The excavator noted that the hands were placed in the pelvic region, apparently passing under and cradling the considerably disarticulated but nearly complete ten-to-twelve-year-old individual placed between the legs of B. 15. It may be noted that this is the second young male found extended supine with immature young placed on top of him.

Immediately underlying Burial 14, but in uncertain association, was found an incomplete immature individual, B. 17. The cranium and mandible were missing, as also were the left scapula and clavicle, ribs, a lumbar vertebra, sternum and patellae. It had been placed with the humeri shoved up in the rib cage and with the fibula and articulated tibia in the pelvic cavity.

Burials 18 and 19 were children younger than ten years, laid next to each other. Roughly between them, thus making it difficult to determine with whom it is associated, lay a band of *Prunum* ("marginella") shell beads, each pierced for attachment. The shells can be seen in Plates XLIX and L, *a*. The portion of the ornaments visible in all these photographs measures about 4 by 11 inches, and about 75 shells can be seen. When fully excavated, the ornament proved to be about 6 inches wide and 15 inches long and consisted of a double thickness of shells that had evidently originally been sewed to a garment or piece of fabric. Nearly 700 beads in all were recovered. A pink color was observed on many of them, suggesting that they had been dyed or painted.

A number of skeletal parts were missing from B. 18 and 19, indicating burial in a highly disarticulated condition. A still greater degree of decomposition is seen in B. 20, a middle-aged female from whose pathological condition a subperiosteal involvement, probably osteomyelitis, is inferred by Eyman. Major parts missing include cranium and a number of vertebrae. Burial 20 can be seen as the parallel bundle of long bones at the far left in Plate XLIX.

To the right of Burial 20 in the same plate is shown the crushed cranium and a number of ribs of B. 21, a child under age eight. Unusual for the site, both patellae were present, although a variety of other skeletal parts were missing.

Burials 22 and 23, located approximately in the center of the ossuary or southeast of B. 21, were children under age five, both lacking mandibles as well as other skeletal parts. They constitute the last burials recovered before the sterile layer separating the top and bottom section of the ossuary was encountered. It can be observed that the deeper down one goes, the greater the degree of decomposition at the time bones were deposited, until, in the bottom section, individuals are encountered all of whose non-osseous parts were gone when they were deposited.

Most of the remaining burials are shown in Figure 29 (p. 204) and Plate L, *b*, where they can be seen to lie at the bottom of the pit, on the black pit lining (presumably decayed bark). Burial 24 (labeled "25" in Plate L, *b)* and Burial 25, above and slightly toward the center of the ossuary and not shown in either figure or plate, were middle-aged females, neither showing significant pathology. Plate LI includes the skull of B. 24. Both had many missing parts, and B. 24 had many fragmented bones. Apparently associated with one of them, although not recognized during excavation, were bones of a fetus.

Burial 26/27 was another middle-aged female, placed in the pit in two bundles. (In the field it was thought to be two individuals, hence the two burial numbers.) It will be remembered that the bundle of long bones, placed vertically along the northern edge of the pit, extended upward to the top level of burials. Except for clavicles and patellae, it was complete.

Burials 28 and 29, on the southern side of the pit, were middle-aged individuals of indeterminate sex, both lacking cranium and mandible as well as many other parts.

Burials 30 and 31, on opposite sides of the pit, were children aged twelve to fourteen and under five, respectively. They were found in relatively complete condition.

The remaining four burials were middle-aged and of indeterminate sex. Burials 32 and 33 lacked cranium and mandible and many other parts; B. 34 consisted of only six bones; B. 35 consisted of a leg and hand and foot bones; and B. 36 consisted of two tibiae. These last three were classed as separate individuals in the laboratory but were not recognized as such in the field.

12.2.1.5 SUMMARY DATA ON FEATURE 11

Burial number 8 was not used; 26 and 27 were one individual; and the fetus was not numbered in the field. The resulting total of 35 can be broken down by sex and age as follows:

Age Group	Sex		
	Male	Female	?
Old	1		
Middle aged	3	4	9
Young adult	3	1	
Teens			1
Prepubescent			8
Infants and fetus			5

Conclusions from study of the skeletal material will be deferred until the other burials from the site have been presented, but certain special features of F. 11 may be discussed at this point.

The pit was clearly in two parts: a lower pit containing bundles, separated by a sterile layer from a larger upper portion containing less decomposed burials.

With regard to condition at time of deposition, the entire range from loose bones to fully articulated individuals is present;

although, at most, only two specimens failed to reveal some dislocation that cannot be attributed to settling of the ossuary pit. The least decomposed individuals occurred at the top of the pit, are mostly males, and constitute four of the five cases of plaque removal as well as the most prominent pathologies. The most decomposed occurred as bundles or disjointed articulated subunits toward the bottom and are mostly subadults and females. This apparent patterning by sex suggests that a factor governing the decision to prepare an ossuary might have been the recent death of a number of adult males of the group.

Both individuals buried with children laid on their bodies in such a way as to suggest close relationship were extended burials of young adult males. Other than avoidance of the prone position, no clear pattern with regard to burial position could be observed.

Individuals buried with artifacts include a middle-aged male (personal kit), a young adult female (miniature pots), and a prepubescent (shell ornament). Thus no pattern or correlation of biological data with inclusion of grave goods can be seen, except insofar as all three cases occurred toward the top of the pit and involved fairly recently deceased persons.

One peculiarity of the ossuary is worthy of note. Great quantities of the tiny terrestrial gastropod *Helicodiscus parallelus* were recovered from among the skeletal remains of F. 11 and the other ossuaries. This species is rare on all other parts of the site. Since these animals are inhabitants of moist forests, not grassy meadows or low bush, one may well inquire how their shells came to be deposited where they were found. On the basis of evidence suggesting that, particularly in the Juntunen phase, the site was not wooded, the probability that the snails naturally occurred in that area seems remote. Further, snails are not known to burrow, yet a great many were found in the ossuaries, in nearly every case in close juxtaposition to skeletal material. The most likely answer seems to be that the snails were brought onto the site along with the individuals that were being buried, and herein may lie a clue to the disposition of bodies between death and secondary reburial. If deceased persons were placed in the woods—on scaffolds, protected inclosures on the ground, or perhaps in trees—until the time for an ossuary ceremony, snails adhering to individuals not fully decomposed would have been brought onto the site with the individuals, and their presence in the ossuaries would thereby be explained.

Feature 11 yielded the most information of all ossuaries excavated, and it was thought worthwhile to devote considerable attention to it. The remainder of the burial features will be treated in somewhat more summary fashion.

12.2.2 FEATURE 34

Just north of Feature 11 (see Fig. 27) was another ossuary, F. 34, that contained eight burials. It was encountered at the very end of the second field season, but was excavated under the direction of Charles Eyman during the course of the brief third summer's work. Its uppermost part occurred at an elevation of 594.8, only 0.3 feet below the surface, and like F. 11 it could not be tied to a habitation layer, but but belongs to the Juntunen phase and is probably approximately contemporary with F. 11. The ossuary cut through a habitation layer of the Mackinac phase, to which the postmolds of Figure 27 (p. 202) belong. At 594.8 feet the tops of a group of large erratic boulders began to appear along with red ocher smears, flint chips, burned fragments of mammal bone (not identified), 14 shells of *Elliptio dilatatus* (the mollusc common on the contemporary beach)—all in a tan gravelly sand matrix that contrasted with the surrounding sand, which was similar in texture but gray in color. These signs of ceremonial attention after completion of the burials contrast with the absence of such indications in F. 11. No human bone fragments were encountered above the burials (again unlike F. 11), although such fragments were encountered close to the surface in an area about three feet distant (where no feature lay below).

The glacial erratic cobbles, shells, and other items ceased at 593.4 feet, when the actual pit outlines in the form of a jet-black lining, preserved as bark by partial charring in places, began to appear. At this point the outline of the oval pit was about 4.5 by 6 feet. Then at approximately 592.8 feet the ossuary proper began to be seen together with more large stones. The appearance of the upper burials is shown in Plate LII, *a-b*.

Burial 1, a female aged sixteen to twenty years, is seen in the foreground of Plate LIII, *a*, and (minus head) at the far left in *b*. As shown in Plate LI, a plaque had been removed from the left side of the head, The trunk was articulated with head, and the limbs were disarticulated from the body. Burial orientation was with head to the south, as with many individuals, notably the top interments, from F.11. A large erratic lay over the lower femur and upper spine. Only the left clavicle and right humerus were missing. No artifacts were found, and the snail shell in the left ocular orbit seems purely accidental.

Burial 2 was classed as a middle-age male. His cranium is the only other case of plaque removal (Pl. LI) from this ossuary. He is also the only individual from the site the cause of whose death is known: a small triangular projectile point was embedded in the centrum of his second lumbar vertebra, clearly having passed through the viscera from the front. Lack of any bone response indicates that death must have resulted. His cranium can be seen in Plate LII at the far left in *a* and at the top in *b*. His state of articulation was reported as being greater than that of B. 1, but orientation was again with head to the south. Only the femora were missing.

Burial 3 was a child of less than three years, buried somewhat below and to the northeast of B.2, extended on its back as a flesh burial.

Field notes and other records were evidently not kept for the remaining five burials; their disposition is therefore unknown, and all that can be done at this point is to present a table summarizing the laboratory findings.

FEATURE 34

Burial No.	Sex	Age	Plaque Removed	Missing Parts
1	F	16-20	X	L. clav., R. hum.
2	M	Middle	X	Femora
3	-	under 3		
4	M	Middle		(Much fragmentation noted)
5	-	12-14		Head, shoulders, feet
6	-	5-8		All but cranium, parts of trunk
7	-	5-8		Mandible
8	-	Infant		

No artifacts are reported for F. 34 other than the projectile point in B. 2. A sketch profile of the ossuary indicates a dark-brown layer lining the pit, so the use of bark both as lining and to separate burials seems to have occurred here as it did in F. 11.

12.2.3 OTHER FEATURES IN THE MOUND AREA

The presence of other ossuaries in the mound area is known from the material removed on earlier occasions, from descriptions by local people of various pothunting explorations, and from pits observed by us from which fragments of human skeletal material could be picked up. The area thus was certainly a focal point for burial activities in the Juntunen phase, but, as will be indicated shortly, burials were not restricted to it. Other features shown in Figure 27 (p. 202) include three hearths (F. 2, 46, and an unnumbered hearth), an apparent row of postmolds, and F. 35-36. All but the last two pertain to the Mackinac-phase occupation; F. 35-36 are probably of the Juntunen phase but were pits of gray and devoid of artifact content, and their function was not determined.

The only other ossuary excavated that closely resembled the two previously discussed occurred at some distance from the mound area.

12.2.4 FEATURE 18

Six individuals were reburied in an ossuary designated F. 18, located in the central area of the site in square 710-210. It lies just outside the rows of postmolds pertaining to the "longhouse," F. 22 (see Fig. 36, p. 234). Because the tops of both postmolds and ossuary were lost in the plow zone, it is hard to determine which has the temporal priority, but, since the edge of the pit comes within a foot of the outermost row of postmolds, it seems unlikely that the pit and the house were contemporary. One post mold appears on square sheet 3 at 0.8 feet below the surface, a depth at which the top of the pit is not yet apparent. Seven postmolds plus the pit appear only 0.1 foot lower on the next square sheet; one possible postmold appears to intrude slightly on the edge of the pit. If these bits of evidence are taken at face value, then the house is later than the pit—though this might mean no more than 50 years.

The maximum dimensions of F. 18 were about 3 by 5 feet, with the long axis parallel to the major surveyed axis of the grid system, meaning that this ossuary departs from the north-south orientation pattern seen in F. 11 and 34. Maximum depth was about one foot. The tendency toward parallel disposition of remains is seen in Plate LIII, in which four stages of excavation are shown. Another point of departure from the pattern of F. 11 and 34 is the absence of any indication of bark lining for the pit or as containment of the burials. There was also, in general, greater disarticulation with this ossuary than was observed with the previous two; F. 18 might be said to resemble most the bundle interments at the bottom of F. 11. Thus, although some articulated subunits—for example, spinal columns (Pl. LIII, *b*)—were intact, there were no cases of entire torsos in articulation.

Burial 1 was an elderly male, the bundle seen most to the left in Plate LIII, *a*. A rather small plaque had been removed post mortem from the right temporal region (Pl. LI). Except for the missing left ulna and the (almost always absent) patellae, the individual was complete, although highly decomposed. Articulated elements included a radius and ulna and the vertebrae. The mandible was broken, and charring was observable on both parts of it.

Burial 2, an elderly individual of indeterminate sex, likewise had a plaque removed from the right temporal, as seen in Plate LI. Missing portions were left clavicle, left radius, innominates, fibulae, sternum, sacrum, all vertebrae, hand and foot bones. This burial is just to the right of B. 1 in Plate LIII, *a*, and was in a virtually complete state of disarticulation.

Burial 3 was a male aged eighteen to twenty, with plaque removal this time on the left side (Pl. LI). The skull is visible as the one numbered *16* lying near the top in Plate LIII, *b*, and in greater detail in *c*. Only the clavicles, left radius, sternum, and hands and feet were missing, but the burial was almost completely disarticulted.

Burial 4 was a child of less than three years, unusual among the child burials on the site for the advanced extent of disarticulation, indicating that by exception it had received the same prior treatment as adults. Only a lower arm was intact. Missing parts were clavicles, sternum, sacrum, and vertebrae. Field notes mention that a few shell beads were found in the vicinity of this individual.

Burial 5 was a fetus lacking only left femur and tibia. It is perhaps to be associated with B. 6, a middle-aged individual of uncertain sex, present in only fragmentary form: right humerus, ulna, and innominate; femora; right tibia and fibula. If association with B. 6 is incorrect, then the specimen must represent an abortion or premature birth. No estimate of age from conception was made.

In general, it was noted that relatively less fragmentation of bone was present in this ossuary compared with the others. A few pieces of bark were observed by the excavators at one edge of the pit, but the great amounts of lining as used in F. 11 seemed to be lacking (see Pl. LIII, *d*, for pit bottom; compare with L, *b*). Considerably fewer snail shells were observed than in F. 11, a circumstance probably to be attributed to the fact that there was little flesh remaining on these specimens at the time of their deposition in the ossuary. Individuals here were not separated by bark as was the case for F. 11, nor did it appear that they had been wrapped as units and deposited as such. The evidence of ceremonial attention in the form of heavy stones and red ocher, found in F. 34, were also entirely missing in F. 18. The temporal relationship with F. 11 and 34 cannot be determined, although there is little doubt that all three pertain to the Juntunen phase.

12.2.5 FEATURE 8

Feature 8 was an ossuary (not mapped in Figure 4) located about 20 feet southeast of Unit 12. It was uncovered by Mr. Juntunen during bulldozing operations and partly removed by him, then later examined and completely excavated by Dr. J. B. Griffin and party in 1959. The skeletal material is discussed by Eyman (N.D.) in a manuscript in the files of the University of Michigan Museum of Anthropology. Eyman noted the following sex and age distribution.

> Crania and cranial fragments indicate that adults are 7-8 in number, probably 8. Two are definitely males, two definitely are females, two are possibly males, and the remaining two are possibly females. The definite adult males seem to be 25 plus and 45-50 years old. The two definite females are 25-28 and 30-35 years old. There were two children, both possibly males [Eyman N.D.].

Dr. Griffin noted the presence of tree branches and part of a log in the pit, all in fairly undecayed state (much fresher than the wood from F. 21), and Eyman noted cranial deformation and extreme tooth wear—absent from the other burials at the site—all of which suggest a date considerably later than for the other ossuaries. On the other hand, the feature was definitely an ossuary like the others, and both Mr. Juntunen, who initially uncovered the ossuary while bulldozing, and Dr. Griffin, who was present only after part of it had been removed, noted bark lining and wrappings, elements observed in the other ossuaries. No artifacts were found. Excavations conducted later in the general area of F. 8 attempted without success to locate a habitation layer that could inferentially be tied in with F. 8.

12.3 BURIALS OTHER THAN OSSUARIES

12.3.1 FEATURE 21

Unique for the site in being the only single-individual burial and in having a peculiar manner of interment, F. 21 consisted of semiarticulated portions of a child in a pit originally covered by a log roof. Two photographs of the pit and its burial (at slightly different stages of excavation) are shown as Plate LII, *c-d,* while Figure 33 is a cross section made at approximately the plane of the wooden support (constructed during excavation) shown in Plate LII, *d.* Portions of the collapsed log cribbing

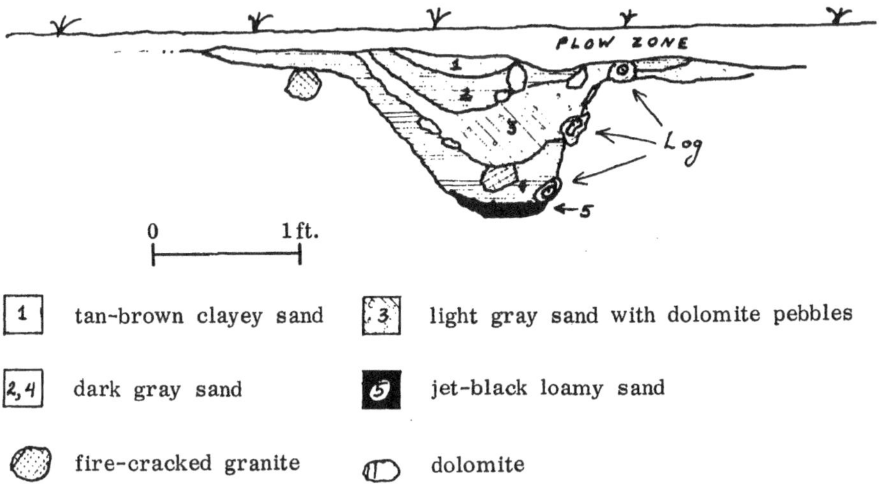

Fig. 33—Profile of Feature 21

were observed at elevation 595.3 feet, close to the surface; the over-all depth of the feature was 1.2 feet. Its dimensions in plan were 3.6 by 2.5 feet, with the long axis pointing a few degrees east of north.

The burial lay in and upon the layer of jet-black loamy sand (5 in Fig. 33) that probably represents decay products of either burial or pit lining. Above it can be seen four layers of earth that filled the pit upon collapse of the log roof.

Although the skeleton was not studied by Eyman, field observation indicated a child of less than five years, at least partly articulated when buried, laid on its right side and partly flexed. The disorientation of many parts is plausibly explained on the basis of disturbance resulting from later invasion of the pit by rodents and from collapse of the wooden roof. The position of the logs can be seen in the photographs and figure.

Artifacts were recovered from all layers within the pit, but the presence of actual grave goods could not be demonstrated. Other than the general habitation debris, such as chert flakes, animal bone, charcoal, and small sherds, layer 2 (Fig. 33) contained a heavy concentration of artifacts, including 25 pieces of copper. Most of it was waste, but there were three awls and one bead. The fact that this square and the one adjoining (700-180) yielded most of the copper from the site suggests accidental intrusion as the explanation. Other artifacts recovered from layers suggest continued utilization of the ground above the pit. As seen in Figure 36 (p. 234), the pit intrudes on postmolds pertaining to the longhouse (F. 22) so it may be concluded that the pit was dug when the house posts were no longer standing.

The remarkably good state of preservation of the log roof—the wood was soft but maintained much of its structure—contrasted with the absence of similar wood from other archaeological contexts (the fresh wood from F. 8 is undoubtedly intrusive) and suggests a very recent date for the feature. In an effort to recover early historic goods such as seed beads and French vermilion, sand from the pit was fine-screened, but with negative results. The sherds are typical Juntunen-phase types—although it should be remembered that most should have fallen into the pit at a later time. It will be noted from Figure 33 that layers 2-5 are truncated by the bottom of the plow zone; the feature therefore preserves layers not present as such on most of the site, where they are compressed into the upper half-

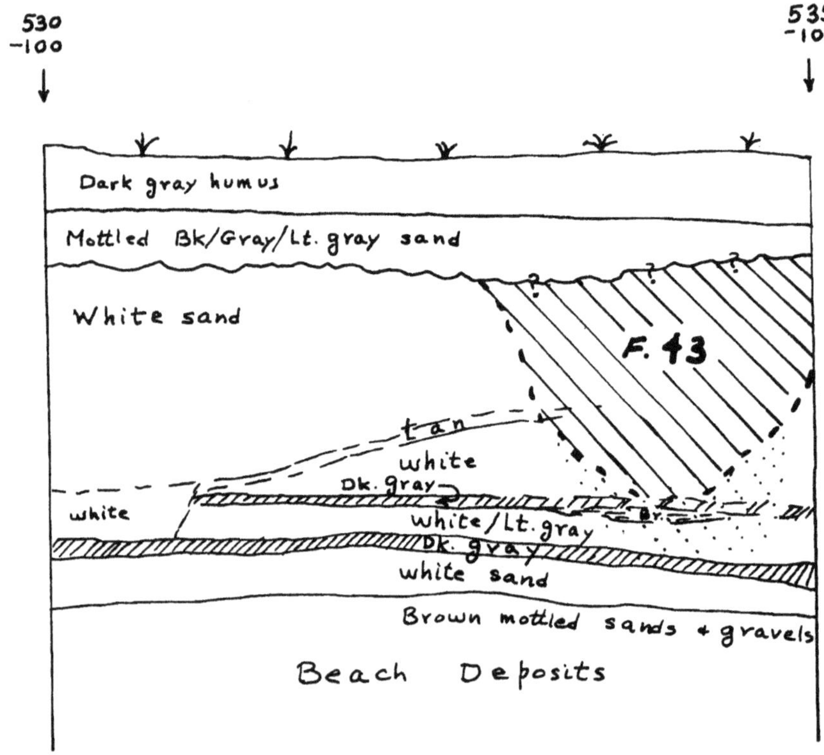

Fig. 34.—Profile of Feature 43

foot or so of deposits. In view of this situation it is of interest that no postcontact material occurred, which certainly supports a prehistoric date for the feature. If this is the case, however, then the wood preservation is unusual, and a date at the very end of the prehistoric period seems most probable.

12.3.2 FEATURE 43

Further indications of Juntunen-phase burial practices are provided by Feature 43, a pit that contained six fragmentary crania, only one of which had appreciable postcranial remains associated with it. The feature was located in square 530-100, shown as Unit 2 in Figure 4 (p. 20), and was excavated during the brief third field season.

A profile of the pit and strata into which it cut is presented as Figure 34, from which it can be seen that the pit was dug from the approximate level of the mottled sand underlying dark-gray humus. The mottled sand bore artifacts of the Juntunen phase, and the form of its juncture with the underlying white sand suggests a meadow-soil formation. The maximum dimensions of the pit in plan were not recorded but may be estimated as about 4 by 5 feet on the basis of the plan drawing of the burials in the feature, Figure 35. Maximum depth of the feature was about 1.6 feet.

The pit fill was evidently somewhat darker than the surrounding white sand, but there was no evidence of bark lining, although bark fragments were reported as encountered in excavating. Plate LIV, *a*, and Figure 35 illustrate the dispostion of materials.

The burials appear to have formed substantially one layer, and those lying below the level of most of the rest are indicated by dotted lines in Figure 35. In the same figure, widely spaced dots surround Area "A", distinguished from other areas in the feature and outside it by the mass of rootlets with which the bones were entangled.

No pattern is apparent in the way the bones were placed in the pit, nor were there any articulated elements other than foot bones of B. 2. The only articles other than the bones were four fairly sizable rocks, a potsherd, a bone awl, and a mammal bone.

Burial 1, a prepubescent, consisted of cranium, left humerus and radius, innominata, and some vertebrae and ribs. The cranium was in two pieces, the calvaria and facial portion at the bottom of Area "A" (Fig. 35), the basal portion nearly two feet away, at the left of Area "A".

Burial 2, a teen-ager, was the only substantially complete interment, lacking right humerus and radius, left ulna, right innominate, left tibia, and fibulae. Articulated foot bones associated with the burial were found adjacent to the cranium of B. 5, but otherwise the bones were quite jumbled.

Burial 3 was a young adult male (the only individual whose sex could be determined), present solely as cranium, regarded as somewhat divergent in many morphological respects from the rest of the cranial series from the site.

Burial 4, probably a young adult was represented by a fragmentary cranium, and B. 5, probably middled-aged, was an even more fragmentary cranium. Burial 6, probably sixteen to twenty years old, was the last cranium.

No evidence from the site or elsewhere permits this feature to be adequately interpreted, but it is notable that the large glacial-erratic rocks are shared with F. 34, and the degree of breakage of the bones—considerably greater than with any of the other ossuaries--may reflect burial after the bones had become brittle through loss of organic components. If so, then the bones had been kept somewhere much longer than was the case with the other ossuaries. It is also suggestive that none of the crania revealed post mortem plaque removal, again indicating initial treatment different from that which most other deceased individuals from the site received.

The maximum precision in dating possible at the present is assignment to the Juntunen phase.

12.3.3 FEATURE 45

The eight burials designated as F. 45 lie just off the southwest edge of the Juntunen site (Unit 7 in Fig. 4, p 20). In terms of location, culture, and date, the feature belongs to the Arrowhead Drive component. A carbon date of A.D. 50 ± 120 was obtained on the skeletal material (M-1392; Crane and Griffin 1965). The bones were excavated and analyzed by Eyman and Bettarel (1965) and Bettarel and Harrison (1962) have published a description of the feature and its materials. The following account will concentrate on comparisons with the other burial features.

Passages from the papers mentioned above are quoted.

> The ossuary was about 8 feet long north and south, and 5 feet wide east and west. The first traces of bone occurred about one foot below the surface and material continued to about 2.5 feet below the surface. No distinct outline of a pit was observed although there were some traces of one here and there. The deposit was undifferentiated sand both within and around the burials. . . .The ossuary contained 7 adults in fully flexed

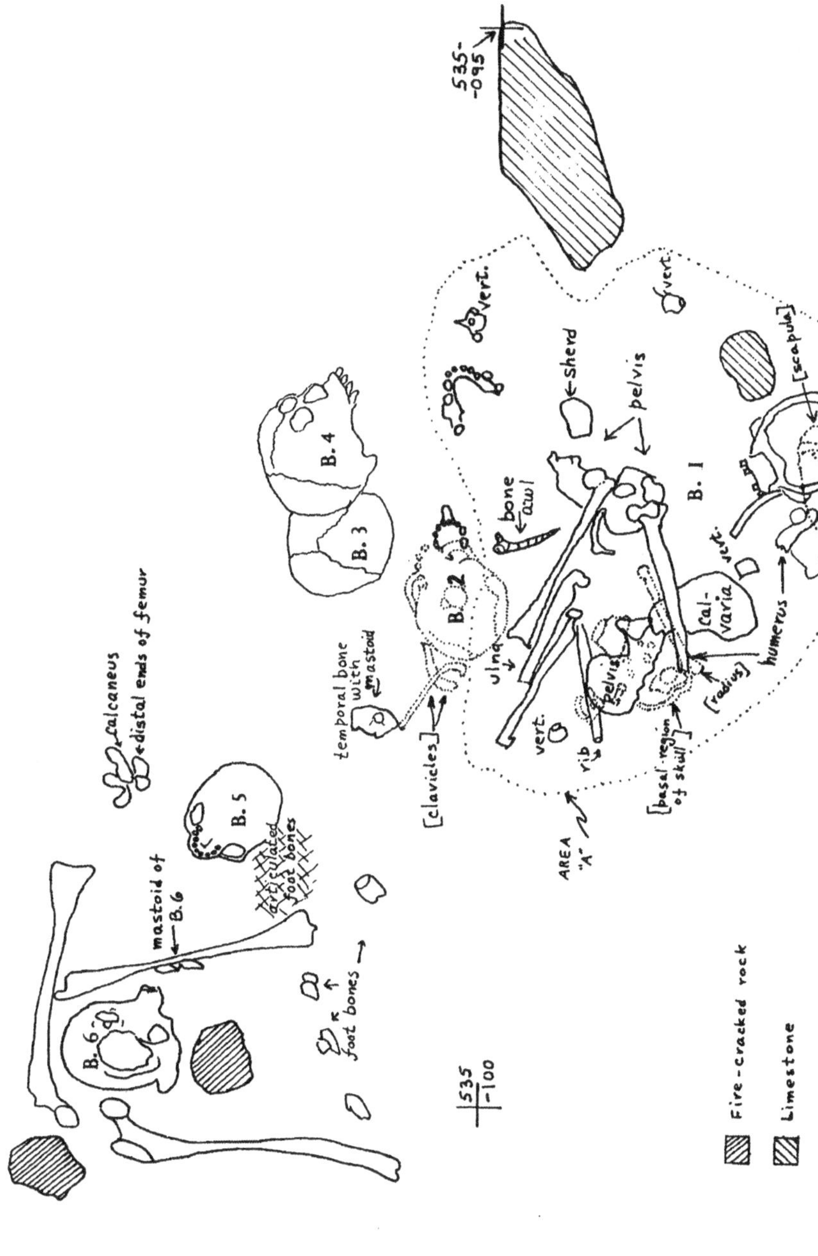

Fig. 35.—Feature 43

> to partially flexed positions with no particular orientation in any direction, and one extended child burial [Bettarel and Harrison 1962:38].
>
> It . . . might be better termed a multiple burial area rather than an ossuary. Two burials represent the fragmentary remains of infants while the other six are adults. The latter consist of two middle-aged males, a middle-aged female, two young adults of indeterminate sex, and a "transitional" adult-subadult male between 17 and 20 years old at death [Eyman and Bettarel 1965:4].

Photographs of the feature are seen in Plate LIV, where *b* shows the uppermost burials in relation to the ground surface. Note in the profile the absence of darkened occupation horizons. The burial pit was in the backslope area of the main dune ridge described by Wright, and the sands, if they are in fact wind-deposited, represent an earlier phase of dune building, upon which very little additional sand was deposited (or from which much was deflated) during Late Woodland times.

Although the burials were in less decomposed condition at the time of interment (as evidenced by articulation) than any of the other burials from the site except those at top of F. 11, they were by no means all complete. Burial 1 lacked all parts above the pelvis; B. 2 lacked innominate and femora; B. 6 and 7 consisted mainly of head, trunk, and portions of limbs. Burials 3-5 and 8 were substantially complete. There was no instance of plaque removal. The bone material was all much softer and in poorer condition than any of the Late Woodland burials.

The most interesting elements in the feature were the included grave goods. At the head of B. 5 was a collection of artifacts including stone projectile points (mostly lanceolate), 2 bone points, 1 spatulate bone chisel, 24 pieces of beaver incisor, 2 pieces of cut and trimmed black-bear maxilla, and nearly 50 pieces of bird and mammal bone, mostly long rectangular fragments. The collection when deposited was inclosed in a skin bag. The absence of hair from the preserved fragments of the skin and its highly wrinkled appearance suggested to Charles Cleland and Charles Eyman, who dissected the collection in the laboratory after it had been encased in plaster in the field and removed as a unit (see Pl. LIV, *d*), that the bag was made of the scrotum of a large mammal, perhaps moose. Illustrations of the artifacts are published in Bettarel and Harrison (1962).

Near parts of B. 4 were found portions of a conoidal-based pottery vessel with plain surface, decorated by shallow incising in a bold crosshatched design. The badly smashed fragments were cemented together by a pink sand, but, since there was no evidence of fire in the vicinity, it was hypothesized that weathering of temper and leaching of poorly fired paste had caused the pink sandy cementation. It seems more likely to me, however, that the vessel was in a fire elsewhere and was later included as pit fill. As can be seen in Plate LIV, *c*, the vessel lies at the outermost periphery of the feature. This vessel is described and illustrated in Bettarel and Harrison (1962).

Also included in the ossuary were a few sherds very much like the other Arrowhead Drive pottery (and quite unlike any of the Late Woodland wares). Decoration was by means of dentate and plain stamp applied in a sort of drag-and-jab fashion, and they can probably be regarded as belonging to the Laurel tradition (cf. Stoltmann 1962).

The other artifact worthy of note was a beaver incisor hafted in a deer antler, very similar to others from the Upper Great Lakes and elsewhere. It was found closest to the child burial, B. 7.

12.4 CONCLUSIONS

Ossuary burials have a wide distribution in the Upper Great Lakes and are of particular interest because in the form of the "Feast of the Dead" they were described by the early missionaries for all the western Iroquoian-speaking groups—the Huron, Neutral, Tobacco, Erie, and Seneca. Many Algonquian-speaking groups adopted this burial practice, some as late as the seventeenth century. The Juntunen examples are of interest in demonstrating the antiquity of these customs, which in the early historic period developed into ceremonies involving the redistribution and destruction of quantities of goods, paralleling in some respects the inferred course of development of the Northwest Coast potlatch. We see at the Juntunen site that the only goods deposited with the dead were personal items associated with an individual through long use. This is a contrast with both the Late Archaic and the Early Historic periods.

Ten burials from Juntunen had a plaque of bone removed from a side of the head. This was already a custom of considerable antiquity in Michigan. Most individuals buried at the Hopewellian Norton Mounds group showed plaque removal, and some of the crania from the Younge site had a disc cut from the rear of the skull. In the Juntunen cases there were no cut marks and no signs of bone response, indicating that "percussion techniques" were employed, post mortem. No such plaques themselves were encountered at the site. The side from which the plaque was removed had no significant association with the sex of the individual, though plaque removal tended somewhat to be associated with males. No children showed the trait. Eyman and Bettarel regard the plaque removal as connected with supernatural beliefs—specifically, the myth of Head-Piercer (Tooker 1964; Hewitt 1895), who removed and ate brains—and also as associated with the idea that removing the brain prevented the soul from preying upon the living. This hypothesis appears to explain the evidence satisfactorily, especially when to it is added the fact that plaque removal is highly associated with semiarticulated burials among the adults, being most often absent from the truly "bundle" burials—individuals who had perhaps died during migratory periods, when the possibility that the dead might "catch up" with the living was less likely.

Some attention can now be paid to Eyman and Bettarel's conclusions with regard to the physical evidence. It can first be said that the sex and age distribution is typical of aboriginal populations. The accompanying table summarizes the findings with respect to pathologies. Typical of aboriginal populations again is the high incidence of dental pathologies. Evidently unrelated to these are the bone conditions. A high incidence of "fungoid excrescenses" and "rough inflammatory lesions"—suggesting osteomyelitis—is present, associated more with females than with males. Bacillary infection is suggested, probably related to the work habits of females, such as gathering in wooded areas, handling carcasses of food animals, especially fish, manufacturing articles from animal and vegetable fibers, and perhaps, removing soft tissues from corpses. Males, on the other hand, exhibit high frequencies of spinal "compression" fractures and compensatory spondylolisthesis, again no doubt reflecting both diet and rigorous work habits. Many of these pathological conditions show an onset earlier than in modern populations, partly attributable to diet.

With respect to metric observations, robust and linear body build and a mean adult height of 1.68 m. ± 3.8 cm. (5'6" ± 1.5") are calculated.

Comparisons with two other skeletal populations were made by Eyman and Bettarel, using population distance formulas as well as discrete traits. Comparison with an early historic ossuary at St. Ignace, Michigan (see map of Straits area, Fig. 2, p. 9), failed to indicate that Juntunen and St. Ignace were different physical groups. Comparison of Juntunen and certain

SUMMARY OF PATHOLOGIES AND ANOMALIES
IN THE JUNTUNEN-SITE BURIALS

Pathology	No. of Individuals
Arthritic pits, exostoses	8
Cervical fossa of Allen	7
Dental caries	11
Vertebral "compression" fractures	8
Post mortem plaque removal	10
Fossa of Civinni	3
Humerus-septal apertures	4
Spondylolisthesis	13
Tooth-socket resorption	6
Spinal fusions	2
Abscesses	6
Non-vert. fractures	2
Ante mortem tooth loss	8
Fungoid excrescences	5
Palatine torus	4
Rough inflammatory lesions	4
Tooth crowding	5
Musculotendinous cuff tear	3
Others	12

Goodall Focus burials of southwestern Michigan did show some interesting similarities and differences. The previously mentioned Norton Mounds burials, with high frequency of plaque removal, are very close physically to the Middle Woodland F. 45 burials—closer than either sample was to the Juntunen-phase burials (F. 11, 18, 34)—which suggest long-term changes in population characteristics, for the time gap between the two Middle Woodland samples is far less than that between those two and the Juntunen-phase sample.

Estimates of human population density were made by Cleland (1962) from the fauna and by Eyman and Bettarel from the skeletal material. Based on a 5 per cent mortality rate, and assuming that families consisted of five individuals, Eyman concludes that an interval of five years between ossuary ceremonies is most reasonable and that a minimum of five families occupied the site at the optimum season. This would indicate occupancy by 25-50 individuals, which is in accord with Cleland's conclusions, although the size of F. 11 is out of accord (if one assumes that ossuaries contained only those individuals dying on the island, even if the unusual number of recently deceased individuals is discounted) and suggests either increase in population size or increase in size of social unit included in one such ceremony. Greater precison with regard to temporal relationship among the ossuaries would be required to advance research into these suggestions.

XIII

HABITATION FEATURES

Features recognized at the Juntunen site other than human burials consisted of hearths, pits, horizontal concentrations, animal burials, and evidences of structures. Since habitations and other structures are of primary importance for study of settlement patterns and often explain the presence of other types of features, evidence for them will be discussed first.

13.1 STRUCTURAL EVIDENCES

Hundreds of small and more or less circular disturbances were observed and recorded on square sheets. On the walls of squares and when square sheets from one square were superimposed (as in Fig. 37), these disturbances stood out as vertical shafts that often became slightly larger toward the bottom. Their approximate range in depth was from 5 to about 60 cm., with most having a diameter between 7 and 12 cm. Some of them were pits, some probably were animal burrows, and others were root patterns. Those classed as "postmolds" were ones that had a total depth greater than 20 cm., that were reasonably vertical, and that lacked both the profusion of fishbones characteristic of the small pits from the site and the horizontal expansion at the base indicative of roots or burrows. Figure 36 maps postmolds in part of the central area of the site. (Refer to Figs. 4 and 5 for orientation.) Excavations in the block of 10 by 10-foot squares shown at the right side of Figure 36 suggested the existence of two parallel lines of postmolds about 22 feet (6.7 meters) apart, oriented parallel to the ridge. The large irregular-shaped excavation unit and those to the left of it were opened when this situation became apparent— characteristically, at the end of the season—and were dug for the most part only to expose postmolds, without sifting for artifacts and without the system of vertical controls used for the rest of the digging. The postmolds considered to belong to the same structure, named Feature 22, are shaded by dotting, while the rest are indicated by outline only.

The elevation at which each postmold was first detected and recorded on a square sheet was used in efforts to determine the occupation level from which it was dug. Other information, such

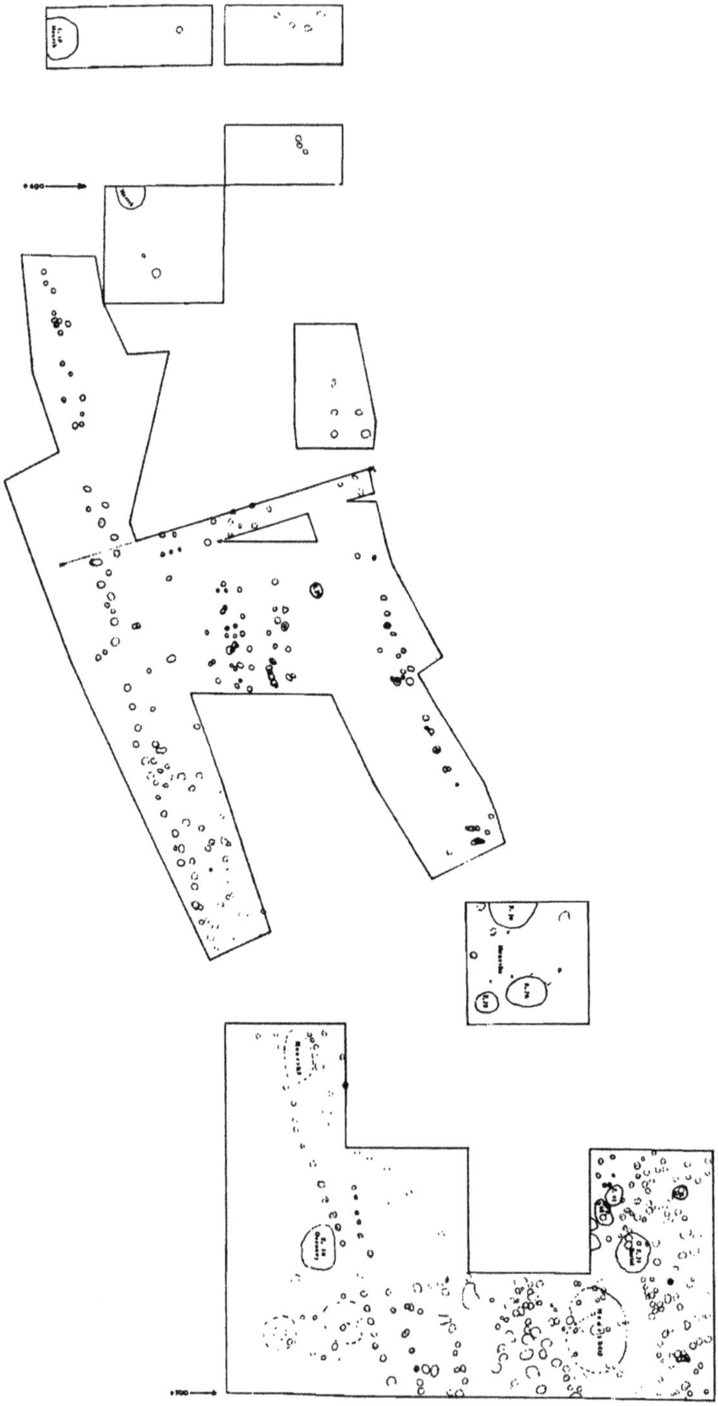

Fig. 36.—"Longhouse" (F.22) and other features

as depth, was obtained by sectioning postmolds in a vertical plane. To this information might have been added other data recorded for each postmold—diameter, dip and strike, color, soil composition, and included artifacts—in order to obtain the optimum separation among the structures. In practice, this whole procedure was not always followed, both because of the time that would have been involved and because the contiguous areas excavated—other than for F. 22—were not large enough to permit other structures to be revealed, and so the rewards would not have justified the effort expended.

Other difficulties in handling postmolds include the fact that gravelly materials from below as well as wind-deposited and culture-bearing materials from above were introduced when the post was removed or decayed. In addition, the derivation of the contents of a number of postmolds was hard to explain. Thus soil composition was of dubious value in any attempt to classify postmolds. Plate LV *c*, illustrates one difficulty with regard to contents. Here is a postmold with part of the post preserved; it is filled with gravel, yet no gravel is now present either above or immediately below the postmold, from which its contents could have been derived. The dark outlines of the postmold in the plate, remnants of the original wood, indicate that at least some posts rotted from the inside out rather than the other way round. But since the post was evidently rotting in place, it could not have been pulled out and the hole filled by gravel brought from elsewhere. Therefore the way in which the postmold was being filled is puzzling.

13.1.1 FEATURE 22, "LONGHOUSE" (?)

Between the two rows of postmolds shown in Figure 36 the artifact content was very high despite the fact that little sifting was done in the left portion. Excavation units on either side of the rows had a pronounced dropoff in artifact density (see Fig. 24). In addition, there was a clustering, between the rows, of other features indicative of intense industrial activity. Most of the copper from the site was concentrated in an area toward the right end of the rows near the hearths, and there were other concentrations, such as the one of flint chips recorded as Feature 29. Finally, the postsherds from the area between the rows were numerous but smaller on the average than those on the rest of the site, suggesting much trampling. The mean sherd weight for all sherds between sheets 3 and 4 of square 710-180 was 2.2 gm., somewhat under the over-all mean of 2.7 for the entire site.

Although the evidence is not conclusive, it is suggested that we are dealing with a habitation, and specifically a "longhouse." This supposition is beclouded by the facts that the outlines of the structure are incomplete; the postmolds peter out at the end shown at the left in Figure 36; the excavations halted abruptly at the right end; and much of the middle was not excavated. No entrances, details of construction, or living arrangements were located. The situation is made worse by the fact that occupations in this area of the site were compressed vertically, making separation among them exceedingly difficult. (Sherds of all periods were found in nearly equal proportions in the units in the left half of Fig. 36.) The supposed "longhouse" was also not the last structure on the site; Features 21, 24-26, and possibly 31, 41, and 42, are intrusive upon the rows of postmolds, as is the "Hearth?" shown at the bottom of Figure 36. Thus assignment of various features, such as hearths, to F. 22 was uncertain.

Based on a study of the postmolds in square 710-180 pertaining to the "longhouse," it is concluded that the structure was built early in the Juntunen phase, was rebuilt or at least reoccupied a number of times, and was succeeded by other structures (of which little evidence is preserved) sometime during this latest aboriginal phase. Figure 37 is a superimposition of square sheets of 710-180, indicating some of the difficulties involved in unraveling the sequence of occupations and structures because of the intrusion of disturbances on each other. Note that numbered features intrude upon all disturbances except the latest (indicated by the heavy black lines). The postmolds considered to belong to Feature 22 begin between 1.0 and 1.5 feet below the surface and extend to at least 2.5 feet below the surface.

Two transects across the rows of postmolds are available. Figure 7 (p. 36) is a profile across the site at about the +700 line (the vertical margin to the far right of Fig. 36). Note the absence of postmolds up to 720-170 and the great number of them to the right of that point. Figure 38 is a profile across the postmold area, located on Figure 36 by the line marked *X-X'*. Both profiles show the highly disturbed nature of the strata in the area of F. 22, the cutting-through of multiple habitation layers earlier than the feature under study, and the shape of postmolds.

Views of the "longhouse" are shown in Plate LV, where *b* is a general view taken with the photographer standing at about the lower left corner of Figure 36. The square with three people standing in it is 710-180. In the same plate, *a* is an earlier stage in excavation of the trench shown in the foreground

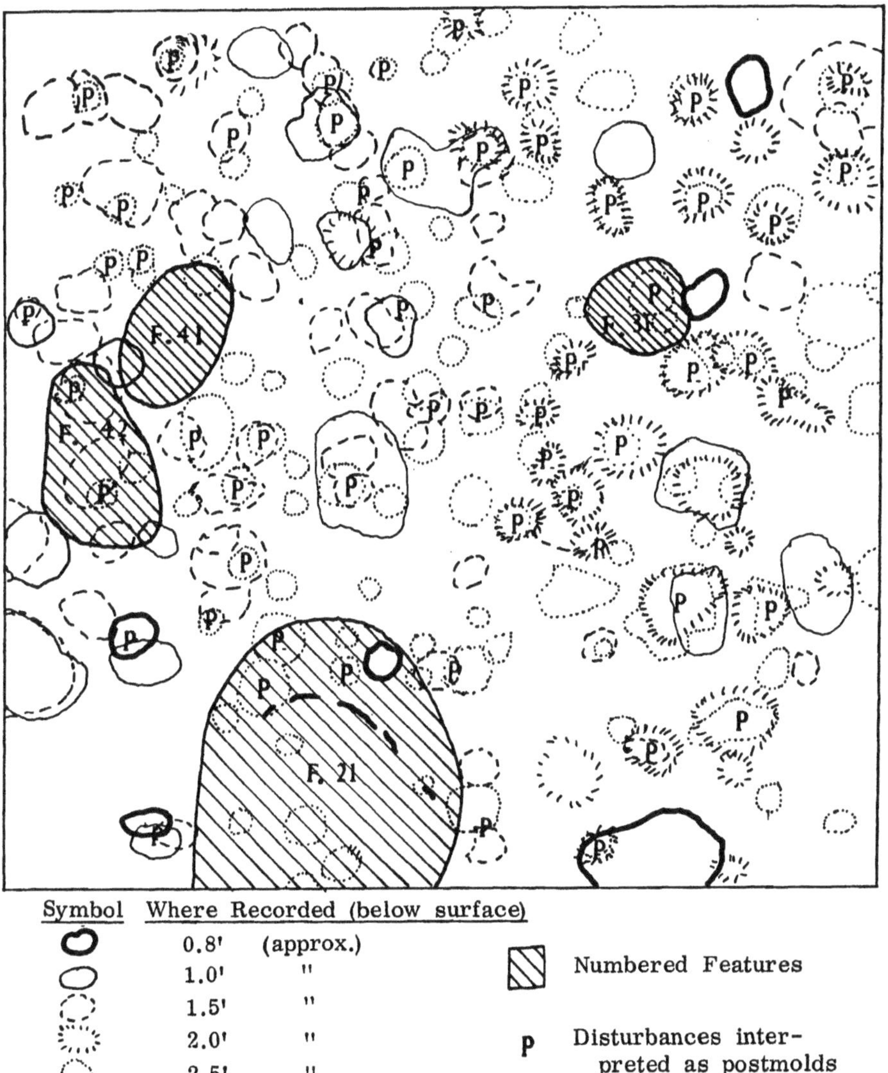

Fig. 37 – Disturbances in square 710-180

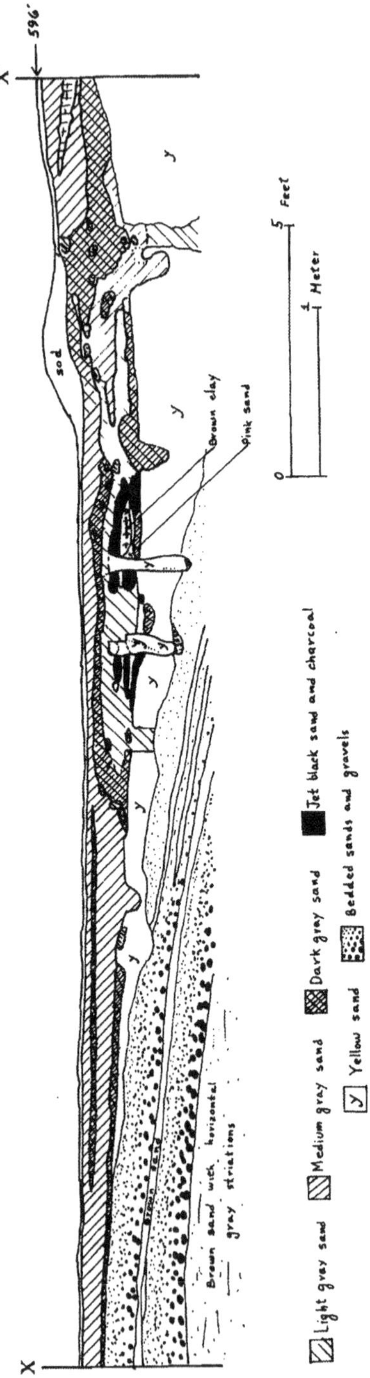

Fig. 38.—Trench X-X' across Feature 22, longhouse

of LV, *b*, and *d* is the right-hand portion of the profile trench $X\text{—}X'$ drawn in Figure 38. The partly decayed postmold in *a* occurred in the upper corner of the trench shown in *a* and *b*, also seen as the upper corner of the lower right leg of the irregular unit shown in Figure 36.

13.1.2 EVIDENCES OF OTHER STRUCTURES

Rows of disturbances, some of which can be interpreted as postmolds, occurred in many other places on the site, but because of the smallness of the excavation units, no actual structure outlines could be seen, not even two corners of one. The row of disturbance and the hearths in the mound area seen in Figure 27 (p. 202) indicate the building of structures in the Mackinac phase in the eastern part of the site. For the rest of the periphery of the site, postmolds were found in Unit 3 (Fig. 4, p. 19) but were absent from Units 1, 4, and 5. None were found in Unit 8; they were extremely sparse in the squares collectively titled Unit 23 and were missing from Units 21, 28, 30, 32-34. In Units 25-27 and 29, however, a considerable number were located, probably of the Mackinac phase. Because of the sizable spatial gap in excavation units between the last named and those in the central area of the site, it is hazardous to draw conclusions, but the evidence as it stands suggests two focal points of activity on the site with concentrations of artifacts, postmolds, and other disturbances: one represented by Units 25-27 and 29, and another in the central area.

13.2 HEARTHS

Disturbances classified as "hearths" typically are basin-shaped features 2-3 feet in diameter and of variable depth, containing jet-black sand with much charcoal ranging from very fine particles to pieces a few centimeters in diameter, with greenish-gray loamy-to-clayey sand interpreted as ashes present in some. Elements reported for other sites that were often missing from Juntunen hearths include rings or other arrangements of stones—although abundant fire-cracked erratics were found on the site—and pink earth under the hearths, the result of heat.

Features 25-26 were located in square 730-190 and are shown in Figure 36. Feature 24, lying partly outside the left side of the square in Figure 36 (p. 234) appeared as a yellow clayey patch approximately 3 feet in diameter about 0.5 feet below the surface; the other two appeared slightly lower. Postcontact materials immediately overlay F. 24, but both it and the others appeared undisturbed, although both F. 25 and F. 26 were penetrated by postmolds. Features 24 and 26, at least, are intrusive upon the line of postmolds pertaining to F. 22. When sectioned, the three were seen to have a maximum thickness of 0.3 feet, to have lenticular profiles, and to contain patches of clayey-feeling soil ranging from yellowish green to brownish gray and lenses of black carbonaceous sand. All three overlay a black layer covering the whole square—perhaps the living floor of F. 22—that was very rich in cultural materials.

Although fires built on the contemporary beach were observed to leave reddened and often hardened layers in the sand beneath them, this element was lacking in F. 24-26 as in most hearths from the site; although patches of pink sand were noted in many places during excavations, they could frequently not be associated with places where fires had evidently been laid. No explanation for this situation is at hand.

Included artifacts from F. 24-26 consist of two Bois Blanc ware and three "other" sherds, all from F. 26, and a total of 16 pieces of copper from all three together. Temporal placement is late (but not latest) in the Juntunen phase.

Feature 32, a tan-gray clayey lens overlying a red-sand lens in square 710-180, was first observed at a depth of 0.9 feet. No diagnostic sherds were recovered, but stratigraphically it should belong to the Mackinac phase.

Feature 38, an apparently undisturbed hearth in 810-225, was found at a depth of only 0.6 feet within the undifferentiated gray-black humus layer that in this area of the site extends from the surface to an abrupt junction with yellow sand. The feature can be seen in plan in the lower left corner of Figure 36 (p. 234). It overlay and was in part clearly separated from the jet-black layer within the yellow sand considered to pertain to F. 22. Diameter of the feature was approximately five feet. It consisted of lenses of yellow clayey material (ash?), pink-to-orange burned earth and sand, jet-black carbonaceous sand, and small amounts of fire-cracked igneous rock. Sherds representing eight vessels were recovered; the types span the typological range from the site and thus offer little help in temporal placement.

Feature 17, first observed 0.6 feet below the surface, with its top evidently disturbed, consisted of an extraordinarily high concentration of small stones—mostly dolomite pebbles—in a black carbonaceous sand matrix containing patches of pink-brown sand and charcoal. Located in 700-180 and contained within the area of the "Hearth(s)" at the top right in Figure 36 (p. 234) its depth varied from 0.5 to 0.8 feet.

Artifacts consisted of 30 pieces of copper in various states of work, including two awls; two scrapers; one bone awl; and sherds of nine vessels, with Bois Blanc ware predominating. In view of the probability that the feature is to be considered part of the arrangements within the "longhouse" (it is located within the postmold rows), and in view of the fact that copper-working was not highly developed in the Bois Blanc phase, the pottery frequencies cannot be accepted at face value in placing the feature temporally.

Feature 1, discovered immediately under the sod in 740-230 and 750-230 (Units 14 and 18 of Fig. 4, p. 19), was a concentration of unbroken and split rocks, portions of broken vessels, and charcoal, about 3.5 by 5 feet in plan, but no thicker than the rocks in depth. The feature was in a matrix of jet-black carbonaceous sand, contrasting with the surrounding soil at the same level, which varied from grayish-black to yellow. There was no apparent pattern to the arrangement of rocks. Below the rocks and black sand were layers of sterile sand and gravel; no ash or reddened soil was observed.

Artifacts included flint chips, numerous body sherds of a red grit-tempered, plain-surfaced Oneota vessel, a few sherds of a Juntunen-ware vessel, and one Blackduck sherd.

From all appearances the feature was basically undisturbed, despite the fact it lay only 4 inches below the surface. Since the area is known to have been the location of a farmyard and earlier a logging camp, it seems likely that more soil must have originally covered the feature and that it was subsequently removed, either by sheet erosion or human agency. At least it can be said that this particular area could not have been plowed with the feature so close to the surface without its having been radically disturbed. Practically no artifacts were found outside the boundaries of the feature.

Three hearths associated with the Mackinac phase were excavated in the mound area (Fig. 27, p. 202). Feature 2 was a saucer-shaped lens of black sand with charcoal and burned bone, a few fire-blackened sherds, and a few small pieces of fired rock. Absent were evidences of ashes, substantial amounts of fired rock and charcoal, and signs of firing in the underlying sand. Dimensions in plan were 3.5 by 2.5 feet. Feature 46 and the unnumbered blackened disturbance in the wall to its left in Figure 27 (p. 202) are also classed as hearths.

13.3 PITS

The disturbances classed as "pits" were certainly unusual in comparison with those found on many sites. Only two (F. 4 and 39) were big enough to suggest that they functioned as storage pits, and most of the rest appeared to be casually dug repositories for fish offal.

13.3.1 LARGE PITS

Feature 4 was encountered in squares 890-190 and 890-200 (Unit 30 in Fig. 4). It was ovoid in plan (2.0 by 1.2 feet), had a maximum depth of 1.6 feet, and a profile as shown in Figure 39. The pit contained masses of pinkish-tan material of a clayey consistency with grit particles, similar to material recovered from a bulldozed pit about half a mile inland from the site. The material is of interest as perhaps representing pottery clay. Between these masses and at the bottom were found stratified layers of black, gray, and yellowish sand containing artifacts. This sand had the same appearance as the sand found in habitation deposits elsewhere on the site, hence it is reasonable to assume that it was derived from them.

The origin and intended function of the pinkish clayey material is uncertain, but it was certainly artifically introduced to the site. The significance is that nowhere else on the site was this amount of possible pottery clay encountered, although a few traces were found here and there. It appears as if the function of the pit may well have been as a repository for clay, where it would have been kept damp and ready for use.

All artifacts were contained in the laminated gray and black sand layers and must therefore have been introduced accidentally as debris. There were 108 sherds in all, including two rims and nine decorated body sherds. All that could be identified are unquestionably of the Mackinac phase. Other than the sherds, 22 pieces of chert were included, with no diagnostic features. Assignment of the pit to the Mackinac phase seems justified. The gray band (Fig. 39) into which the pit intrudes bore extremely few artifacts, but such as were found were all likewise Mackinac-ware types. Wares later than Mackinac were in general rare in the units in which the feature was found.

There were other signs of habitation in the units mentioned, but no postmolds were found, and the occupation seems not to have been very intense. It is not clear whether the top of the feature is intact or whether, after abandonment, erosion occurred. There appears to be continuity with a thin band of dark-gray-to-black sand at the left, but it is not present on the right side as seen in Figure 39; if the band represents the occupation floor at the time the pit was dug, then we can conclude that the pit remains generally intact.

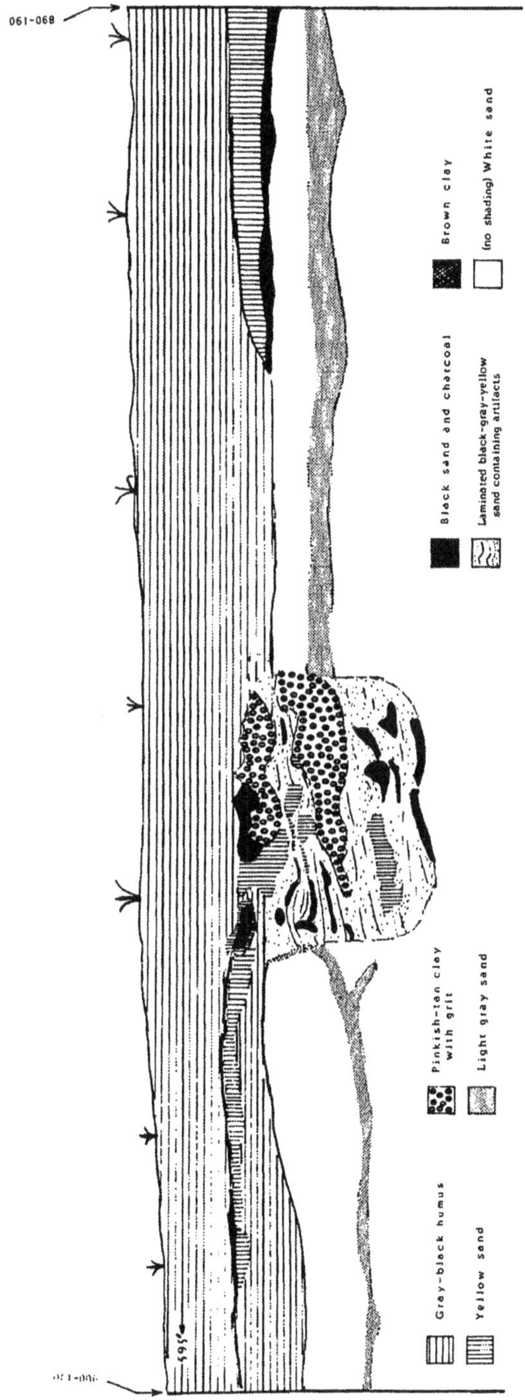

Fig. 39.—Feature 4, pit

Feature 39 was the largest pit encountered; it was located in 700-160 (Unit 9 of Fig. 4, p. 19). A profile of F. 39 is provided in the lower left corner of Figure 7 (p. 35). Its maximum dimensions were 3.8 feet in diameter and 3.6 feet in depth. Its fill was predominately light-gray sand, with some pebbles, gravel and habitation debris. Despite the occurrence of two discontinuities in the fill—concave jet-black lenses overlying tan sand that indicate changes in the conditions under which the pit was being filled—no significant differences were noted in the different layers of pit fill other than that more artifacts were encountered at the top than at the bottom. Artifacts were rather sparse for a refuse pit, and all elements were disorganized and jumbled, suggesting a casual filling with general habitation debris rather than a purposeful utilization as repository for broken pots, garbage (in which semiarticulated animal skeletal portions might be expected), or other refuse. Unless the habitation debris represents the intended fill, the original purpose of the pit is unknown.

The earliest element in the pit was a thin layer of black material (shown unshaded in Fig. 7, p. 35) lining portions of the wall at left as seen in Figure 7, material that extends from near the top to the bottom. Its remaining in position throughout the period (however long or short it may have been) during which the pit was being filled up warrants attention, and I suggest that it may have been a pit lining designed to protect the original contents from contact with the sand walls.

The pit may be correlated with levels in the same square by stratigraphy and by matching sherds. Seven sherds of one Mackinac Punctate pot could be fitted together. They were as follows:

Feature 39	4 sherds
700-160, sheets 3-4.	1 sherd
700-160, sheets 6-7.	1 sherd
700-160, sheets 7-8.	1 sherd

On the assumption that it is more likely for sherds to be displaced upward than downward and on the basis of quantity, F. 39 would be contemporary with the layers represented by material between square sheets 6-7 or 7-8 (these may actually not be separated in time). All vessels from the feature were Mackinac-ware types, as were those from sheets 6-8, hence assignment to the Mackinac phase is reasonable. Locating the level with which the feature is to be temporally associated is important in that one sherd from sheet 6-7 of the same square matched another from F. 23 (to be discussed shortly) and that, while there were many disturbances in the square that could be interpreted as postmolds, the tops of a series forming a line across the square were at approximately the level of square sheet 7, thus providing the largest connected sample of features of the Mackinac phase. Unfortunately, square 700-170 was not excavated, and the postmolds from the one square (700-160) are insufficient to permit reconstruction of the inferred structure or even to indicate the relationship of pit to structure.

Feature 40 was a pit in the opposite corner of the same square (700-160) but of later date. Its maximum diameter was about 3.5 feet, maximum depth about 5 feet. Fill consisted of gray sand, and the included artifacts were non-diagnostic. The pit was evidently not a depository for refuse, and its function is unclear.

13.3.2 SMALL PITS

A number of other pits were encountered, quite different from those just discussed; they were small and usually contained a dark-gray to jet-black carbonaceous "greasy" fill with many uncharred fishbones. Data on those assigned a feature number are summarized in Table 27. They averaged 1.1 feet in diameter and could seldom be traced vertically for more than 1.5 feet, although precision in this respect is impossible because the tops of many were lost in the homogeneous uppermost layer of black sand found on the site, which kept the pits from being visible until the surrounding material was of a lighter color. They were not postmolds—almost no postmolds were of black sand, and the diameters of the pits were too large. They were not simple depressions or undulations in the habitation surface, for they had more or less vertical sides and their fishbones and scale content was usually much greater than that of ordinary habitation debris; also the texture of the fill was less compacted and "crisp" than that of habitation surfaces and usually had a different feel. These may have been pits dug as needed to serve for disposal of refuse, especially fish offal, or for ceremonial usage—an explanation that might be supported by the animal burials from the site, although neither explanation seems satisfactory. My impression is that perhaps three times the number discussed were present without being recognized or without exciting sufficient attention to cause a feature number to be assigned—largely because of their lack of distinctiveness.

TABLE 27

SMALL PITS

Feature No.	Square	Depth (ft.)	Diameter (ft.)	Phase	Contents
3	890-190	1.1	0.7	Mack.	Shiny jet-black sand—perhaps 50% charcoal, a few blackened rocks, a few chert chips.
9	890-190	0.9	1.1	Mack.	Brown-black sand with much fishbone and scales.
13	700-200	1.2	2.0	Mack. ?	Jet-black sand with great concentrations of fishbones; two sherds out of 38 identifiable as Mack. Cord impressed.
19	600-130	0.4	0.8	Junt.	Black sand with much fishbone; partly completed harpoon (Pl. L, *g*); about 175 chert chips ranging in size from about 1 cm. to about 1 mm., all of the same material.
27	700-130	0.4	0.8	Junt.	Gray sand with masses of fishbone and scales. Of 11 sherds, the only identifiable one was Oneota.
31	710-180	?	1.5	B.B. ?	Gray sand, fishbone, chert chips, a few unidentifiable sherds, a streak of pinkish clayey sand, dolomite pebbles, fire-cracked granite; and an entire miniature pot, placed inverted in the pit (Pl. XXIV, *d*).
41	710-180	2.2	1.1	Junt.	Dark-gray to jet-black carbonaceous sand, fishbones, dolomite pebbles; 68 sherds (none identifiable), 22 chert flakes (all but one of exotic materials), 2 scrapers, and 2 awls, one copper and one bone.

13.4 ANIMAL BURIALS

Cleland's (1966) study of the animal burials was cited earlier (secs. 11.3.2., 11.3.4.) These burials will be discussed here in the broader context of the other features from the site.

Feature 5 consisted of three apparently deliberate burials of small animals—a young dog, articulated; a snowshoe hare, partly articulated; and 133 limb-bone fragments of a bald eagle. The three burials formed a triangle; in the middle, black and red sand and green-brown clay (ash?) indicated that a fire had been built. The burials, however, were not charred. All elements were found only 0.6 feet below the surface in square 970-185 (Unit 32 of Fig. 4, p. 19). The feature is shown in Plate LVI, *a*, where it can be seen that the feature occurred at the edge of a shallow round pit (F. 6) dating to the early part of the nineteenth centruy, judging from the U.S. Infantry enlisted man's button of the period 1816-21 (described in chap. 10) that was found in it. From the square sheets it is clear that F. 6 is intrusive upon F. 5 and not the other way round. On the other hand, no undisturbed habitation level from which the pits could have been dug was encountered, no doubt because of the proximity to the surface. Sherds occurring at the same level as the burials were of all periods, but, if the burials had been dug from the lowest part of the black layer extending to the sod seen in the profile of Plate LVI, *a*, they would have occurred deeper, so it seems that they should be associated with the upper part of the black layer, and assignment to Intermediate II or the Juntunen phase seems the best choice. No other aboriginal features occurred in this block of units, but, since the black soil in the pits with the animal burials contained fishbone, the pits must have been dug through an occupation deposit, perhaps that of the people doing the burying. Several small round discolorations were also found in the square. They were not fishbone pits and probably not postmolds but may have resulted from occupation activities.

Feature 28, an eagle burial (Pl. LVI, *b*), was encountered during rapid operations to reach a lower occupation level in 700-120, and its associated occupation layer is not known; but from comparison of its elevation with the adjacent profiles, assignment to the Bois Blanc phase or Intermediate II is reasonable. The eagle bones were mostly the extremities, thus, as Cleland suggests, were probably the burial of a preserved skin that retained the more distal skeletal elements.

Other inclusions were two bone awls, of which one was a 50-mm. tip fragment made of unidentified bird bone and the other a complete 125-mm. awl of loon longbone. Some chert flakes, dolomite pebbles, fire-cracked rocks, and 19 sherds were also found. Only two sherds—representing two vessels—could be identified; they were Mackinac Punctate. As much of the feature as was preserved is illustrated in Plate LVI, *b;* note that one talon can be seen to be in articulation and that all limb bones were broken. Dimensions in plan were 2.2 by 1.4 feet.

Feature 16 was a pit in 870-100. It was 1.1 feet in diameter and 1.6 feet deep, commenced at a depth of 1.3 feet from the surface, and contained portions of an eagle skeleton plus typical refuse: firecracked granite, fish bones, sherds (non-diagnostic). Had it not been for the eagle bones, it would have been classed as a "small pit". The feature indicates either that eagle bones were sometimes not accorded special treatment or that some "small pits" had, at least on occasion, a more than purely utilitarian function. Cleland identified a few eagle bones from general village refuse deposits, but there seems to have been a decided preference for burying eagle remains.

13.5 HORIZONTAL ARTIFACT CONCENTRATIONS

Two concentrations of artifacts on habitation surfaces were assigned feature numbers because of their unusual nature. Both occurred on the lake side of the area of heavy occupation and appear to have been short-term dumps.

Feature 23 was the only unmistakeably pure Mackinac-phase feature recovered that also yielded a good artifact sample. Located in Unit 8 (in Fig. 4, p. 19), parts of it can also be seen as the floor in Plate IV, but Plate LVII, *a*, illustrates it better. It formed part of the next-to-lowest cultural deposit. In places it cut into gravel deposits representing the latest beach formation at this locus; and it lay only about 20 feet inland from a scarp that may represent close proximity to the water's edge at the time the feature was deposited.

The feature can be described as a very dense concentration of large Mackinac-ware pottery pieces—several vessels or large parts of them having been broken and left in place—with dolomite cobbles, fire-cracked rocks up to half a foot in maximum dimension, chert chips, fishbone, charcoal, an unfinished celt (Pl. XXXVI, *a*), and a hammerstone. All this was deposited on a low rise on an occupation level of yellow sand mottled with charcoal flecks but sparse in artifacts, assigned by Wright to level *V*.

The concentration might be a dump area, an explanation supported by the pottery, which consisted of about 1,200 sherds representing only eight vessels, five encrusted with cooking residue and three that had never been used for cooking. But under this hypothesis it is hard to explain the large numbers of dolomite pebbles and cobbles and large pieces of angularly cracked granitic rock, presumably firestones. The mean sherd weight was 6.7 gm., over twice as high as the 2.7-gm. mean for the site as a whole, indicating fairly rapid covering-over of the feature by sand. Thus the feature perhaps represents a house floor, with indications of walls not recovered. Satisfactory explanation of the feature will probably not be at hand until more of the occupation surface is exposed, but it may be noted at this point that other squares on the lake side of the area of major occupation activity also yielded large sherds, sometimes in white sand with no sign of an occupation layer, suggesting that they were dropped between the water's edge and the habitations, an area not subjected to heavy foot traffic. Such was the case with the reconstructible vessels illustrated as Plate XII, *a*, and Plate XIV, *a-b*.

Feature 20 (Pl. LVII, *b)* was a somewhat similar heavy concentration of pottery about 4 by 6 feet in a thin horizon seldom more than two sherds thick. It occurred in square 700-140 only 0.6 feet below the surface, was separated from the gray humus "plow zone" by a thin layer of tan-white sand, and was completely undisturbed. It had been deposited on top of a nearly sterile white sand-dune formation (Layer XXIV in Table 2, p. 33; F. 20 would be Layer XXV_3), which it dates. A radiocarbon estimate of A.D. 1330±100 (M-1391; Crane and Griffin 1965) was obtained on charcoal from the feature.

The pottery consisted of large fragments from seven vessels plus a number of unassociated sherds, a total of 356. This total weighed 5.5 kg., giving a mean sherd weight of 16 gm., strikingly higher than the 2.7-gm. mean for the site as a whole and also considerably higher than the mean for F. 23. The largest vessel, of which about two-thirds of the sherds could be fitted together, is illustrated in Plate XXI, *a*. No vessel was complete, and all showed encrustations of charred cooking residue. Lying in and on top of the feature and continuing for about a foot beyond it to one side was a compact layer of fishbone and scales. Some vertebral columns were in articulation, and of these some had ribs articulated. Some bones were charred. Associated with the fishbones were pieces of charcoal, charred wood, and what may be charred bark. From the fact that the vessels were smashed flat but the bones not seriously disturbed or crushed, it can be inferred that their deposition was not simultaneous. Their occurrence together, however, does indicate that the area functioned for a short time as a dump. The fish-bones suggest a rapid covering-over of the feature.

All pottery from the feature was Juntunen Drag-and-Jab, and it may be pointed out that the feature was the only unmistakably pure Juntunen-phase feature recovered from the site.

13.6 SUMMARY

Evidence of two walls of one structure (F. 22) was located; it is inferred to have been a longhouse, occupied in either Intermediate II or the Juntunen phase but definitely not pertaining to the latest aboriginal occupation of the site. Within the area of the walls, great concentrations of artifacts were recovered, with copper in considerable quantity. Because the feature was not completely excavated, little idea of interior arrangements is available. The mulitple rows suggest rebuilding or reinforcement and indicate occupation over several years.

Cache or storage pits were rare, supporting other indications that storable foods such as maize formed at all times a relatively minor part of the diet. Small pits were apparently dug as required, some perhaps serving as receptacles for fish offal. But in a few others certain animals, notably eagles, were buried, with strong implications of ceremonial activity. It is conceivable that most such pits served a religious function, related to sanctions governing the disposal of certain animal bones, although this hypothesis is not well supported by ethnographic data.

Concentrations of artifacts, particularly crushed partial or entire vessels, were encountered on the edge of the site toward the water, where well-defined habitation surfaces were absent. Some finds suggest vessels dropped and left where they lay broken, perhaps while water was being fetched. Such concentrations were not observed on the edge of the site away from the lake.

PART III
INTERPRETATIONS AND CONCLUSIONS

XIV

DISTRIBUTIONAL AND FUNCTIONAL ANALYSIS

In this chapter, data on the distribution of artifacts and features will be employed in three ways. We will consider differences in the relative frequencies of different artifact classes through time, horizontal distribution of artifacts, and relative differences in horizontal distribution. The chapter will conclude with a depositional history, in which artifacts, distributions, time, and the geomorphology will be integrated.

14.1 CHANGES IN ARTIFACT FREQUENCIES THROUGH TIME

The relative frequencies of most artifacts are displayed in Figures 17, (p. 127), 40, and 41, all of which are graphs done in terms of frequency per cubic foot, a conversion made to standardize the data and eliminate the effect of the differences in total cubic footage excavated from each of the three phases; thus artifact "densities" are actually being presented. Differences in absolute density from phase to phase can be observed in nearly every artifact class. The most prominent exception is formed by pottery vessels, which remain nearly constant through time, as seen in Figure 41. Most other artifact classes show more pronounced variation. While vessels remain constant or decline slightly in frequency in the Bois Blanc phase, the frequency of sherds shows the opposite effect, and it is apparent that this variation cannot be explained in terms of different degrees of breakage, that is, different average sherd weights, because the relation between frequency and weight of sherds remains relatively constant through time. A chi-square test of the independence of sherd and vessel frequencies in the three phases yielded a value of 14.8, significant (with two d. f.) at the .01 level, so we cannot assume that the difference in behavior of sherds and vessels with respect to each other is solely the result of chance. Mackinac and Juntunen have more pots but fewer sherds than expected, while Bois Blanc has more sherds and fewer pots than expected. This situation calls for an attempt at explanation. The simplest reason seems to be that more unidentifiable sherds

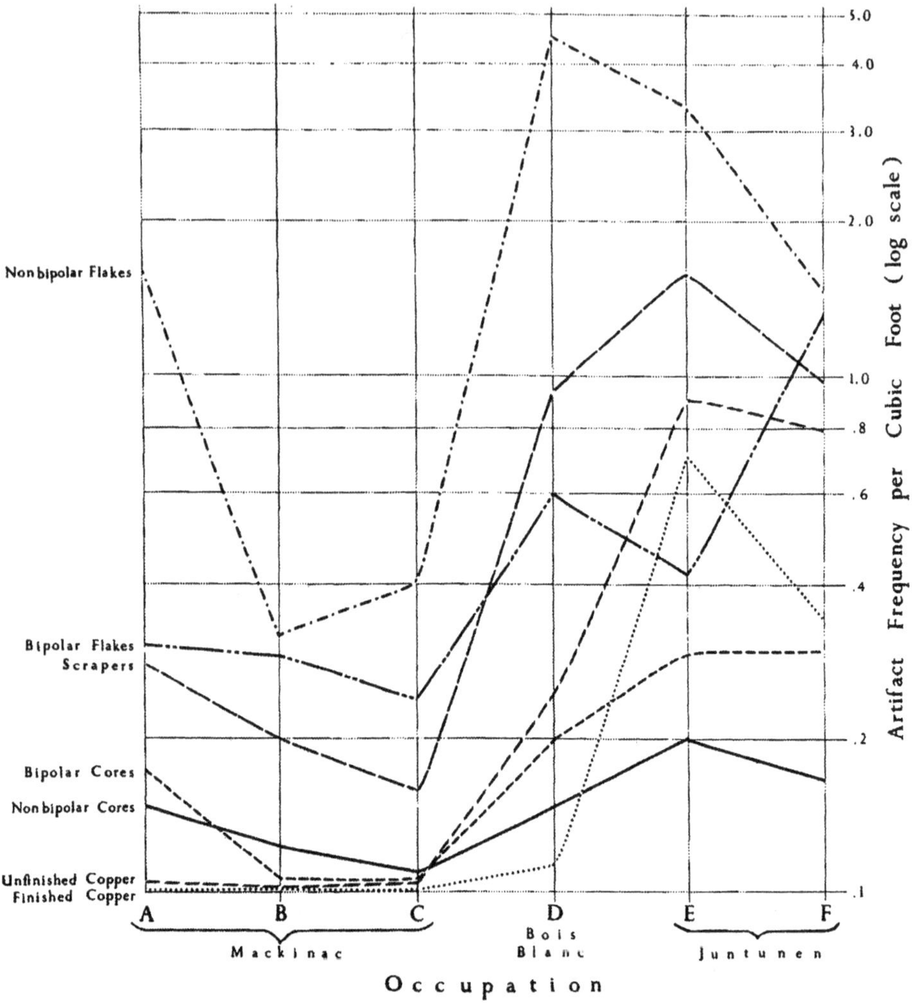

Fig. 40.–Relative frequencies of some artifact classes, by occupation.

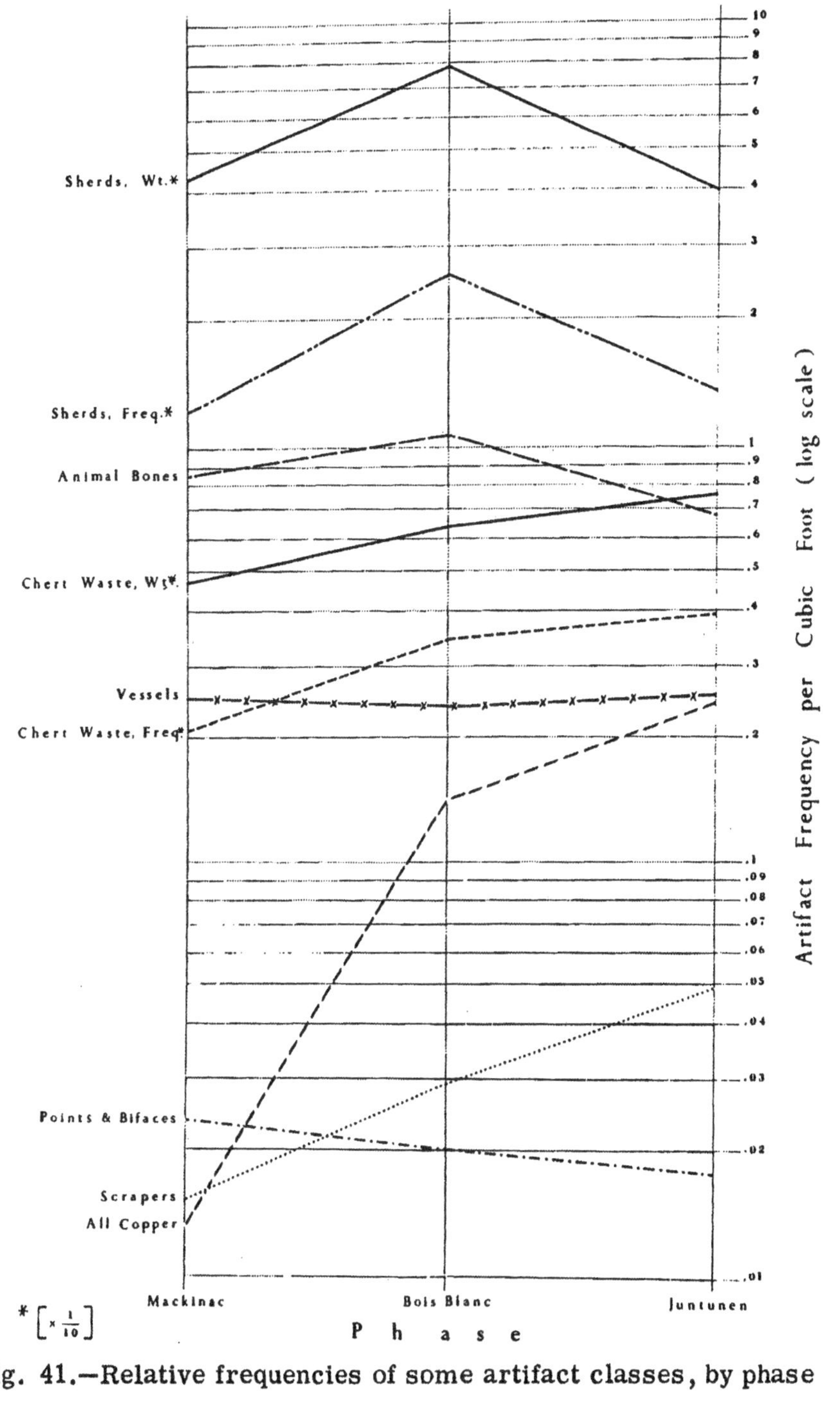

Fig. 41.—Relative frequencies of some artifact classes, by phase

were recovered from Bois Blanc-phase units rather than that the mean sherd weight in Bois Blanc was lower than in either of the other two phases. Pronounced differences in sherd size were observed between excavation units and levels in excavation units, with small sherds predominating in areas where aboriginal activities had been intense and large sherds in areas where either traffic was light or dune building had rapidly covered-over dropped vessels and large fragments. So that mean sherd weights could be obtained, the total number of sherds and their weight were recorded for every provenience unit that contained five or more sherds weighing a total of ten or more grams.

Table 28, produced by the BIMD 23 program on the IBM 7090, distributes the resulting 336 provenience units in a scattergram according to size and weight of the sherds. We note a pronounced skew, largely the result of the vast number of tiny sherds recovered. To correct the skew resulting from this concentration at the low end, a log transformation was applied, again using the BIMD 23 program, and we see in Table 29 that the severe skew has been eliminated and a normal distribution is approximated. We can now observe in the new scattergram an abrupt halt in the distribution as we move in the direction of "small sherds." The line of halt represents a mean sherd weight of close to two grams, evidently reflecting the minimum size of sherds collected. There is more scatter moving in the "large sherds" direction, representing the nearly complete vessels recovered in several large pieces.

To date, the work done with the sherd-weight data allows me to conclude only that there is a slight trend toward lower mean sherd weight as we move from early to late in the sequence on the site, as seen in the accompanying table.

Phase	Mean Sherd Wt. (gm.)
Juntunen	2.96
Bois Blanc	3.13
Mackinac	3.44

The difference does not seem great enough to explain the discrepancy between the sherd and vessel curves in Figure 41; however, no tests of significance were applied.

Under the hypothesis that low mean sherd weights indicate heavy foot traffic, the mean-sherd-weight measure could be used to plot areas of intense activity on the site, in which case the measure would represent an "index of trampling," but perhaps

TABLE 28

DISTRIBUTION OF PROVENIENCE UNITS BY SHERD FREQUENCIES AND WEIGHTS

Frequency	Weight (Grams) 1-500	501-1000	1001-1500	1501-2000	2001-2500	2501-3000	3001-3500	3501-4000	4001-4500	4501-5000	5001-5500	5501-6000	6001-6500	6501-7000	7001-7500	7501-8000	8001-8500	8501-9000	Total
4001-4500																	1		1
3501-4000													1					1	2
3001-3500																			0
2501-3000									1										1
2001-2500												2							2
1501-2000			1	1			2			1									5
1001-1500			1	2	1	2		1	1								1		9
501-1000		1	6	6	8					1			1						23
1- 500	211	56	14	5	4	2						1							293
Totals	211	57	22	14	13	4	2	1	2	2	0	3	2	0	0	0	2	1	336

TABLE 29

DISTRIBUTION OF SHERD FREQUENCIES AND WEIGHTS IN LOG$_e$ TRANSFORMATION

Log$_e$ Sherd Frequency	Log$_e$ Sherd Weight															Total
														1	2	3
													2	3	1	6
											3	5	3		1	12
										1	3	8		1		13
									1	5	7	4		1		18
								1	3	15	8	7	1	1		36
							2	9	14	14	2	1				42
						1	5	10	15	9						40
					2	6	11	12	8	1	2					42
					4	8	15	9	3			1				40
				2	7	7	8	2	1							27
		2		8	9	4	1		1			1				26
			3	3	2	1		1								10
	1	2	2	1	3	1										10
	2		3					1								6
	1	1	1			1										4
				1												1
Totals	4	5	9	15	27	29	42	45	46	45	25	27	6	7	4	336

Small Sherds ↖

Large Sherds ↘

the most important use would be in intersite comparisons. Mason (1966:27) indicates, for example, that 1,276 rim and body sherds represented 61 vessels at the Heins Creek site. This contrasts by an order of magnitude with the situation in the contemporary Mackinac phase at Juntunen, where 1713 rim and decorated body sherds (including, it is true, *all* fitted sherds from the seven reconstructible vessels) represented 631 Mackinac-ware vessels. An explanation for the striking difference would be furthered if we had mean sherd weights for the Heins Creek pottery to indicate whether Mason's sherds were markedly smaller than the Juntunen ones or whether other variables—such as, for example, that in judging when sherds belong to a common vessel—are involved.

If we assume that the constancy observed through time in vessel frequency represents a real situation indicative of stability in an industrial activity, not an unreasonable assumption if there was long-term stability in group size and in food-storage and preparing techiques, then it is the deviations from this essentially horizontal line (as seen in Fig. 41) that require examination. Other than vessels, the only artifacts stable in relative frequency through time were bone awls (not shown in the graphs). Their relative frequencies closely parallel those of vessels, and it seems reasonable to see in them, as in vessels, an artifact of basic importance, the need for which did not vary during the period of occupation of the site.

All other artifact classes show significant shifts in frequency. Chert waste increases in frequency through time (Fig. 41). Comparing weight and frequency, it appears that pieces were somewhat heavier on the average in the earliest phase. By referring to Figure 17 (p. 127) we see that the ratio of Bois Blanc to non-Bois Blanc cherts changes through time, the non-Bois Blanc chert types having a higher relative frequency in the two later phases. We also see that this situation correlates with changes in the ratios of bipolar and nonbipolar techniques. Thus the greater average weight in the Mackinac phase is largely to be explained by the prevalence of nonbipolar techiques used on Bois Blanc cherts. Figure 40 breaks down the two techniques into flakes and cores and distributes them by the occupations established by H. Wright (1962). Since fewer provenience units could be assigned to occupations than to phases, this graph is less reliable than Figure 41, based on phases, but it is suggestive at least to see that the most marked difference between occupations E and F is in the frequency of bipolar flakes, which rises sharply from E to F while practically everything else is declining. One would logically expect the frequency of bipolar cores to rise in a parallel fashion, but while this frequency does not actually decline from E to F, neither does it increase. Still, the apparent increase in total bipolar element can surely be regarded as real.

The two stone artifact types plotted on Figure 41 behave differently through time; points and bifaces gradually decline, while scrapers rise. The decline in points and bifaces is actually very slight; a chi-square test on points and bifaces versus vessels yielded a value of 1.12, whose probability of .50 at 2 d.f. does not lead us to suspect that points and bifaces are behaving differently than vessels through time. With regard to scrapers, the matter is different, and the chi-square value of 8.04 with probability of .02 at 2 d.f. in a test of independence between scrapers and vessels does suggest that more than sampling error is involved. An even higher chi-square value would obviously be obtained in a test of indèpendence between scrapers and points.

The complementary behavior through time between scrapers and points may reflect a widespread trend in the late prehistoric period. Thus Hall suggests that "the proportion of end scrapers relative to triangular points increases toward recent times and toward the Plains area" (1962, I: 121-22). The same trend is seen at Juntunen, as shown in the accompanying table, but it is not suggested that the obtained indexes can be used to fit Juntunen into

Phase	Juntunen Points	Scrapers	Index*
Juntunen	19	51	268.4
Bois Blanc	12	17	141.7
Mackinac	39	25	64.1

*Scrapers x 100/Points.

Hall's (1962, II:139) sequence. If this were attempted, Juntunen would appear to be several hundred years later than all other signs indicate. It is nonetheless of interest that a similar trend can apparently be detected in both areas. Hall makes no attempt to explain the trend, and it may well be that it occurred for different reasons in the Oneota area, on the Plains, and at Juntunen. Figure 40 suggests a reversal in the trend, if the decline from occupation E to F reflects cultural activities and not sampling error or geology. Mason (1966) also indicates that the Mero site does not fit well into Hall's sequence.

The copper industry shows the most spectacular change through time of all the artifact classes. The total number of pieces is plotted by phase in Figure 41 (p. 253), and the pieces are broken down into finished and unfinished (scrap) and distributed by occupation in Figure 40 (p. 252). From the latter figure it appears that the copper industry underwent its heyday in occupation E and declined in F, although, if this graph can be relied on, the decline is evidently mainly with respect to finished pieces. Perhaps more finished products were being traded out in F.

Food-animal bones decline after the Bois Blanc phase, thus providing a rough parallel with the behavior of sherds, but, while there may be a correlation here, it would seem a priori that in terms of life at the site a comparison of the animal-bone curve with that of points would be more likely to reveal a functional relationship. The decline in both through time compared with vessel frequencies (slight but significant) suggests an increase in the importance of vegetable foods.

14.2 HORIZONTAL DISTRIBUTIONS

Horizontal distributions of artifacts were studied for indications of loci of specialized activity and to delimit the area occupied at different periods. Several lines of approach were followed.

It was thought that some artifact types might be evenly distributed over the site, while others would show "clustering" in certain areas. Vessels showed the least change in vertical distribution but horizontally might be distributed either evenly or unevenly at any one time. The accompanying table shows that there

Phase	No. of Provenience Units	Vessels (observed)
Juntunen	98	269
Bois Blanc	53	161
Mackinac	194	425

$\chi^2 = 3.60$
$p = .20$

is no reason to suspect a changing distribution with respect to the provenience units from phase to phase. That is, in no phase are pots found in fewer or in more provenience units than would be expected under the hypothesis of random distribution. This essentially corroborates the picture as seen in Figure 41 (p. 253).

The same is not the case, however, with scrapers. The accompanying table shows that there are significant differences from phase to phase: fewer scrapers than expected are found in the Mackinac phase, about the number expected in Bois Blanc, and more than expected in Juntunen.

Phase	No. of Provenience Units	Scrapers	
		Observed	Expected
Juntunen	98	51	32
Bois Blanc	53	17	15
Mackinac	194	25	46

$\chi^2 = 24.5$
$p < .01$

We can go one step further and compare the frequency of scrapers with the number of units in each phase containing one or more scrapers, as in the accompanying table, from which the principal fact to be noted is that whereas in the Mackinac phase 25 scrapers are spread over 19 units, in Juntunen over twice the

Phase	Provenience Units with Scrapers	No. of Scrapers	Ratio of Scrapers to Units
Juntunen	20	51	2.6
Bois Blanc	8	17	2.1
Mackinac	19	25	1.3

number of scrapers are spread over only 20 units, from which we infer that the spatial organization of work in the latest phase differed from that in the earliest. In other words, in the Juntunen phase there were certain locations where scrapers tended to be left behind, and there were others where it was less the case.

Another strong case for horizontal clustering on the site is provided by copper. Data on copper distribution was presented earlier (sec. 7.5; see esp. Tables 20 and 21, p. 172). Figure 24, *c* (p. 174), plots the distribution, with two major areas of concentration encircled.

14.3 COMPARATIVE DISTRIBUTION

We may now compare the distributions of artifact classes with one another, making reference to the maps of Figure 24 (p. 174). (The numbers indicate actual frequencies, except that in Fig. 24, *a*, the frequencies should be multiplied by 100 to obtain actual counts.)

If we initially concentrate attention on the row of units along the +700 line—the same transect considered with respect to the "longhouse" (F. 22), whose profile is shown in Figure 7 (p. 36)—we observe moderate densities of artifacts from the point nearest the lake until the area of the "longhouse" is approached. (The exceedingly low densities in the square second from the top result from the fact that this unit was dug quickly for the first three feet without sifting or collecting artifacts—its frequencies should be disregarded.) We note that copper becomes densest in 700-180 (232 pieces), while sherds have a remarkable peak (23,000 sherds) in 700-190. The latter square also holds the record for pipes (5), projectile points (14; Fig. 24, *d*, p. 174), and Mackinac-ware vessels (79; Fig. 42, *b*). The only artifact class peaking in the adjacent square, 700-200, is scrapers (37). It is notable that all these peaks fall between the two rows of postmolds believed to form the walls of a house. The peak in Mackinac-ware vessels is important to consider because, in this area of maximum disturbance, the early-phase materials cannot be sorted out, as is evident from the "disturbance chart" of Table 30. The

TABLE 30

LINKS BETWEEN SQUARE-SHEET LEVELS AND SQUARES THROUGH MATCHING SHERDS

Level	Square						
	710-140	700-160	700-180	710-180	700-190	700-200	710-200
1*				d	a	s	v
2					b g	s	
3		f	h		abcdefghijk q		djkmqsuvw
4			l	em	bcdef qr		j s vw
5		f	fh m	em	bcdef h	n q	
6	b	f	h		bc		u
7			h		bcd g p	cinopqr	n
8	s		l	em	c no q		
9			f		a e		
10							
11					a		

* Level 1 = "Surface to square sheet 1" material, Level 2 = "Square sheets 1 to 2" material, etc.

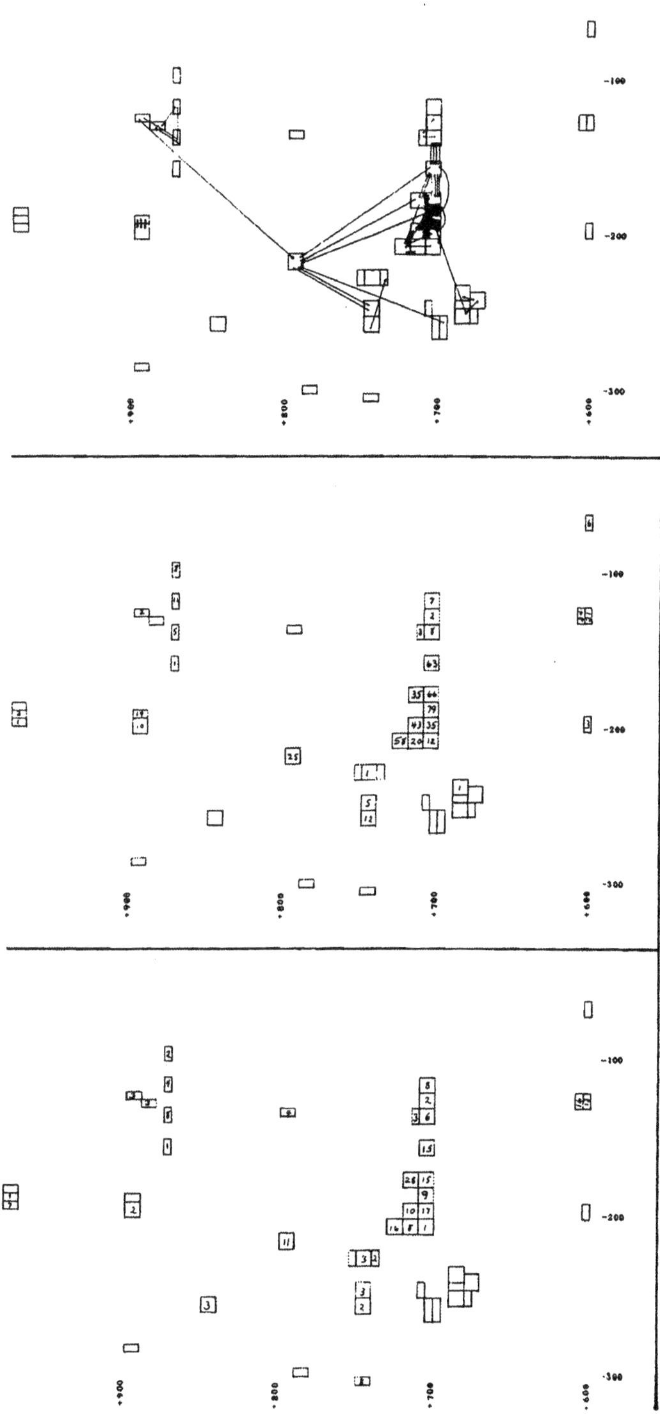

a—Units linked through matching sherds

b—Distribution of Mackinac-ware vessels

c—Distribution of Juntunen-ware vessels

Fig. 42

square-sheet levels of the line of squares being discussed are indicated in the left column, and it should be realized that "level 4" (square sheets 3-4) in one square cannot be equated with "level 4" in another square; these levels bear no necessary relation to each other except insofar as they all begin with zero at the surface. How many square sheets were drawn depended on the nature of the stratification and the sensitivity of the excavators.

Each letter in Table 30 represents a vessel, sherds of which were found in different levels or squares. We immediately see that 700-190 has the most links both vertically and horizontally; thus sherds of vessel "a" were found in the top and in the bottom levels. A sherd of vessel "m" was found in 700-180 and 710-200, over 20 feet away. In all but a few cases, the vessels represented at both top and bottom are early types, indicating that many more sherds were brought up from earlier levels than descended from top to bottom.

The foregoing class of information was used to assess the reliability of provenience units. We conclude from the "disturbance chart" that the vertical position of any artifact in 700-190 cannot be relied on at all; the whole square, with the exception of certain concentrations in hearths, is badly disturbed, and almost none of its provenience units could be assigned to phases. Figure 42, *a*, shows the same situation horizontally, the ends of each line representing two sherds of the same vessel. Square 700-190 has by far the most sherd links with other squares. The widest horizontal distribution of all vessels on the site was enjoyed by the vessel indicated as "f" in Table 30 (illustrated as Pl. XIX, *c*). Two sherds of this vessel were recovered from squares separated by 220 feet: 870-160 and Feature 11. The vessel is Bois Blanc ware, but I suspect that the scattering occurred in the Juntunen phase both because the most far-flung sherds occurred in deposits of that period and because F. 11 dates to that phase.

Figure 42, *b-c*, compares the horizontal distribution of Mackinac and Juntunen wares, presented in terms of actual frequencies. In terms of its occurrence on the whole site, Mackinac ware should outnumber Juntunen ware in a ratio of 2.2 to 1. We see that this is so for some units, but not for others, and the total picture suggests differences in areas intensively occupied in the two phases. The units along the +700 line that form a group nearest the lake (Unit 8 in Fig. 4, p. 19) are low in Mackinac ware; this was the area of Mackinac-phase Feature 23, after the deposition of which considerable dune building occurred with only sporadic occupational indications, until after stabilization of the dune in the Juntunen phase more occupations took place. At the landward end of the +700 line, squares 700-200 and 700-210 show a high ratio of Mackinac- to Juntunen-ware vessels; Unit 6 (Fig. 4, p. 19) had Mackinac and Bois Blanc occupations but none in the Juntunen phase. These facts suggest that the center of the site shifted toward the lake with time. But there are other indications that, at least sometime during the last phase, occupation took place on the area of the Arrowhead Drive site, for, in the latter area, the only pottery type other than Middle Woodland types found are Juntunen-ware types, of a subvariety that seems to me closest to the vessels recovered from the Round Island site. But they occur in the first few inches of soil, and there are no signs of occupation, hence the over-all picture of occupation moving in a lakeward direction is not contradicted.

14.4 DEPOSITIONAL HISTORY

Chapter 4 presented a depositional history based on the geological studies of H. Wright (1962). At this point, the archaeological and ecological data will be integrated and the over-all sequence of events reconstructed.

Layer I (see sec. 4.2), the bedded sands and gravels underlying all Late Woodland occupations, cannot be dated, nor is the subsequent sequence of dune formations clearly understood. Low dunes formed on the lakeward side of the site presumably at a later date than the one stabilized by the time of Juntunen phase, and deposits of sand, much of it evidently deposited by wind, blanket much of the area landward of the site from the backslope well up into the woods, probably representing wind deposits coeval with beach formations farther toward the lake. Dune formation was not observed in many other areas near the shore on the island, where leaf mold and a very thin gravelly soil over-lie gravels and weathered bedrock and where there is a high frequency of windfallen trees with roots that penetrated vertically no more than a few inches. As a result of these conditions, while the temporal relationship of the Arrowhead Drive site to Juntunen is known, thanks to carbon estimates, the environment at the time of the Middle Woodland occupation—particularly the lake level—is unknown. The water's edge cannot have been farther inland than Feature 45, the Arrowhead Drive-period burials (Unit 7 of Fig. 4, p. 19); it *may* not have been much less inland than the middle contour line of the three 594-foot contours shown on Figure 4 that run the length of the site, because the only Arrowhead Drive sherds recovered from the entire site were the few—probably of one vessel—found in Unit 15. But the length of time intervening between elevation of the beds underlying the site and the first Late Woodland occupation is unknown. It would be of great interest to know whether the lowering of lake level that created the offshore shallows and other features was a relatively sudden event or occurred gradually.

There was clearly an occupational gap between Middle and Late Woodland that may have been up to 800 years in duration. Whether before or during this period (by about A.D. 600, according to Wright's estimate) the lake had retreated with the result that by about A.D. 800 what had once been an offshore bar was dry land blanketed by deposits of beach sand and covered by forest growth—trees undoubtedly had been advancing with the retreating shoreline as a climax element in a pattern of floral succesion since some time after the island emerged following the high-water stage. The forest cover by A.D. 800 was dense enough and had stood long enough to permit the formation of a pronounced soil of the northern podzol type. The growth of this soil was terminated by fire, for which there is evidence in the form of a layer of jet-black sand containing much charcoal in many areas on the site.

The first occupation—"A" of the Mackinac phase—occurred as a meager scattering of artifacts in and on this burned layer, so it is suggested that the fire may have been set deliberately. On the other hand, other areas on the island show charcoal-rich strata, and the aerial photographs show various stages of forest succession in local areas, indicating that small forest fires occurred with some frequency, not necessarily caused by human agency.

In most areas of the site the burned layer is preserved only sporadically, having mostly been broken up and disturbed by later occupations or perhaps in part deflated by wind action. In the southern part of the site it is not visible at all. The zone overlying the jet-black layer consists of lenses of sand, and on them occur the first really intense occupation, to which can be assigned features F. 2, 23, and 39, as well as some postmolds. A carbon estimate of A.D. 835±75 (M-1142; Crane and Griffin 1961) was obtained for this occupation (H. Wright's layer V.) Cleland noted among the fauna some species that did not occur in later levels, such as porcupine, marten, and squirrel. The only vegetal remains recovered were birch-bark and hazelnut (which also appear in the other occupations) and two maize kernels.

Toward the end of occupation A, there are indications that the forest began to encroach, with attendant podzolization. After occupation A, a transgression of water on the lowest part of the site appears to have occurred, as evidenced by black laminae in water-deposited sand overlapping cultural deposits and by a few water-worn sherds in one square in the most lakeward part of the site. Certainly both an end to human occupation and a deposition by wind of much sand over the site took place, preserving intact such features as the occupation floor of F. 23. During this period of deposition several very brief occupations occurred, leaving thin layers containing virtually nothing but fish scales in dune deposits on the foreslope area and meager deposits of artifacts elsewhere. The low density of artifacts is displayed by Figures 17 and 40. Two occupations are recognized by Wright, termed B and C. Wright infers that C occurred during a temporary halt in sand deposition. Because of the paucity of artifacts and the difficulty in assigning provenience units to B and C, it was not possible to demonstrate significant formal differences in artifacts between A, B, and C, hence they were all lumped as the Mackinac phase. The latest part of occupation C is carbon dated at A.D. 910±75 (M-1141; Crane and Griffin 1961). The only species first appearing in occupation C is the dog.

We can generalize over the Mackinac phase by stating that an intense occupation—either many people at one time or fewer people repeatedly over a longer time—was succeeded by several light and poorly attested occupations. The pottery is early Late Woodland, defined as Mackinac ware for the site, and is most similar to contemporary pottery in Wisconsin. The fish bones and scales and the two harpoon heads indicate that the site was a fishing village from the start. (We lack evidence of exploitive activities on the Arrowhead Drive site.) No burials assignable to the Mackinac phase were located.

At the end of the period during which wind-blown sand was being deposited on the site, another major occupation, D, or the Bois Blanc phase, took place. There are indications that the forest was again encroaching in some places and that in other areas on the site a meadow soil was forming; plant stabilization of the dune is thus indicated. A carbon estimate of A.D. 1070±75 (M-1140; Crane and Griffin 1961) was obtained for this phase.

The frequency of artifacts per cubic foot of matrix was high in the Bois Blanc phase, probably because little sand was being deposited. Sherds, animal bones, and chert wastage are densest in this phase. The vessel count, on the other hand, shows a slightly lower density than for either of the other phases.

The Bois Blanc phase marks the first appearance of a number of animal species, and it is of sigificance that, of them, deer and turkey do not reappear later. Cleland (1966) sees a trend from occupations B to D involving increase of the Carolinian-province species, with a return to predominance of Hudsonian fauna in E. Taken together, these factors suggest a slight climatic change about A.D. 1000, probably with a higher mean annual temperature; alternately a change of flora may be indicated, but for this there is no evidence from the site. Although it cannot be demonstrated, the animal bones also suggest that the mammals were of somewhat greater importance in subsistence than fish during this phase.

No features could be securely assigned to the Bois Blanc phase, presumably because it occurred on the site mostly in the central and western areas. In the central area, disturbance from later occupations and the telescoping of strata made it hard to assign features to a phase; in the western area, not enough area was uncovered to sample features adequately, No burials could be assigned to the phase.

Following the Bois Blanc phase, a period of severe erosion took place during which some sand was redeposited as lenses in depressions in the surface of the site. A few brief occupations on the surface of erosion could be detected, all denoted by H. Wright as occupation E and probably characterized by pottery called Bois Blanc Castellated Corded, Juntunen Linear Punctate, and perhaps some Juntunen Drag-and-Jab pottery. As seen in Figures 17 (p. 127) and 40 (p. 252), the artifacts occurred densely, a condition probably to be explained in part by concentration of artifacts attendant upon deflation, much as the low densities in B and C can be explained by the fact that they occurred during periods of sand deposition. Scrapers and copper in E *appear* to have particularly high densities, and it is conceivable that the copper industry was of higher intensity in occupation E than in F, but, in view of the evidence of much copper-working from around hearths of late occupation F, I suspect that the density indications are misleading—especially since all other signs point to E as being a light and sporadic occupation, evidenced in only a few areas on the site.

Yarnell (1964) originally concluded that the first maize kernels appeared in E, but the reassignment of provenience units to the more reliable phases showed that two kernels came from two definite and undisturbed Mackinac-phase units, hence the late date for introduction of corn to the site becomes questionable, although E may mark the beginning of its increased importance. Cleland's data suggest the beginning of a cooler phase beginning with E; Figure 25 shows that the Bois Blanc phase appears to be a reversal in species predominance, followed by a return to animals preferring cooler and moister habitats in E, the first part of the Juntunen phase. This coolness would seemingly argue against a first introduction of maize in E.

Occupation F yielded an abundance of charred seeds, most of them appearing for the first time in this occupation. There are a number of berries and various weed seeds—*Chenopodium*, *Galium*, and *Rumex*—which, together with the soil profile, suggest that the site was well cleared of trees, with grassy meadow covering much of the area and bushes growing around the periphery. Yarnell noted that the plant remains tended to cluster in F—that is, when they occurred, nine or ten plants tended to be found together rather than occurring alone in a deposit.

The earliest of the stratigraphic levels assigned by H. Wright to occupation F (XXV_3) includes Feature 20, for which we have a carbon estimate of A.D. 1330±100 (M-1391; Crane and Griffin 1965). The feature contained portions of seven vessels, all of the Juntunen Drag-and-Jab type. The carbon date is essentially identical in age with the A.D. 1320±75 date on material from Feature 11 (M-1188; Crane and Griffin 1963). The F. 11 ossuary as well as at least three others, F. 18, 34, and 43, appear to have been dug during this intense occupation, which was probably also the period of the building of the "longhouse," F.22. F seems in addition to have had the main copper-working occupation. It also shows the highest frequency of bipolar flakes.

Because of deflation, erosion, land-leveling, and plowing in later times and because deposition of wind-blown sand had ceased by occupation F, it and all succeeding ones, except in a very few places, are telescoped together and cannot be separated stratigraphically. Toward the end of occupation F, people making Oneota-style pottery appear to have inhabited the site. Unfortunately, it is impossible to be precise about the relationship, temporal or cultural, between the Oneota pottery-makers and the people making Juntunen ware, although the pottery does not indicate mixing of the two highly disparate traditions. If F. 11 is a Juntunen-phase feature, then the two miniature vessels from it—one Oneotoid, the other Mackinac-ware in style, together with the absence of any Juntunen ware from the feature, present a puzzle.

Subsequent occupations appear to have been sporadic and short-termed, judging from stray sherds of Iroquois Linear, Lalonde High Collar, and of a few unidentified but evidently late wares, encountered mostly in the plow zone. Thus it can be said that the Juntunen phase was the last period of important use of the site as a fishing station and that the site was in use for about 600 years.

Trends over the 600-year period can be detected. There was a slight decrease in mean sherd weight, a slight decrease in points and bifaces, and a marked increase in the frequency per cubic foot of scrapers. After the Bois Blanc phase, the copper industry becomes of increasing importance, while there is an apparent decrease in the mammalian fauna—both a decline in density and a decrease in the number of species present. Among the fish, sturgeon declines and whitefish increases in frequency.

These trends are all rather slight—except for the copper—and do not contradict the basic point about the site, namely, that a stable adaptation to a resource whose occurrence can normally be expected at certain seasons of the year is indicated for the whole period of occupation, in an environment that except for a minor climatic fluctuation about A.D. 1000-1100 was also stable.

XV

EXTERNAL RELATIONSHIPS AND DATING

The present chapter will complete the archaeology of the Juntunen site by comparing its materials with those from other sites in the Upper Great Lakes, utilizing a temporal framework based on radiocarbon age estimates. Chapter 16 will attempt a cultural reconstruction with the aid of the ethnographic record.

There are several well-attested sequences for nearby areas that are of particular interest in terms of parallels with the Juntunen series. Of all known sites, Mason's (1966) sequence from the Door Peninsula near Green Bay, Wisconsin, has the most intimate connection with the earlier Juntunen-site phases (Mackinac and Bois Blanc) and considerable interaction around the top of Lake Michigan is indicated for this time period. For the Bois Blanc and Juntunen phases, the developments in Ontario as seen in Wright's (1966b) analysis are the most closely similar. Wisconsin Oneota can be brought in at the late end of the Juntunen sequence. There are also many manifestations part of whose formal or temporal range can be fitted into the Juntunen sequence: Blackduck, Madison ware, the Clam River Focus, Isle Royale sites, and the Pic River site. A logical procedure is to consider these manifestations from the point of view of the Juntunen sequence, beginning with the Mackinac phase. Figure 43 illustrates the temporal relationships.

15.1 MACKINAC-PHASE RELATIONSHIPS

Looking first to the west of the Straits, one finds that some Mackinac-ware pottery is close to the Heins Creek ware of the Door Peninsula (Mason 1966). Mason characterizes Heins Creek as having cord marking as a "virtually universal surface finish" (1966:14) and as showing the use of cord-wrapped objects. As with Mackinac ware, undecorated body sherds could not be sorted into types. Mason's description of the physical features, such as paste and temper, tallies closely with Mackinac ware. Statistics on body-sherd thickness are presented in the accompanying table. There is probably no significant difference in body thickness.

Heins Creek Corded Stamped has no close analogue in Mackinac ware, although some similarity is seen in Mackinac Punctate. Heins Creek Cordwrapped-Stick Impressed, on the other hand, is exceedingly close to Mackinac Banded.

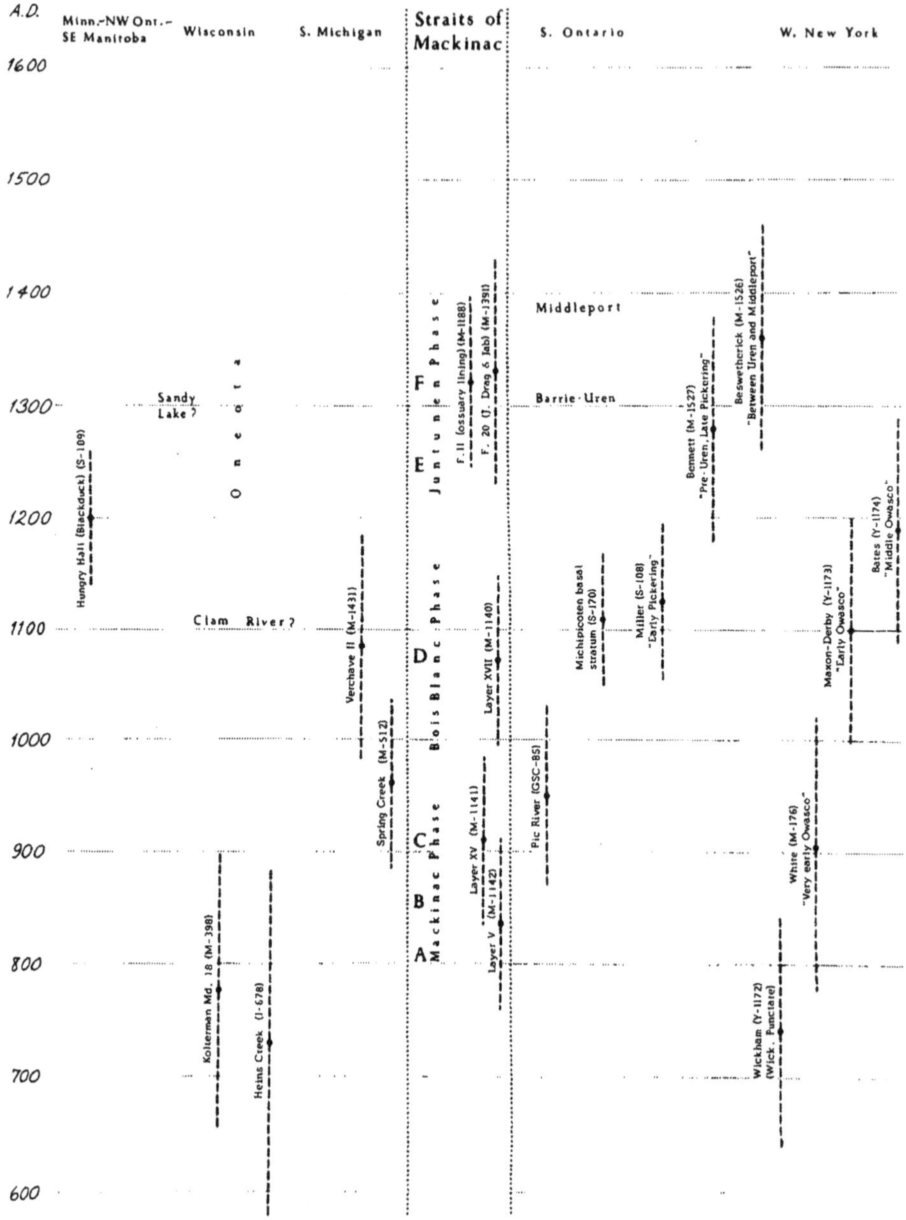

Fig. 43.—Comparative chronology of some Upper Great Lakes manifestations

Pottery Ware	Body Sherd Thickness	
	$\bar{X}$ (mm.)	s (mm.)
Heins Creek*	6.9	1.3
Mackinac**	6.3	1.4

*Data from Mason 1966:14.
**Excluding Mackinac Undecorated.

Madison Cord Impressed on the Door Peninsula is very much like Mackinac Cord Impressed. The Madison Cord Impressed sherds from sites excavated by Baerreis that I examined in the collections of the Department of Anthropology, University of Wisconsin, differed from the same type in the Door Peninsula largely in terms of thickness—the former were notable for extreme thinness, averaging about 4 mm. Both varieties, however, shared such traits as a row of punctates commonly found as the bottom design element, horizontal bands of linear cord as the most common motif, a tendency toward thinner vessel walls approaching the lips, and a common absence of lip decoration. The aberrant "punctated pottery" from Heins Creek is similar to Mackinac Punctate, while the few sherds of incised pottery are reminiscent of the unique cord-impressed and crosshatched incised vessel from Juntunen illustrated as Plate XIV, *a*.

The splayed lips common to Mackinac ware are not commonly seen in Wisconsin; they are absent from Heins Creek ware, and the only examples I observed in the Milwaukee Public Museum collections were on sherds from Sheboygan County, collected (according to the catalog) from dunes at a depth of about one foot below the surface.

Similarities between Door Peninsula Late Woodland and the Mackinac phase other than in ceramics can be seen in several other artifact classes. Projectile points from Heins Creek were all triangular; of the 12 recovered, 8 were unifacial. Of the 118 classifiable points from Mero, 78 were triangular; of these, less than half were bifacially worked. In terms of size and shape, while no statistical tests were performed, the Door Peninsula points appear to have a slightly lower length-to-width ratio than the Juntunen Triangular point but otherwise are within range. It is notable that they are all of non-local chert, like the Juntunen points—an unusual feature for Wisconsin, where the uniform use of a brown quartizite from Plano times through Late Woodland is a prominent feature of many stone industries.

A few cores from Mero suggest the presence of the bipolar technique; according to Binford and Quimby (1963:305), bipolar materials occur as far south along the Wisconsin shore as Sturgeon Bay.

Although McKern (1963) regards the Clam Lake Focus of northwestern Wisconsin as extremely late in the prehistoric sequence, the stylistic characteristics of the pottery as well as many of the burial traits suggest an earlier temporal placement. The evidence from Juntunen and other sites in Wisconsin and Minnesota indicates that Clam Lake might be contemporary with at least the later part of the Mackinac phase, as early as A.D. 1000. Thus the vessel from the middle stratum of the Clam Lake mound illustrated by McKern (1963, Fig. 27), has thickened lip, interior and lip decoration in cord-wrapped stick edge, and is very close to Mackinac Undecorated. McKern's Figure 29 (referred to in the text as "Fig. 36") has exterior decoration in horizontal bands of cordwrapped object but is otherwise rather close to Madison Cord Impressed. Figure 36 (referred to in the text as "Fig. 29") has decoration similar to Mackinac Banded. Two very small vessels strongly resemble the miniature vessel from Juntunen Feature 31 herein illustrated as Plate XXIV, *d*, and tentatively assigned to the Bois Blanc phase.

In the uppermost stratum of the same Clam Lake mound—a "cumulative" mound in which burials were added at intervals—a vessel was found for which McKern proposed the name Burnett Stamped Conoidal. As described by him and illustrated in Figure 34 of his report (1963), the vessel clearly differs from the other vessels in the mound and may perhaps be related to certain sherds of the Selkirk Focus, particularly those named Alexander Fabric Impressed by MacNeish (1958; see esp. the latter's Pl. XVIII). If so, then the Clam Lake Focus should be roughly contemporary with Blackduck and with late Madison-ware pottery.

Corroborative evidence for this temporal placement is provided by the pipes from the Clam Lake mound (McKern 1963, Fig. 21), which certainly look more like early Late Woodland pipes than ones from the late end of the sequence, and by the perforations of the long bones, a trait shared with the early Late Woodland Younge site of southeastern Michigan (Greenman 1937, Pl. VI; Fitting 1965) but not seen in Oneota burials or the Juntunen ossuaries. These ideas are confirmed by the carbon date of A.D. 1110±100 obtained on charred bone from Burial 18, Stratum 3, Spencer Lake Mound (Michigan XII, in press).

Looking to the south in Michigan we find that Mackinac ware occurs at various sites near Cross Village on the eastern shore of Lake Michigan only a short distance south of Fort Michilimackinac and probably as far south as Little Traverse Bay. It occurs in various places in Emmet, Cheboygan, and Presque Isle Counties and no doubt in many other localities around the shores of Lakes Michigan and Huron at the top end of the lower peninsula of Michigan.

In southeastern Michigan, some sherds of the Riviere au Vase and Younge phases, notably Wayne Cord-marked (Fitting 1965, Pl. IV), are clearly related to Mackinac-ware pottery, but the typical southeastern Michigan vessel shape—like a pendulous bag and reminiscent of pottery to the south of the Great Lakes—differs strongly from the squat Mackinac vessels, which are more similar to vessel shapes from the Plains.

Pottery related to Mackinac ware is found along the north shore of Lake Michigan; similarly, submerged sites on the south shore of Lake Superior ought to yield such pottery. In general, however, the area to the north of the Straits seems to have been pre-empted by Blackduck ware, which although not as early in its appearance as Mackinac ware is still evidently the earliest Late Woodland pottery in much of the area (and is also, according to some, the pottery persisting until historic times). The dating of Blackduck in all areas is in some confusion; the Pic River carbon date of A.D. 950±80 (GSC-85; Dyck and Fyles 1963) and the Hungry Hall date of A.D. 1200±60 (S-109; McCallum and Wittenberg 1962) are perhaps the most reliable. The former dates a Blackduck level that also yielded other artifacts similar to ones from Juntunen. I observed* a few Pic River sherds that were very close to Mackinac Banded and Mackinac Zigzag Lip. The Pic River projectile points fit perfectly into the Juntunen Triangular and Juntunen Notched categories. Scrapers—some made on cherts very similar to ones used at Juntunen—show a wider variety of sizes and shapes than at Juntunen. The collection contains some shaped like the little "thumbnail" scrapers from Juntunen. A few small bladelets—down to 15 mm. in length—suggest the possible presence of a bipolar technique. There were a few copper pieces: some rather poorly made awls, a few rolled-sheet beads, and one copper knife about 10 cm. in length, with outline like the specimen herein illustrated in Plate XXX, *b*.

The four carbon dates for Minnesota Blackduck sites range from A.D. 800 to A.D. 1490. These Minnesota dates (I-789,790,794,796,

*In collections from the Pic River site in the National Museum, Ottawa, studied through the courtesy of Dr. James V. Wright.

unpublished) were "obtained on materials excavated in the 1930's... and kept in open storage" (Elden Johnson, personal communication), hence the time spread could well be the result of contamination, perhaps from fallout. Taking into account the standard deviations, the spread is probably too great for the carbon estimates to be statistically considered to have come from a common population, but nevertheless if one calculates an arithmetic mean for the age estimates, the resulting date of A.D. 1213 is remarkably close to A.D. 1200 (S-109) for Hungry Hall in the Rainy River region, a Blackduck site. Therefore, alignment of Blackduck with Juntunen's late Mackinac and Bois Blanc phases seems most reasonable and is in accord with the Juntunen stratigraphic evidence as well as with the situation at the Pic River site, in the lowest level of which Wright (1966a) found early Pickering sherds in association with Blackduck.

Looking to the east of the Straits, we find poorly reported Point Peninsula and Owasco-like materials in southern Ontario for the period of the Mackinac phase, while in New York State the period is that of the transition from manifestations that Ritchie groups as Late Point Peninsula to those he classifies as Early Owasco.

At a number of locations in the Upper Great Lakes—the Mero site on the Door Peninsula of Wisconsin (Mason 1966), the Juntunen site, the Lucas or Inverhuron site (Kenyon 1959; Lee 1960), and various stations along the north shore of Lake Superior (Wright 1963, 1966b)—a gap has been found to exist between Middle and Late Woodland occupations. The gap is both spatial and cultural; the evidence for it ranges from sterile layers to complete areal separation of components and includes shifts to lower beach levels, changes in types of terrain chosen for sites, as well as changes in settlement patterns and in the formal characteristics of most artifacts. A temporal gap in occupation of considerable duration is inferred from such evidence.

Such a gap is not seen at Frank Bay on Lake Nipissing (Ridley 1954), the site closest to the north shore of Lake Superior and to the Inverhuron site. If the transition from late Point Peninsula to Early Owasco in New York is to be equated with one from Middle to Late Woodland, then the transition occurs there about three hundred years later than elsewhere (see Fig. 43, p. 270), and one is led to question the meaning of the transition from Middle to Late Woodland in New York State. While resemblances of Juntunen pottery to types in New York State are greater in the Mackinac phase than in any other phase at Juntunen, the resemblances are split between those to Late Point Peninsula, notably the Kipp Island phase (Ritchie, personal communication), and those to early Owasco, notably Carpenter Brook.

A fairly smooth transition from Middle to Late Woodland is seen in southern Michigan (Quimby 1952:104-5). In Wisconsin, there is controversy as to the transition. Baerreis in 1953 regarded Madison ware as part of the Effigy Mound complex and thought that it began in Middle Woodland while Mason's data place it in the Late Woodland period. The question arises as to what we mean by the transition from Middle to Late Woodland. Are we talking of pottery styles, settlement patterns, ethnic groups, subsistence patterns, or climatic shifts? The only place where the transition apparently involves an unbridgable temporal and cultural gap is the north-central part of the Upper Great Lakes. This is indeed a marked contrast with Wisconsin, Lower Michigan, New York, and their respective southern ties.

Did parts of the Upper Great Lakes become uninhabited for a number of centuries? If so, can we see in the Juntunen site vis-a-vis parts of the Blackduck area a temporal gradient in reoccupation, such that the Juntunen site contains early Late Woodland, while Blackduck pottery, apparently later than the earliest Mackinac-ware pottery, is the first to appear in a broad area to the north—and perhaps appears in this broad area suddenly, as suggested by the typological unity of Blackduck wherever found?

If these ideas should be found to bear weight, then the shift from Middle to Late Woodland in the Canadian biotic province—the area where the temporal gap is notable—may indicate, first, very low-density occupation of the area by Early and Middle Woodland groups whose adaptation was not quite adequate to the particular conditions, leading ultimately to population decline. The increasingly successful Late Woodland occupation may have been the result of better adaptive devices (these need not all have been only on the technological side) developed to the south of the Canadian biotic province but then found to be well adapted to the Canadian province itself. The introduction or development of new varieties of maize may be one factor in the shift, particularly if, as the Juntunen evidence suggests, maize was a part of the culture of all groups, in areas where it could be grown, from the beginning of the Late Woodland period.

15.2 BOIS BLANC-PHASE RELATIONSHIPS

While a number of changes between the Mackinac and Bois Blanc phases suggest a minor climatic shift (see sec. 11.5 and 14.1), the changes in pottery styles do not show a sharp break with the Mackinac tradition. The main change is from splayed lips to braced rims and the appearance of castellations. The relatively high degree of continuity contrasts with the transition from the Bois Blanc to the Juntunen phase, in which a number of discontinuities can be seen.

The over-all picture in the northeastern United States and southeastern Canada in the period between about A.D. 700 and A.D. 1000—the period of the Mackinac phase—is one of evenly grading crosscutting clines in pottery style attributes. Thus, disregarding for the moment minor points of difference, we can observe an overriding generic similarity with rareness of sharp stylistic breaks. This situation has been commented on by Byers, who says that

> Corded pottery of one sort or another, including corded-stick impressed and corded-paddled, extends from Nova Scotia to Saskatchewan.... Pottery of this general style is widespread in an area traditionally Algonkian .... It does not appear to me that the Iroquois can take all credit for this. We are here dealing with something much larger than developing Iroquoian cultures [Byers 1961:47-48].

I would enlarge the area he discussed.

A blending of attributes and an absence of sharp geographic borders thus seems to prevail with respect to pottery styles for the early Late Woodland period over a broad area, linking together areas as widely separated as tidewater Virginia and the northern Plains. Beginning about A.D. 1000, however, regional differences start to become more marked, and they continue to increase in the area as a whole until obliterated in many areas by the spread of the Mississippian and Iroquoian traditions. Bois Blanc-phase pottery looks less like a regional type than like a geographically intermediate ware. It shares attributes of distinct traditions: in Wisconsin, Point Sauble Collared; in the area to the north, Blackduck.

About the only linking trait across most of the Upper Great Lakes at this time (aside from the Blackduck area) is seen in a rim shape variously called "vee-shaped," braced," "cambered," or "filleted". Such rims are seen in Bois Blanc Braced Rim and B.B. Beaded (see profiles *l-x* in Fig. 9, p. 57). The attribute appears in southeastern Michigan (sec. 5.7.3.1) and in the Saginaw Bay area. The portion of a vessel found near Flat Rock, Michigan and illustrated by Fitting (1965) as Plate II, is remarkably similar to the Bois Blanc Braced Rim fragments illustrated herein as Plate XVIII, *a*. In Wisconsin the attribute is seen in Hahn Cord-Impressed and Point Sauble Collared; the "braced" rim shape is about the only attribute linking these pottery styles with the Glen Meyer and Pickering pottery of southern Ontario (Wright 1966b), although it may also be noted that castellations occur on both Bois Blanc and Glen Meyer pottery. This trend toward rim thickening, perhaps leading ultimately to the collars on the rims of many Late Woodland wares toward the end of the prehistoric period, is a very widespread phenomenon, appearing in Canton Ware of Iowa about A.D. 1000, and in Dillinger of Illinois (as folded rim). In New York State it occurs on Jack's Reef Corded Collar and Levanna Corded Collar. Braced rims do not offer a very good link between pottery in western New York State and southwestern Ontario. The New York styles of rim treatment are in fact closest to some Wisconsin vessels, a point mentioned earlier (sec. 5.7.4).

Thus regional traditions in pottery increased in importance between A.D. 1000 and A.D. 1300. The geographic shadings in stylistic traits in the earlier period give way to more clearly-defined boundaries, and wares such as Point Sauble, Aztalan Collared, Glen Meyer, and Pickering appear to lack the great internal variability of the earlier wares in their respective areas. Within-group variability is being reduced, while between-group variability is considerably increased; in general it can be said that attributes show more pronounced clustering.

Of all the pottery of this period that has been considered, Bois Blanc ware maintains the greatest internal variability, which indicates the continued operation of the "crossroads effect" and also suggests that Juntunen pottery may be a sensitive indicator of trends in a number of surrounding areas.

Bois Blanc ware was observed to occur on several sites at the north end of Lake Michigan that were reported by Binford and Quimby (1963) to have a bipolar chipping industry. The distribution of this technique—between the Door Peninsula of Wisconsin and the Eastport site in Michigan (see Fig. 2, p. 9) and probably as far north as the Pic River site—as well as its absence from the flint industry from the Oakfield site in western New York State that I examined in Buffalo,* is of great interest in indicating that both the technique and the Bois Blanc pottery style were distributed over a limited area. One chert piece** from the Too site (Glen Meyer) in southern Ontario was a bipolar core of the flat variety (see sec. 6.1.2.2). Battering was evident on

*Through the courtesy of Dr. Marian White.

**Examined at the National Museum of Canada, Ottawa.

both ends; one end had been reduced to a ridge, while the other was the original flat cortical surface of the pebble from which the core had been derived. A number of parallel flake scars occurred on the more convex face of the core. A distribution study of the bipolar technique compared to a similar study for ceramics should be of importance for study of male-culture versus female-culture diffusion patterns (see Owen 1965). This matter will be developed further in the next chapter.

It is worthy of mention that palisaded villages first began to appear between A.D. 1100 and A.D. 1200 at Glen Meyer, Pickering, and Owasco sites. The Miller site at the north shore of Lake Ontario, dated A.D. 1125±70 (S-108; McCallum and Wittenberg 1962), is a fortified village with large elongate oval houses; one was 24 by 57 feet with five central hearths. It appears that fortifications do not occur in northeastern Michigan until at least 200 years later. Thus the Linseman-Walters Earthwork Enclosure in Ogemaw County is dated A.D. 1350±75 (M-779), and the Mikado Earthwork Enclosure in Alcona County is dated A.D. 1450±75 (M-777). Both are discussed in Moll (1958). Increases in population density in Ontario and possibly New York State may have preceded such changes in Michigan. In western New York, the earliest longhouses appear to be seen at the Bates site and the Oakfield site, both dating about A.D. 1300.

15.3 JUNTUNEN-PHASE RELATIONSHIPS

As seen in Figure 43, (p. 268) the transition to the Juntunen phase occurs at about the same time as the shift in Ontario from the Glen Meyer and Pickering Branches of the Early Ontario Iroquois to the Middle Ontario Iroquois (using Wright's [1966] terminology). Uren is an early substage of Middle Ontario Iroquois, and Middleport (Wintemberg 1948; Wright 1960) is a late horizon. It is in Middleport that Wright begins to be able to detect signs of the historic Iroquoian-speaking divisions. The time spread of Barrie-Uren is bracketed by the A.D. 1280±100 date from the late pre-Uren Bennett site (M-1527) and the A.D. 1360±100 date for Beswetherick, considered just post-Uren (M-1526). The time relationships in Figure 43 (p. 270) suggest that occupation E, the brief earliest Juntunen-phase occupation, occurred before the time of the Uren substage of the Middle Ontario Iroquois. Although Wright (1966b) considers Uren to have developed out of his Late Pickering and Glen Meyer stages, the occurrence of only some of the Uren traits in the Juntunen phase suggests that Uren may in fact represent a blending of two traditions that developed separately: one consisting of diffused elements seen in pure form at Juntunen and another consisting of elements that are in fact phylogenetic developments out of Glen Meyer and Pickering.

Ceramic similarities between the Juntunen phase and the Ontario sites, Barrie and Uren, (Ridley 1958; Wintemberg 1928) include vessel shapes and decoration. Vessels of both wares have more or less rounded bottoms, developed collars, and castellations. Shared decorative techniques and motifs include linear punctations and drag-and-jab, both applied commonly in horizontal bands on collars, with a row of punctations at the base of the collar. Decoration is commonly applied to rim interiors and lips, but the addition of decoration below collars is uncommon. Uren pottery attributes, shared with Glen Meyer-Pickering but not seen in Juntunen, include trailing and incising, ribbed paddle and check-stamp impressing, and some decorative motifs.

Juntunen ware marks a typological break with the previous pottery tradition in the Straits of Mackinac, and the break is accompanied by a number of other changes. The fauna of the site shows a return to the moister and cooler conditions of the Mackinac phase. Bipolar flakes increase in frequency, and copper-working becomes an industry of major proportions for the first time. It is important to note that the strongly marked typological similarities with Wisconsin seen in the two preceding phases are completely absent in the Juntunen phase; the occurrences of Oneota ware suggest a brief occupation by people who made this pottery rather than a blending of traditions as is suggested for the earlier phases. If in fact "Woodland" traditions persisted in Wisconsin during the Oneota dominance, their influence is not seen at Juntunen (except for the miniature vessel in F. 11), nor is the Selkirk Focus pottery that follows Blackduck in south-eastern Manitoba and northwestern Ontario in evidence at Juntunen. My examination of sherds excavated from sites on Isle Royale* suggests that while a great time range is present, some Isle Royale components are Uren-like, with a number of sherds fully conforming to the Juntunen Drag-and-Jab type.

In my opinion, then, the orientation of the Juntunen site was rather unspecific in the Mackinac phase, inclined more to Wisconsin in the Bois Blanc phase, but shifted strongly in the opposite direction, toward the area of incipient Iroquois-style pottery development, in the Juntunen phase.

---

*Studied in the University of Michigan Museum of Anthropology through the courtesy of Tyler Bastian.

It is of interest that no ossuary on the Juntunen site can be placed earlier than the Juntunen phase (except for the Middle Woodland group burial, F. 45). Secondary bundle burials occur in the Kathio focus of Minnesota (Wilford 1955), considered transitional between Middle and Late Woodland; also at Kratz Creek (Barrett and Hawkes 1919); and in the Clam Lake Focus of Wisconsin (McKern 1963). The Blackduck McKinstry Mound 2 on the Rainy River contained primary burials with a portion of the occiput removed; here we see another occurrence of plaque removal antecedent to that at Juntunen.

In Wisconsin the Clam Lake and Spencer mounds (McKern 1963) contained bundle burials surrounded with bark. The mounds contained a number of such burials but differed from ossuaries in having burials spaced at some distance from one another and interred over an extended period of time. Some were placed in pits below the mound floor, some on the mound floor, and others on the surface of the previously erected mound, with a surmounting earth cover then added.

It appears that the traits out of which ossuary burial, as seen at Juntunen, was composed came into use over a large area at about the same time. It may be asked why this congeries of traits was diffusing over the Great Lakes at about the same time that one sees in the Juntunen pottery attributes a marked diminution of contacts with the Wisconsin-Minnesota area and a concentration of similarities with the east. This problem will be considered in the next chapter.

XVI

ANTHROPOLOGY AND CULTURAL ECOLOGY OF THE JUNTUNEN SITE

With the completion of description of artifacts and features, establishment of a chronological sequence, and comparison of the material remains with those from other sites, I shall now attempt (as Edmund Leach says somewhere) to dress the bare bones of archaeology (an attempt foredoomed to failure, according to Leach); that is, to convert archaeological data into ethnography and then compare the result with the ethnographic record. We are on fairly sure ground at Juntunen, where we are dealing with a cultural entity that was similar in many important respects to the cultures in the same area described by the early missionaries and traders. Out of no entrenched theoretical bias but because some system has to be used, I have found it convenient to make a threefold division of the cultural system: technology, sociology, and ideology.

16.1 TECHNOLOGY

Subsistence technology at Juntunen clearly revolved around fishing, evidenced by the offshore shallows, faunal remains, harpoon heads, and probably the hard deposits of carbonized material on vessels that suggest gluey residues from fish boiling. It seems likely that fish were netted as well as speared, although direct evidence for the use of nets is lacking. Nets were certainly used in the historic period. They are mentioned for the early seventeenth-century Huron by Champlain (Rau 1884). Jenness (1935:16) still saw nets of false nettle with cedar floats and stone sinkers, stone weirs, and spears in use among the Ojibwa. Hearne saw only angling and netting in the 1700's (Rau 1884:275). Grant, writing in the early 1800's, talks of sturgeon-fishing with a "kind of drag-net or *seine*....dragged between two small canoes" (1890:345). On the other hand, Skinner says that "some old Salteaux claim that nets are not an aboriginal but a European invention.... [They] were probably formerly made of spruce root bark....They are weighted down with unworked pebbles" (1911:137). Kohl saw fish mostly speared: "the huge sturgeon and the little herring—often, too, even smaller fish" (1860:328). As seen at the Juntunen site, the increase through time in the ratio of whitefish to sturgeon—if statistically significant—may mean that netting became increasingly important. Sturgeon are easily speared, but whitefish are said by some not to be. Jenness, on the other hand, says that in October the Parry Island Ojibwa used to "spear the trout and whitefish that were spawning close to shore. The men fished at night by torchlight.... On a favourable night a man frequently captured as many as twenty large fish. Formerly his wife dried most of them for the early winter..." (Jenness 1935:15).

Rostlund (1952) points out that aboriginal fishing in the Great Lakes was inefficient compared with modern methods because of inability to fish in deep waters; nevertheless, it is evident from numerous historical accounts that at certain seasons fish constituted a very rich resource indeed. Marquette wrote in 1671: "This place is the most noted in these regions for the abundance of its fisheries; for, according to the Indian saying, 'this is the home of the fishes'" (quoted in Strickland 1860:40-41).

Although the number of mammal bones recovered from the site was far less than that of fish, it must be realized that one moose produces about 400 pounds of meat as against 36 for a sturgeon and about 10.5 for a whitefish. Cleland (1966) calculates from such considerations that fish accounted for about 60 per cent of the total summer diet; mammals, about 20 per cent; plant foods, 15; and others—birds, turtles, shellfish, etc.—about 5 per cent. These percentages would have fluctuated greatly both with the season (the several classes of food resources becoming seasonally and geographically available at different times) and with the years; "bad years" for one resource or another are proverbial among northern hunters and gatherers. Jenness (1935:4) says that moose were too lean in summer for the Indians to bother about if anything else was available.

Fish have important advantages as a food source. They (at least theoretically) come to certain places to spawn at known intervals and so do not have to be tracked down; they do not fluctuate in abundance from year to year as greatly as do the large mammals, such as barren-ground caribou, elk, deer, and moose. Rogers says that in south-central Quebec "[mammalian] species appear to vary greatly from one section of the country to another for no apparent reason" (1958:134). Fish can be taken through the ice in winter—Jenness believed that ice-fishing at Parry Island produced "only a very slim harvest" (1935:11), yet it was important at Fort Michilimackinac (Henry 1901; Maxwell and Binford 1961). Most important of all, fish become available with the ice breakup in early spring at a time when the thaws enforce immobility upon hunting groups and animals. So, if a group got to the fishing place before the thaw, it could stay in place and avoid starvation in the most meager season of the year. Rogers (1958) indicates that the Mistassini return from hunting camps in time to avoid the spring thaw.

Skeletal pathology at Juntunen reveals the rigors of the life. Many abnormalities suggest inadequate protection from the cold. In historic times the netting of fish, other than in commercial operations, was mainly the work of women when it could be done standing in shallow water. This is noted by Hilger (1951), Landes (1937, 1938), and Densmore (1929). Rogers (1958, 1962) states that most net fishing of the Mistassini and the Round Lake Ojibawa, however, was conducted by men.

The sexual division of labor is reflected in the Juntunen skeletons: more men than women suffered "athletic" troubles: fractures, spinal "compression" fractures, and soft-tissue responses on the long bones of the legs. The last-mentioned suggests that legs were lifted high when walking, presumably over rough terrain or with snowshoes. Women, on the other hand, showed a number of bone and joint pathologies, some of which suggest osteomyelitis to Eyman, who considers the condition related to work habits—less physically straining than the work of men, but subjecting them to sources of bacillary infection, perhaps through handling certain types of material. Among other tasks, women would have probably gathered plant foods and firewood; handled fish and other animal carcasses (some no doubt in states of decay); prepared skins and plant fibers for clothing, containers, and textiles, and possibly defleshed decaying human corpses.

Containers at the site undoubtedly included birchbark boxes or makaks; birchbark was the most frequently encountered botanic remain. Skin and twined-fabric bags were also made, as seen by the personal kit from Feature 11. The impressions in pottery show that a wide variety of twines and cords were made; they were probably mainly used to make nets. Hilger says that bowstrings were made either of sinew or of "inner bark of the nettle ...the same as that used in making cords for fish nets...[and that] the inner bark of the basswood [was also used]" (1951:119-25). Pottery vessels ranged in size from some holding a little under a gallon to some holding about 2.5 gallons. Different types for different functions do not seem to have existed, and also there was evidently no special class of storage vessels. Most vessels of all types showed signs of use in cooking.

Storage techniques are not evidenced from the site, although it seems highly probable that fish were both preserved and stored. Preservation techniques frequently mentioned in the historic accounts and ethnographies include drying, smoking, and freezing. Storage in birchbark boxes seems to have been common; such a method of storage does not conflict with the Juntunen evidence. I encountered no mention of underground storage of preserved fish. Salting techniques were not used even in historic times.

Pits were certainly dug by the Ojibwa, but their use seems to have been restricted to caches of meat, maize, and other foodstuffs during winter hunts (Quimby 1962) and, at the spring camps, storage of maple sugar. Thus Jenness says that by the middle of April at Parry Island the women "stored away all their maple sugar in pits lined and covered with birchbark and heaped over with earth" (Jenness 1935:13).

With regard to the question of the months of the year during which the site was generally occupied, it was pointed out earlier (sec. 11.4) that occupation by early spring—the sturgeon spawning time—and lasting till late autumn—whitefish spawning time—is indicated and that remains of berries that become available only in late summer found at the site suggest occupation during the period between spring and autumn. There certainly may have been trips away from the site during this season; it may have been occupied successively by different groups; and the period of occupation no doubt varied, but at least there is no evidence suggesting a winter occupation. It is of interest that burbot, which spawn in winter, were not recovered from the site.

A number of factors support the idea that the site was abandoned in the dead of winter. The exposure of the site on the shore to the severities of winter, including strong winds and storms, makes a retreat at least into the relative protection of the inland forests seem likely. Food resources would have shifted from fish to inland game, yet mammal bones and points were not especially plentiful on the site. Firewood around the site would also have been rapidly depleted.

On the ethnographic side, all accounts indicate abandonment of summer camps, where several families had spent the summer, and breakup into smaller units for winter trapping and hunting. This is the pattern even at the present with the Round Lake Ojibwa and Mistassini (Rogers 1962, 1958). Jenness observed that the "hunting season was the winter from November until the end of March, during which period the Parry Island natives dispersed into individual families" (Jenness 1935:4). Even at the present, the winter season is fraught with hardships and dangers. Rogers writes for the Mistassini:

> The period from the freezing to the thawing of the lakes (November to May) is the most difficult part of the year. Throughout this period, it is hard to secure the necessities of life. The large quantity of firewood required is obtained only by great expenditure of labor and time. Hunting is hazardous because of climatic conditions and animals are often difficult to locate. Fishing is curtailed. This is due not only to the fact that fish remain somewhat inactive in deep water, but the ice is so thick that by February, it sometimes takes nearly a whole day to set one net. Formerly, the small amount of European food brought in by the group in the fall was consumed by mid-winter. Even today, some families have no flour by early spring.
>
> Illness during this period is particularly disruptive, since a husband curtails his hunting if his wife is ill, or ceases hunting if sickness strikes him [Rogers 1958:177-78].

A detailed picture of the seasonal movements of a post-fur-trade family to some extent dependent on the Michilimackinac trading post is provided by Alexander Henry (1901; summarized in Quimby [1962]). Henry spent a year with the family in A.D. 1763-64, hence after the disruptions produced by the fur trade in its heyday. The account is of particular interest because the groups spent part of the summer on islands in the Straits, so must have been within hailing distance of the Juntunen site on a number of occasions. There is no mention of Bois Blanc—in fact I have not located any historic mention at all of Indians on Bois Blanc Island. It is worth noting that Schoolcraft (1851) located a village site and an ossuary on Round Island, but makes no reference to adjacent Bois Blanc.

Henry and the Chippewa family spent the latter part of summer "taking sturgeon" at an encampment on St. Martin Island together with an unspecified number of other families. Toward the end of August the family prepared to go to the winter camp. They obtained supplies, including two bushels and a bag of maize, at Fort Michilimackinac and the Ottawa village of l'Arbre Croche (where maize was grown to supply the fort), then proceeded down the east coast of Lake Michigan to the mouth of the "river Aux Sables," where the head of the family

> took a dog, tied its feet together, and threw it into the stream uttering at the same time, a long prayer, which he addressed to the Great Spirit, supplicating his blessing on the chase, and his aid in the support of the family, through the dangers of a long winter [Henry 1901:123, quoted in Quimby (1962:223)].

Camping 15 miles above the mouth of the river, the family hunted, dried meat, and prepared hides until December 21, 1763, when the family moved farther inland; Quimby (1962:225) estimates that they got into Osceola County. Here they engaged principally in elk hunting, although other animals, such as beaver, were also taken. In late February or early March of 1764 the group commenced the return journey west, which they accomplished in a number of stages, transporting "blankets, cooking and eating utensils, guns, axes,... furs, animal skins, six porcupine skins full of bear oil and strips of dried bear meat, some 4,000 pounds of dried venison, and one infant, all of which had to be carried by seven people" (Quimby 1962:228). Arriving near the Lake Michigan shore, they engaged in making maple sugar, having been joined by other Chippewa families, "most of whom were of the family [clan or band] to which I belonged, and had wintered near us. The lands belonged to this family [clan or band], and it had therefore the exclusive right to hunt on them" (Henry 1901; 142, quoted in Quimby [1962:229]). Henry mentions that he "was treated very civilly by all the lodges," evidently a marked difference from the scornful treatment he had received from the other families at St. Martin Island the previous summer. Whether this difference is to be explained by anti-British feelings on the part of the families at St. Martin or by differences in the social relations of the family with whom he was living vis-a-vis the other families at St. Martin and at the sugaring camp respectively is not clear. Since Henry mentions the existence of some social ties with the people at the sugaring camp but not at the fishing station, one might suspect that rights of certain groups to use fishing stations either never existed or else had been broken down as a result of the contact situation. The problem cannot be solved from the existing data, but it is one of obvious importance for inferring the social relations of groups occupying the Juntunen site.

At the sugaring camp great quantities of maple sugar were consumed. Quimby says that "in the previous year at the same season Henry had been one of a party of eight people who consumed about 300 pounds of maple sugar in a month..." (Quimby 1962:231). One naturally wonders whether such sugaring was carried on in prehistoric times; there is no affirmative evidence from Juntunen or any other site known to me. One also wonders whether the dental abscesses and caries noticed on the Juntunen skeletal sample might reflect such repeated periods of heavy sugar consumption.

On April 25, 1764, the sugaring camp broke up, and after three weeks at the Michigan shore the families moved north again by canoe into the Straits of Mackinac. About May 6, Henry and the family again went to St. Martin Bay to fish and hunt.

Thus, during the course of the year the family co-resided for periods of more than a few days with four groups of other families. It is not clear whether these were four different groups, but there were at least two—Henry contrasts the hostility of the St. Martin group with the amicability of the sugaring-camp group. It would be difficult to identify any definite group that could be called "the band" from Henry's account, although it must be remembered that the fur trade, epidemics, and other factors had wrought havoc with aboriginal organization.

The area around l'Arbre Croche was evidently important for maize production in the eighteenth century. Such archaeological data as exist from the northwestern coast of Michigan's lower peninsula suggest that the area from Little Traverse Bay to Cross Village was heavily occupied in the Late Woodland period; pottery of the Mackinac phase is particularly prominent. Alexander Henry noted, as he canoed west across the top of Georgian Bay and Lake Huron, small fields of maize and tobacco growing. Thus the problem whether maize was cultivated at or around the Juntunen site or was obtained in another way cannot be solved. The botanical evidences of more extensive clearing in the Juntunen phase may suggest that cultivation was being practiced, but the evidence is anything but conclusive.

Certain materials were introduced to the site—by the occupants through collecting trips or as part of the seasonal cycle or else by trade. In order of frequency, these materials include exotic cherts, copper, and shell items. The shells are the only items necessarily acquired through exchange. Trade in such items by Huron and Ottawa groups displaced to Green Bay in the middle of seventeenth century is mentioned by Radisson: "they went to the farthest part of the bay to trade for light earthen pots, woven girdles, and small sea shells with which they trimmed their pelts" (Kinietz 1940:245).

Information on the houses and other structures at the site is inadequate. The only outline that could be discerned was the pair of postmold rows about 22 feet apart, designated as Feature 22. Postmold evidence indicates that houses were built on a limited area of the site and suggests that very few houses were in existence simultaneously. The many shallow disturbances considered not deep enough to have pertained to houses may indicate such structures as drying racks, smokehouse, "shaking tents," and the like. The depth of the bona-fide postmolds and their rounded and somewhat belled bottoms indicate that they were dug, presumably by the bare hands, rather than being produced by forcing pointed poles into the soft sand: deeply anchored poles would clearly have been required to support house walls.

Many perishable classes of goods noted in historic times—in particular, matting—were not preserved at all from the site, although a number of the large and rather blunt "awls" very likely were in fact matting needles.

16.2 DEMOGRAPHY AND SOCIOLOGY

16.2.1 DEMOGRAPHY

Cleland (1962), arguing from the number of pounds of meat that could have been supplied by the minimum number of animals inferred from the bones at the site, suggests that, if the site was normally occupied by 30 people for about 200 days a year, five occupations could have been supported. This is of course based on the excavated sample; by applying a correction using my estimate of the percentage of the site excavated (6 per cent), the number of occupations can be increased to 80. But since much more of the richest area of the site was excavated than the poorest area, this figure ought to be reduced by a factor that I would guess should be at least four, resulting in a minimum total of about 20 occupations of 30-odd individuals over the 600 years the site was used. This is not badly out of accord with the stratigraphic indications, although great fluctuations in group size at any one occupation and in length of occupation are indicated by the stratigraphy of the site as well as by the ethnographic data for later Algonkian groups in the Upper Great Lakes.

The figure is apparently out of accord with some artifact frequencies, however. Applying the same arithmetic operations to the total vessel count, for example, each family would have used 57 pots over the course of one spring/autumn season! Two possible explanations for this apparent absurdity may be proposed. It may be that the high pot count results from the breakage characteristics of pottery and the subsequent kicking around of sherds. I noted, for example, that a flowerpot dropped and broken on the University of Michigan campus in an area of heavy foot traffic was scattered within a week over a zone so big that sherds were separated by as much as 25 feet. Thus the vessels-per-cubic-foot count for the site may be much too high. On the other hand, the high pot count may indicate larger groups or more occupations than my figures suggest.

The calculations applied to points yield 6 dropped or lost on the site per family per yearly occupation. For scrapers the figure is 8.5. I regard these figures as being within reason, particularly if most points and scrapers were made, used, and lost away from camp, whereas the center of "pot activity" was in the camp.

Eyman and Bettarel (1965) approach the problem of yearly-population estimate from the ossuaries and conclude that Features 18, 34, and 45 are in keeping with Cleland's estimate but that Feature 11, with its 35 burials, is aberrant, assuming a five-year interval between burial ceremonies. Their argument assumes further that the ossuaries contain only those individuals who died on the island—an assumption clearly open to question.

16.2.2 THE "FEAST OF THE DEAD"

The Juntunen ossuaries bear certain formal resemblances to the famous ceremonial gatherings involving reburials of bones, noted particularly in the Jesuit Relations for the Huron and Iroquois but also reported for some Algonkian groups. The similarities include the digging of a pit, placement of bundle burials of individuals who had been disinterred from some sort of initial burial, wrapping in bark-fiber coverings, and inclusion of the recently deceased as flesh interments without prior burial. The most striking differences are the paucity of grave goods from the Juntunen ossuaries and the rather small size of the ossuaries compared with the historic ones.

Hickerson finds that "the only Algonkians who, so far as we know, ever celebrated the Feast of the Dead were some of those who had direct contact with the Huron during the first half of the 17th Century" (1960:87). He suggests that the practice had probably been introduced to the Algonkians "by the Hurons or their trading partners, the Nipissing" (1960:81).

The sociological function of ossuary burial seems clear: the boundaries of the ossuary symbolize the boundaries of some kind of social unit, perhaps based on kinship, perhaps extending beyond kin "as an instrument to initiate alliances" (Hickerson 1960:92) or to perpetuate them. People placing their relatives in a common grave become allied in the same way that parents-in-law become allied upon the marriage of their children.

Let us look for a moment at the historic Huron ceremony, with an eye to making inferences with respect to the prehistoric period. As summarized by Hickerson:

> . . . the ceremony was held every ten or twelve years at a village selected by a council of chiefs. The remains of those who had died since the last ceremony were buried in a common grave. Great wealth in trade goods, and in beaver robes and other articles of Indian production, were expended as grave goods and as presents exchanged by visitors and hosts. Members of outside groups were invited to the Feast and

> these honored guests were feted and given valuable presents. Games, dancing, and feasting accompanied the rites, which culminated after ten days in the sanctified atmosphere of the burial. Alliances through joint participation among the several villages of the Huron and outsiders were solemnized by the mingling of the bones of the dead from all the Huron villages and were reinforced through the exchange of articles of wealth among the living [Hickerson 1960:88].

The historic Huron ceremony thus involved, on the social side, creation and solidification of ties and, on the economic side, redistribution and destruction of property. The seventeenth-century Feast of the Dead thus bears a certain similarity to the historic-period potlatch ceremonies of Northwest Coast Indians, in which likewise "great wealth in trade goods" was involved. It appears as if similar causes could be called upon for explanation in both cases, despite the geographic separation and the differences in political integration represented.

I suggest that the Juntunen (and other prehistoric) ossuaries represent the original form of the ceremony and strengthen the argument that historic Huron Feasts of the Dead show how an original rite that functioned to solidify ties was greatly transformed in function as a result of the influx of trade goods with the fur trade.

The Huron Feast involved a very large area: "all the men of the country assist to designate the spot where the festival is to take place" (Champlain, quoted in Kinietz 1940:100). Brebeuf writes that "Twelve years or thereabout having elapsed, the Old Men and Notables of the Country assemble, to deliberate in a definite way on the time at which the feast shall be held to the satisfaction of the Whole Country and of the foreign Nations that may be invited to it.... Usually there is only a single feast in each Nation; all the bodies are put in a common pit" (Kinietz 1940:110).

In an application of the "direct historic approach," Kenneth Kidd (1953) excavated a large Huron ossuary that he was able to identify as the one recorded by Brebeuf for 1636 (JR 10:279-305). Brebeuf estimates that about 2,000 persons were in attendance at the ceremony; Kidd estimates that the excavated bones represented about 1,000 deceased individuals. This ceremony was apparently one of less than normal size; Brebeuf, quoted above as saying that "usually there is only a single feast in each Nation" goes on to say that, in the year he is describing the feast, "the kettle has been divided; and five Villages of the part where we are have acted by themselves, and have put their dead into a private pit" (Kinietz 1940:110).

Brebeuf somewhat reproachfully remarks that the dining, feasting, dancing, gift-giving, and other merriment overshadowed the supposed solemn chief purpose of the get-together. There was competition among important individuals in giving parties: "each Captain makes a feast for the souls in his Village—the most considerable and most magnificent having been that of the Master of the Feast" (Kinietz 1940:110). It may be supposed that, if it took a year to prepare for a Feast, the "Captains" must have expended considerable effort manipulating social relations so as to accumulate goods for the event; I suggest that the Captains may have obtained their name and status from their activities in organizing village-wide feasts, somewhat after the fashion of Melanesian "big-men" (Sahlins 1963).

Brebeuf notes that a considerable portion of the goods were deposited with the dead. Many beaver robes were used up in preliminary activities: when the bodies were disinterred in the first place, "they cover them with handsome Beaver robes quite new; finally, after some time they strip them of their flesh, taking off the skin and flesh which they throw into the fires along with the robes and mats in which the bodies were wrapped" (Kinietz 1940:111). The impression gained is that new robes were used at each successive stage of preparation, the old ones being discarded or destroyed. The burial pit itself was lined with "fine large new robes, each of ten Beaver skins...each entire body, besides the robe in which it had been enveloped, had another one, and sometimes even two more, to cover it" (Kinietz 1940:115). Later, "the greater part of the robes in which the souls had been wrapped were cut into pieces, and thrown...into the midst of the crowd, for any one who could get them" (Kinietz 1940:116).

Kidd (1953:364) notes that the other grave goods deposited included items of both European and native origin. Aboriginal items included beads and other shell artifacts, stone projectile points, pigments, textile fabrics, and pipes. Of the beads, "cylindrical wampum beads were the most common variety, and two outstanding forms of ornaments made of it were found. One of these consisted of a length of beaded band..." (1953:364). European goods included ornaments—beads, bracelets, rings—and utility goods such as kettles and knives. The amount of goods is certainly not overwhelming for an ossuary containing 1,000 "souls."

Comparing the Juntunen and Huron ossuaries, the contrast between the near absence of grave goods at Juntunen and their relative abundance in the historic period is at first striking, but the difference probably reflects the relative abundance of items of adornment in the cultures in question. Thus there were very few ornamental objects from the Juntunen site as a whole, whereas they are fairly common on Huron village sites. It is worthy of note that the one definite ornament from Juntunen Feature 11, the band of shells, is similar to the band of cylindrical wampum beads found in the Huron ossuary. Projectile points were also found in both ossuaries.

A major difference in grave goods consists in the use of many beaver robes in the Huron ossuary; there is no evidence for such an item at Juntunen—but this is only to be expected for the aboriginal period; the correlate at Juntunen is the bark used to line some of the pits and to wrap burials.

From the sociological point of view, a major contrast is in terms of size. The Huron ceremony obviously integrated a vastly greater number of people and social units than is indicated for any of the Juntunen ossuaries, although in the Juntunen case one problem is that we cannot determine the interval between ossuary ceremonies. For the middle of the seventeenth century, there are three estimates (cited in Hickerson 1960) for the interval among the Algonkians living close to Huronia. Radisson says "every seven years"; Beschefer says "every seven or eight years"; Perrot says the ceremony was held annually, although, as Hickerson suggests, he is probably speaking not of one particular group but of the entire Algonkian area. As was noted earlier (sec. 12.4), Eyman and Bettarel (1965) suggest an interval of five years for the Juntunen ossuaries.

Judging from the size of the Juntunen ossuaries, the largest social unit that could possibly be supposed to have included their dead would seem to be the "band," and the number of burials at Juntunen is not high enough to suggest that this maximum was reached except possibly for Feature 11 with its 35 individuals. On the other hand, there is evidence from the early historic period that not all the people invited to an Algonkian Feast of the Dead brought their dead but that some joined only in the gift-exchanges and festivities; this may well also have been the case at Juntunen, although it seems improbable that gift-exchange was as prominent as it was in the historic period. The prehistoric event probably consisted of little more than a ceremonial meal and dance in addition to the actual preparation of the ossuary and deposition of bones, and the bones probably represented a social unit no larger than an extended family, as suggested by Eyman and Bettarel (1965).

Some supportive evidence for burial ceremonies of this nature is provided by Steward, who writes:

> Death observances were matters of private ritual among most of these patrilineal bands, but the Shoshoneans of southern California developed them into a ceremony which greatly strengthened group cohesion. An annual mourning ceremony was held under the direction of a special ceremonial leader, while images of the deceased were burned and myths were recited to commemorate the dying god. This ceremony seems to have contributed greatly to the cohesion of the Shoshonean bands, and it may partly explain why the bands continued to regard themselves as kin groups and to practice exogamy after they became dislocated from their territories, scattered, and lost geneological knowledge of their relationship to one another [Steward 1955:141-42].

It seems likely, then, that the Feast of the Dead had been considerably transformed by historic times among both the Huron and the Algonkians participating in the fur trade, with its emphasis shifted from burial ceremonialism to trafficking in "surplus commodities." The ceremony may perhaps be regarded as functioning to reduce the quantity of goods through simple destruction and through redistribution of the proceeds of the fur trade, serving as a mechanism to forestall the social disruption that was occurring as a result of the enormous change in economic relations.

There is one further feature of the Juntunen ossuaries worthy of note in connection with social structure: in all cases of children found placed in direct association with an adult, the adult was a young male. Since with patrilocal band organization the people who are related other than by marriage are members of a "father's group" (Service 1962:69), the situation makes one wonder whether deceased wives were buried in the ossuary of the band into which they had married, or were returned to the band that contained their family of orientation. It may well be, of course, that in the Juntunen cases the juxtaposition of children with young adult males is purely fortuitous.

16.3 IDEOLOGY

Religious activities at the site are evidenced by the burials of animals, particularly eagles (secs. 11.3.4, 13.4); by the human burial patterns; and possibly by the "fishbone pits" (sec. 13.3.2). Inferences as to the ideological importance of most of these traits were presented in the appropriate sections, but some ideas may be summarized at this point. Since it was mostly the extremities of eagles that were buried, it is inferred that the preserved skin and feathers were utilized in some unknown way before ultimate burial. The feathers may well have been used for arrow fletching. Dogs are frequently reported in the ethnographic literature as elements in magicoreligious practices; an example is the dog sacrifice mentioned by Alexander Henry (sec. 15.1). No taboos about the disposition of waste animal bones could be discovered at the site; bones were found charred from fires in the general village refuse. The little "fishbone pits" may have served some such taboo, but, if so, then it is hard to understand why fishbones and scales were also very abundant in the village refuse.

With regard to burial practices, while ossuaries were the modal form, the unusual Feature 43 may be cited as an exception. This burial contained the disarticulated and incomplete remains of one individual together with five isolated crania. It could be regarded as an ossuary of which five individuals are represented solely by the cranium, or it might be conjectured that the individuals had died under such circumstances—perhaps during the winter hunt—that only the cranium could be brought back. In the absence of other data, nothing positive can be stated.

The "personal kit" included with Burial 3 in Feature 11 is of exceptional importance for its combination of utilitarian and magicoreligious items. Most of the latter suggest "medicine," but the otter skull and the shells—while they might be personal "medicine" like the loon wings and other items—do also appear in historic times as parts of the gear of members of the Midewiwin. The Mide sack was often made of an otter skin, and it contained, among other objects, the *migis* or shell used in the initiation ceremony. As described by Hoffman (1891), the shells were mostly of exotic species.

In the Juntunen kit from Feature 11, the otter skull was found near but not in the container, which—as indicated by preserved hairs—was of moleskin; further, the shells are of the common mollusc found on the beach. Nevertheless, the inclusion of a kit with this one individual does suggest that he was special in some way. Possible evidence for the Midewiwin among the seventeenth-century Huron is provided by the short description by Brebeuf of a ceremony similar in some respects to the Mide initiation ceremony (cited in Kinietz [1940:160]).

The removal of a piece or plaque of bone from the cranium seen on ten out of the sixty-five-odd burials from Juntunen is a practice of respectable antiquity in Michigan. As pointed out in section 12.4, it appears logical to suppose that it was connected with a supernatural belief, such as the notion that removing the brain prevented the soul from preying upon the living. Why plaque-removal was not performed on all adults cannot be explained, although the fact that no fully "bundle" burials showed the practice suggests that proximity of the deceased to the living during the period before the ossuary ceremony may have been the deciding factor. No such plaque-removal or other post mortem alteration of the skeleton has been observed east of Michigan, nor was any such reported for any tribe in the historic period. We can therefore regard it as an element in a localized prehistoric tradition.

XVII

SUMMARY AND CONCLUSIONS

17.1 SUMMARY

In the foregoing chapters, the archaeological materials were analyzed according to the dimensions of form, space, and time (Spaulding 1960). Analysis according to formal attributes included the use of computer techniques to describe the variability present and to compare the pottery taxonomy that I set up on the basis of "skill and judgment" with ones produced by the computer. Although the results were not entirely satisfactory, the computer did reveal some pottery types to be poor categories and produced output from which two-dimensional plottings of the types could be drawn, permitting typological "distance" between types to be seen. Further experiments with such techniques are in progress.

The chipped-stone industry contained projectile points of generally triangular shape characterized by the minimum of aesthetic standards, and scrapers uniformly of the "thumbnail" variety—both classes being made on high-quality cherts. The debitage revealed that two distinct knapping techniques were in use. Fairly thick flakes with large flat striking platforms were struck from cores of the coarse local chert, and thin bladelets were produced from very small cores of high-quality chert by a poorly controlled blade technique called "bipolar" from the inferred practice of resting the core on a hard anvil when striking it, which resulted in crushing or battering at both ends of cores and often of flakes as well. It should be pointed out that the term "bipolar" is used in the European literature to describe a quite different technique whose products only superficially resemble the Juntunen bladelets and cores.

Copper-working was absent from the earliest phase but of considerable importance in the latest phase. Only small pieces of raw material were used; they were sometimes hammered directly into artifacts but more often hammered into thin sheets from which larger artifacts were then made by rolling and pounding together a number of sheets. The final products were restricted to small awls, knives, and beads. Several hundred pieces of copper in all stages of working were recovered from the site, largely from around hearths.

The burial pattern consisted of secondary reburial in ossuaries that at the site contained from 5 to 35 individuals in various stages of decomposition. Grave goods were extremely rare, but one man—evidently a primary burial, for almost all skeletal parts were in articulation—was buried with a twined fabric and skin bag containing utilitarian items such as projectile points, awls, and fire-making equipment, and "medicine," such as the wings of a loon. Plaques of bone were removed from the side of the head of some of the adults, particularly from those who at burial were relatively less decomposed.

Although the changes through time in frequencies of artifacts were often significant in the statistical sense, the subsistence pattern remained essentially the same through the 600 years of occupation, and from the areas of the site occupied at different times it appears that group size remained about the same. The site thus represents stable adaptation to the exploitation of fish. Certain broad trends in artifact frequencies can be detected: projectile points decline while scrapers increase over time, and copper appears suddenly in the last phase. The ratio of mammals to fish being exploited may have risen slightly during the middle (Bois Blanc) phase, concurrent with an inferred slight climatic amelioration. But it does not appear that any of these changes greatly affected the basic activity at the site, fishing.

What is true of artifacts and attributes functioning in technological contexts is not necessarly true of other contexts, however. In the techniques and designs of decoration on pottery vessels, very pronounced and (one assumes) "non-functional" changes through time are apparent. Not only did motifs and techniques of execution change, but there was marked change as well in the over-all amount of variability present. In the early phase the amount of variation was so great, and the degree to which decorative attributes tend to occur together so weak, that great difficulty was experienced in pursuing the work of taxonomy and classification along traditional lines. The great lability of the Mackinac phase pottery attributes contrasts sharply with the almost rigid uniformity in the Juntunen phase and suggests that, whatever the causes accounting for the amount of variation present, important changes were occurring. It was noted that the stylistic change represents a shift in the area with which similarities are greatest from the upper Lake Michigan basin in the early phase to southwestern Ontario in the last phase.

If we can assume pottery-making to be a female occupational specialty, then it seems possible to hypothesize from the pottery data that changes occurred in the female composition of the local groups represented at the site. On the basis of the change from great to slight variability, a shift is postulated either to uxorilocal residence from virilocal or to agamy from local exogamy. I suggest that the shift (1) reflects the changes occurring in south-western Ontario, (2) indicates increased interaction with the latter area, and (3) may well show the gradual formation, three hundred years before contact, of patterns of trading relations between sedentary horticulturists and fisher-hunters that formed the basis for the trading networks of the historic period (cf. McPherron N.D.).

17.2 CONCLUSIONS AND COMMENTS

This study has raised more questions than it has attempted to solve, and, of those attacked, most proposed answers range from the tentative to the speculative. The sketchiness of the total picture derived from study of the excavated part of the site rests ultimately upon inadequacies such as the small amount of site that was dug and the lack of comparable excavated sites in the area. Unfortunately, too, many of the questions broached in the preceding chapters arose only after the excavations had been completed.

At the moment, in the absence of comparable sites, the Juntunen site is of significance by reason, first, of its geographic position in the center of the Great Lakes drainage basin and its central location with respect to the lakes themselves, the land bodies, and the biotic provinces; second, its stratigraphic sequence, exceeded in comprehensiveness only by the Frank Bay site on Lake Nipissing (Ridley 1954). The geographic factors give Juntunen the appearance of a "crossroads" sensitive to developments in a number of directions. The factors that led to multiple occupations on the same area with separation resulting from wind-deposited sands resulted in good preservation of features, particularly in the earlier phases, of which only inadequate samples were excavated.

The Juntunen sequence contains a number of gaps, and the minimum total of 20 yearly occupations do not evenly sample the passage of time. There is a gap—either between occupations D and E or between E and F—that might well make the switch from corded to drag-and-jab pottery less sudden than the sequence itself suggests. In addition, because of the lack of systematic horizontal sampling, it is possible that such phenomena as the Juntunen-phase dating of all excavated ossuaries do not represent the real situation. It is perfectly possible, for example, that in the Mackinac phase similar ossuaries were dug—but in an area where we did not dig. At least this possibility cannot be discounted.

The Juntunen site also does not represent a "culture," but only one phase in a sequence of seasonal rounds. We are not in a position to talk of "settlement system" except by means of analogies from the ethnographic record, and for all we know the length of the season in which the site was used may have changed greatly over time. It is worth noting that most of the seeds recovered that indicate summer and particularly late-summer occupation are from occupation F. We shall not be able to *demonstrate* what the settlement system was until we can locate and excavate all the stops in the seasonal round of one group of people in one year—which is as much as to say that in all probability we shall always have to infer from the ethnographic record—and the latter of course represents a culture much altered from the aboriginal pattern.

It is expected of all reports that the phrase, "Further work is needed," be included. But while *any* "further work" will enable many points of the temporal sequence as well as of horizontal distribution to be understood better, it must be added that certain types of work might be more profitable than others. If the purpose of further work is to explore the archaeologically unknown, no exception can be taken in this poorly studied area, but it should be realized that if certain steps are taken during the planning of archaeological surveys, the results could be used in the furtherance of such objectives as clarification of intergroup relations over a wide area. The importance of these problems is obvious from the cultural-ecological standpoint and has been stressed from divergent points of view by Lesser (1961) and Binford (1964).

As an example, an intensive controlled sampling project around the Lake Michigan shore should enable clines in artifact attributes—such as pottery decorative modes and projectile point metrics—to be studied. If time could be controlled, a set of synchronic pictures of interband relations plus a set of diachronic and related changes in attributes would result, both of which could be related to ecological factors—natural and cultural. I do not regard such a proposed project as visionary, although it might require the sacrificing of some other classes of information normally obtained from archaeological field work.

A second example of a project involving study of a broad area is with respect to Blackduck pottery. This ware has a wide distribution, mostly just north and west of the Upper Great Lakes. Control of the time factor is an obvious first necessity; but after this had been accomplished, existing collections could be compared, perhaps using techniques analogous to generalized population distance formulas, and the observed "distance" related to geographic, sociologic, and ecologic factors. I suggest as an initial hypothesis that Blackduck ware spread very rapidly over a wide area beginning about A.D. 900; if this is so, the causes of such a spread need to be analyzed.

A third problem that merits further study is the interaction of peoples making pottery called "Prehistoric Iroquoian" (people inferred to be involved in the development of the historic Huron and Iroquois) with peoples to the north subsisting by hunting and fishing. The Juntunen evidence suggests that contact led to acculturation of some of the northern peoples; other examples are clearly needed before this evidence can be more than provocative.

The chapter devoted to ceramic analysis contained the results of some work conducted with experimental computer programs. Some comments at this point seem desirable.

First, comparisons were made between traditional methods of classifying artifacts and those done mechanically. Service's remarks on these two types of judgment are worth quoting.

> There is a modern tendency to regard judgments. . . [based on the "feel" or the "understanding for the material"] as somehow subjective and therefore out of place in a science seeking greater objectivity through the use of statistics and measurement. But this "subjectivity" is really intelligence, skill, and experience applied summarily. . . .It does not follow that this form of judgment should be abandoned in favor of the mechanical scientism now so fashionable in the social sciences [Service 1964:372].

I agree with this statement but might add that, when a great amount of unfamiliar material is being studied, it is very difficult to maintain consistency over time. In studying artifacts, one "learns"; with practice, finer discriminations become easy, and cases that would have been difficult to classify at first become easier later. Conversely, categories that seemed unified at the outset come to appear "bimodal" as the sorting proceeds. It is situations of this sort that "mechanical scientism" can help overcome, although even here it is obvious that mechanical aids can operate only with the discriminations initially provided by the "attribute list." In most cases a computer cannot decide during the course of computing that "parallel" and "perpendicular" (for example) are insufficient categories and that a third, "diagonal," ought to be provided for, then go back and redo the analysis on that basis. So the archaeologist's judgment and skill are, in the last analysis, the crucial factor. A computer does maintain consistency, however, and can sometimes expose poor judgment; thus a regression analysis of pottery attributes revealed that some types I had set up on the basis of "judgment and skill" were exceedingly poor.

Second, while an individual may become internally consistent in his judgments, it is a trüism that comparison of site reports requires a classification and "taxonomy of the archaeologists themselves" to make the data comparable. Criteria for discrimination that are not explicit and never rise above the "feel for the material" are also not easily communicated from one worker to the next.

APPENDIX

ATTRIBUTE LIST FOR JUNTUNEN POTTERY WITH DESCRIPTIVE STATISTICS ON ATTRIBUTE FREQUENCIES

I. CONTINUOUS VARIABLES	n*	$\bar{X}$	range	s.d.
A. Lip thickness	165	8.5	4-16	2.1
B. Body thickness	165	6.3	2-10	1.4
C. Outside diameter at lip	64	246.0	80-380	68.0

II. DISCRETE ATTRIBUTES (See figure at end of Appendix)

A. Vessel finish	n	f
1. External surface treatment	688	
a) Plain		79
b) Fabric impressed		215
c) Cord-wrapped paddle (fine cord)		129
d) Cord-wrapped paddle (coarse cord)		257
2. Interior surface treatment	1691	
a) Brushed		60
b) Polished		150
c) Sandy or gritty		275
3. Treatment of area to be decorated	1691	
a) Smoothed		843
b) Brushed		2
c) Unaltered		468
B. Lip-rim complex		
1. Rim cross section	1843	
a) V-shaped		122
b) Thin toward lip		78
c) Even thickness		788
d) Folded over or fillet applied		81
e) Splayed		774
2. Angle subtended between lip and rim exterior surfaces	1691	
a) Acute		151
b) Right		165
c) Obtuse		224

* n: Number of specimens measured
$\bar{X}$: Arithmetic mean
s.d.: Sample standard deviation
f: Frequency of occurrence of an attribute

Attribute	Total	Count
3. Angle subtended between lip surface and plane of vessel orifice	500	
a) Insloping lip		11
b) Lip parallel to orifice		58
c) Moderately outsloping lip		426
d) Lip outsloping, nearly normal to orifice		5
4. Lip eversion	1691	
a) None		771
b) Slight		479
c) Moderate		84
d) Extreme		9
5. Rim Flare	1691	
a) Incurving sides		32
b) Straight sides		775
c) Moderate outflare		209
d) Pronounced outflare		33
6. Shoulder	1691	
a) Smoothly rounded		1320
b) Angular		27
7. Collar	1856	
a) Absent		1365
b) Folded or applied thin fillet		39
c) Cambered rim ("incipient collar")		178
True collar, height:		
d) <2 cm.		59
e) 2-4 cm.		191
f) >4 cm.		24
8. Castellations	1692	
a) Absent		1453
Present:		
b) 4-8 along lip		288
c) wavy-edged lip (usually >16 peaks)		11

C. <u>Decorative techniques</u>

Attribute	Total	Count
1. Pointed-tool devices (except punctations)	1691	
a) Incising		20
b) Trailing		12
c) Interrupted linear		5
d) Drag and jab ("push and pull", "stab and drag")		318
e) Linear punctating		25

2. Punctating 2065

a) Occurrence
- (1) Sole decorative element 287
- (2) Part of basic decorative motif 287
- (3) Superimposed on basic dec. motif 93
- (4) Below basic dec. motif 179
- (5) Other 21

b) Tool used
- (1) Knot or loop of cord 47
- (2) Rod with flattened end 189
- (3) Flat ended stick with oblong or oval cross section 482
- (4) Unfinished or irregular ended stick with rectangular section 345
- (5) Flat ended stick with square or triangular section 27
- (6) Corner of cord-wrapped object 44
- (7) Turtle scute edge or suture 50

c) Depth of impression
- (1) Shallow 886
- (2) Deep—boss or node raised on vessel interior 269
- (3) Punching 29

3. Cord and fabric 1691

Cord impressing:
- a) Separate two-strand cord 385
- b) Double-twisted two-stranded cord 138
- c) Fabric, apparently twined 30

4. Cord wound objects 1691
- a) Hard core—stick, paddle, dowel 498
- b) Flexible core—cord, babiche, plant 107

D. Decorative motifs

1. Dominant or "basic" motif on rim and neck (typology shown in Fig. 11, p. 61)

Motif No.	f	Motif No.	f
(plain)	541	9	23
1	372	10	22
2	241	11	20
3	120	12	16
4	113	13	10
5	62	14	8
6	49	15	2
7	25	"Others"	45
8	24	Not recognizable	472

2. Decoration below "basic" motif (presence or absence)
3. Lip decoration
4. Interior decoration

III. TENTATIVE TYPE DESIGNATION (45 initial "tentative" types)

IV. CARBONIZED FOOD REMAINS (Presence or absence)

V. IDENTIFICATIONS AND OTHER DATA

A. UMMA (University of Michigan Museum of Anthropology) catalog number. The same number was used for all sherds from a provenience unit.

B. Provenience-unit vessel serial number. Starts from 1 for each provenience unit, and all sherds from one vessel are assigned the same number.

C. Number of sherds by which the vessel is represented in that provenience unit.

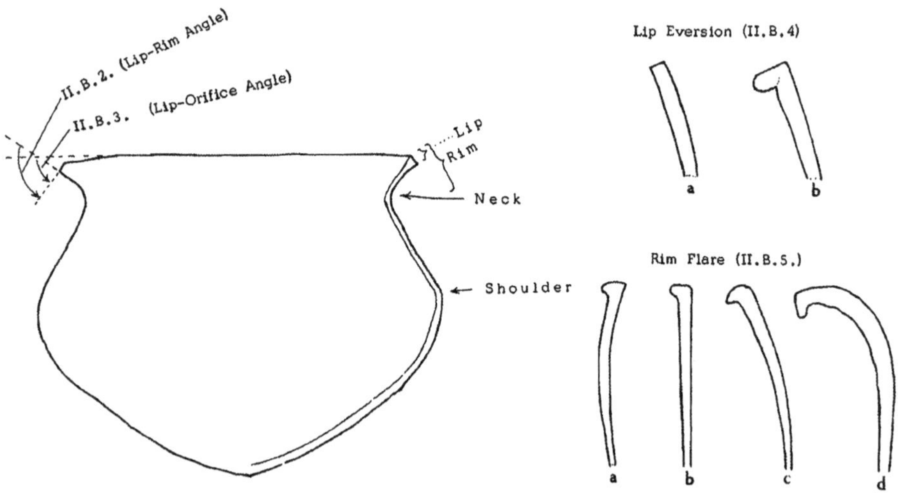

Explanation of terms used in description of pottery

REFERENCES CITED

Ayers, John C.
1962 Great Lakes waters, their circulation and physical and chemical characteristics. *In* Symposium on Great Lakes basin, H.J. Pincus, editor. American Association for the Advancement of Science, Washington, D.C.

Baerreis, David A.
1953 The Blackhawk village site (Da5), Dane County, Wisconsin. Journal of the Iowa Archeological Society 2: 5-20. McGregor.

Baerreis, David A., and Joan E. Freeman
1958 Late Woodland pottery in Wisconsin as seen from Aztalan. Wisconsin Archeologist 39: 35-61. Lake Mills.

Barrett, S. A., and E. W. Hawkes
1919 The Kratz Creek mound group. Bulletin of the Public Museum of the City of Milwaukee, Vol. 3, No. 1, pp. 1-138. Milwaukee.

Bettarel, Robert, and Sidney Harrison
1962 An early ossuary in Michigan. Michigan Archaeologist 8: 37-42. Ann Arbor.

Binford, Lewis R.
1962 Archaeology as anthropology. American Antiquity 28: 217-225. Salt Lake City.
1963 A proposed attribute list for the description and classification of projectile points. *In* Miscellaneous studies in typology and classification. University of Michigan Museum of Anthropology, Anthropological Paper 19, pp. 193-221. Ann Arbor.
1964 A consideration of archaeological research design. American Antiquity 29: 425-441. Salt Lake City.

Binford, Lewis R., and Mark L. Papworth
1963 The Eastport site, Antrim County, Michigan. *In* Miscellaneous studies in typology and classification. University of Michigan Museum of Anthropology, Anthropological Paper 19, pp. 71-123. Ann Arbor.

Binford, Lewis R., and George I. Quimby
1963 Indian sites and chipped stone materials in the northern Lake Michigan area. Fieldiana: Anthropology 36: 277-307. Chicago.

Borko, Harold
1962 Computer applications in the behavioral sciences. Englewood Cliffs, N.J., Prentice-Hall.

Braidwood, Robert J.
1932 Manuscript report of site on Bois Blanc Island dated August 25, 1932. *In files of* Archaeological Survey of Michigan, University of Michigan Museum of Anthropology, Ann Arbor.

Brainerd, Goerge W.
1951 The place of chronological ordering in archeological analysis. American Antiquity 16: 301-313. Salt Lake City.

Byers, Douglas S.
1961 Second comment on William A. Ritchie's "Iroquois archeology and settlement patterns." *In* Symposium on Cherokee and Iroquois culture, Fenton and Gulick, editors. Bureau of American Ethnology Bulletin 180. Washington, D.C.

Callender, Charles
1962 Social organization of the Central Algonkian Indians. Milwaukee Public Museum Publications in Anthropology, Vol. 7. Milwaukee,

Cleland, Charles
1962 The fauna of the Juntunen site. Unpublished manuscript in the files of the University of Michigan Museum of Anthropology, Ann Arbor.

Crane, H. R., and James B. Griffin
1961 University of Michigan radiocarbon dates VI. Radiocarbon 3: 105-125. New Haven.
1963 University of Michigan radiocarbon dates VIII. Radiocarbon 5: 228-253. New Haven.
1965 University of Michigan ratiocarbon dates X. Radiocarbon 7: 123-152. New Haven,

Deetz, James J. F.
1966 The dynamics of style change in Arikara ceramics. Illinois Studies in Anthropology, No. 4. Urbana.

N.D.a. A non-typological approach to the analysis of archaeological materials. Dittoed.
N.D.b. Cultural patterning of behavior as reflected by archaeological materials. Dittoed.

Densmore, Frances
1929 Chippewa customs. Bureau of American Ethnology, Bulletin 86. Washington, D.C.

Dice, Lee R.
1943 The biotic provinces of North America. Ann Arbor, University of Michigan Press.

Dunning, R. W.
1959 Rules of residence and ecology among the Northern Ojibwa. American Anthropologist 61: 806-816. Menasha.

Dyck, W., and J. G. Fyles
1963 Geological Survey of Canada radiocarbon dates II. Radiocarbon 5: 39-55. New Haven.
1964 Geological Survey of Canada radiocarbon dates III. Radiocarbon 6: 167-181. New Haven.

Evans, G. Edward
1961 Ceramic analysis of the Blackduck ware and its general cultural relationships. Proceedings of the Minnesota Academy of Science 29: 33-54. Minneapolis.

Eyman, Charles E.
1964 Physical anthropology of the Juntunen site. Unpublished paper read at the 1964 meetings of the Society for American Archaeology, Chapel Hill, N.C.
N.D. Report on analysis of skeletal material recovered from an ossuary at the Juntunen site excavated under the direction of Dr. J. B. Griffin in 1959. Unpublished manuscript in the files of the University of Michigan Museum of Anthropology, Ann Arbor.

Eyman, Charles E., and Robert L. Bettarel
1965 Physical anthropology of the Juntunen site, 20Mk1, Bois Blanc Island, Michigan. Unpublished manuscript in the files of the University of Michigan Museum of Anthropology, Ann Arbor.

Fitting, James E.
1965 Late Woodland cultures of Southeastern Michigan. University of Michigan Museum of Anthropology, Anthropological Paper 24. Ann Arbor.

Ford, James A., and Clarence H. Webb
1956 Poverty Point: A Late Archaic site in Lousiana. Anthropological Papers, American Museum of Natural History, Vol. 46, Pt. 1. New York.

Frake, Charles O.
1962 Cultural ecology and ethnography. American Anthropologist 64: 53-59. Menasha.

Grant, Peter
1890 The Sateux Indians about 1804. *In* Les Bourgeois de la Compagnie du Nord-Ouest, L. F. R. Masson, ed., Vol. II, pp. 303-366. Quebec, De L'Imprimerie Générale A. Coté et Cie.

Greenman, Emerson F.
1937 The Younge site. Occasional contributions from the Museum of Anthropology of the University of Michigan, No. 6, Ann Arbor.

Griffin, James B.
1949 The Cahokia ceramic complex. *In* Proceedings of the Fifth Plains Conference for Archeology, John L. Champe, editor. Mimeo.

Griffin, James B. (editor)
1950 Prehistoric pottery of the Eastern United States. Ceramic Repository for the Eastern United States, University of Michigan Museum of Anthropology, Ann Arbor.
1952 Archeology of Eastern United States. Chicago, University of Chicago Press.

Haag, William
1948 An osteometric analysis of some aboriginal dogs. University of Kentucky Reports in Anthropology, Vol. 7, No. 3. Lexington.

Hall, Robert L.
1950 A style analysis of Wisconsin Woodland pottery. Wisconsin Archeologist 31: 1-42. Lake Mills.
1962 The archeology of Carcajou Point. Madison, University of Wisconsin Press.

Harrison, Sidney
1963 Petrological identification of archaeological materials, with particular discussion of the Juntunen site, 20Mk1. Unpublished manuscript in the files of the University of Michigan Museum of Anthropology, Ann Arbor.

Henry, Alexander
1901 Travels & adventures in Canada and the Indian Territories between the years 1760 and 1776, by Alexander Henry, fur trader. James Bain, editor. Toronto, George N. Morang & Company, Ltd.

Hewitt, John N.B.
1890 Iroquois superstitions. Amercian Anthropologist 3: 388-389. Menasha.

Hickerson, Harold
1960 The Feast of the Dead among the seventeenth century Algonkians of the Upper Great Lakes. American Anthropologist 62: 81-107. Menasha.

Hilger, M. Inez
1951 Chippewa child life and its cultural background. Bureau of American Ethnology, Bulletin 146. Washington, D.C.

Hinsdale, Wilbert B.
1931 Archaeological atlas of Michigan. Ann Arbor, University of Michigan Press.

Hockett, Charles F.
1964 The Proto Central Algonquian kinship system. *In* Explorations in cultural anthroplogy in honor of George Peter Murdock, W. H. Goodenough, editor. New York, McGraw-Hill Book Company.

Hough, Jack L.
1958 Geology of the Great Lakes. Urbana, University of Illinois Press.

Jenness, Diamond
1935 The Ojibwa Indians of Parry Island, their social and religious life. National Museum of Canada, Bulletin 78. Ottawa.

JR
1896-1901 The Jesuit Relations and allied documents. . . .R. G. Thwaites, editor. Cleveland, Burrows Brothers Company.

Karpinsky, Louis C.
1931 Bibliography of the printed maps of Michigan 1804-1880. Lansing, Michigan Historical Commission.

Kent, Barry, and Ronald Vanderwal
1962 The copper industry at the Juntunen site. Unpublished manuscript in the files of the University of Michigan Museum of Anthropology Ann Arbor.

Kenyon, Walter
1959 The Inverhuron site. Royal Ontario Museum, Art and Archaeology Division, Occasional Paper 1. Toronto.
1961 The Swan Lake site. Royal Ontario Museum, Art and Archaeology Division, Occasional Paper 8. Toronto.

Kenyon, Walter, and Nancy S. Cameron
1961 The Brock Street Burial. Royal Ontario Museum, Art and Archaeology Division, Occasional Paper 3. Toronto.

Keslin, Richard O.
1958 A preliminary report of the Hahn and Horicon sites, Dodge County, Wisconsin. Wisconsin Archeologist 29: 191-273. Lake Mills.

Kidd, Kenneth E.
1953 The excavation and historic identification of a Huron ossuary. American Antiquity 4: 359-379. Salt Lake City.
1954 A Woodland site near Chatham, Ontario. Transactions of the Royal Canadian Institute, Vol. 30, Pt. 2, pp. 141-178. Ottawa.

Kinietz, W. Vernon
1940 The Indians of the western Great Lakes, 1615-1760. Occasional contributions from the Museum of Anthropology of the University of Michigan, No. 10. Ann Arbor.

Kohl, J. G.
1860 Kitchi-Gami, wanderings around Lake Superior. London, Chapman and Hall.

Laidly, W. T.
1962 Regimen of the Great Lakes and fluctuations of lake levels. *In* Symposium on Great Lakes basin, H. J. Pincus, editor. American Association for the Advancement of Science, Washington, D.C.

Landes, K. K., G. M. Ehlers, and G. M. Stanley
1945 Geology of the Mackinac Straits region. Dept. of Conservation, Geolgoical Survey Division, Publication 44, Geological Series 37. Lansing, Michigan.

Landes, Ruth
1937 The Ojibwa of Canda. *In* Cooperation and competition among primitive peoples, M. Mead, editor. New York, McGraw Hill.

Lee, Thomas E.
1960 The Lucas site, Inverhuron, Ont. National Museum of Canada, Bulletin 167, pp. 29-65. Ottawa.

Lesser, Alexander
1961 Social fields and the evolution of society. Southwestern Journal of Anthropology 17: 40-48. Albuquerque.

Lingoes, James C.
1963a MAXPAC—an IBM 7090 program for maximizing prediction and classification. Behavioral Science 8: 368. Ann Arbor.
1963b A taxonomic optimization procedure—an IBM 7090 classification program. Behavioral Science 8: 370. Ann Arbor.
1963c Sequential dependency analysis—an IBM 7090 program for factoring nonlinear or nonmetric data. Behavioral Science 8: 370. Ann Arbor.
1963d MAXPAC-TOP-SDA: an IBM 7090 general program for analyzing non-linear or nonmetric data. Computation report, University of Michigan Computing Center, No. 1, March 15, 1963. Ann Arbor. Ditto.

1964 New computer developments in pattern analysis and nonmetric techniques. Mimeo expanded version of paper presented at IBM symposium, "Computers in psychological research," Blaricum, Netherlands, November, 1964.

MacNeish, Richard S.
1952 Iroquois pottery types: a technique for the study of Iroquois prehistory. National Museum of Canada, Bulletin 124. Ottawa.
1958 An introduction to the archaeology of southeast Manitoba. National Museum of Canada, Bulletin 157. Ottawa.

McCallum, K.J., and J. Wittenberg
1962 University of Saskatchewan radiocarbon dates III. Radiocarbon 4: 71-80. New Haven.

McKern, W. C.
1930 The Kletzien and Nitschke mound groups. Bulletin of the Public Museum of the City of Milwaukee, Vol. 3, No. 4, pp. 417-572. Milwaukee.
1931 Wisconsin pottery. American Anthropologist 33: 383-389.
1963. The Clam River focus. Milwaukee Public Museum Publications in Anthropology, Vol. 9. Milwaukee.

McPherron, Alan
1963 Late Woodland ceramics in the Straits of Mackinac. Papers of the Michigan Academy of Science, Arts, and Letters, Vol. 48, pp. 567-576. Ann Arbor.
1965 Ionic removal of corrosion from copper. Michigan Archaeologist 11: 53-55. Ann Arbor.
N.D. Pottery style clustering, marital residence, and cultural adaptations at an Iroquoian/Algonkian border. New York State Museum. Albany. (In Press)

Maher, Robert A., and D. A. Baerreis
1958 The Aztalan lithic complex. Wisconsin Archeologist 39: 5-26. Lake Mills.

Mason, Ronald J.
1964 Comment on I-678 (Isotopes IV). *In* Radiocarbon 6: 278. New Haven
1966 Two stratified sites on the Door Peninsula of Wisconsin. University of Michigan Museum of Anthropology, Anthropological Paper 26. Ann Arbor.

Mason, Ronald J. and Gregory Perino
1964 Microblades at Cahokia, Illinois. American Antiquity 26: 553-557. Salt Lake City.

Maxwell, Moreau S., and Lewis R. Binford
1961 Excavation at Fort Michilimackinac, Mackinac city, Michigan, 1959 season. Publications of the Museum, Michigan State University, Cultural Series, Vol. 1, No. 1. East Lansing.

Moll, Harold W.
1958 Earthwork enclosures in Ogemaw, Missaukee, and Alcona counties, Michigan. The Totem Pole, Vol. 41, No. 3. Detroit.

Owen, Roger C.
1965 The patrilocal band: a linguistically and culturally hybrid social unit. American Anthropologist 67: 675-690. Menasha.

Papworth, Mark L., and Lewis R. Binford
1962 A guide to archaeological excavations. Southwestern Lore 28: 1-24. Boulder, Colorado.

Parker-Rhodes, A. F., and R. M. Needham
1960 The theory of clumps. Mimeographed paper, Cambridge Language Research Unit, Cambridge, England.

Perino, Gregory
1960 The micro-drill industry at Cahokia. Central States Archeological Journal 7: 117-120. St. Louis.

Pincus, Howard J. (editor)
1962 Symposium on Great Lakes Basin. American Association for the Advancement of Science, Publication 71. Washington, D.C.

Porter, James
1962 Report of petrographic analysis, No. 4. Manuscript paper, Lithic Laboratory, Southern Illinois University, Carbondale.

Potzger, J. E.
1946 Phytosociology of the primeval forest in central-northern Wisconsin and upper Michigan, and a brief post-glacial history of the Lake Forest Formation. Ecological Monographs 16: 211-250. Durham, Duke University Press.

Powers, William E.
1962 Drainage and climate. *In* Symposium on Great Lakes basin, H. J. Pincus, editor. American Association for the Advancement of Science, Washington, D.C.

Quimby, George I.
1952 The archeology of the Upper Great Lakes area. *In* Archeology of Eastern United States, J. B. Griffin, editor. Chicago, University of Chicago Press.
1960 Indian life in the Upper Great Lakes, 11,000 B.C. to A.D. 1800. Chicago, University of Chicago Press.
1961 Cord marking versus fabric impressing of Woodland pottery. American Antiquity 26: 426-428. Salt Lake City.
1962 A year with a Chippewa family, 1763-1764. Ethnohistory 9: 217-239. Bloomington, Indiana.

Rau, Charles
1884 Prehistoric fishing in Europe and North America. Smithsonian Institution Publication 509, and Smithsonian Contributions to Knowledge, Vol. XXV, pp. 1-342. Washington, D.C.

Ridley, Frank
1954 The Frank Bay site, Lake Nipissing, Ontario. American Antiquity 20: 40-50. Salt Lake City.
1958 The Boys and Barrie sites. Ontario Archaeological Society, Publication 4. Toronto.

Ritchie, William A.
1945 An early site in Cayuga County, New York. Researches and Transactions of the New York State Archaeological Association, Vol. 10, No. 1. Rochester.
1961 A typology and nomenclature for New York projectile points. New York State Museum and Science Service, Bulletin 384. Albany.
1965 The archaeology of New York State. Garden City, N.Y., The Natural History Press.

Ritchie, William A., and Richard S. MacNeish
1949 The pre-Iroquoian pottery of New York State. American Antiquity 15: 97-124. Salt Lake City.

Robinson, W. S.
1951 A method for chronologically ordering archeological deposits. American Antiquity 16: 293-301. Salt Lake City.

Rogers, Edward S.
1958 Mistassini hunting groups and hunting territories. Unpublished doctoral dissertation, University of New Mexico, Albuquerque.
1962 The Round Lake Ojibwa. Royal Ontario Museum, Art and Archaeology Division, Occasional Paper 5. Toronto.

Rostlund, Erhard
1952 Freshwater fish and fishing in native North America. University of California Publications in Geography, Vol. 9, Berkeley.

Sahlins, Marshall D.
1963 Poor man, rich man, big-man, chief. Comparative Studies in Society and History 5: 285-303. The Hague.

Schoolcraft, Henry Henry Rowe
1851 Personal memoirs of a residence of thirty years with the Indian tribes on the American frontiers. Philadelphia, Lippincott, Grambo and Co.

Semenov, S. A.
1964 Prehistoric technology. New York, Barnes and Noble.

Service, Elman R.
1964 Archaeological theory and ethnological fact. *In* Process and pattern in culture, Robert A. Manners, editor, Pp. 364-375. Chicago, Aldine Publishing Company.

Simpson, George Gaylord
1963 The meaning of taxonomic statements. *In* Classification and human evolution, S. L. Washburn, editor. Chicago, Aldine Publishing Company.

Skinner, A. B.
1912 Notes on the eastern Cree and northern Salteaux. Anthropological Papers, American Museum of Natural History, No. 9, Pt. 1. New York.

Spaulding, Albert C.
1953 Statistical techniques for the discovery of artifact types. American Antiquity 18: 305-313. Salt Lake City.
1960 The dimensions of archaeology. *In* Essays in the science of culture, Gertrude Dole and Robert Carneiro, editors. New York, Thomas Y. Crowell Company.

Stephenson, Robert L., and Alice L. L. Ferguson
1963 The Accokeek Creek site: a Middle Atlantic Seaboard culture sequence. University of Michigan Museum of Anthropology, Anthropological Paper 20. Ann Arbor.

Steward, Julian H.
1955 Theory of culture change. Urbana, University of Illinois Press.

Stoltmann, James B.
1962 A proposed method for systematizing the modal analysis of pottery and its application to the Laurel focus. Unpublished master's thesis, University of Minnesota, Minneapolis.

Strickland, William P.
1860 Old Mackinac; or, the fortress of the lakes and its surroundings. Philadelphia, J. Challen & Son.

Taggart, David
1962 Preliminary analysis of Juntunen site chipped stone artifacts. Unpublished manuscript in the files of the University of Michigan Museum of Anthropology, Ann Arbor.

Taylor, William E., Jr.
1962 A distinction between blades and microblades in the American arctic. American Antiquity 27: 425-426. Salt Lake City.

Teilhard de Chardin, P., and W. C. Pei
1932 The lithic industry of the Sinanthropus deposits in Choukoutien. Bulletin of the Geological Society of China, Vol. 11, No. 4: 317-365. Peiping.

Thompson, Warren O.
1937 Original structures of beaches, bars, and dunes. Bulletin of the Geological Society of America 48: 723-752. Washington, D.C.

Tooker, Elisabeth
1964 An ethnography of the Huron Indians, 1615-1649. Bureau of American Ethonology, Bulletin 190. Washington, D.C.

Trigger, Bruce Graham
1963 Settlement as an aspect of Iroquoian adaptation at the time of contact. American Anthropologist 65: 86-101. Menasha.

White, Marian E.
1961 Iroquois culture history in the Niagara Frontier area of New York State. University of Michigan Museum of Anthropology, Anthropological Paper 16. Ann Arbor.

Wilford, Lloyd A.
1955 A revised classification of the prehistoric cultures of Minnesota. American Antiquity 21: 130-142.

Wintemberg, W. J.
1928 Uren prehistoric village site, Oxford County, Ontario. National Museum of Canada, Bulletin 51. Ottawa.
1948 The Middleport prehistoric village site. National Museum of Canada, Bulletin 109. Ottawa.

Witthoft, John
1957 The art of flint chipping. Ohio Archeologist 7: 17-20, 35, 42-46, 80-88, 92, 122-127.

Wittry, Warren L.
1959 Archeological studies of four Wisconsin rockshelters. Wisconsin Archeologist 40: 137-267. Lake Mills.

Wright, Henry
1962 The geology of the Juntunen site. Unpublished manuscript in the files of the University of Michigan Museum of Anthropology, Ann Arbor.
1963 The setting and geomorphology of the Juntunen site. Unpublished paper presented at 1964 meetings of the Society for American Archaeology, Chapel Hill, North Carolina.

Wright, James V.
1960 The Middleport horizon. Anthropologica 2: 1-8. Ottawa.
1963 An archaeological survey along the north shore of Lake Superior. National Museum of Canada, Anthropological Paper 3. Ottawa.
1966a The Pic River site. National Museum of Canada, Bulletin 206. Ottawa.
1966b The Ontario Iroquois tradition. National Museum of Canada, Bulletin 210. Ottawa.

Wright, James V., and J. E. Anderson
1963 The Donaldson site. National Museum of Canada, Bulletin 184. Ottawa.

Yarnell, Richard A.
1964 Aboriginal relationships between culture and plant life in the Upper Great Lakes règion. University of Michigan Museum of Anthropology, Anthropological Paper 23. Ann Arbor.

PLATE I

Views of the Juntunen Site

a

b

a—Juntunen site in August, 1960, at the end of the first field season. Shot taken from a position facing a few degrees east of north. UMMA Neg. 13885. b—Juntunen site in August, 1960. Shot taken with the photographer facing a few degrees north of west, standing at approximate location of square 1 of Figure 4. The lake can be seen in the distance. UMMA Neg. 13884.

PLATE II

a

b

a—Lakeward-dipping lenses of sand and gravels (Layer I) underlying podzol formation in sand that in turn underlies the earliest Late Woodland occupations (Layer III). UMMA Neg. 14515. b—Burned root pattern of a tree in Layer $IIIA_2$, central foreslope zone (Square 700-120), suggesting burning off of vegetation of earliest occupation of site. UMMA neg. 14536.

PLATE III

a

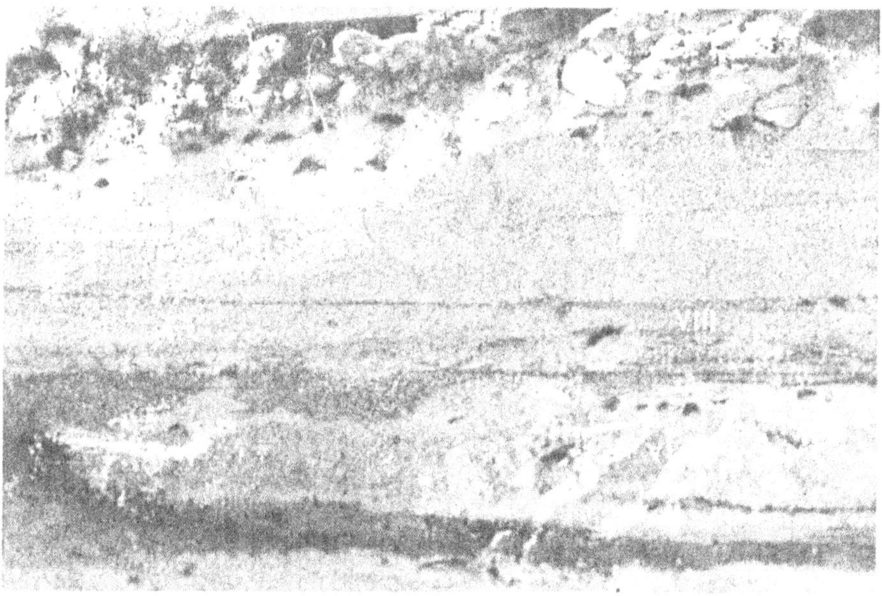

b

a—Profile from +875-100 to +875-090, southwest zone, showing transgression of lake over cultural deposits. Layers VI-X overlap Layers III-V. Note black laminae. UMMA Neg. 14421. b—Detail of the black laminae shown in *a*, above (Layers VI-VIII). UMMA Neg. 14425.

PLATE IV

Profile from 700-110 to 700-140, central foreslope zone, showing dune formation in Layers XI-XVI, truncation of uppermost portion of dune, and overlying strata (Layers XVII-XXV). UMMA Neg. 14521.

PLATE V

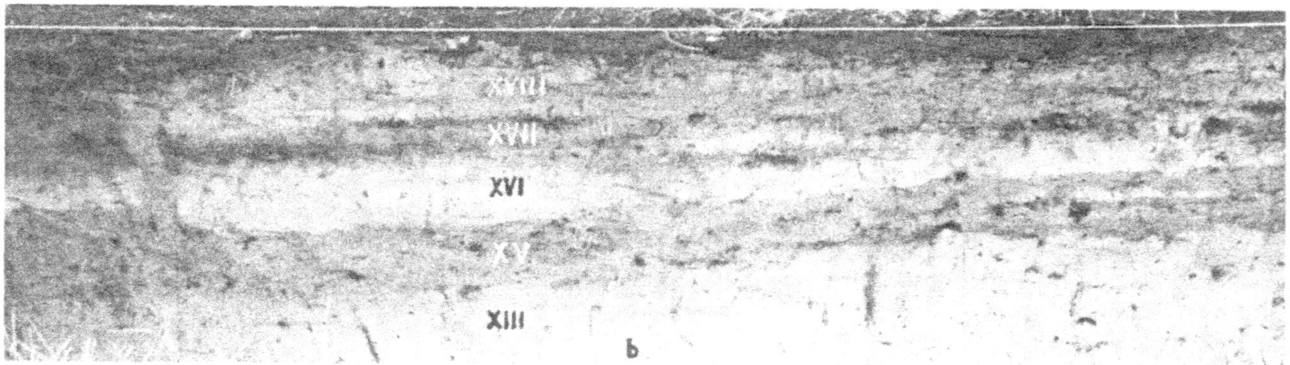

a.—Profile from 720-180 to 720-170, central topslope zone, illustrating Layers II-V, XI-XIII, XV-XVII, and XXIII-XXV. Note degree of disturbance, mostly by posthole digging. UMMA Neg. 13844. b.—Profile from 890-125 to 880-125, southwest foreslope zone, illustrating Layers XIII, XV-XVII. UMMA Neg. 13843.

PLATE VI

Sherd casts showing cord-loop impressing

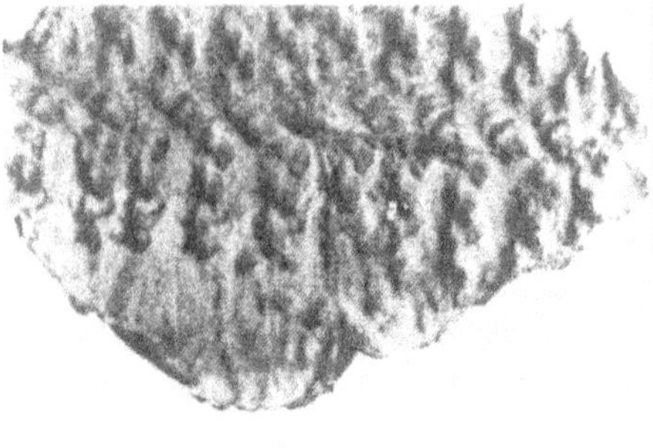

a

a'

Scale (cm)

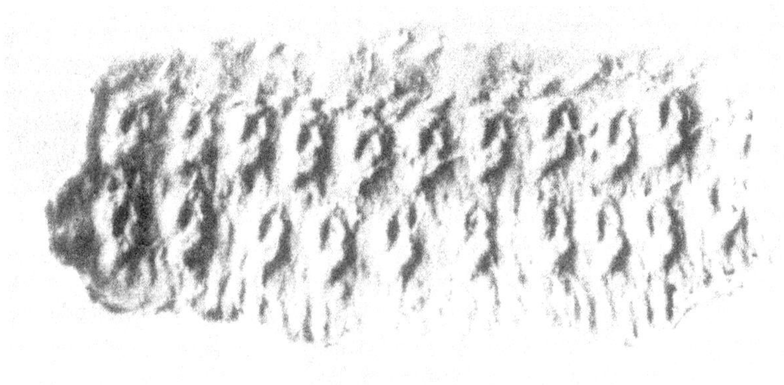

b

a.—Latex cast of doubled two-strand twisted cord. a'.—Sherd from which the cast was taken. b.—Latex cast of another sherd showing twisted cord-loop.

PLATE VII

Sherd Casts Showing "Cord-Wrapped Cord" Impressions.

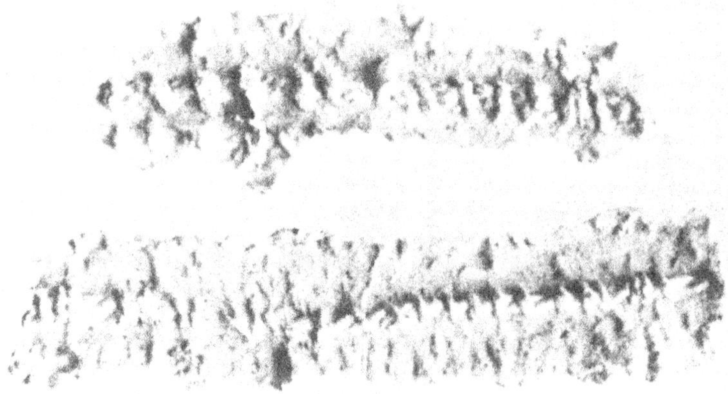

a
b

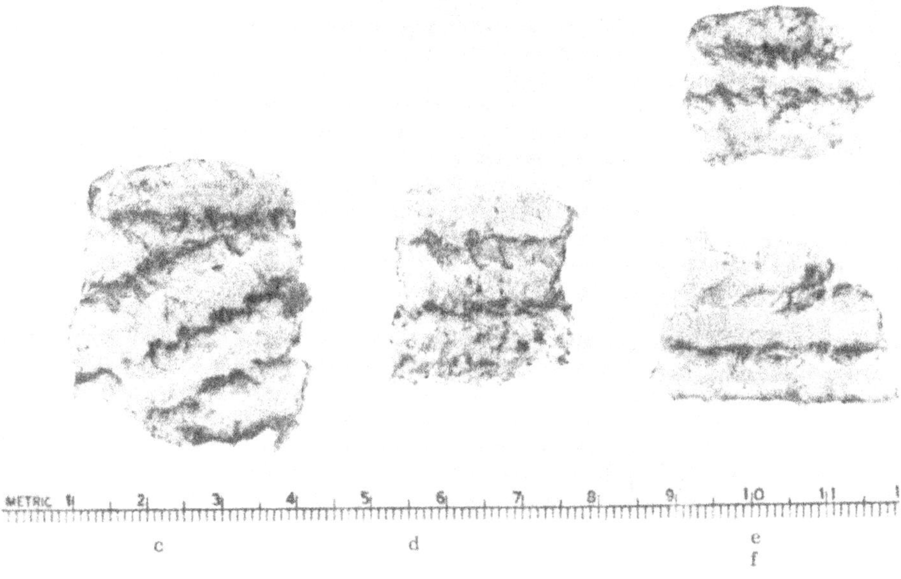

c d e
f

a-e.—Cord-wrapped cord in which the underlying core is evident. f—Unusual cord-wrapped-cord in that the core is very loosely twisted, and the cord that goes around it appears to bind it together.

PLATE VIII

"Cord-wrapped-object" impressions on sherds

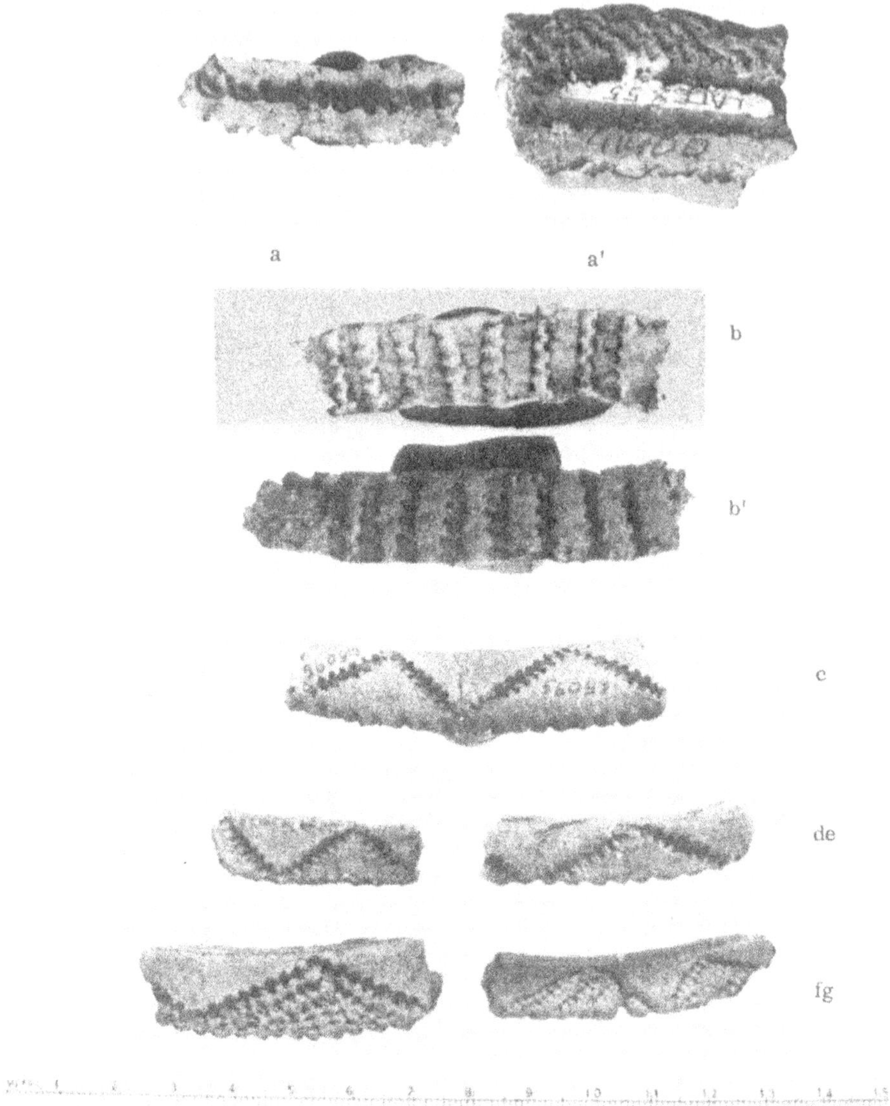

a-a'.—Cord-wrapped cord on vessel interior. Latex cast is shown as *a*. b-b'.—Impressions of cord wrapped around untwisted core (thin blade or perhaps thong). Cast is shown as *b*. c—g.—"Zigzag lip" decoration with cord-wrapped thin blade or paddle. Note smoothness of lips prior to application of decoration.

PLATE IX

Some examples of relatively elaborate decoration. Exteriors and interiors of each sherd are shown.

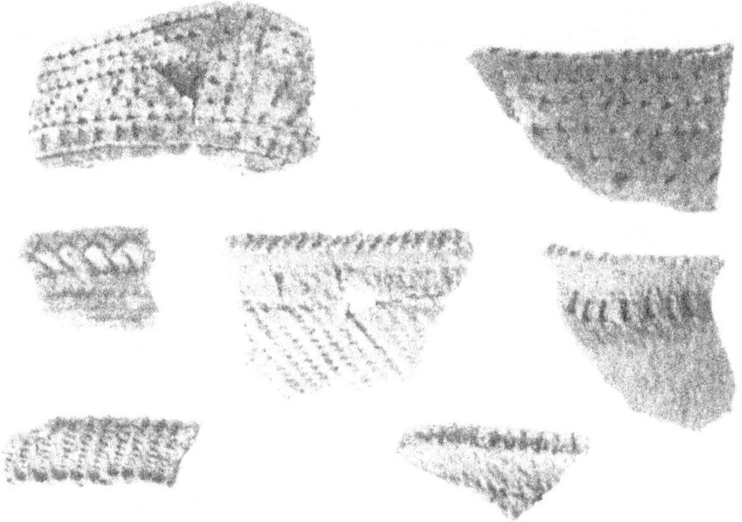

ab

cde

fg

a'b'

c'd'e'

f'g'

Interiors

a-a'.—UMMA Cat. 62968. b-b'.—UMMA Cat. 41567. c-c'.—UMMA Cat. 41512. d-d'.— UMMA Cat. 41562. e-e'.— UMMA Cat. 40737. f-f'.— UMMA Cat. 62947. g-g'.—UMMA Cat. 41512.

PLATE X

Rare vessel rim treatments

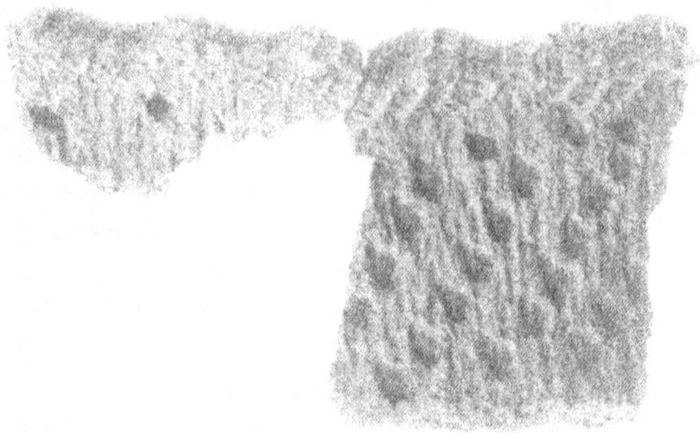

a

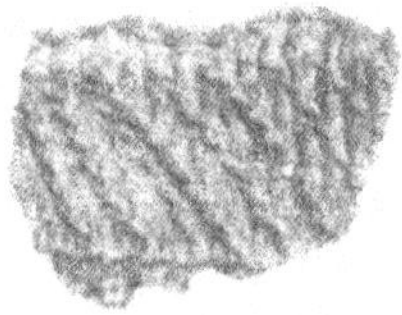

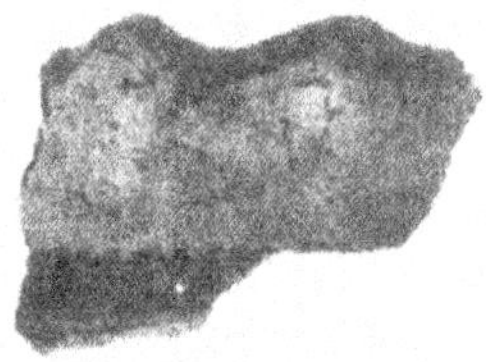

b c d

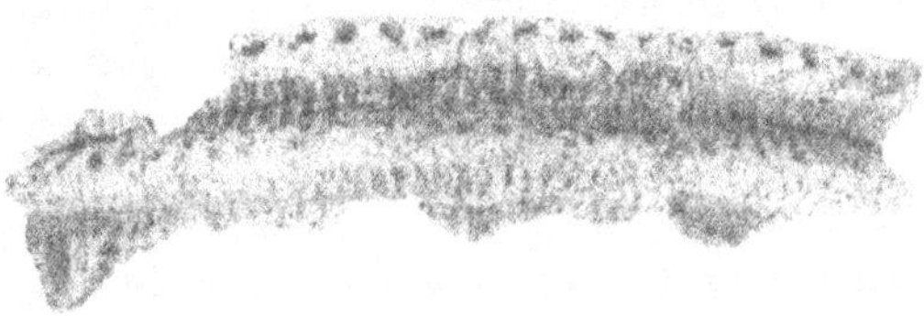

e

a, c-d.—Scalloped or undulating lips on sherds with decoration otherwise most like Mackinac ware. b.—Castellation on sherd otherwise like Mackinac ware. e—Exceedingly thick beading or fillet. a.—UMMA Cat. No. 65108, 65121 (glued together). b.—UMMA Cat. No. 62950. c.—UMMA Cat. No. 41590. d.—UMMA Cat. No. 41397. e.—UMMA Cat. No. 65089, 091, 096, (glued together).

PLATE XI

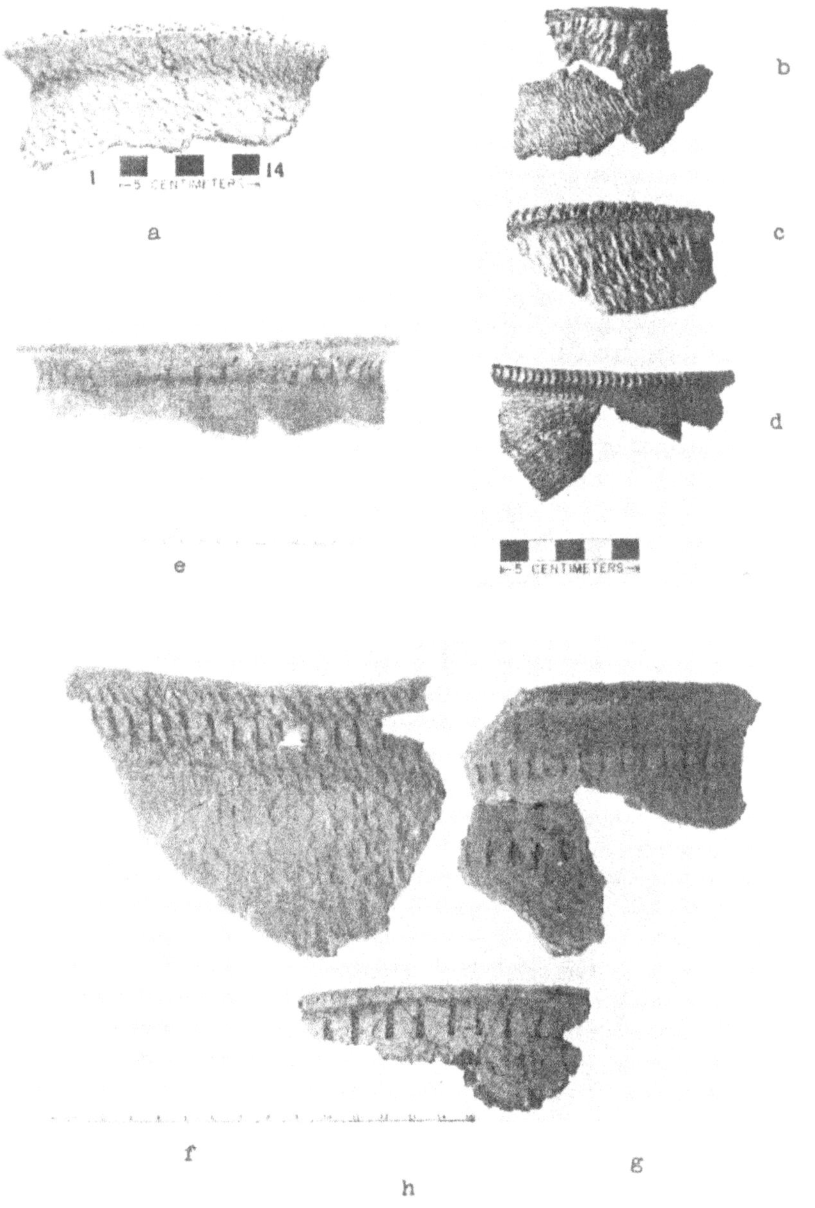

a, c, d.—Mackinac Undecorated. b, e-h.—Mackinac Punctate. a-d.—UMMA Cat. No. 41512. e.—UMMA Cat. No. 40834. f.—UMMA Cat. No. 41799, 41804. g.—UMMA Cat. No. 41787, 41793, 41805. h.—UMMA Cat. No. 41580.

PLATE XII

Mackinac Punctate vessels and sherds

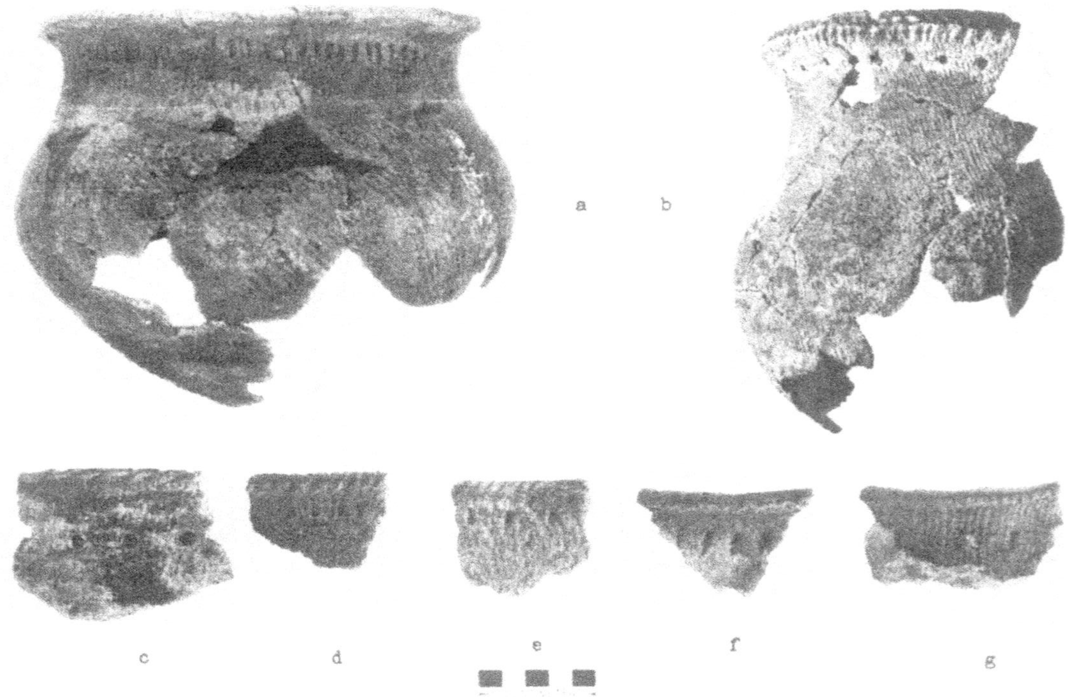

a.—UMMA Cat. No. 41588. b.—UMMA Cat. No. 41512. c.—UMMA Cat. No. 65096. d.—UMMA Cat. No. 62854. e.—UMMA Cat. No. 65096. f.—UMMA Cat. No. 62854. g.—UMMA Cat. No. 41071.

PLATE XIII

Mackinac Ware

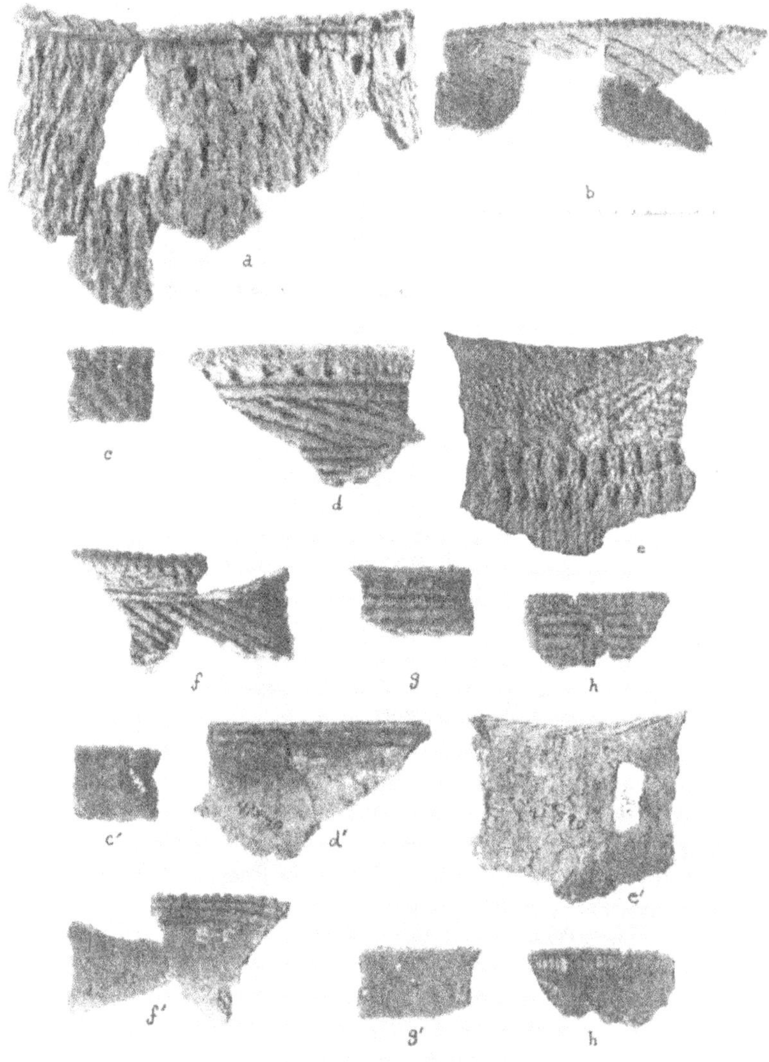

a.—Unusual straight-sided vessel fragment, assigned to Mackinac Punctate type. b, e-e', h-h'.—Mackinac Cord Impressed. c-c', d-d', f-f', g-g'.—Mackinac Banded. a.—UMMA Cat. No. 41611, 70. b.—UMMA Cat. No. 41760. c.—UMMA Cat. No. 41399. d.—UMMA Cat. No. 41542. e.—UMMA Cat. No. 41590. f.—UMMA Cat. No. 41075. g.—UMMA Cat. No. 65127. h.—UMMA Cat. No. 40818.

PLATE XIV

Partly restored Mackinac Banded vessels

a.—Height 19.5 cm.; maximum diameter 24 cm. UMMA Cat. No. 41795. b.—Height 29.1 cm.; diameter at lip 25.6 cm.; maximum diameter 34 cm. UMMA Cat. No. 41582.

PLATE XV

Mackinac Banded decorative styles. Item *d* is aberrant in having a slightly *in*curving rim; *e* is aberrant in lacking lip thickening or eversion.

PLATE XVI

Mackinac Banded exteriors and interiors, showing the variability in interior decoration

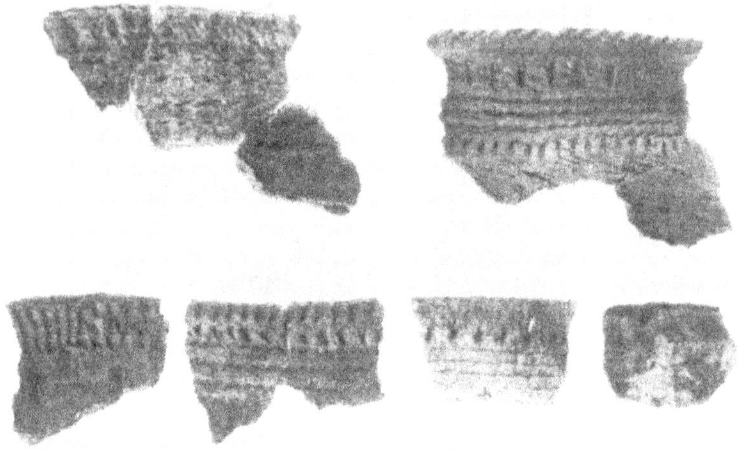

a b

c d e f

a' b'

c' d' e' f'

a.—UMMA Cat. No. 65086, 91, 93. b.—UMMA Cat. No. 62947. c.—UMMA Cat. No. 41527. d.—UMMA Cat. No. 41400. e.—UMMA Cat. No. 64992. f.—Surface collection.

PLATE XVII

a-c

d

SCALE:
(3/4 Size)

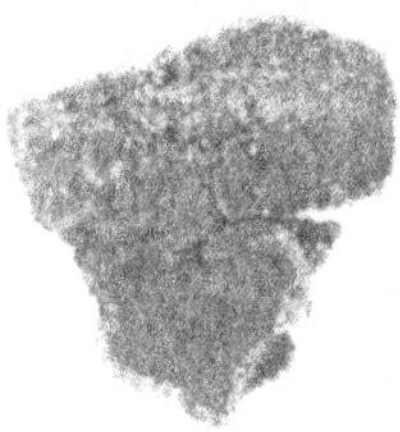

e

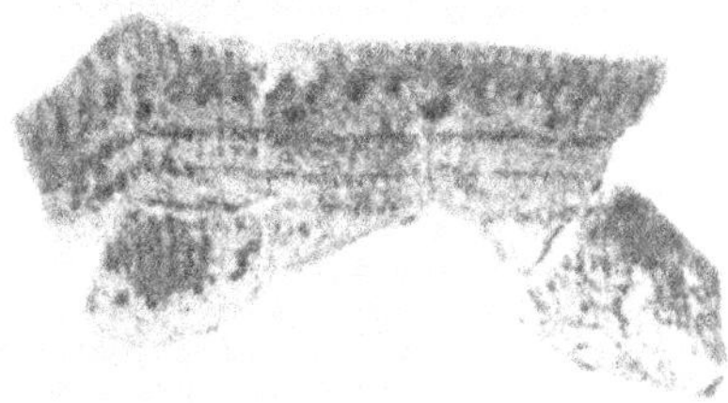

f

a.—Blackduck Banded. UMMA Cat. No. 40711. b.—Blackduck Banded. UMMA Cat. No. 62810. c.—Blackduck Banded. UMMA Cat. No. 40703, 40737. d. Blackduck Banded sherd with vertical brushing. e. Bois Blanc Braced Rim. f. Bois Blanc Braced Rim. This example has all attributes of the type except for the "bracing".

PLATE XVIII

Bois Blanc Braced Rim

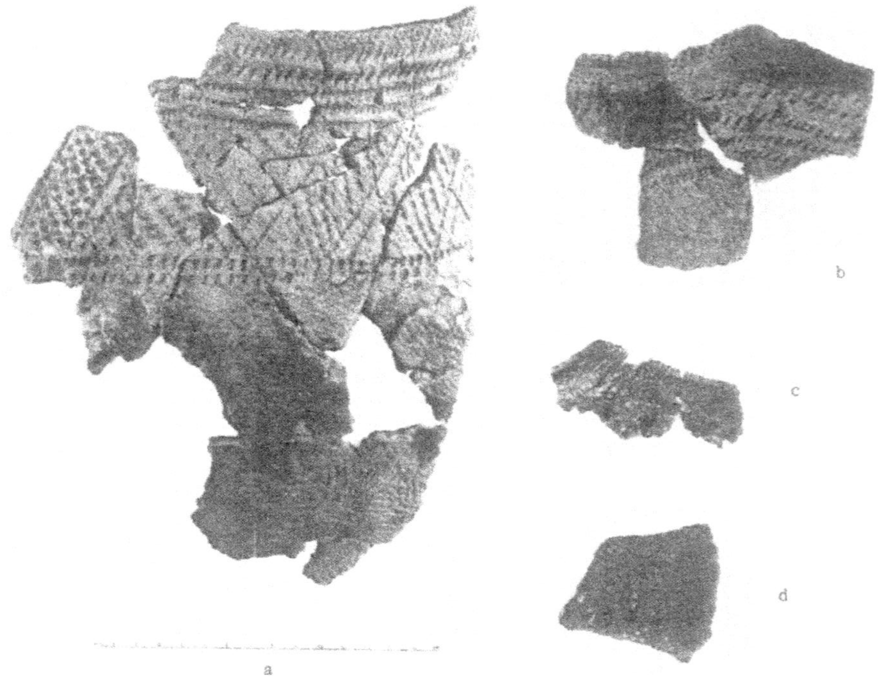

a.—Unusual example with corded devices and punctations used on top portion of rim, and with drag-and-jab used in a different motif below. UMMA Cat. No. 41059, 41491. b.—Sherds of a vessel found in many units. UMMA Cat. Nos. 40696, 40703, 40724, 40737, 40770, 41399. c-d.—Examples with "simulated fabric impression" (closely-spaced cord-wrapped stick edge impressions).

PLATE XIX

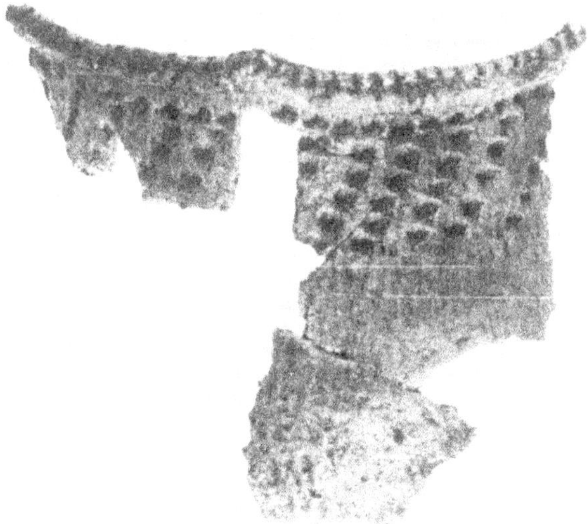

a

b

c

a.—Bois Blanc Braced Rim fragments with decoration similar to that found on some Blackduck vessels. UMMA Cat. Nos. 41540, 41839. b.—Aberrant Vessel. Close to B. B. Braced Rim but considered just out of range. Vessel came from 18 separate provenience units, being thus the most widely-scattered vessel from the site. c.—Considered "typical" B. B. Braced Rim. UMMA Cat. No. 41059.

PLATE XX

a

b

c

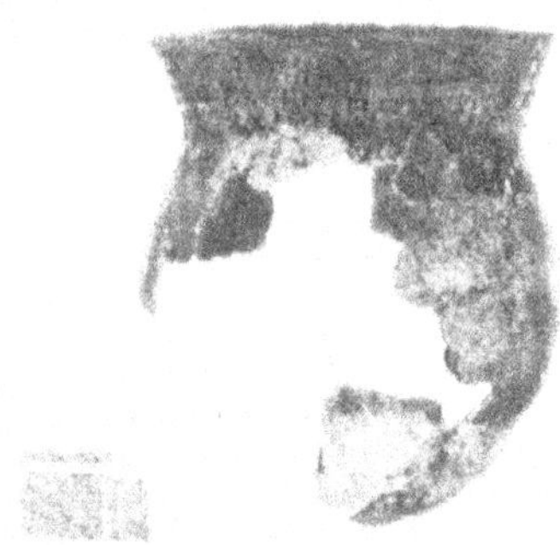

d

a.—Bois Blanc Beaded. A rather unusual specimen of the "thin beaded" variety, with deep punctations—often punched through—"superimposed" on the motif. UMMA Cat. No. 41037, 40. b. Bois Blanc Castellated Corded. Note turtle-suture impressions forming crosshatched design near lip, and both cord and interrupted linear punctating in alternating triangles on the major motif. UMMA Cat. No. 40703, 11, 19. c.—Bois Blanc Castellated Corded. The lip is rising toward a castellation at the left. Note cord-wrapped object decoration. d.—Juntunen Linear Punctate.

PLATE XXI

Juntunen Drag-and-Jab

a.—Restorable vessel from Feature 20 (UMMA Cat. No. 41594). Note secondary motif below collar. b.—Elaborate decorative treatment. UMMA Cat. No. 62947. c.—Linear punctate technique on collar, but drag-and-jab on secondary motif (similar to that seen in *a*, above,) below collar. UMMA Cat. No. 40962.

PLATE XXII

Juntunen Drag-and-Jab

a.—Doubled-twisted cord decoration, a rarity. b-b' through d-d', f-f' through i-i'.—Some of the variety in drag-and-jab decoration. e-e'.—Interrupted linear technique. a.—UMMA Cat. No. 40687. b.—UMMA Cat. No. 41835. c.—UMMA Cat. No. 62839. d.—UMMA Cat. No. 62782. e.—UMMA Cat. No. 62944, 47. f.—UMMA Cat. No. 64970. g.—UMMA Cat. No. 41171. h.—UMMA Cat. No. 62796. i.—UMMA Cat. No. 41077.

PLATE XXIII

Mississippian Tradition Pottery

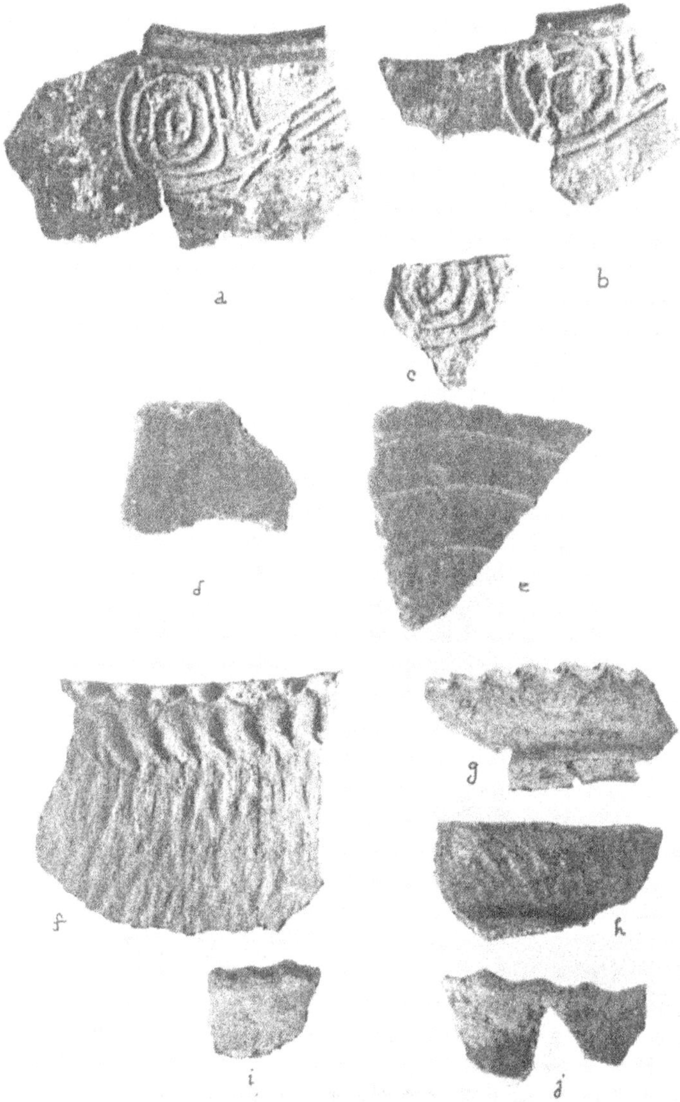

a-c.—Like Ramey Incised. Shown 2/3 size. d-e.—Shell-tempered Upper Mississippian-like sherds. Shown 2/3 size. f-j.—Grit tempered Oneota-like sherds. Shown 1/4 size. a-c.—UMMA Cat. No. 41399. d.—UMMA Cat. No. 41817. e.—UMMA Cat. No. 41835. f.—UMMA Cat. No. 40568. g.—UMMA Cat. No. 40962. h.—surface collection. i.—UMMA Cat. No. 41168. j.—UMMA Cat. No. 41152.

PLATE XXIV

Miniature and Children's Vessels

a-b.—Mortuary vessel from Feature 11, with Woodland-like decoration. Found inverted over *c*, below. c.—Mortuary vessel from Feature 11, made in an oneotoid pattern. d.—Miniature vessel from Feature 21. The photograph does not show the rounded base. The only entirely complete vessel from the site. e-f.—Children's vessels. UMMA Cat. Nos.: *e*, 41581; *f*, 40818. Note: Scale below *f* applies to *d*, *e*, and *f*.

PLATE XXV

Rare and Unique Sherds

a.—Iroquois Linear. b.—Ontario Oblique (?). c.—Lalonde High Collar. d.—Castellated sherd with vague decoration near lip. e-f.—Unique sherds. Note: All except *a* are shown 3/4 size.

PLATE XXVI

Pottery Pipe Fragments

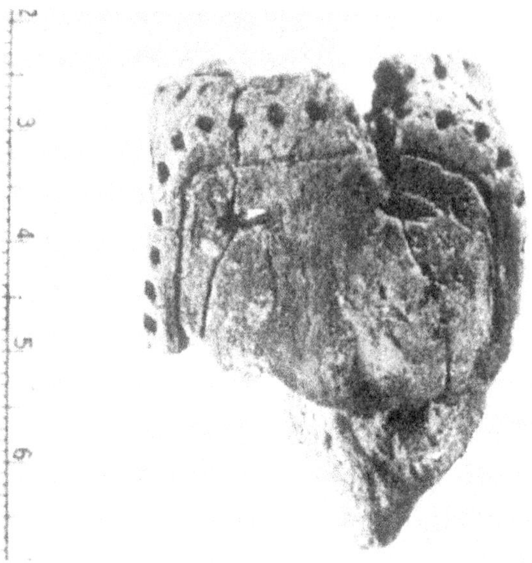

a

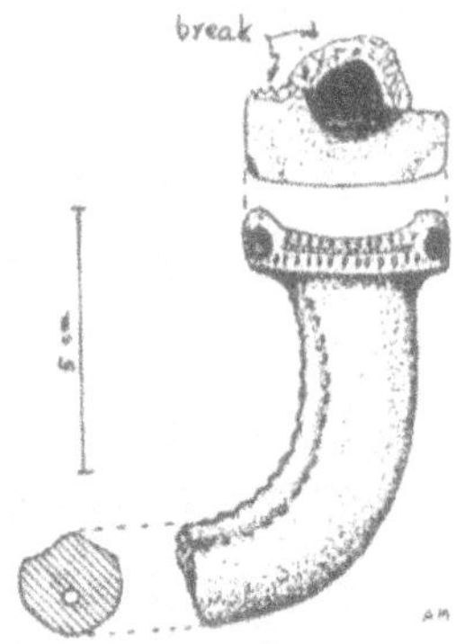

b

c
f

d
g

e
h

a.—The only human representation from the site. Intermediate I phase. b.—Square-bowl Huron pipe. Juntunen phase. c, f.—Mackinac-phase bowl fragments. d.—Very fine cord-wrapped object decoration. Not assignable to phase. e.—Bois Blanc-phase fragment with cord-wrapped object decoration. g.—Cord-wrapped object and punctations on bowl fragment. Not assignable to phase. h.—Incised bowl fragment. Not assignable to phase.

PLATE XXVII

Polyhedral Bipolar Cores

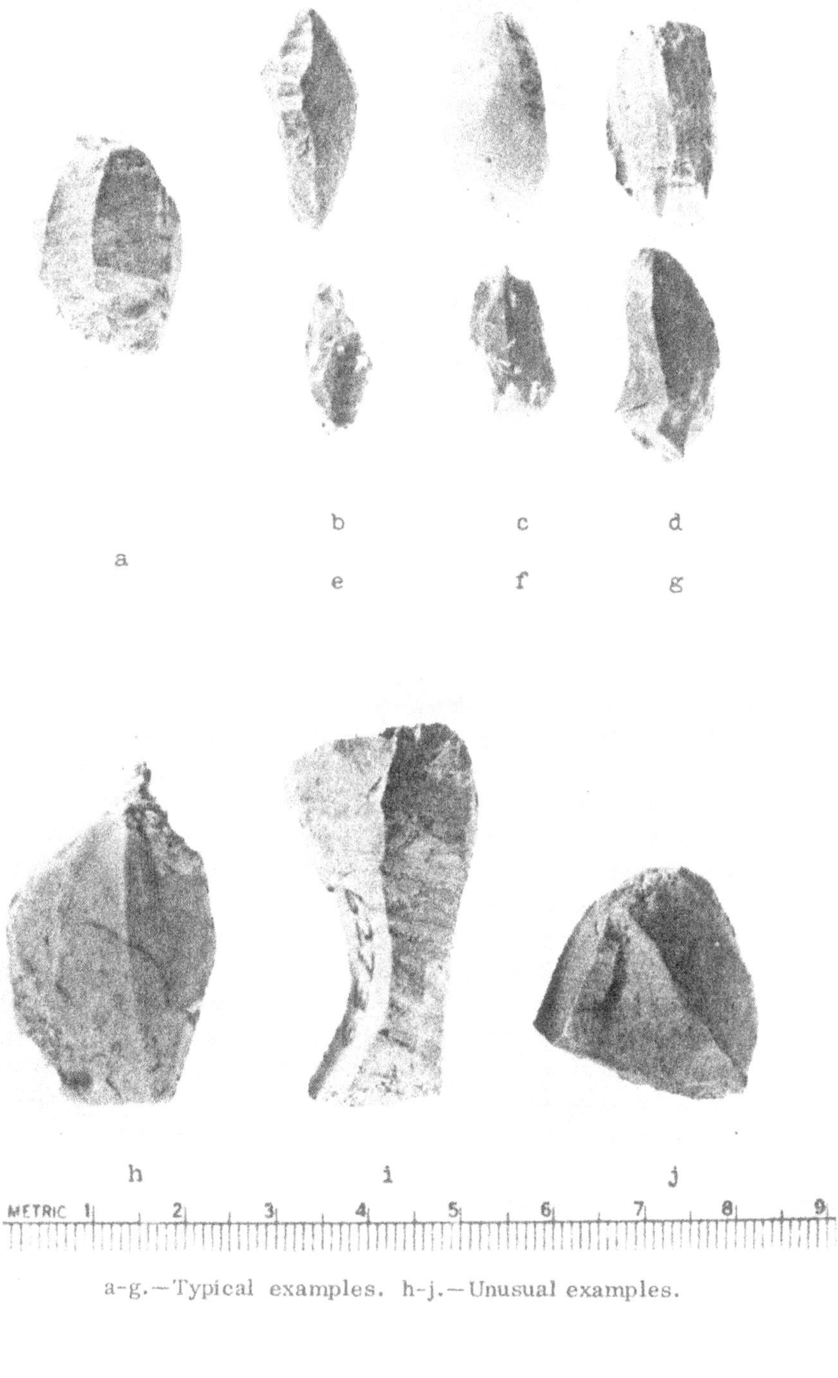

a-g.—Typical examples. h-j.—Unusual examples.

PLATE XXVIII

"Gouged-End Artifacts"

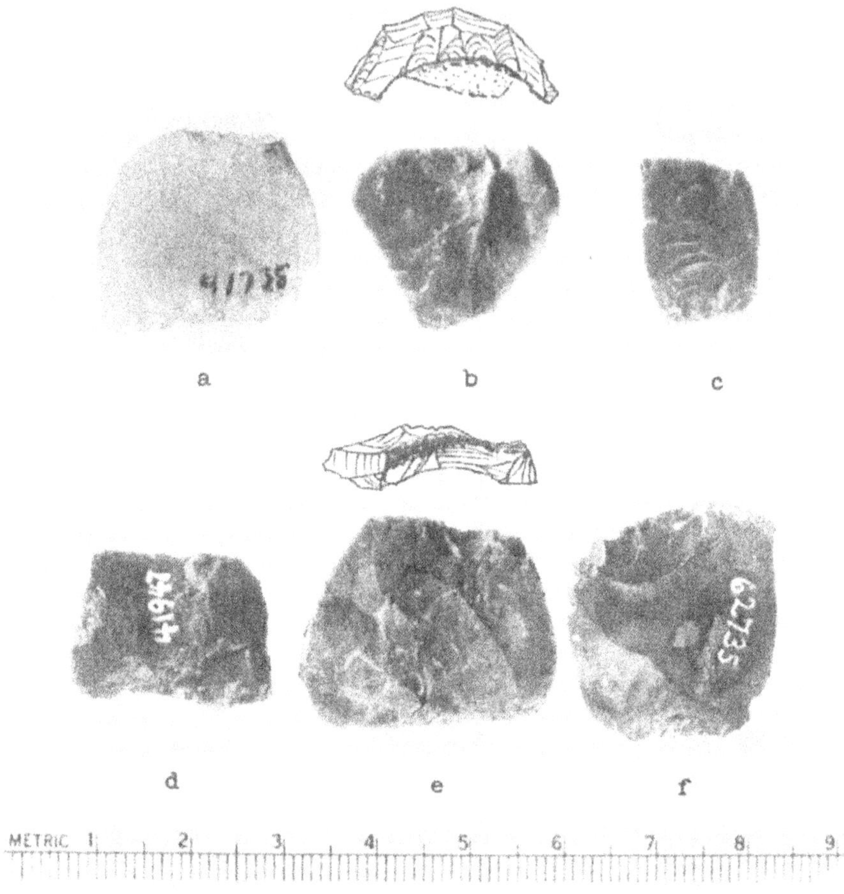

a.—Unique quartz specimen. b.—Steep retouch toward dorsal surface preceded the flaking that resulted in the "scooped-out" appearance on the ventral surface. c-f.—These specimens have two opposed battered ridges; one is shown in an end view in *e*.

PLATE XXIX

Bipolar Bladelets

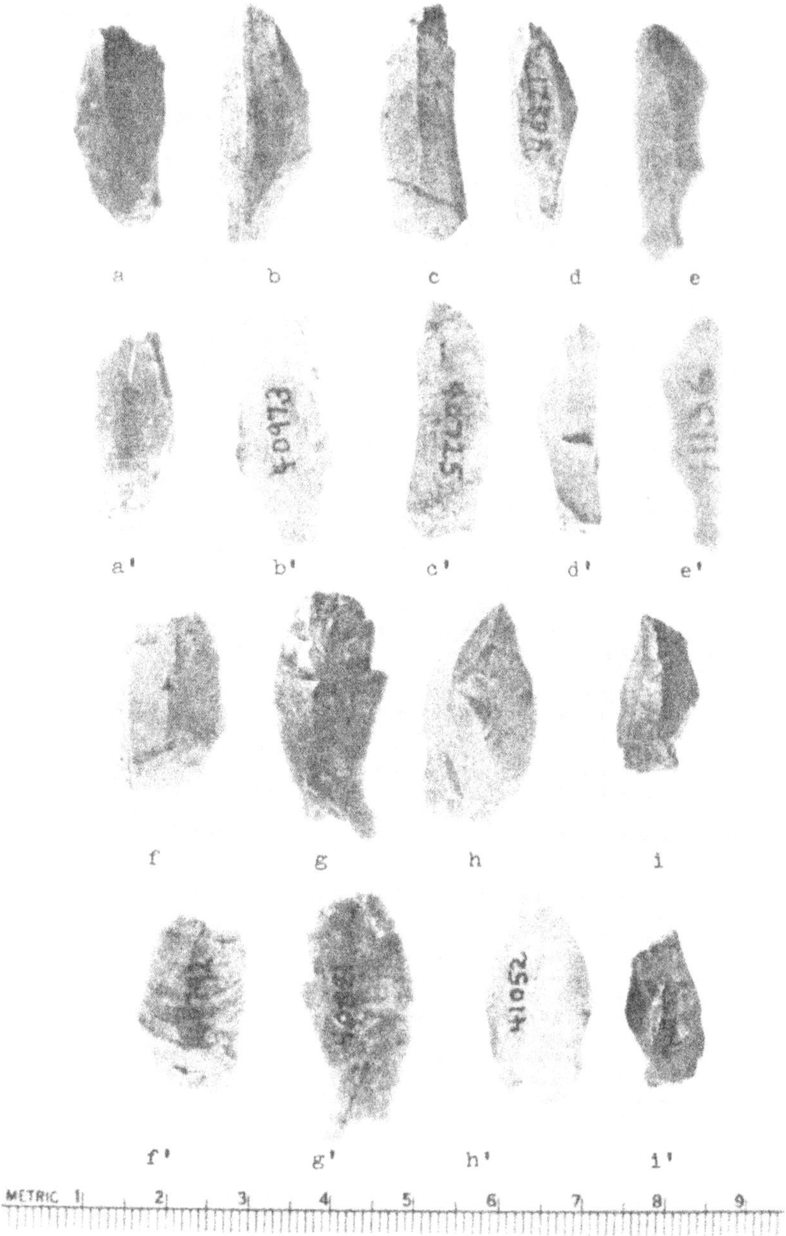

Representative bladelets produced by the bipolar technique. Two faces of each specimen are shown. Note the variety of "exotic" cherts employed and the frequent battering at one or both ends.

PLATE XXX

Largest bladelets from the site produced by the bipolar technique.

PLATE XXXI

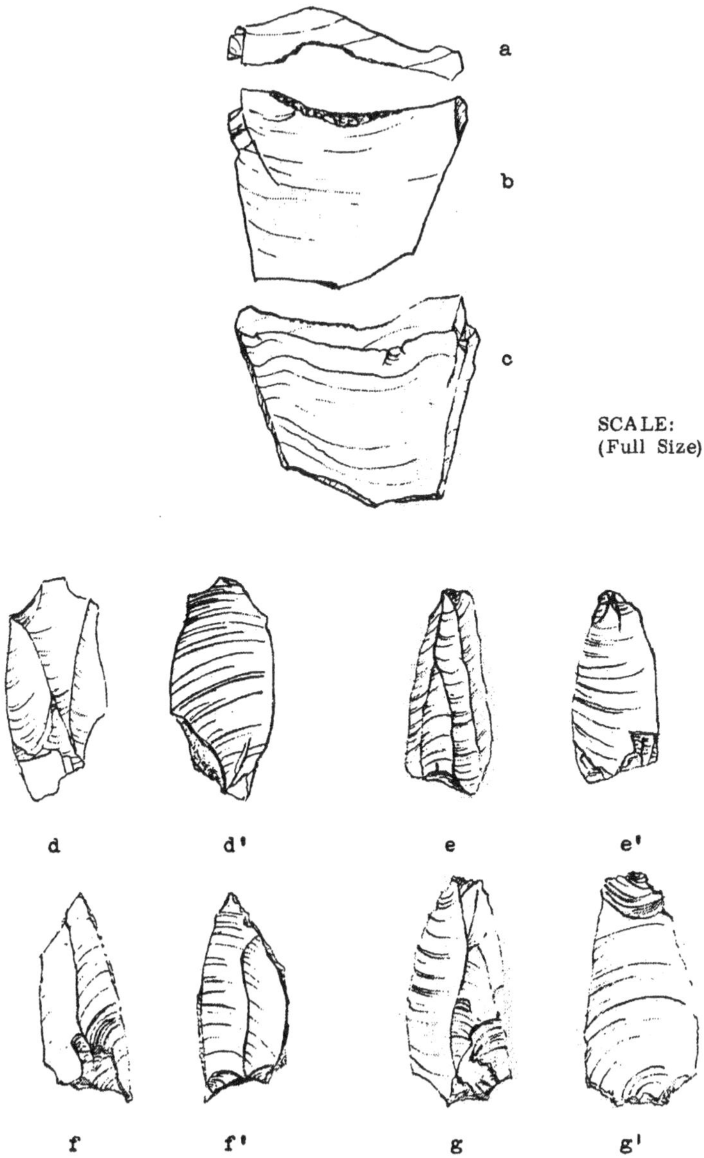

a-c.—Unique artifact of Eastport chert, produced by a non-bipolar technique, with chipping similar to that found on some "gouged-end artifacts." d-d' through g-g'.—Drawings of bladelets produced by the bipolar technique.

PLATE XXXII

Juntunen Points

Row 1 (a-f).—Juntunen Triangular points. Row 2 (g-m).—Juntunen Triangular Points (g-h, j-l); Juntunen Notched point (i); Levanna point (m). Row 3 (n-t).—Juntunen Triangular points. Row 4 (u-z).—Graver (u); Juntunen Notched points (v-y); Aberrant point (z). Row 5 (A-H).—Juntunen Notched points (A-C, E-H); Aberrant point (D).

PLATE XXXIII

Medium and Large Points

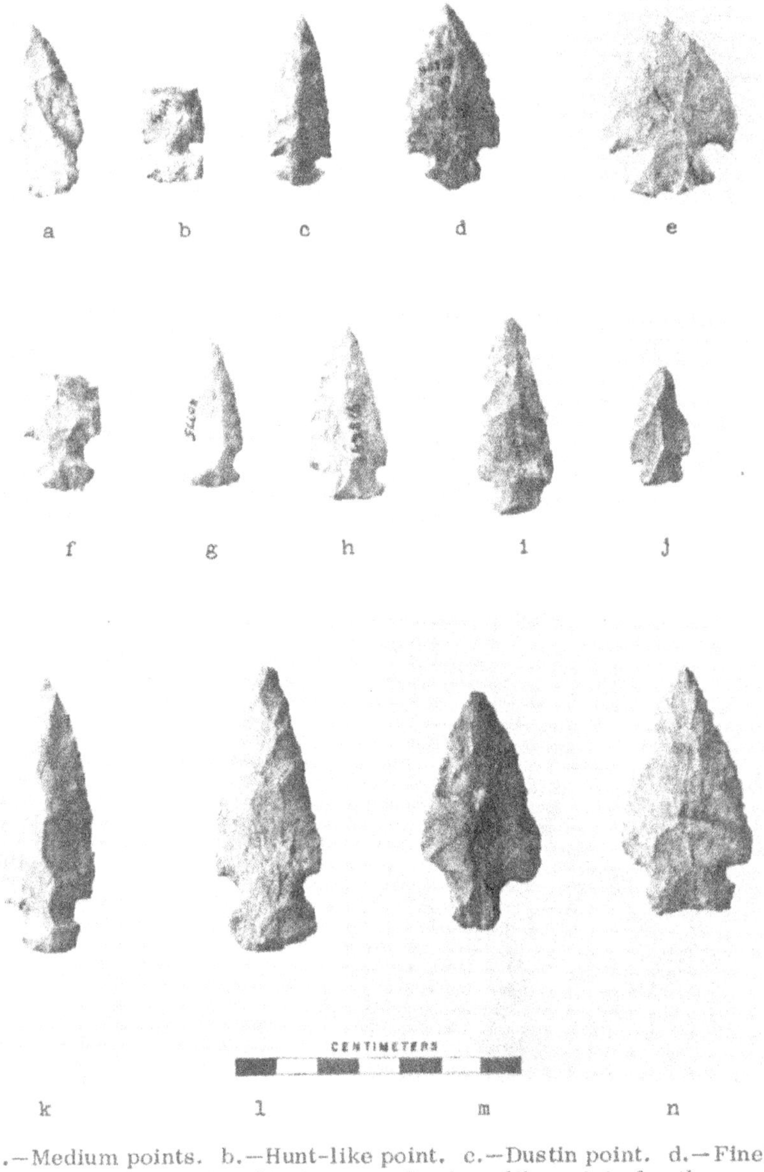

a-i.—Medium points. b.—Hunt-like point. c.—Dustin point. d.—Finely-flaked point from Arrowhead Drive. e.—Snyders-like point of rather coarse pinkish chert, found at locality on island near the Nipissing beach (see sec. 6.1.3.1.B). j.—Juntunen notched point. k.—Large point with diamond-shaped cross section, from Arrowhead Drive site. l-n.—Large points from Juntunen site.

PLATE XXXIV

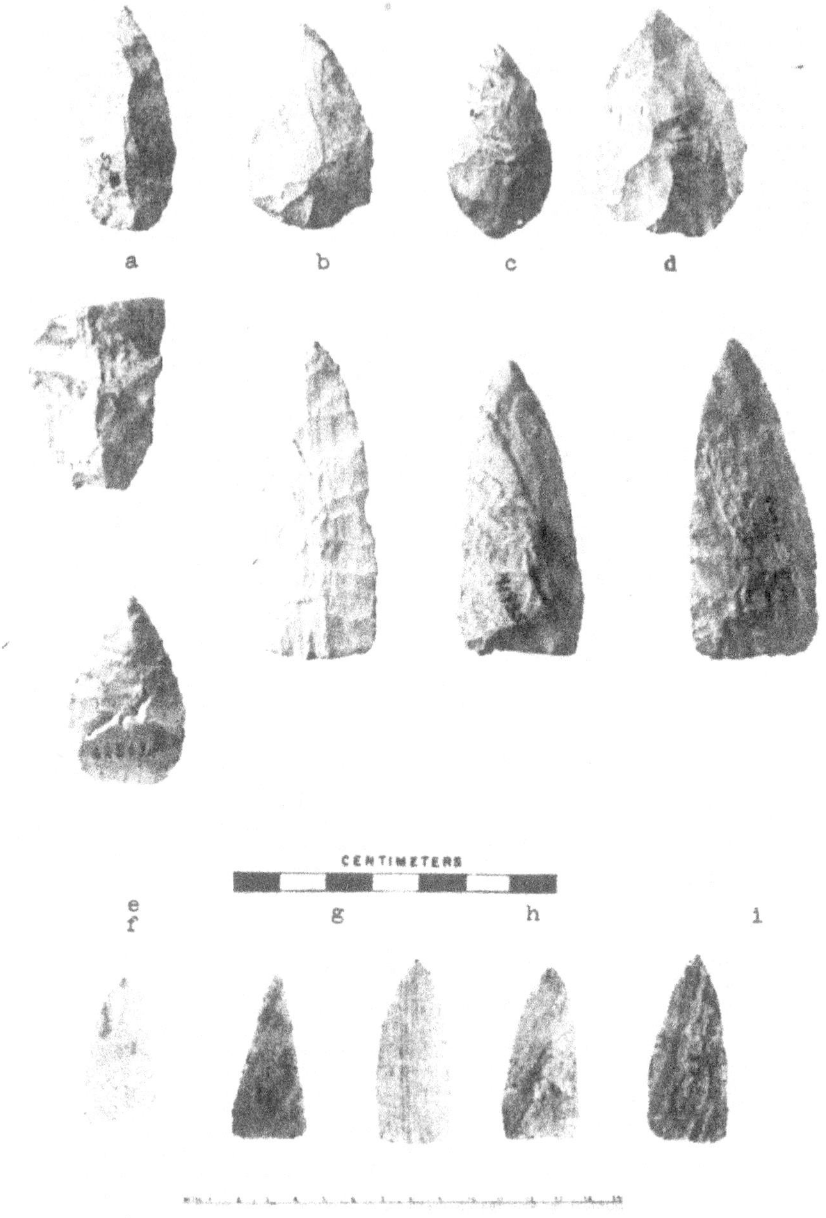

a-f.—Bifacial ovates. g-n.—"Cache Points." Items *g-i* and *l-n* are the same points, with *m-n* showing the opposite sides of *h-i*.

PLATE XXXV

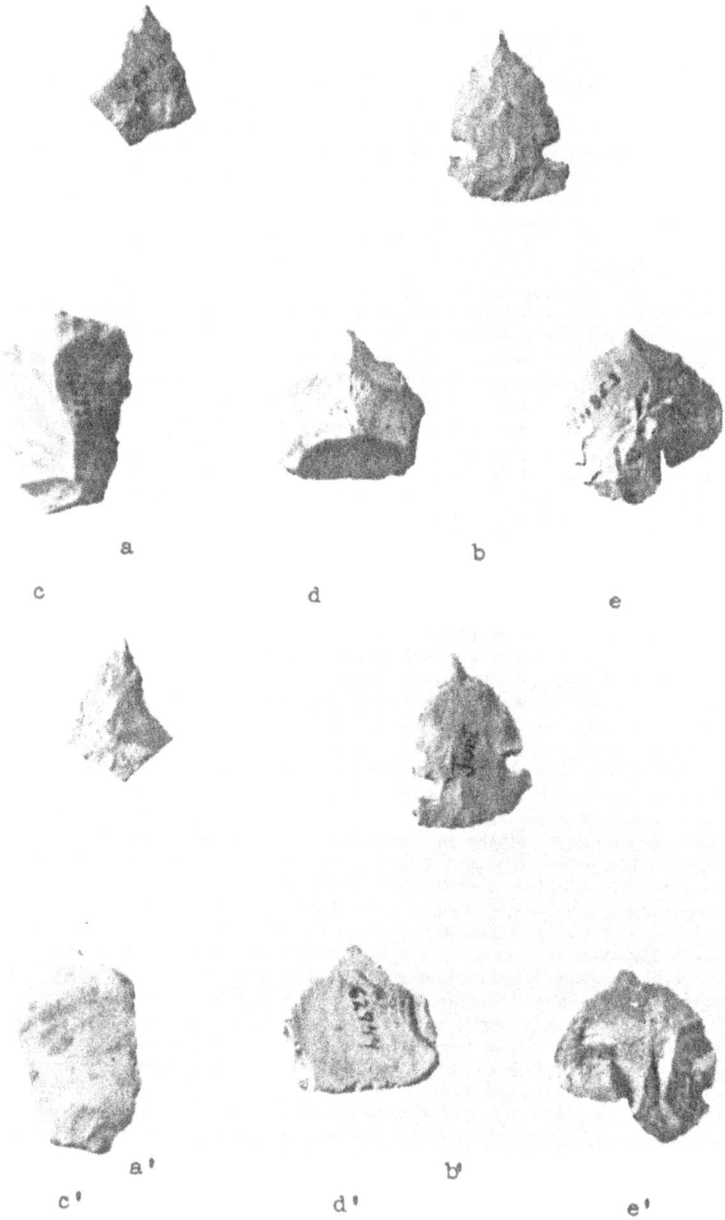

The five gravers—all those recovered during the excavations—are shown, obverse and reverse. Note that *b* was also illustrated as Plate XXXII, *u*. The artifacts are shown 3/4 size.

PLATE XXXVI

Scrapers and Ground-Stone Objects

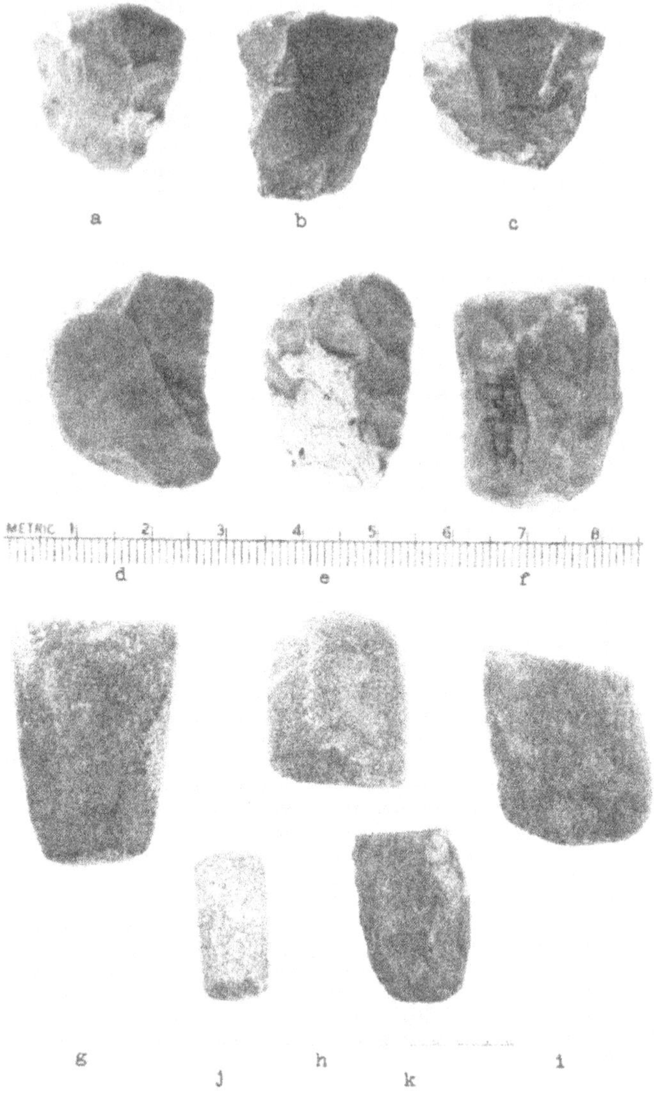

a-c.—Typical range of shapes of scrapers. d.—Scraper retouched nearly all around. e.—Scraper retouched on two edges plus the special rounded area at upper right. f.—Scraper retouched on three edges. g.—Unfinished ground stone celt. h.—Finished gound stone adze, broken cleanly across. i.—The broken end of a crudely bifacially worked object of an iridescent material with some laminar properties. j.—An apparently unbroken artifact of roughly quadrangular cross section. k.—A broken, crudely bifacially-worked tool of a black laminar slatey material.

PLATE XXXVII

a

b

c

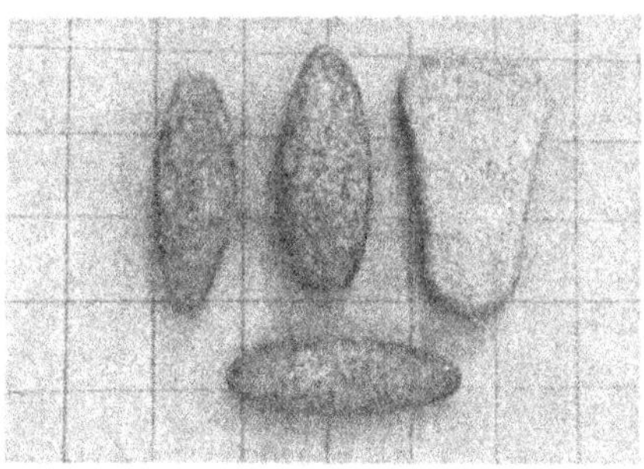

d

a.—Palette, gorget, or whetstone from personal kit, Feature 11. b-d.—Except for the adze in upper right of *d*, these are bipointed pecked objects of unknown function. Items *b* and *c* were included with the personal kit from Feature 11. The items in *d* are all from the collection of Mrs. John Bible, Bois Blanc Island. Items *a-c* are shown 3/4 size; the items in *d* are laid on a one-inch grid.

PLATE XXXVIII

Juntunen Copper Artifacts
(All but *g-j* were electrolytically cleaned*)

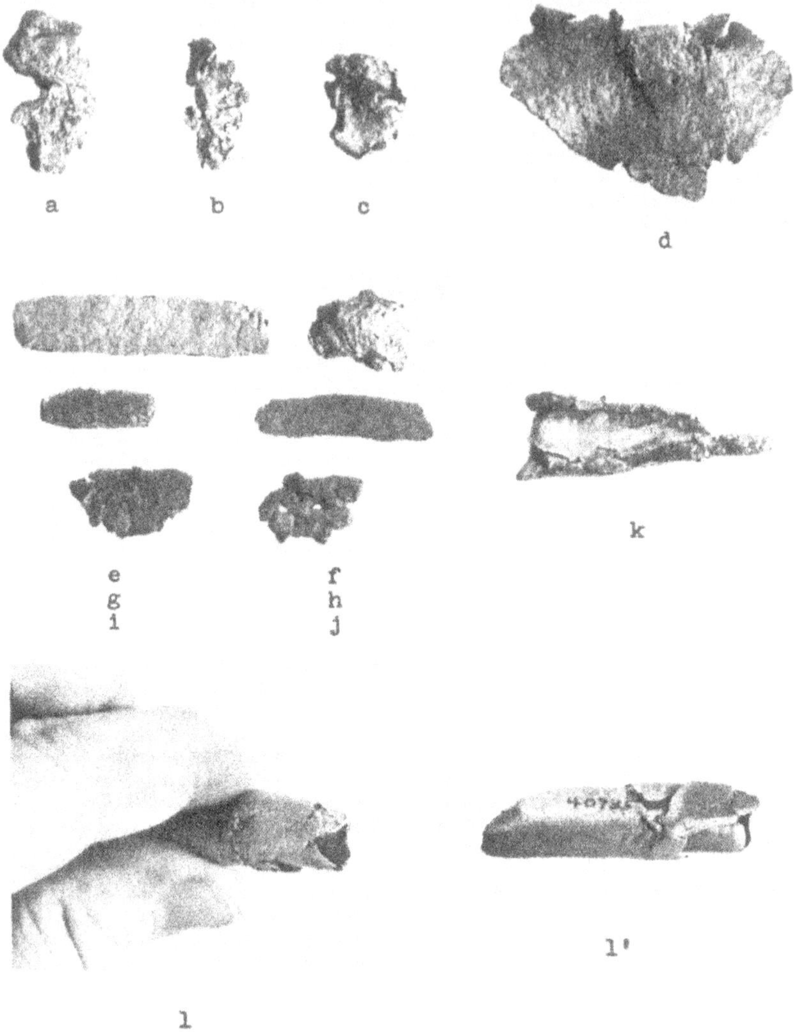

a-c, j.—Nearly unworked lumps. f—h.—Reject fragments from stages in making solid-lump tools. d,i.—Thin sheet. e.—Flat bar made of rolled sheets, pounded and ground. k.—Several sheets overlapped and folded over to produce a thick object. l-l.'—Largest bead recovered from site. Note: All artifacts are shown 3/4 size.

*Process described in McPherron (1965).

PLATE XXXIX

Juntunen Copper Artifacts
(All but *b*-*c* were electrolytically cleaned)

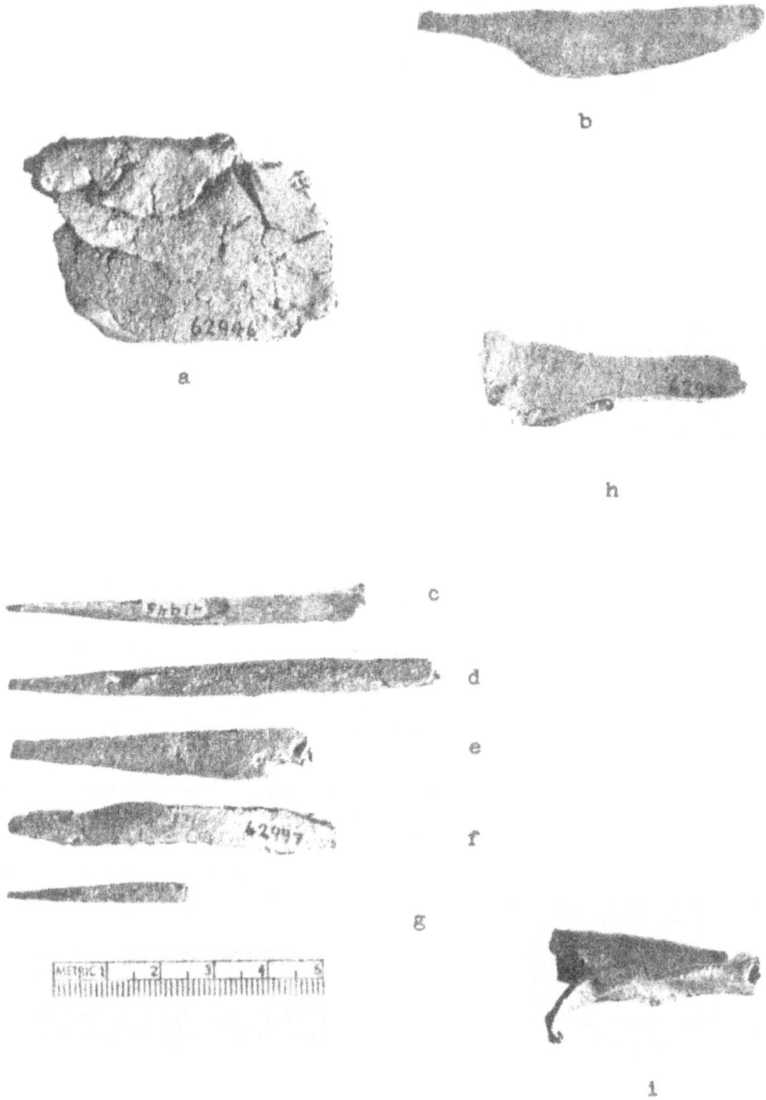

a.—Flat piece about 7 mm. thick made of several sheets folded together and pounded. b.—"Butter knife." End of tang bent over, presumably for securing into a handle. c-h.—Awls. Note laminations indicating the "sheet-metal process" in *d*-*g*. i.—Unclassified artifact. Note: All are shown 3/4 size.

PLATE XL

Bone Awls (No letter designations)

PLATE XLI

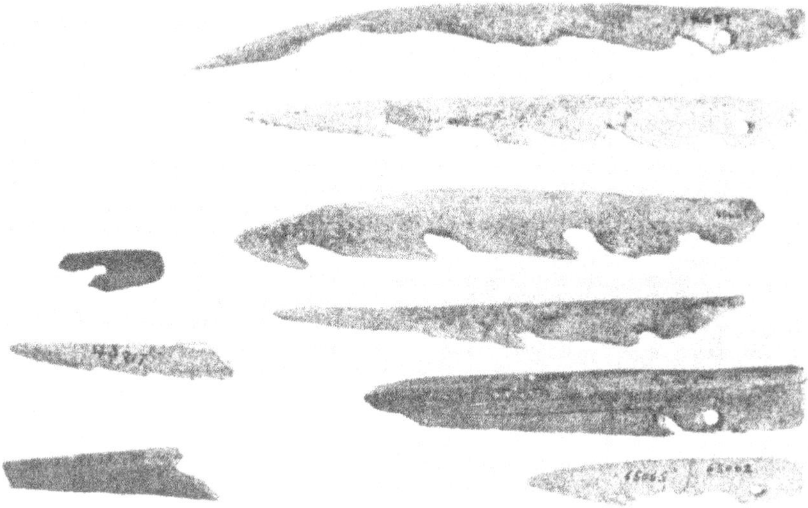

d a
b
f c
e
h g
i

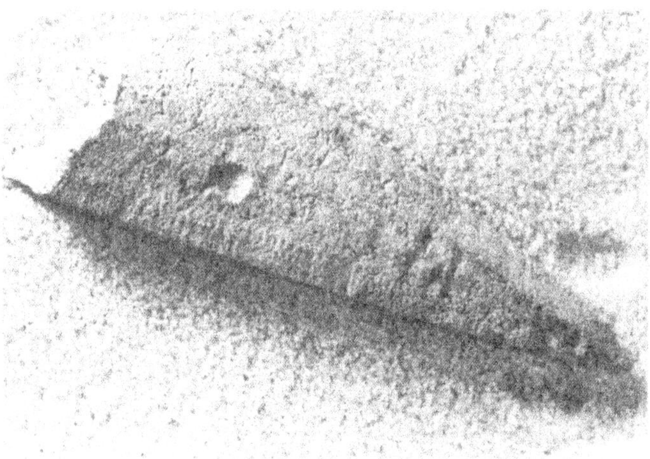

j

a-i.—All of the harpoon heads and fragments recovered. j.—Broken pointed bone object showing facets and chatter marks from scraping.

PLATE XLII

a

b

a.—Heaped gravels (basket loads?) in mound area. The black layer immediately overlying yellow sand is of the Mackinac phase. See Figure 28. UMMA Neg. 13875. b.—Loose human bone near surface above Feature 11. UMMA Neg. 13878.

PLATE XLIII

Feature 11

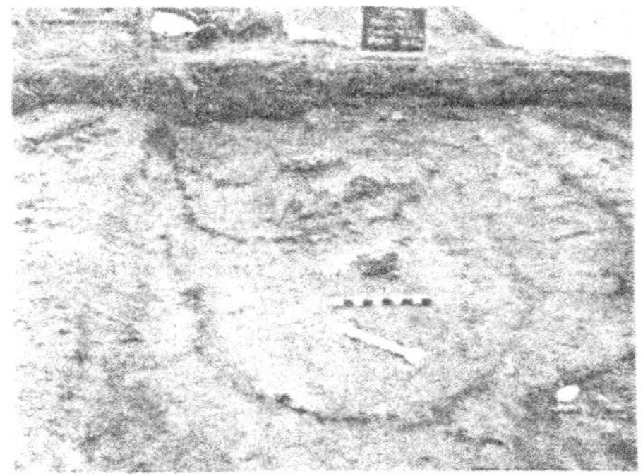

a

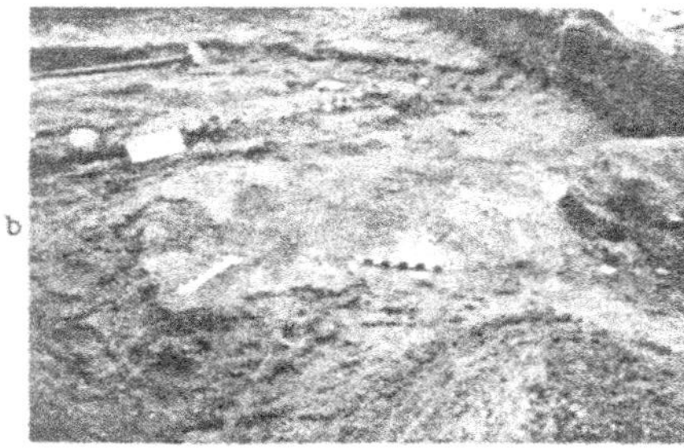

b

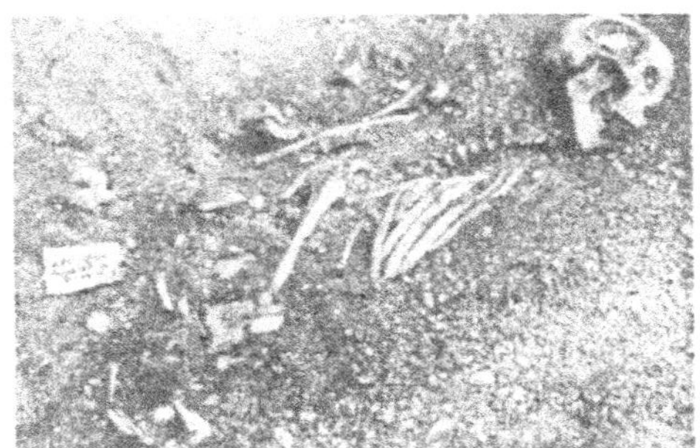

c

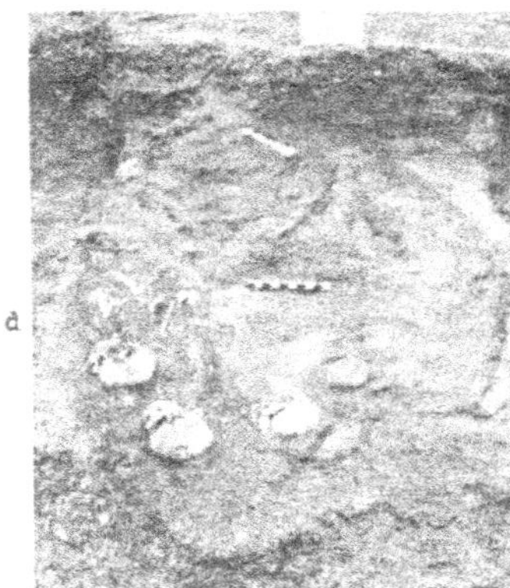

d

a.—Bark pit lining appearing. UMMA Neg. 13957. b.—Uppermost burials, showing nearby row of postmolds (compare Fig. 27). UMMA Neg. 13966. c.—Burial 3 showing "personal kit" above pelvic region. Note plaque of bone removed from skull. UMMA Neg. 13882. d.—Uppermost burials, as *b* (above). Compare Figure 30. UMMA Neg. 13963.

PLATE XLIV

a

b

Personal kit found at pelvic region of Burial 3, Feature 11. Two stages of excavation are shown by *a* and *b*. Compare Figure 31. UMMA Neg. Nos: *a*, 13962; *b*, 13839.

PLATE XLV

a

b

a.—Burial 3 (Feature 11) after removal of personal kit. UMMA Neg. 13968. b.—Burial 2 (Feature 11). UMMA Neg. 13970.

PLATE XLVI

Items from "Personal Kit" (F. 10) associated with Burial 3, F. 11

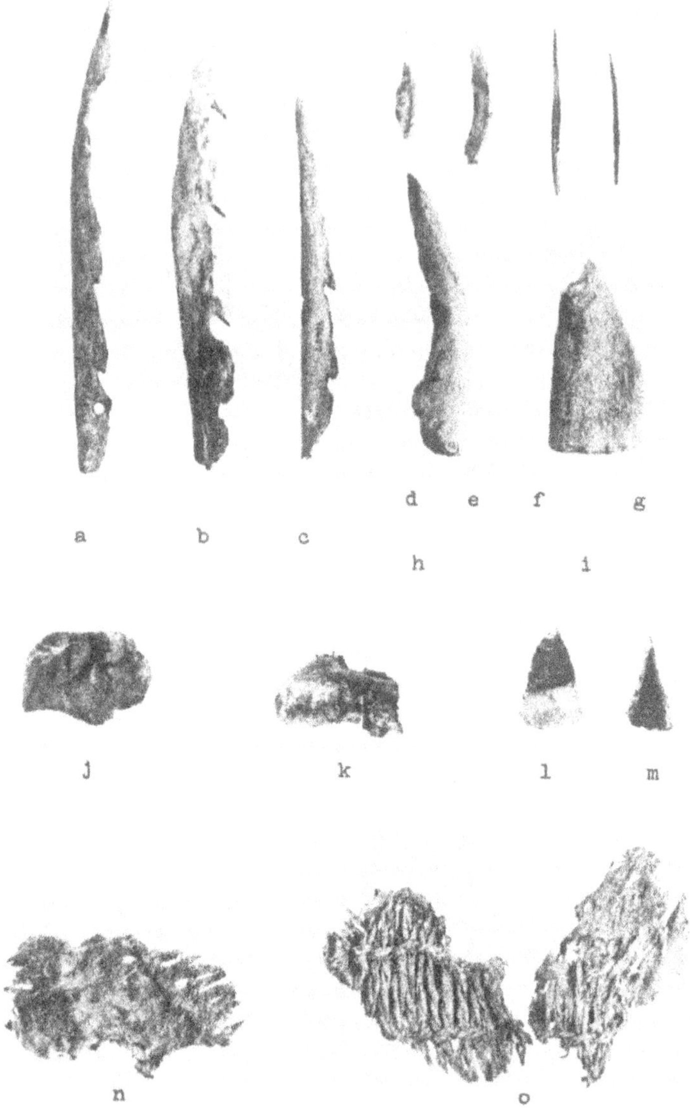

a-c.—Harpoon heads. d-e.—Cut beaver incisors. f-g.—Bone awls. h.—Deer antler tine. i.—Bone "chisel". j.—Chert striker (with *k*, forms strike-a-light). k.—Remnant of stone that contained iron pyrites. l-m.—Juntunen points. Item *l* is stained by iron oxide from the decayed pyrites; *m* is a decortication flake with edge trim only. n.—Mole fur and fabric o.—Twined fabric. Scales a-m: x 1/3; n-o: x 1-1/3.

PLATE XLVII

Feature 11

a

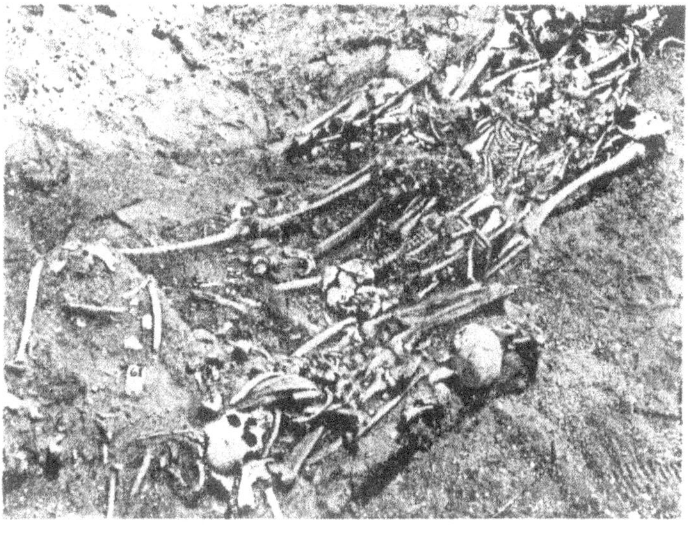

b

a.—Top left to right: B. 7, 6, 1. In the middle: B. 9-10 on top of B. 1. UMMA Neg. 13974. b.—General view of ossuary at stage at which Figure 30 was drawn. UMMA Neg. 13982.

PLATE XLVIII

Feature 11

a

b

a.—At left, uppermost burials being excavated; at right, first stages of excavation. UMMA Neg. 13981. b.—The two miniature mortuary vessels are seen with the larger superimposed over the smaller, above the skull of B. 5. UMMA Neg. 13825.

PLATE XLIX

Feature 11

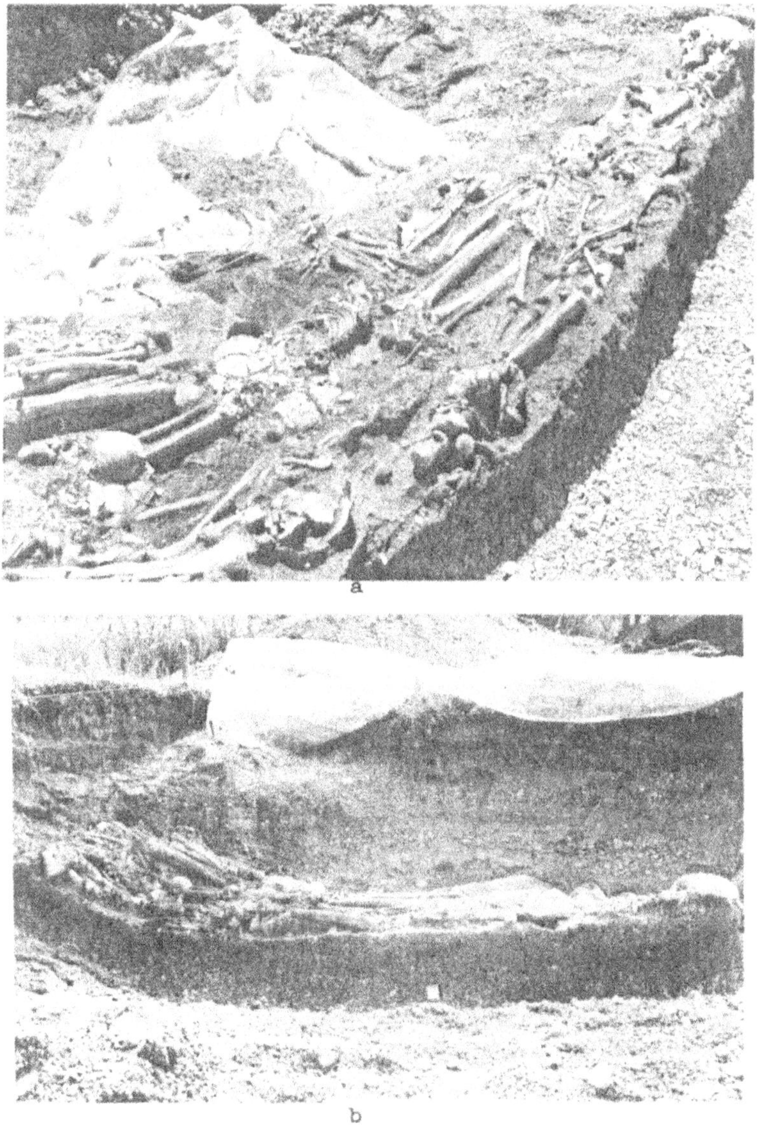

a

b

Two views of upper level of F. 11 at a slightly later stage of excavation than shown in Plate XLVIII. Burials 2, 3, and 6 have been removed. Burial 1 is seen at top right, with two children (B. 9 and 10) across his body. Band of shell beads is seen at bottom left. a.—UMMA Neg. 13831. b.—UMMA Neg. 13828.

PLATE L

Feature 11

a

b

a.—Band of *Prunum* beads lying above skull of B. 5. UMMA Neg. 13826.
b.—Bundle burials lying on bark (?) layer in bottom of ossuary pit. UMMA Neg. 13836.

PLATE LI

The Best-Preserved Juntunen Crania

F. 11, B. 1

F. 11, B. 2

F. 11, B. 3

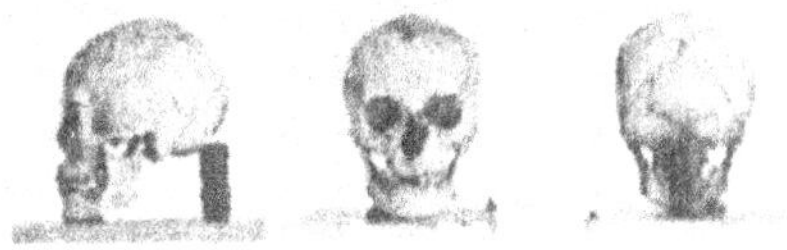

F. 11, B. 4

F. 11, B. 5

F. 11, B. 6

F. 11, B. 7

F. 11, B. 15

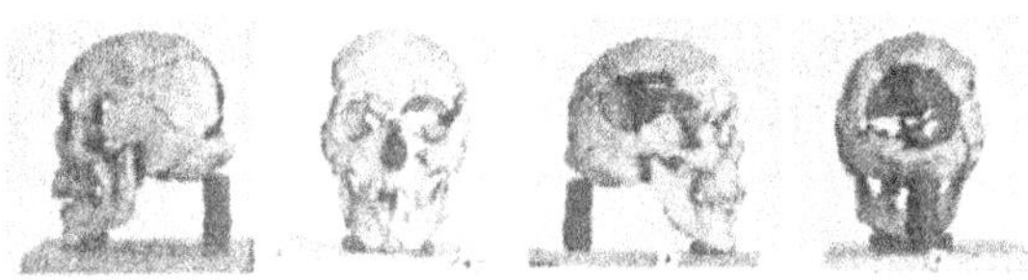

F. 11, B. 24

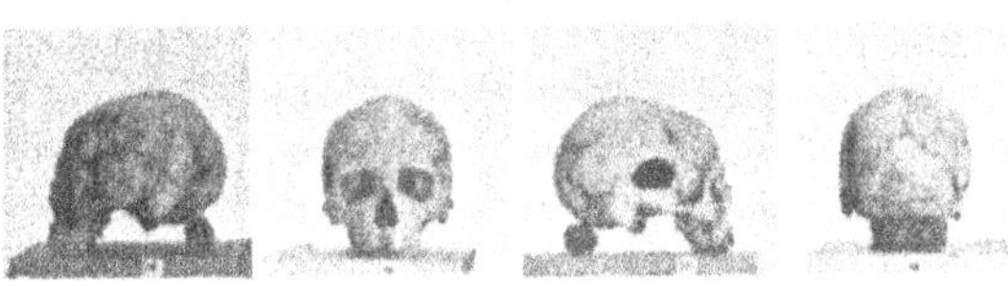

F. 18, B. 1

F. 18, B. 2

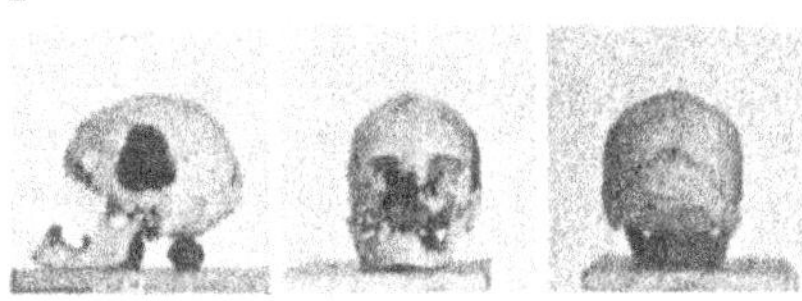

F. 18, B. 3

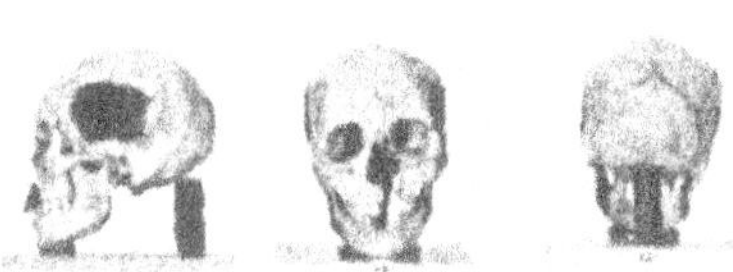

F. 34, B. 1

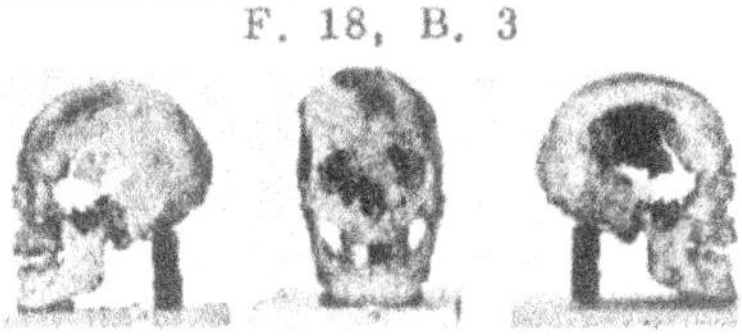

F. 34, B. 2

PLATE LII

Features 34 and 21

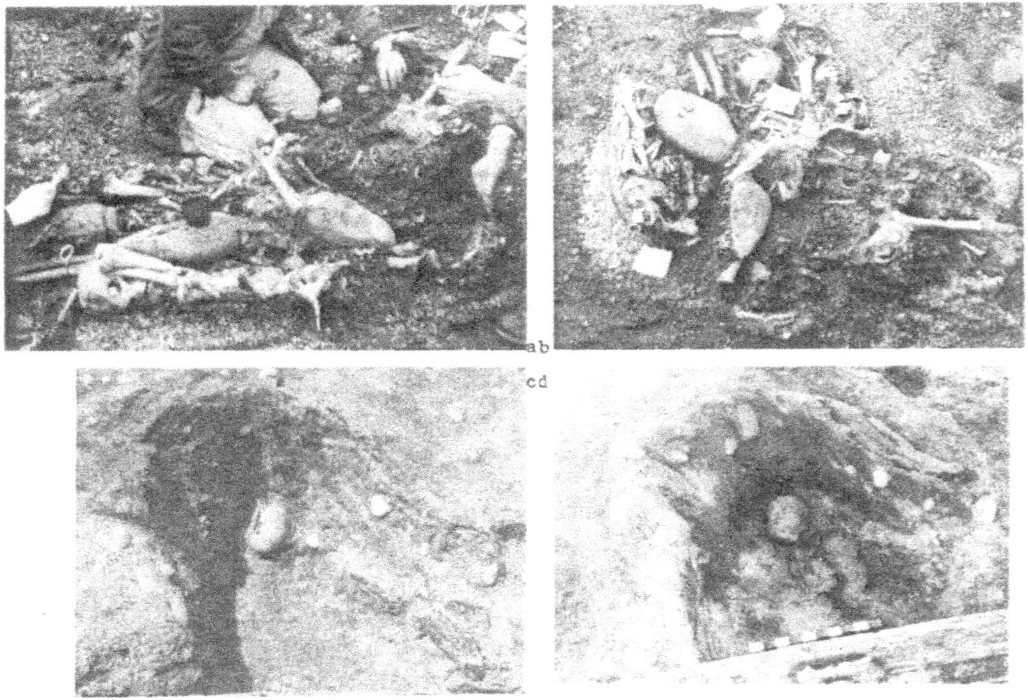

a.—Top part of Feature 34 during excavation, showing large stones amid burials. UMMA Neg. 15154. b.—Feature 34; as *a* but seen from above. UMMA Neg. 15147. c.—Feature 21. Note log cribbing. UMMA Neg. 14492. d.—Feature 21 with pit bottom exposed. UMMA Neg. 14506.

PLATE LIII

Four Stages in the Excavation of Feature 18

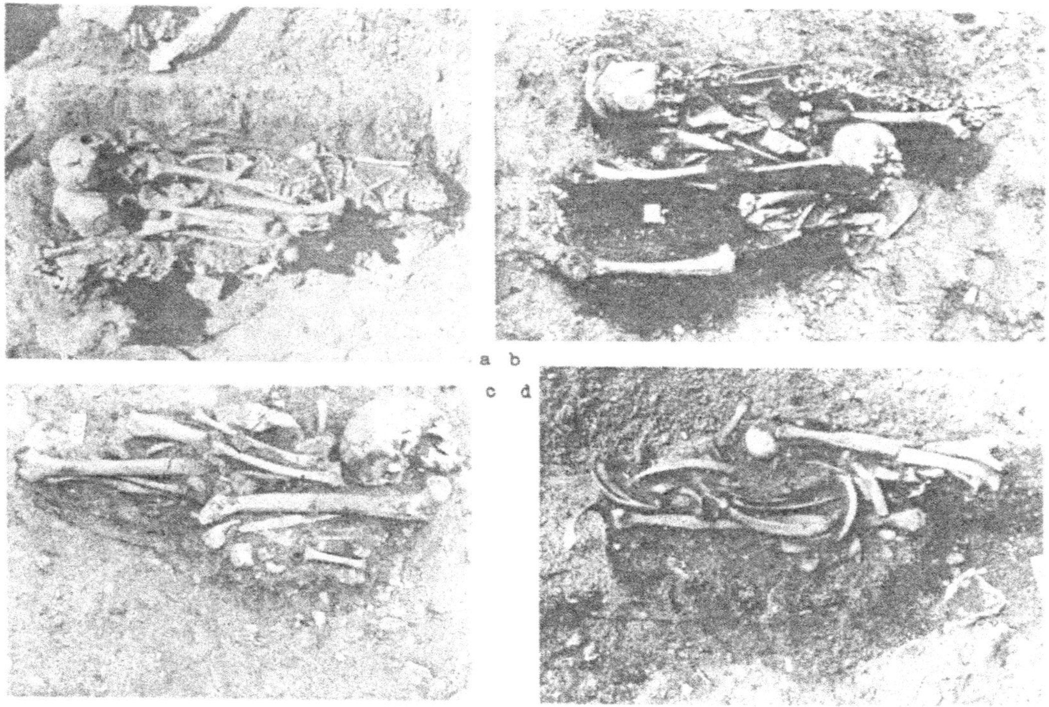

a.—Top of ossuary with all burials in situ. UMMA Neg. 14436. b.—Some burials removed. Note articulated spinal column. UMMA Neg. 14455. c.—Burial 3: nearly complete but highly disarticulated. UMMA Neg. 14458. d.—Pit bottom. UMMA Neg. 14461.

PLATE LIV

Features 43 and 45

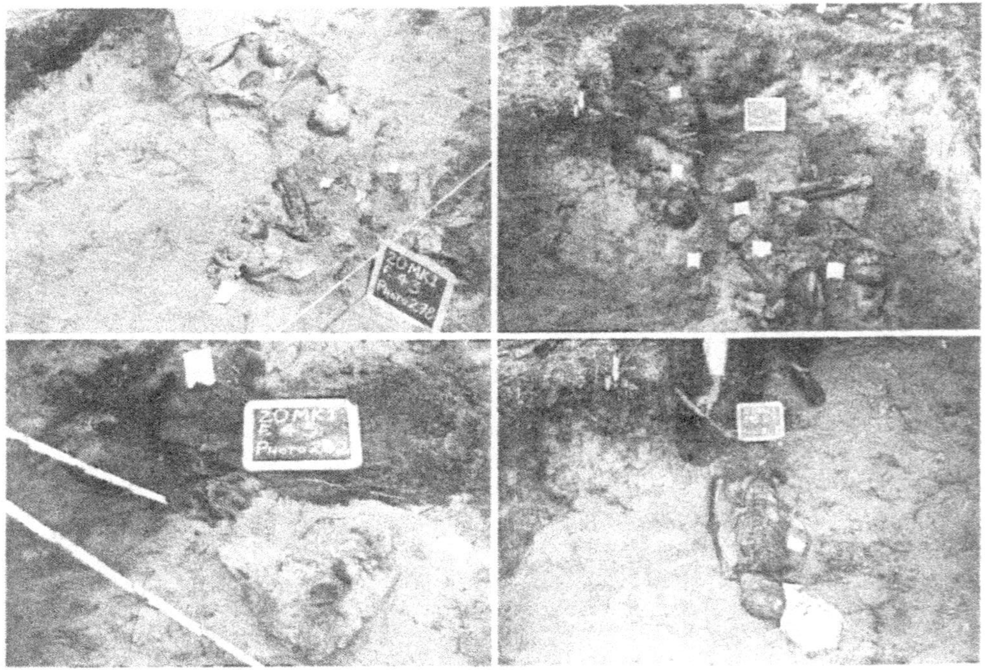

a.—Feature 43: burial of six crania. UMMA Neg. 15165. b.—Feature 45: multiple burial of the Arrowhead Drive component, but on spacial limits of Juntunen site. General view. UMMA Neg. 15187. c.—Feature 45. Fragmentary vessel near Burial 4. UMMA Neg. 15185. d.—Feature 45, showing kit of items at head of B. 5 encased in plaster for removal as unit. UMMA Neg. 15159.

PLATE LV

a.—Postmolds of part of longhouse (F. 22). UMMA Neg. 14502. b.—View of site during excavations in August, 1961, showing in foreground, a later stage of excavation of postmolds of previous photograph. UMMA Neg. 14508. c.—Postmold with decayed part of original post preserved at edges. UMMA Neg. 14541. d.—Part of profile cut across longhouse. Compare Figure 38. UMMA Neg. 14526.

PLATE LVI

a

b

a.—Feature 5: burial of dog, hare, and eagle. The arrows point to the burials, which form a triangular arrangement. The square is a 10 by 10 foot one. UMMA Neg. 13948.. b.—Feature 28: eagle burial. UMMA Neg. 14520.

PLATE LVII

a

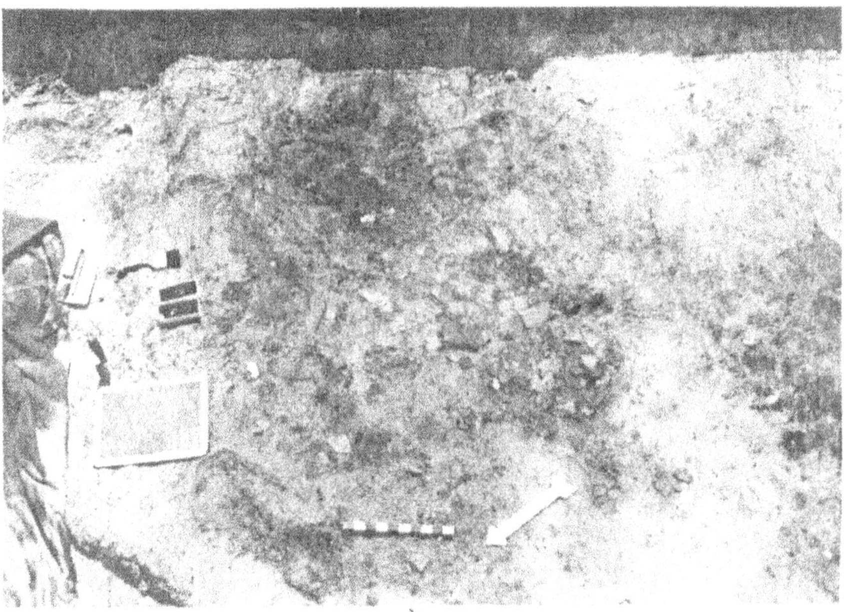

b

a.—Feature 23, Mackinac-phase dump with much pottery and charcoal. UMMA Neg. 14504. b.—Feature 20, Juntunen-phase dump of pottery and fish scales. UMMA Neg. 14471.

www.ingramcontent.com/pod-product-compliance
Lightning Source LLC
LaVergne TN
LVHW050020250826
846302LV00008B/35
9780915703685